Gooey Media

For Clare and Saad

Gooey Media
Screen Entertainment and the Graphic User Interface

Nick Jones

Edinburgh
University Press

Edinburgh University Press is one of the leading university presses in the UK. We publish academic books and journals in our selected subject areas across the humanities and social sciences, combining cutting-edge scholarship with high editorial and production values to produce academic works of lasting importance. For more information visit our website: edinburghuniversitypress.com

© Nick Jones, 2023

Edinburgh University Press Ltd
13 Infirmary Street, Edinburgh, EH1 1LT

Typeset in 12 on 14pt Arno Pro and Myriad Pro by
Cheshire Typesetting Ltd, Cuddington, Cheshire

A CIP record for this book is available from the British Library

ISBN 978 1 3995 2276 2 (hardback)
ISBN 978 1 3995 2277 9 (paperback)
ISBN 978 1 3995 2278 6 (webready PDF)
ISBN 978 1 3995 2279 3 (epub)

The right of Nick Jones to be identified as author of this work has been asserted in accordance with the Copyright, Designs and Patents Act 1988 and the Copyright and Related Rights Regulations 2003 (SI No. 2498).

Contents

List of Figures   vii
Acknowledgements   xi

Introduction   1
    At the interface   4
    Web of connections   8
    Chapter GUIde   12

1. Screen Mirroring   19
    Getting to the GUI   21
    Gooey media   27
    Screen share   36
    Conclusion   51

2. Interface Realism   52
    The myth of total resolution   55
    Bazinterface   59
    Workflow cinema   63
    Frames win games ...   72
    ... Not films   77
    Conclusion   83

3. Listen Mode   85
    Ping   88
    Gooey listening   93
    Collision boxes   95
    In sync   102
    Conclusion   113

4. Seamless Composites   115
    Asset management   117
    Breaking down the breakdown   120

Narrow viewports	131
The breakdown in history	134
Media (dis)assemble	136
Conclusion	144
5. Graphic Urban Interface	**147**
Altered urbanism	149
Personal space	152
Screening source code	156
Procedural rhetoric and spatial flexibility	160
Where do you want to go today?	165
Conclusion	172
6. Programming Matter	**175**
Animate form	177
Transforming Packard	186
Polymer visions	197
Conclusion	205
7. Empathy Machines	**208**
Getting to VR	210
Dirtying up the faceless interface	212
VRealities	217
Milking it	219
Looking through the Aperture	226
Conclusion	232
Conclusion: Stuck In	**234**
Back to where it all started	237
Stay away from marketing	241
Time off screen	244
Bibliography	247
Index	264

Figures

I.1	One of the unlockable suits in the videogame *Spider-Man* (2018) is a recreation of the animated suit seen in the television show *Spider-Man: The Animated Series* (1994–8)	8
I.2a	Spider-Man soars through the air above New York in the videogame *Spider-Man* (2018) …	9
I.2b	… a composition which closely replicates that seen in *The Amazing Spider-Man 2* (2014)	9
I.3	The map of New York accessed during gameplay of *Spider-Man* (2018) in order to navigate to tasks and identify collectibles	11
1.1a	The cluttered desktop from *Unfriended* (2014), in which Skype, Spotify playlists, Facebook profiles, background images, and private messages all contribute to story and character information	38
1.1b	Narrative events and their aftermath play out simultaneously across multiple layered program windows in *Unfriended* (2014)	38
1.2a	Multiple windows open on a desktop to demonstrate the range of fan videos of the shooting of *Transformers: Age of Extinction* (2014), in *Transformers: The Premake* (2014)	43
1.2b	Kevin B. Lee reveals his own editing timeline at the culmination of *Transformers: The Premake* (2014)	43
1.3a	Multiple tabs on a mac desktop in Jessica McGoff's *My Mulholland* (2020)	45
1.3b	McGoff includes webcam footage of herself on the desktop in *My Mulholland* (2020)	45
1.4a and 1.4b	The player's phone screen is synonymous with the videogame *Sara is Missing* (2016)	49
2.1a	A mac desktop cluttered with icons	68
2.1b	*Gravity*'s (2013) terrifying orbital mise-en-scène	69

2.1c	Stone looks on at the chaos in *Gravity* (2013)	69
2.2a	Stone begins to lose hope in *Gravity* (2013) …	70
2.2b	… and the camera racks focus to a single tear floating in front of her	70
2.2c	The Launchpad function on a mac computer, revealing application logos and throwing the background heavily out of focus	71
2.3	The website for Nvidia's 'Frames Win Games' advertising campaign. From Nvidia, n.d.	75
3.1	The crafting menu from *The Last of Us Part 2* (2019)	98
3.2	A WhatsApp group message chat is the setting of the lyric video for Katy Perry's 'Roar' (2013)	111
3.3	The chaotic but carefully orchestrated visual field of the 100 gecs 'ringtone' lyric video, including an internet-sourced image of a 'barking dog'	112
4.1a	An outdoors scene from *Little Women* (2019) …	123
4.1b	… fades into a LIDAR scan of this environment in the VFX breakdown for the film	123
4.2	A rudimentary model of New York has detail added to it through a rain of spherical camera data in the VFX breakdown for *The Avengers* (2012) (Industrial Light and Magic 2013)	124
4.3	The VFX breakdown for *Shanghai Fortress* (2019) swings out from the final image to show layers arrayed in front of it in three-dimensional space (CGF 2019)	125
4.4	The VFX breakdown for *Wonder Woman* (2017) undertakes a similar manoeuvre, showing layers of detail making up an explosion (UPP n.d.)	125
4.5	And, once again, in the VFX breakdown for 'Hardhome' (El Ranchito Imagen Digital 2015)	126
4.6a, b and c	The VFX breakdown for *Wonder Woman* (2017) begins in a rudimentary Piccadilly Circus, pulling back as layers and detail accumulate, with the final position (and shot) barely showing the initial space (UPP n.d.)	129
4.7	The various iterations making up the character of the Hulk and their relationship to facial capture data drawn from actor Mark Ruffalo are all demonstrated simultaneously in the VFX breakdown for *The Avengers* (2012) (Industrial Light and Magic 2013)	130
4.8	A typical Maya viewport with a central viewport and numerous surrounding panels	133

4.9	In the credit sequence of *Black Panther* (2018) the names of production personnel fly around digital models of the key vehicles and action of the film	137
4.10	Windows' Flip 3D program window shortcut resembles the swing-out shots of Figures 4.3, 4.4, and 4.5 (Sanjiv Creation 2016)	145
5.1	The player of *Echochrome* (2008) manipulates space in order to keep a constantly strolling figure from falling	155
5.2	New York is easily modified and duplicated by the sorcerers of *Doctor Strange* (2016)	159
6.1	The Guggenheim Museum Bilbao, designed by Frank Gehry. Photograph by Jeremy Jones	178
6.2	The fluxing, metallic form of the T-1000 from *Terminator 2: Judgment Day* (1991)	184
6.3a and b	During a Chicago-based battle in *Transformers: Dark of the Moon* (2011), the CCTV Building briefly dominates the skyline (in the right-hand side of (a) and the background of (b))	188
6.4	The flexible matter Transformium is demonstrated in *Transformers: Age of Extinction* (2014)	191
6.5	The proposal for the Center for Fulfillment, Knowledge, and Innovation depicts parametric digital structures glomming onto the Packard Plant (Framestore 2016)	194
6.6	Physical and virtual cameras glide through the Packard Plant and its digital additions (Framestore 2016)	194
6.7	The proposal for the Center for Fulfillment, Knowledge, and Innovation centres ideas of transformation and robotic circulation among post-industrial ruins (Framestore 2016)	195
6.8	A Transformer leaps across the roofs of the Packard Plant in *Transformers: Age of Extinction* (2014)	195
6.9	London King's Cross Train Station redevelopment by John McAslan and Partners. Photograph by Jeremy Jones	199
6.10	In *SimCity BuildIt* (2014), the world turns polished white when the player explores possible spatial additions or rearrangements (EA n.d.)	201
6.11	The City of Glass from *Mirror's Edge* (2008), a sparse and CAD-inspired terrain	202
6.12	The Tower from *NieR: Automata* (2017), a nonhuman environment of digital polymers crystallised, rudimentary structures	204

7.1	Pinchas Gutter is composited into the Majdanek concentration camp in *The Last Goodbye* (2017), directly addressing the viewer as he discusses his experience	222
C.1a and b	An aerial view of the city created by (and used to announce and advertise) Unreal Engine 5 in *The Matrix Awakens* (2021), offering the user/player/viewer/experiencer the option to toggle visual attributes	235
C.2	Synthespian versions of Keanu Reeves and Carrie-Ann Moss state that they sometimes miss 'these younger versions of us' in *The Matrix Awakens* (2021)	242
C.3	AI generated image of the prompt 'Neo and Trinity from the Matrix missing the younger versions of themselves', made using DALL-E 2 (labs.opeai.com)	244

Acknowledgements

This book is the result of interfaces with many people. The project grew in large part out of my role at the University of York, where I taught both Film and Television Production students and Interactive Media students; working on these subjects in tandem allowed me to consider their overlaps, and this was in no small part further encouraged by students who had little time for the kind of disciplinary or medial boundaries that predominate in academia. I also had a hugely stimulating session teaching on York's Centre for Modern Studies MA programme, and the enthusiasm of those students (and module convenor J. T. Welsch) for these ideas around the interface was heartening. My thanks to all of you.

In bringing this manuscript into the world I have benefitted from the superb editorial work of Gillian Leslie and Sam Johnson – both always punctual and both always helpful – as well as the anonymous reviewers of the initial proposal who gave me so many valuable suggestions and, perhaps more importantly, reminded me of my own enthusiasm for the project. Thanks so much.

Over the last few years, various colleagues generously gave up their time to help me understand a host of subjects which were new to me: Alessandro Altavilla talked to me about audio software over a coffee (and offered some incredibly stimulating responses to Chapter 3); Joe Cutting and I spoke productively on interface design; Laura McLaren kindly chatted to me via email about lyric videos and Katy Perry; and Liam Moloney got me thinking about sonification and microwaves. Thanks everyone for being so kind and charitable.

Closer to home, these pages were shaped by the professional and personal encouragement of many dear friends. Rebecca Benzie was always willing to be a sounding board and co-working buddy; Hannah Bungard buoyed me up when I sorely needed it; Tasos Giapoutzis worked much the same magic; Saad Maqbool never let me leave a thought unexplored (and taught me how to spell Magikarp); Jenna Ng was a consistently fierce and welcome ally;

Jon Swords helped me climb the walls; and Lara, Jim, Bram, and Wren all showed me endless patience. My brother Jeremy even jumped in with some of his photography skills to help flesh out the visuals of Chapter 6. I sincerely appreciate you all.

Much of the manuscript was drafted during the COVID-19 lockdowns of 2020 and 2021. A horrendous time for many, I am eternally indebted to Clare Whitehead and Ben Woodiwiss in particular for their support through these years and beyond. So, to both of you: it is truly impossible to say how much you guys mean to me. It was hard going there for a bit, but you always helped me see the light at the end of the tunnel. I'll never forget it.

Of course, any and all errors in what follows remain the product of my own sticky fingers.

Material that forms parts of Chapters 5 and 6 has been published previously as 'The Flexible Urban Imaginary: Postindustrial Cities in *Inception*, *The Adjustment Bureau*, and *Doctor Strange*', in Johan Andersson and Lawrence Webb (eds), *The City in American Cinema* (London and New York: I. B. Tauris, 2019), although it appears here in much revised form. The same is true for sections of Chapters 5 and 7, which have been published previously in 'Empathy Machines, Indifference Engines and Extensions of Perception', in Lucy Bolton, David Martin-Jones and Robert Sinnebrink (eds), *Contemporary Screen Ethics* (Edinburgh: Edinburgh University Press, 2023). I am grateful to the editors for their permission to reprint this material here.

Introduction

We get stuck to our screens for many reasons. Watching television, taking photos, creating albums, filling baskets, messaging friends, playing games, writing documents, mapping journeys: all can all be undertaken using the same screen in the space of a few minutes, or even simultaneously. This functional convergence is extremely convenient. The screen-based desktop interface becomes a one-stop shop, our go-to destination for a range of work and leisure tasks. It also makes this interface a crucial element of contemporary visual and aural culture, the centre of a gelatinous web bonding together various media.

This book is about the aesthetic cross-pollination that occurs as a result of this integrated screen culture. The graphic user interface, or GUI, is installed as standard on the vast majority of the world's desktop computers and smartphones.[1] Whether using Windows, macOS, Android, or some other brand of technology, it is overwhelmingly a GUI of some sort which provides access to the applications which furnish us with our media environment. Through a GUI we can open a Chrome internet browser to watch Netflix; through a GUI we can access the Android app store to download Google Earth; through a GUI we can load up Steam to play a videogame; through a GUI we can use Maya to design buildings and even entire cities. The many tabs of an internet browser and the multiple programs scattered upon a typical desktop all testify to the multiplicity inherent in today's interfaces, the convergence they enact by bringing a range of media and functions together in a single 40-, 14-, or 4-inch screen. As a result, the GUI becomes gooey. The GUI sticks a multitude of media together, such

---

[1] Graphic user interface is the label most often found in media studies, as well as wider cultural discussion. However, it is necessary to note that an alternative formulation, graphical user interface, is also sometimes used, in particular in the field of human–computer interaction. I take these to be interchangeable descriptions, and use the former.

that these media not only blend and interact with one another, but also increasingly adopt a fluid mass of aesthetic attributes that they share with the GUI itself.

For the last few decades, media scholars have been attentive to the ways in which consumer agency, corporate ownership, and industrial strategy have shifted thanks to digital production and distribution. Aesthetics have also been explored, but in less holistic ways. Several commentators have noted how, for instance, videogames import aesthetic qualities from cinema, and sometimes even seek critical validation through this process of appropriation (with 'cinematic' being synonymous in some videogaming cultures and scholarship with 'good'). In the other direction, films have adopted many videogame traits, both in terms of aesthetics (say, the many long-take action sequences that evoke first person shooter gameplay) and narrative construction (action sequences as levelling up; morality as a series of binary player choices). And in a less noted example of emulation, videogames have begun to mimic televisual release patterns, with new content dropping into popular games just like a new series or season will drop onto a streaming service. While significant, such examples are just the boot-up screen of much more extensive overlaps. As the media ecosystem has undergone a convergent march in the digital era, processes of aesthetic coalescence have gone far beyond unidirectional borrowings or bidirectional intermedia influence.

Writing in 2006, Anne Friedberg proposed that 'the once distinct material differences between cinematic, televisual, and computer screens have vanished', and as a result the 'the segregation of histories of telephony, moving-image, and computing technologies appears – in postmillennial retrospect – to have been a set of arbitrary separations that disregarded the intermedial complexity of technological development' (Friedberg 2006: 236). This is certainly the view that I take in the pages that follow, as I argue that these distinctions (and others) are in many ways even more arbitrary than they were at the time of Friedberg's writing. This is not, though, to propose that boundaries have vanished and that specific screens don't matter. Friedberg's own work is highly sensitive to the contextual nature of any media delivery, and likewise Haidee Wasson (2007) is instructive in encouraging us to address the way that technological circulation and variable viewing settings alter media content. As she puts it, 'Moving images may be increasingly fluid but their fluidity is not limitless nor can it be fully understood without recourse to the expanded viewing contexts and the enduring screens which enable their visibility' (Wasson 2007: 91). For all the industrial rhetoric today of frictionless content circulation and limitless access, screens and their specificities still matter.

Enduring screen forms and the fluidity of media imagery were the subjects of Jay David Bolter and Richard Grusin's *Remediation*, a book which influentially explored how new media refashion old media in the digital age. Published in 1999, it described the twinned approaches of 'immediacy' – a 'you are there' approach in which mediation seeks to disappear – and 'hypermediacy' – a cacophonous visual field of decoration, user appeals, and other conscious signs of mediation – which the authors argued were simultaneously at work in visual culture (Bolter and Grusin 1999: 5). These forces are not new: painting long sought immediacy, while medieval manuscripts could be hypermediated in their decoration. But computational media are novel thanks to 'the particular ways in which they refashion older media and the ways in which older media refashion themselves to answer the challenges of new media' (Bolter and Grusin 1999: 15). The GUI is a key example of this: it seeks both transparency in its appeal to 'windows', its employment of the desktop metaphor, and its skeuomorphic components, yet it is also markedly hypermediated in its multiplicity of tiles, overt interface components, and possibilities for user interaction (Bolter and Grusin 1999: 23, 33).

In the twenty years since Bolter and Grusin wrote *Remediation*, the GUI has become ever more culturally embedded. A media form which facilitates and defines endless work and leisure activities, the development of the GUI's aesthetic is indebted to cinema (Manovich 2001) and television (Harpold 2009: 83–4). It has also made its own interventions in visual culture, inaugurating what Friedberg calls a 'new visual vernacular': from the inclusion of multiple windows within a single frame, to the gravity-defying imagination of a desktop which hangs in the air on the vertical axis, to the conflation and confusion of flatness and depth, the GUI offers a media experience that is 'multiple, adjacent, postperspectival' (Friedberg 2006: 22). This vernacular, moreover, is not only visual – the desktop generates noises as much as images, and this sonic terrain is similarly influential across media culture.

What happens if we look (and listen) for this new vernacular in a range of other media forms, forms that would seem on the surface to operate in very different ways to the GUI? Since the 1970s, the graphically representational desktop has become increasingly central to instrumental action and time-swallowing distraction. As such, it is not surprising to find overlaps between its aesthetic traits and those of films, videogames, television, and even built space. As the GUI has become indispensable, unignorable, yet frequently invisible, its visual and sonic qualities have subtly but significantly altered those media with which it interacts, and for which it often provides a container. Yet the magnitude of these overlaps is frequently concealed beneath increasingly outdated media boundaries and delineations. *Gooey Media* seeks to redress that by paying particular attention to the desktop interface as an influential aesthetic environment in its own right, and by connecting this environment to those of a wide range of other media.

At the interface

In their book on the key concepts of new media, Nicholas Gane and David Beer foreground the importance of interfaces to today's media environment: 'interfaces are to be found at the very centre of new media systems and infrastructures' (Gane and Beer 2008: 54). Yet moving our critical attention to the interface can be a difficult task. Digital media theorist Jacob Gaboury states that screens are so ubiquitous that they are 'often taken for granted in all forms of computational interaction', resulting in a 'screen essentialism' in which 'the screen stands in for, and thereby occludes, the deeper workings of the computer itself' (Gaboury 2018: 25). But even if we look at screens rather than these deeper workings, we often still don't really *look* at the screen.

The interface, after all, is not designed to be visible. Indeed, this is the very thing that can make an interface an interface. Philosopher of technology Alexander Galloway (2012) proposes that an interface is not a *thing*, it is always an effect. Interfaces work to bring things together, yet they also assert boundaries and boundedness. As Galloway (2012: 33) states, the interface 'is that moment when one significant material is understood as distinct from another significant material', a distinction asserted precisely because of the need to translate between these two materials. But the act of translation itself is usually hidden or marginalised. In the case of the computer screen, the interface between user and computer allows for a series of further interfaces, as the user can move from one media (plat)form to another, from blog post to film clip, from news article to image gallery, all while remaining within the same single interface that is the screen. But our conscious attention is on the programs, not the GUI. As videogame theorist James Ash (2015: 16) notes, the interface is inherently ambiguous or paradoxical: it is simultaneously a site of contact – in which different parts of a system come together and share information – and a site of separation – in which the various operations, languages, and affordances of multiple systems must be negotiated.

Galloway asks that any thinking about the interface as a window, door, or other threshold to a virtual world must be aware of this paradox: the more successful an interface is, the less visible it is, the apparently less present it is. If the interface provides users access to a space-beyond (that is, if it is working as a window or door), then its capacity to provide access is directly connected to its ability to *disappear* in the user's eyes. This colours a wealth of media theory, which looks through the screen at the represented content upon it. And yet, as an effect not a thing, the interface enacts change. In Lev Manovich's (2001: 65) words, by '[s]tripping media of their original distinctions, the interface imposes its own logic on them'. Similarly, Steven Johnson (1997: 102) calls the interface 'a metaform, a mediator, a filter. It is a window looking out into dataspace, separating user and information, but also shaping that information in all sorts of subtle and not so subtle ways'. For Aylish Wood (2007: 11), the interface is a key component of digital media more generally, as this media is always a composite collection of elements that the viewer/user encounters or negotiates, just as they encounter a composite series of screens in their daily lives.

The interface is an important element of the 'convergence culture' described by Henry Jenkins (2006), even if the interface itself is little discussed by Jenkins directly. Pointing to the shift away from the unidirectional media systems of the twentieth century, convergence culture names 'the flow of content across multiple media platforms, the cooperation between multiple media industries, and the migratory behavior of media audiences who will go almost anywhere in search of the kinds of entertainment experiences they want' (Jenkins 2006: 2). For Jenkins, convergence is a way of understanding new or evolving ways in which media consumers and media companies interface. Through convergence, consumers seem to gain more agency, becoming 'produsers' who can point, click, and comment in real time, and who can work together on a global scale to project their voices further and louder. Corporate entities, meanwhile, can adjust their business practices to nurture, repel, or cautiously integrate this consumer activity, all with healthy profit in mind.

For Jenkins (2006: 3), convergence is something predominantly born of the negotiation between old media and new media, and he is clear that it 'occurs within the brains of individual consumers and through their social interactions with others', and resolutely 'does not occur through media appliances, however sophisticated they may become'. If we follow Jenkins, then, the blurring together of media within and thanks to multi-purpose screens is not the convergence culture that he outlined in the first decade of this millennium. But it *is* convergence, and it *does* trace the increasing prominence and importance of the GUI to the wider media environment.

The computer screen, after all, enables and propagates these new relations in the first place, and so we must take it into account in any discussion of today's media. Screens, as Wasson puts it,

> are not blank frames but active forces. Moreover, screens take on fuller meaning when understood alongside the material and institutional conditions that surround and embolden them. Screens are implicated in identifiable institutional formations and also inextricably linked to multiple systems. Screens, in other words, are not autonomous sites but windows connected to complex and abstract systems: corporate, aesthetic, and political. (Wasson 2007: 90)

The result, in short, is that we need new, or at least newly joined up ways of thinking about screen culture today. Nanna Verhoeff is clear in her own study of contemporary screens that their mixed media use calls for new tactics of study:

> Where film theory, television theory and new media theory have focused on the specific nature of these scenes and practices, the current screen culture of intermediality, transmediality, crossmediality and remediation requires a reconfiguring of divergent theoretical approaches. This is necessary in order to explore the convergence of perspectives that are currently often segregated, separated by virtue of different objects of investigation, such as television, cinema and mobile phones. (Verhoeff 2012: 18)

This kind of theoretical reconfiguration, while certainly underway, still has a long way to go to catch up with the screen culture of the twenty-first century.

Take, for instance, the discipline of Film Studies, which has in particular wrestled with the nature of its subject in the digital era. In the early 2000s, Manovich claimed that cinema was a kind of Rosetta Stone or source code of digital media more generally, as it had become '*the* cultural interface, a toolbox for all cultural communication, overtaking the printed word' (Manovich 2001: 86; emphasis in original). Understanding cinema would therefore help us to understand computer use, because '[c]inema's aesthetic strategies have become basic organisational principles of computer software'; in short, 'what was cinema is now the human-computer interface' (Manovich 2001: 86). This work helpfully stressed the centrality of cinematic ways of organising visual information to a wider range of media and functions. But it also points to the danger apparently posed to cinema through its intermingling with other media, a growing fear of the end of cinema as cinema.

This kind of eschatological thinking abounded in the late 1990s, and beyond. A 1996 piece in the *New York Times* by Susan Sontag (1996) on the 'decay' of cinema still reverberates to some extent in Film Studies, as the discipline contends with hard drives, Netflix, iMovie, TikTok, and selfie sticks. To quote the title of a 2014 article by scholar of film technology and aesthetics John Belton, 'If Film is Dead, What is Cinema?' As Belton is aware, to equate cinematic media with both the space of the cinema and the material of celluloid film is to historicise it. In such a model, the arrival of digital technology and wider and wider possibilities for reception and participation can only ever be a kind of threat. If cinema becomes software, what remains of cinema? What even is film in an era of streaming platforms, YouTube supercuts, and transmedia MCUniverses?

Yet it might be better to think of the 'ends of cinema' that have been wrought by digital technology as less temporal than spatial. This is not so much the end of cinema as a historical media, than it is the end of cinema's geographical boundaries. Cinema, after all, continues to flourish across 'multiple discursive constellations' (Szczepaniak-Gillece 2020: ix). Post-cinema emerges as a useful term here, naming the migration of cinema beyond the cinema, beyond celluloid, and even perhaps beyond even human perception (Denson 2020a). The result is a post-cinematic affect which embodies neoliberal ideals of flexibility, responsiveness, and sensation (Shaviro 2010).

But post-cinema still centres cinema, even as it describes cinema's displacement and refraction in a networked digital ecology. Cinema may be a key model for audio-visual media generally, and it may be influential as an industry, a discursive framework, and a visual and sonic language, but it must not take automatic priority in models of media analysis. Despite my own background in Film Studies, I therefore seek to displace the centrality of these theories in what follows. The cinema, as so many scholars acknowledge, is not the exclusive standard operating system of screen culture anymore. This is not an obituary, but a reality, and an opportunity. I contend that we must move our gaze from the cinema to the desktop interface in order to fathom the unfolding present of screen media, from film to television to videogames to apps to virtual reality and beyond.

To do this, I shall seek to draw attention to the interface while also thinking through the way its structure and workings have shaped not only the content it is used to design, access, or view, but also some content that exists seemingly beyond its borders, like the planning and navigation of urban space. As I will argue, the fact that various media and functions are now consistently situated within a single screen grants them all an essential equivalence. Their mutual co-existence as so many mutual program windows and browser tabs inevitably leads to bleed and cross-contamination between diverse media forms, with the GUI playing a central role in not only propagating but also managing these intersections.

Web of connections

To provide some further sense of the scale of this sticky web of media connections, a web which has the GUI at its centre, let's take a slightly more detailed look at a recent incarnation of a particularly adept webslinger. The character of Spider-Man originated in comic books created by Stan Lee and Steve Ditko for the publisher Marvel in the 1960s. The superhero and his world have been adapted for endless films, television shows, and videogames since this debut. A big-budget part of this unfolding stable, *Marvel's Spider-Man*, a videogame for the PlayStation 4 developed by Insomniac Games and published by Sony Interactive Entertainment, was released in 2018 to general acclaim.

In the game, the player swings through an open world New York City, collecting items and completing missions. The story draws on a wealth of Spidey lore, with both major plot points and throwaway details drawing on the long transmedia history of the character. The savvy Spider-fan is further rewarded with intermedial echoes within the gameplay: one of the many unlockable suits in the game is a recreation of the style and look of the 1990s animated TV series, for instance, while another replicates the character's metallic Iron Spider Suit from his appearance in the multi-billion-dollar Marvel Cinematic Universe franchise (Figure I.1). This is a case of comics, films, and games all intermingling: the player swings the title character through the streets

Figure I.1 One of the unlockable suits in the videogame *Spider-Man* (2018) is a recreation of the animated suit seen in the television show *Spider-Man: The Animated Series* (1994–1998). Frame enlargement from PS4 gameplay.

of Manhattan in shots which, in their digital fluidity and spectacle, resemble action set-pieces from *Spider-Man* (2002) or *The Amazing Spider-Man 2* (2014), and which also evoke the liberating compositions of the early comics (Figures I.2a–b). But there is more going on here: the player's media experience is not that of 'playing a film', nor even of swinging through a comic book come to life, but of interfacing with a diverse selection of media experiences, all of which are familiar from the GUI.

The game's images indicate possible interactivity through overlain information and icons which specify where the player can shoot a web, or

Figure I.2a Spider-Man soars through the air above New York in the videogame *Spider-Man* (2018) ... Frame enlargement from PS4 gameplay.

Figure I.2b ... a composition which closely replicates that seen in *The Amazing Spider-Man 2* (2014). Frame enlargement from Blu-ray.

whether we can pick up an object. Like hovering a cursor over a program button and receiving pop-up text about that button's function, these icons invite the user to interact with a highly legible, functional set of options. Similarly, when battling a group of enemies, we know a specific henchperson is targeted thanks to a white outline, a marker of selection reminiscent of the outlines that appear when hovering over program windows in the Launchpad function of a macOS. Throughout the game, predictable outputs accompany our inputs, as the player is trained to undertake similar or identical actions in repeating scenarios: just as pressing save on a program will always produce the same result, pressing x in the same situation in *Spider-Man* will always result in the same confident kick from the titular hero.

This combat is predictable not only functionally and visually but also sonically. The same noises play when we punch or kick, and we soon come to learn that certain music cues indicate the presence of danger, their disappearance signifying our victory over enemies even when we have not looked around to check if we are the last one standing. Just as the pings and beeps of our tablets, screens, and laptops help us understand the success of our desktop navigation, so too the aural universe of the game acts as a series of sonic notifications, orienting the player's interactive experience and aiding the legibility and predictability of this interaction.

To level up, we are encouraged to scour the extensive, photorealistic Manhattan for noted landmarks to photograph, at which point the game resembles both Google Earth and Street View, and even geocaching games (Figure I.3). The player toggles between an abstract 3D aerial map and a pedestrian perspective, plotting their way around the city like a real New York commuter with Google Maps in hand (albeit with the welcome capacity to web-sling fleetly above the teaming crowds). The verisimilitude and authenticity of this environment, meanwhile, renders the game a kind of architectural exercise in replicating an existing urban terrain. Like a city from the SimCity videogame series, Manhattan has been both recreated in minute detail but also remixed and re-ordered to suit the designers of Spidey's battles with a variety of foes.

When collecting special items around this city we are prompted to view them within an interface menu, where we can rotate them as though we are a visual effects artist working in a program like Maya, checking the all-around acceptability of our work. This menu is essentially a personalised GUI, one that we must use to succeed at the game. This in-game interface provides familiar operating system functionality around activities and record-keeping, actions which explicitly improve the character's (and so

Figure I.3 The map of New York accessed during gameplay of *Spider-Man* (2018) in order to navigate to tasks and identify collectibles. Frame enlargement from PS4 gameplay.

the player's) performance at a range of tasks. To neglect the in-game GUI is to stymie one's chances of finishing or even remotely enjoying the game. Tapping into another web, there is even the option to peruse a fictional social media feed to monitor how the game's citizens feel about Spider-Man and the choices you have made while wearing his suit.

It may not seem all that radical to propose that navigating this videogame requires digital media literacy. We could prove this perhaps by handing the controller to someone who has not played a videogame since the 1980s and watching them struggle. Yet the scale of the required literacy indicates the extent to which the visual environment, audio cues, and functional affordances of this game are all intimately connected to more general screen practices. *Spider-Man* interfaces with other media: it is inspired by, reliant on, and integrated within a wider media ecology. In saying this I seek to emphasise not transmedia migration – the movement of characters, settings, plots, or whatever from media to media (Schiller 2018) – nor media convergence – the transformation of media culture that Jenkins (2006) describes above as occurring thanks to participatory structures and global networks. Rather, I am pointing to the aesthetic blending that arises through the prioritisation of the GUI in today's screen culture. The graphic user interface sits at the centre of this web and functions as an interactive and aesthetic model of task management and media engagement.

Chapter GUIde

Beyond *Spider-Man*, how can we get stuck into this gooiness? Perhaps it is best to begin with the usual couple of caveats as to what this book is not. The screens we interact with today are overwhelmingly liquid-crystal display (LCD) screens, with or without touchscreen functionality (Dunmer and Sluckin 2014: viii). They employ active matrix technology to feed electrical current to a grid of pixels that make up the screen, and are constructed from layers of glass, liquid crystal arrays, mercury-vapour backlights, polarising filters, and circuitry. Posing significant challenges in terms of recycling and ecological sustainability (Cubitt 2011: 23), these screens have superseded the cathode ray tubes of earlier eras (see Chapter 1). The selfsameness of this LCD technological substrate across laptops, computers, televisions, smartphones, videogame devices, and more is certainly pertinent to the pollination I discuss throughout *Gooey Media*, as it helps drive the convergences described in the following pages. But my focus is for the most part not in this material reality, as crucial as it may be. As such, descriptions of the physical structure of screens themselves – while they do arise in Chapter 1 and Chapter 7 – are relatively brief.

If the manufacturing industry is important, then so are the industries of media production which create content to fill these technological devices. If, for Jenkins, fans drive convergence, then we can equally see this amalgamation and fluidity propagated by media conglomerates hungry to create densely populated textual networks and proliferating consumer access points. For instance, the latest Doctor Strange film is quite the media multiverse, and to truly 'get' everything in it you might feel compelled to watch two related TV shows on Disney+, pick through several YouTube explainer videos, skim some comic books on ComiXology, and even browse news sites for information about corporate mergers and the ownership of character IP. Meanwhile, pervasive internet connections and the glorification of on-the-go access to any and all media propel the fluid migration of content across screens: once it hits streaming, you can watch *Multiverse of Madness* (2022) on your smartphone, tablet, laptop, or television. Relatedly, the cycles of technological obsolescence that are crucial for yearly profit margins compel the creation of particular screens that can adopt more and more of the attributes of other screens (TVs with Skype in them, smartphones with access to videogame libraries, and so on). Again, while all this industrial terrain is essential for the aesthetic interlinking traced in this book, it nonetheless falls out of the direct purview of my methodology, and so only manifests relatively briefly within Chapters 4, 7, and the Conclusion.

With those deficiencies forewarned, what approach *does* this book take in order to make its claims? The focus is primarily aesthetic: I trace the visual and aural linkages across various media and how these linkages are also indebted to or taken up by the desktop interface. In this way, I attempt to map aesthetic connections in ways that foreground the presence of the GUI and its status as a powerful force shaping the look, sound, and feel of media content today. I will examine a range of images and sounds in detail (admittedly emphasising the former). I will note points of overlap across contexts, and will propose historical, cultural, and at times industrial and political reasons for these pervasive associations (and, occasionally, their absence).

As indicated, this requires a wide theoretical reach, and what follows will touch upon histories of technology, debates about labour practices, Marxist urban theory, architectural discourse, and models of ethical action, among other things. The search history of this book might therefore be a little unorthodox, bringing together the likes of *'Apple Computer, Inc. v. Microsoft Corp.* ruling', 'myth of total cinema', 'high frequency trading', 'Tom Cruise motion smoothing', 'lyric videos', 'Houdini particle effects', 'performative cartography', 'CCTV Building Chicago?', 'parametric architecture/NURBS', 'witnessing texts', 'This Person Does Not Exist', and more into one incongruous list. Rather than the cacophony of a poorly curated social media feed, though, I hope that the following chapters address all these topics and tangents in a manner that forms a mucilaginous whole, a polymorphous but singular entity.

Through this work, I aim to build an understanding of the many ways that visual culture has been shaped by the goo of the desktop interface. If the 2018 *Spider-Man* gives us a sense of the wend and weave of this adhesive web, of the way multiple media forms intersect in a single text, then this is not because the wall-crawler is special in this regard. The videogame is, rather, a friendly neighbourhood example of the importance of the GUI to analysing any media text today.

How can we explore all this gooiness? Clearly, chapters on discrete media forms would cut against my intention. This could never be a book with respective chapters on film, television, and videogames: such an approach would reinstate those medial boundaries that I seek to avoid. Instead, these media must all intermingle, as they do on our desktops. As a result, I have structured what follows in a way that seeks to foreground connections rather than distinctions. Each chapter places the GUI alongside a range of other media, exploring some overlapping aesthetic or functional traits. I aim to apply a kind of medium agnosticism, placing the visual and aural elements of interfaces, videogames, films, television, apps, programs, and other media all on equal footing. We might think of this as keeping all these usually discrete media open on the desktop at a single time, with analysis jumping from window to window, or keeping several windows all in view simultaneously. For some readers, this may be an unwelcome diffraction of attention through some conceptual lenses and textual examples that they consider less relevant or even unnecessary. For others, my sought-for media impartiality may not go far enough, as there are many forms of screen and interface that I do not find room to discuss in the following pages (to take just one example, the profusion of advertising and information screens in urban centres is unfortunately an un-clicked pop-up in what follows). But hopefully, for some, the balance will be just right, with the various media forms that are discussed all productively informing and intermingling with one another, just as they do during particularly productive periods of desktop multitasking.

The start-up screen for this work must be a detailed understanding of the aesthetic of the graphic user interface itself, and an unpacking of its history. To do this, Chapter 1 first explores the GUI's lineage and describes how its development was influenced by other screen media such as cinema, television, and videogames. It then identifies the way the GUI cross-pollinates with these other media today. Such overlaps can be subtle, as in the case of TV guide interfaces and the split-screen compositions of digital cinema, or overt, as in the case of texts which openly remediate the look, sound, and affordances of the GUI. These latter – which include films like *Unfriended* (2014) and mobile videogames like *Sara is Missing* (2016) – may seem marginal, but they reveal the extent to which the desktop and various forms of narrative entertainment screen media are, as it were, all compatible files.

Part of the reason for this compatibility is the sought-for representational realism of the desktop, a realism which brings it into close dialogue with other representational or photographic media. The GUI works hard to create and sustain the illusion that the screen is not a site of code and technics but a three-dimensional space that users can effectively access. Chapter 2 accordingly suggests that the GUI can be usefully read through film theorist André Bazin's influential 'myth of total cinema'. But, as the GUI borrows codes of representational realism from cinema and other visual media, so too these other media increasingly emulate the aesthetic traits of the GUI. Television, cinema, and videogames present visual data across ever-denser layers and arrangements of virtual space, a gooification which is most overt in a film like *Gravity* (2013). However, while the GUI certainly sits at the centre of this aesthetic web, it's important to note that there are limits to gooiness. After all, not everything glues together: display technologies like stereoscopic 3D and high frame rates, for instance, are not universally adopted across the digital screen ecology. For all the industrial support they have received, technologies like this fail to stick for all audiences and all screens. With this in mind, the chapter ends by proposing that such piecemeal uptake – too often blamed on poor technology or creative limitations – actually reveals the contingent and disputed nature of realism and interactivity across diverse media forms.

In Chapter 3, we access our screen's sound settings. Just as the visual features of the GUI echo across other media, so too the audio organisation of the desktop reverberates through the wider aural culture of screen-based entertainment. In films, television, and videogames, multi-layered soundtracks and spatially placed sound objects function as sonic equivalents of so many high-resolution navigable windows, while blended soundtracks increasingly use music, sound effects, and dialogue in concert to generate an audioscape which is tightly bound to the contents and movements of its associated imagery. The result is an audio environment which functions a series of notifications or highly complex 'pings' designed to draw the viewer's attention to distinct elements of the visual field. From videogames like *The Last of Us Part II* (2020) to the films of the Marvel Cinematic Universe and even lyric music videos, the sounds and images of contemporary digital media are bound together in order to aid navigable synchronisation in a manner entirely familiar from the GUI.

Returning to the visual field, Chapter 4 addresses digital visual effects, and the way these are produced and advertised. Crucial to today's media ecology, VFX are produced using the GUI, but their manufacture is also marketed to viewers through VFX breakdowns on sites like YouTube. Short videos which claim to show the extensive, expensive processes by which large scale effects shots in films, television, and even videogames are created, VFX breakdowns present layered, malleable 3D spaces of creative digital generation that are indebted to GUI visuality. As such, even though they are little commented upon in scholarship, breakdowns are in fact one of the most visible manifestations of the way that GUI practices and aesthetics have informed wider imaginations about digital media in the twenty-first century. This is further shown through an analysis of the ways in which the breakdown's representational strategies, borne from the GUI, have themselves become crucial parts of mainstream cinematic language.

Chapters 5 and 6 then consider how the GUI has influenced both representations of built space as well as ideas of space itself. Chapter 5 navigates urban form, and the flexibility urban space is granted by films and videogames like *Inception* (2010), *Doctor Strange* (2016), and *SimCity* (1989 – ongoing), among others. The cities in these texts propagate an urban ideal of literal and metaphorical flexibility: characters wave their hands and reorganise city blocks like so many program windows. Disregarding material restrictions and messy complexities, and instead bestowing physical structures with instant flexibility and personalisation, these representations seek to endow built space with the same malleability that we find in the GUI. This imagination of urban space is then also found in navigation technologies like Google Maps and Google Street View, which create individualised and interactive augmentations or replacements of lived urban space. The result is the inculcation of a graphic urban interface – an experience of urban navigation indebted to desktop use. Unfortunately, such graphic urban interfaces are only a dream of digital urban possibility, and this chapter critiques some of the ways in which such a visuality disregards the realities of unfolding urban histories and the lived experiences of urban inhabitants.

Chapter 6 in some senses narrows focus from city planning to architecture, but architecture is here used as a vehicle to think about matter itself. I begin by discussing parametric and topological architectural discourse; that is, the idea that computers enable the design of excitingly pliant and complex buildings. The work of Greg Lynn is key here, as he represents a broader field of architects (and others) who posit that computer-aided design (CAD) tools are changing the very nature of built space. I take the liberty of extending the connections that Lynn himself draws between cinematic CGI and architecture, seeing echoes of his claims in the *Transformers* film franchise. If these seem incompatible, then there is more here than meets the eye: both Lynn and the blockbuster films use digital images to revitalise postindustrial wastelands, namely the Packard Plant in Detroit. Computational possibility is sacrosanct in both contexts, and so they each in their own way trace the eruption of desktop editability into (images of) the real world. The chapter ends with a discussion of the polymer-like aesthetic of Lynn's work and related depictions of 'programmable matter', tracing how and why this matte-like, textureless finish also appears in other media.

In Chapter 7, I consider an interface which is often thought not to be an interface at all. While still relatively marginal, virtual reality (VR) is increasingly prominent as a form of media delivery and is often positioned as providing an experience which goes beyond the screens of cinema, television, and the desktop computer. If the GUI is a space to browse media and accomplish tasks, VR is a place for total immersion: the spectator/user is perceptually transported into another realm, where they seem to have interactive agency with space itself. But rather than leaving the GUI behind,

I here propose that VR just wraps us even more tightly within its representational coordinates. To reveal this connection I think about the content of VR as a 'gameworld interface' – a manifestation of system information with which we can interact, even if only through head movements. Through close attention to 'immersive journalism' (experiences in which the user is framed as a witness to some urgent political issue, as in *Clouds Over Sidra* (2015), which is set in a refugee camp), I connect scholarly critiques of VR with this book's focus on GUI aesthetics in order to dismantle some of the hype concerning the medium's ethical potential.

Through these chapters and their diverse case studies, I aim to show not only how the GUI is central to visual culture, but also how a proper accounting of its influence forces us to consider a wealth of further topics like media ethics, labour relations, and the nature of built space. I also aim to explain the existence of a media object such as *The Matrix Awakens* (2021), the case study taken up in the Conclusion. This object – not quite videogame, not quite game engine, not quite product demo, not quite television, not quite film – is an appropriate place to end this book, as it indicates the urgent need for the media agnostic model of gooey media proffered in its pages (and even – inevitably – indicates how much more work there is to do in this area).

In brief, then, there is much at stake in our interfaces. Like other tools, they are often only noticeable when they fail (and this failure is always a temporary interruption, fixed with a software update, reboot, service resumption, or a new device). But they are far from neutral, as they shape our access to digital media culture, its access to us, and even – crucially – what this culture looks and sounds like in the first place.

1
Screen Mirroring

Accepting a prompt to restore information on the device I'm holding, I swipe right, accessing the phone's home screen. The intelligent assistant suggests that I look through the available programs to identify the location of the phone's owner, Sara. I scroll through the text messages, read the emails, and scour the photos that belong to this stranger. In doing so, I encounter dissatisfied mothers, quirky friends, and dumped boyfriends. This all seems fairly innocuous, apart from some casual mentions of witchcraft, midnight meetings, and deadly viral media (and then there's the Siri-like assistant, which seems oddly pushy …). Suddenly, my investigations are interrupted as the phone rings and, without thinking, I answer. A muffled, desperate voice asks if I'm Sara. Before I can reply, the call cuts off. A few minutes later, after more investigative work and coaching from the phone itself, I find myself having to choose which of two strangers is killed. The predictive text I'm using to communicate my decision only allows me to state one of their names – there is no option to protest.

This is *Sara is Missing* (2016), an immersive sim for Mac, Android, and Windows. If played on a smartphone, the game takes over the entirety of the user's screen, and mimics many of the operations and expectations of this kind of interface. Answering a call in-game requires the exact same swipe on the same screen that the player would undertake to answer a call coming in from their actual life (which could well also occur as they play). The result is a videogame that finds deeper leverage in the player's reality than might be expected given its more outlandish elements, leverage achieved precisely because the game's diegesis overlaps with, or rather *consists openly and entirely of* a specific interface, the one of the device on which it is being played. That the game can mimic a smartphone screen so successfully, and yet still function as a videogame, hints at the extent to which computing interfaces overlap with other media.

As discussed in the introduction, the screens we use to watch media, do our jobs, and plan and enact our social lives are in many cases not discrete, single-use devices. Whether a phone, laptop, tablet, or even a television, screens are multipurpose, whatever their size. At the grander end of the spectrum, a cinema may predominantly be used for screening theatrical narrative feature films (as well as the preceding commercials), but it might also be the vehicle for filmed theatrical performances, sporting events, and concerts, among others. And on the smallest scale, even smartwatches communicate health goals, live biometric data, maps, and social media feeds alongside a choice of digital timekeeping facades on their tiny screens. Most commonly, the average mobile phone has since the early 2010s consolidated media viewing, media capture, videogame play, and internet browsing – all of which *Sara is Missing* cannily exploits.

If this versatility is an inescapable feature of today's media environment, then it does not just impact exhibition and reception. The act of viewing these intermingled screens, while crucial, is less my focus than the aesthetic consequences of this intermingling. As I will describe in more detail near the end of this chapter, the videogame *Sara is Missing* only works because the contemporary smartphone is simultaneously mobile communication device and game platform, media depository and life journal, social map and surveillant apparatus par excellence. These features do not just co-exist on the same screen, they look, sound, and feel similar, and their functionality relies on common (if seemingly unlearned and intuitive) rules and affordances. As such, sufficiently analysing this game requires us to pay attention to the cross-medial nature of its screen, and of all screens.

The same is true, as this chapter will ultimately show, for other media texts that work in similar ways, whether they are videogames, narrative fiction films, short documentaries, or whatever. In the examples explored below, screens mirror one another in unexpected but productive and telling ways, as the GUI is copied and pasted into other media formats, adapting to these affordances but also reshaping the media into which it has been imported. Mirroring our desktops, these texts reveal much about our experience of the GUI and its importance in a host of other contexts. An analysis of them is, therefore, a vital first step in this book's later exploration of a wider array of cross-pollinations. Indeed, while the focus of this chapter is those texts which directly quote the GUI interface, this is just the brief thumbnail prompt of a much larger process of borrowing and amalgamation. As the remaining chapters will hopefully make clear, *any* media text today partakes in this overlapping economy of multi-purpose screens. The inevitable result is a certain amount of stylistic bleed, whether overt or not. Yet before I can turn to these related media, it is necessary to provide a history and brief analysis of the GUI itself.

Getting to the GUI

Today, screens and computers are fused together technologically and culturally – if it's a computer, it'll probably have a screen attached, and if it's a screen it'll likely have some kind of computing power. But this was not always the case, and screens and computers have separate histories before their convergence. This is perhaps obvious in the case of screens: cinema screens were mechanical and chemical long before they were also electronic and digital. Histories of film often emphasise the media's lineage in optical illusions, parlour toys, and painting, rather than in engineering and calculation. A site of creative leisure activity first and foremost, the screen is more a development of illusionistic art than an interface-in-waiting.[1]

Meanwhile, the earliest computers – the difference engine and later analytical engine of Charles Babbage and Ada Lovelace in the 1820s and 30s – were designed to print the output of their equations onto reams of paper, punch cards, or copper plates. Even into the 1940s, machines like the ENIAC (Electronic Numerical Integrator and Computer) – which calculated artillery trajectories and was used to test the viability of a hydrogen bomb – employed card readers and punch cards to input and output data. The workings of machines like this were monitored through careful observation of a cornucopia of blinking lights, with nary a screen in sight.

The application of cathode ray tube (CRT) displays to computers in the 1950s introduced more recognisable interfaces, as they united the computer with a form of rectangular visual display. But despite CRT technology being integral to the development of television, when used for computing these screens were not initially representational. As Gaboury (2018: 26) states, 'despite the prevalence of screen technologies for televisual and cinematic images, these could not be readily adapted for use with computational technology because computer graphics, unlike film and television, do not begin as images'. Instead of showing virtual worlds and manipulable icons, early computer screens provided command-line interfaces: illuminated lines of text on a black screen, with keyboards used to enter data and navigate through programs and lines of code.[2]

---

1 As a valuable counterpoint to dominant histories of cinema, Luci Marzola (2021) has stressed the engineering basis of early twentieth-century Hollywood.
2 Some computer screens of the 1950s and 1960s did allow for some forms of direct manipulation. The US military's SAGE (Strategic Air Ground Environment), a program for tracking missiles, required operators to 'tag' suspect elements shown on the screen (which was fed by radar) using a light gun. Charlie Gere (2006) uses SAGE as an

If command-line interfaces only enabled typed commands and coded language strings to be inputted and displayed, then as a result computers in the 1960s and 1970s were effectively opaque black boxes, reliant on and mostly used by those few people who were able to type readable commands and interpret the displayed textual responses. To compute, you had to speak the language of the computer.

The migration of computers beyond highly specialised military, university, and corporate contexts and into a wider array of commercial and domestic spaces demanded a move away from these command-line interfaces. Crucial to the computer's widespread adoption was the shifting of a user's interactions from an overtly coded, semiotic, specialised process to one that was imagistic, representational, and even perceptually tactile. The core machine itself might remain reliant on complex strings of binary code, but for today's embrace of screen culture to take place the computer had to present itself in more accessible, visually intuitive ways. As Steven Johnson (1997: 14) puts it in his book *Interface Culture*, 'For the magic of the digital revolution to take place, a computer must also *represent itself* to the user, in a language that the user understands'. This not only expands the machine's user base but even invokes feelings of power and mastery (Chun 2011: 62–3).

The GUI provided this in the 1980s, but it did not emerge from nowhere. Archaeologies of the interface identify a series of precursors to this graphical data-space, including the vapourware of Vannevar Bush's 1940s Memex machine and a legendary 1968 presentation at the Association for Computing Machinery/Institute of Electrical and Electronics Engineers joint conference in San Francisco by Douglas Engelbart. Both predict and celebrate GUI-style functionality, and were themselves inspirations for GUI design in the 1980s.

As head of the US Office of Scientific Research and Development in 1945, Bush published an essay in the magazine *The Atlantic* in which he called for a solution to the overwhelming amount of information being produced by global scientific and commercial industries. To him, this profusion of material was unmanageable with the presently existing laborious ways of accessing it, meaning much of its possible use was being unexploited. Imagined as a machine whose job was to store a user's files and offer instant access to them, Bush's proposed Memex was not a computer as it would have been understood then, although its ability to find specific information

---

example of the importance of the radar screen in the development of the contemporary GUI interface.

from within the depths of vast sets of numbers and letters did evoke the kind of data processing such machines were used for at the time. Never built, the Memex nonetheless appears in numerous histories of the GUI and the internet.[3] It anticipates a world of screen interfaces, databased and customised links, and active individual users. The Memex, in Bush's description, provides not just information, but trails and digressions, annotations and suggestions, and it foreshadows the idea of the computer as a storehouse of easily navigable, highly personalised, and digitally sharable material. This material is, of course, accessed using the visual interface of a personal screen.[4]

Meanwhile, Engelbart's presentation at ACM/IEEE twenty years later is colloquially referred to as 'the mother of all demos' because it seems so prescient in identifying and even performing elements that would become foundational for mainstream computer use. It even yokes these possible functionalities to recognisable user intentions and actions. Updating and actualising the Memex, the demo shows a multipurpose computer that was visually lively and intuitive. Key ideas put forward in the demo include bitmapping and direct manipulation, which shifted the screen from a site of textual updates to a cartographic and tactile environment. Such interactive strategies therefore amplified immediacy, even though, as Johnson (1997: 21) states, they technically added yet a further layer of abstraction between user and information. Wendy Chun (2011: 87) describes how this demo, which was for many the origin of 'interactive real-time interfaces', installs a 'promise of transparent technologically mediated contact' at the core of computer use.

Through this demo, the screen interface became a synecdoche for the machine itself, a frame of interpretation that would become effectively unthought with the widespread adoption of the GUI in the 1980s. Across this decade, computers in governmental, institutional, and consumer contexts increasingly employed graphical user interfaces. Apple led the charge here, creating a desktop which was not only graphical, but which, for many commentators, had *character*. This kind of interface was not just usable, but, thanks in part to the application of insights such as those put forward

---

3 For example, see Johnson 1997: 116–23; Chun 2011: 75–81; and Hillis, Petit and Jarrett 2013: 129–36.

4 From late in the essay: 'A touch brings up the code book. Tapping a few keys projects the head of the trail. A lever runs through it at will, stopping at interesting items, going off on side excursions. It is an interesting trail, pertinent to the discussion. So he sets a reproducer in action, photographs the whole trail out, and passes it to his friend for insertion in his own memex, there to be linked into the more general trail' (Bush 1945).

by psychologists like James J. Gibson in *The Ecological Approach to Visual Perception* (1979), pleasurable. In Johnson's words, Apple's interfaces 'displayed a masterful integration of form and function, of course, but there were also instances of *gratuitous* form, art for art's sake' (Johnson 1997: 49; emphasis in original). His examples of this artistry alight on the way program windows zoom and 'twirl', and the customisability of the on-screen components. All this salvaged the desktop from implications of bureaucracy or corporatisation: 'No longer a lifeless, arcane intersection point between user and microprocessor, it was now an autonomous entity, a work of culture as much as technology' (Johnson 1997: 50).[5]

If Apple have for a long time been iconic for their interface design, their path to ascendancy was not uncontested. As a major development in visual culture, the GUI was a high-stakes piece of technology, an idea with enormous commodity value. This was made clear by a copyright lawsuit in the early 1990s, in which Apple sought to prohibit market competitor Microsoft from too closely evoking their distinctive 'character'. Never mind that Apple had themselves taken many of their desktop functions and aesthetics from Xerox several years earlier, leading Xerox to file their own suit against Apple. All that mattered was that Apple protected what they had come to see as their intellectual property. They did not just want to perfect the GUI, they wanted to own it as a concept.

The case against Microsoft needed to define exactly what a GUI was. It distilled the definition to five elements:

> [1] use of windows to display multiple images on the computer screen and to facilitate user interaction with the information contained in the windows; [2] iconic representation of familiar objects from the office environment; [3] manipulation of icons to convey instructions and to control operation of the computer; [4] use of menus to store information or computer functions in a place that is convenient to reach, but

---

5 Lev Manovich agrees with Johnson on the character of Apple products, stating that their design of both hardware and software became ever more focused on aesthetics throughout the 1990s. In this respect, the release of OS X and its interface Aqua in 2001 are crucial: 'Aqua's icons, buttons, windows, cursor, and other elements were colorful and three-dimensional. They used shadows and transparency. The programs announced their start by opening their windows via an animation. The icons in Dock playfully increased in size as the user moved a cursor over them. And if in OS 9 the default desktop backgrounds were flat single-color monochrome, the backgrounds that came with Aqua were much more visually complex, more colorful and assertive – drawing attention to themselves rather than attempting to be invisible' (Manovich 2012: 281).

saves screen space for other images; and [5] opening and closing of objects as a means of retrieving, transferring and storing information.[6]

Here, right at the moment the computer was becoming intrinsic for social, cultural, political, and economic life, the precise aesthetic ways in which we would use it for these purposes were being carefully defined, and fiercely contested.

Neither the Apple lawsuit against Microsoft nor the Xerox lawsuit against Apple was wholly successful, though. Apple may have claimed the 'look-and-feel' of their GUI was original, but the court ruled that it consisted of elements that were, in themselves, not protected by copyright law. The *ideas* of the GUI – the icons, the manipulability, the openings and closings – could not be owned, even if their particular *expression* – exact shapes of icons, for instance – might be. Microsoft may have copied Apple (just as Apple earlier copied Xerox), but, as Joseph Myers (1995) states in his casenote on this ruling, Apple did not have 'a right to the exclusive use of those elements'. Apple could not win the 'GUI Wars', and so this form of computer access, along with those elements that seem to personify it, became usable across a wider range of products.

Those features outlined in 1995 remain fundamental to desktop use today, testifying to the keen way in which Apple and their legal team understood the central visual attributes of the GUI. Apple and Microsoft therefore both popularised a particular imagination of the computer, an imagination which is predominantly representational and realist.

The GUI represents a move in computing towards the structuring interpretation of the screen as window. Across the five legally defined elements listed above is a focus on images, icons, representation, and the maximising of screen space. A pictorial form of communication rather than a linguistic one, the GUI organises information visually and spatially rather than (solely) linguistically, and works to evoke the handling of real objects in non-computer-mediated spaces. The visual space of the screen contains discrete objects arranged on a vertical 'desktop', and the user can layer elements of this environment as they see fit. Both the virtual objects themselves and our interactions with them are heavily skeuomorphic – visual and audial cues provide connection to and evocation of analogue equivalences to an item or function. For instance, many diary management programs visually resemble physical notebooks, while the sound of a shutter click usually accompanies the taking of a screenshot. Users are granted a sense of 'immediacy'

---

6 *Apple Computer, Inc. v. Microsoft Corp.* (1995), 35 F.3d 1435 (9th Cir).

thanks to the way operating systems like the appropriately named Windows do not require them to input semantically opaque language but instead prompt them to manipulate virtualised representations.

If this technical and legal history implies that the GUI developed in a vacuum, this of course isn't the case. The GUI evolved in explicit and implicit dialogue with a range of other screen media, and these media shape the GUI as much as the GUI soon began to shape other media. For instance, at its outset, the GUI adopted traits of another fast-domesticating media device, the television. Since the CRT was being used for both computers and TV broadcasts in the 1970s and 1980s, conceptual slippage between them is not surprising. The domestication of TV may have played its own part in acclimatising developers and consumers to the concept of a small box with a representational surface that provided instantaneous access to many discrete visual worlds (referred to as programs in both televisual and computing contexts). In the other direction, the development of teletext in 1970s Europe imagined the television as a kind of part-time command-line computer: semantic commands (inputted numbers) allowed the television owner to access pages of information, offering a kind of nascent internet of news, weather reports, program listings, and even train timetables (Holyer 2019).

Scholars have in particular called attention to the bleed between cinema and the GUI, with the development of the representational language of the latter informed by the existence and cultural longevity of the former. Friedberg (2006: 194–200), for instance, contextualises the GUI with a discussion not only of video art and split-screen installations but also film sequences. Meanwhile, Manovich (2001: xv) compares the aesthetics and organisation of the desktop with both established and emerging film grammars, suggesting that 'cinematic ways of seeing the world, of structuring time, of narrating a story, of linking one experience to the next, have become the basic means by which computer users access and interact with all cultural data'.[7] This is not to downplay the connections between the GUI and other media forms which are not primarily about screen entertainment. For instance, Charlie Gere (2006) and Bernard Geoghegan (2019) each in their own ways stress the need to rescue the GUI's indebtedness to military radar technology from its contemporary association with ideas of media entertainment convergence.

---

7 Thanks to the unusual structure of the book's opening this quote is also found at pp. 78–9; it has been excerpted by Manovich and included up front along with a still from Dziga Vertov's documentary *Man with a Movie Camera* (1929), indicating the importance he wishes to grant this concept.

Gooey media

Through its transformation from command-line to GUI, the screen changed from a site of regulated text into a simulated deep space that was navigable with a cursor. Computers therefore subtly moved from abstract processing machines to a kind of alternative reality. In 1965, Ivan Sutherland – a key presence in the development of computer graphics – called for what he called an 'ultimate display': a computer screen which functioned as 'a window through which one beholds a virtual world', a virtual world designed to look, sound, and act as 'real' as possible (Sutherland 1965: 508).

If the GUI would end up providing just such a display, the 'reality' of this world was not instantaneously achieved. As Terry Harpold (2009: 100) states, in the 1980s and 1990s, the GUI expressed a tension between realist aspirations and technical affordances: 'During that period, limited screen resolution and color depth, performance bottlenecks, and the primitive state of graphic design meant that users were confronted by images that bore at best a cartoonish resemblances to windows, desktops, and folders'. Just as there was no confusing the pages of teletext with those of a TV show, at this time there was a vast difference between the representational images of film and photography and the icons of the GUI. This representational gap did not last long, though, and the GUI soon developed its own form of photorealism, allowing it to more powerfully integrate with a predominantly photographic visual culture.

Yet, even in its early days, the GUI inaugurated the computer's logic of virtuality. As Friedberg (2006: 226–7) stresses, the translation from bits to space allows seemingly direct (but actually metaphorical) access, as the user directly manipulates virtual versions of what they command: 'the user selects, drags, drops, opens, closes, copies, deletes, puts in the trash'. This direct manipulation begets other features. Since the alternate reality of the GUI relies upon the management and navigation of the z-axis, layering becomes common. Early desktops may not have allowed program windows to overlap, but today's desktops depend upon it. Organising programs atop one another, like sheets of paper on a physical desk, allows for more programs to be accessed without the screen itself needing to grow larger. This space is, in Friedberg's (2006: 227) description, 'both deep and flat', and so layering and overlaps become key to accomplishing tasks, as they allow engagement with multiple programs within the relatively limited area of the screen's constricted flat rectangle. Program windows peek out from behind one another, reminding us of their presence and possibility, without needing to take up a large chunk of the entire visual field. As a result, the GUI not only expands access to the computer – in that it allows more than just computer programmers to use and even program computers – it also expands the perceptible space that the user can access within the now-layered screen.

In the next chapter, I will delve into such visual strategies in more detail, unfolding the GUI's increasing verisimilitude. Here, though, I would like to continue establishing quite broadly how the GUI cross-pollinates with other media. This work can be undertaken by focusing on pronounced functions and some quite generalised aesthetic qualities which echo across media, rather than by paying attention to any specific texts. As such, this section will provide a foundation for the remainder of the book, with the following chapters offering more sustained discussions of textual examples under more specific thematic nuclei. But in order to get to that deeper analysis, I need to convince you that we undertake GUI-style interfacings in a range of non-computational contexts, and that we do so with staggering frequency. Whether using a phone, a TV, a laptop, a tablet, or even a VR headset, our entertainment media and ancillary infrastructures of access are deeply imbued with the look, feel, and functions of the desktop interface, as I hope a short tour through some of these media devices and their affiliations with the GUI will be able to demonstrate.

The most obvious place to begin mapping these connections is probably videogames. Symbiotic with both the computer and interactivity, we should not be shocked to find that videogames overlap with the GUI in terms of aesthetics and operability. Early text-based multi-user dungeons (MUDs) provided digital gameplay in the era of the command-line interface, but the development and broad embrace of the desktop turned games into (for the most part) virtual spaces: as the GUI adopted spatial cues and layered organisation, so too did games. The move from 2D representational space in 1980s side-scrollers to 3D movement in 1990s platformers, and then to the highly detailed and photorealistic environments of the 2000s and 2010s, all closely aligns with the changes to operating system aesthetics across this time. The game world, running parallel with the interface, shifts from textual system to (seemingly) habitable environment, adopting similar developments in, for instance, representational contour and shading.

The interactivity of videogames is also synonymous with that of GUI use. New media, as Manovich (2001: 183) has argued, change viewers into users, demanding that we move into the images they provide through our clicking, zooming, and selecting. Videogames rely on an identical form of active engagement, whatever the genre. This isn't just about particular forms of exploration, discovery, problem-solving, or enemy-obliteration. Rather, the very visual and aural space of any videogame is dependent on player agency.

As Aylish Wood (2012) argues, game spaces should not be thought of as pre-existent and stable, but rather as being constantly generated through the confluence of player, game code (software), and gaming system (hardware). Wood (2012: 88) stresses how the processes of exploration and negotiation undertaken by the gamer lead to the rendering of space in the first place, all surroundings being 'actively created when a gamer becomes entangled with the game world and the possibilities of a game's code'. To play a game is by necessity to interact with and personalise it. If all game space is 'recursive' – a series of object relations not just revealed but actively shaped the player's every input choice – then the same is true of the desktop interface, which relies on its user to open and reposition programs, select from multiple options, and generally create the visual space through which they navigate.

Moreover, because games often combine elements of a representational world with operational menus and markers that help the player navigate this world, they stage an encounter between photographic realism and digital data in a way that directly evokes how the same process plays out in the GUI environment. Illusions of photographic and haptic fidelity found in the GUI (buttons that depress, shadows cast by program windows) reappear in game menus and even in some cases the way operational information is embedded in the diegesis of the videogame world. Every time a number indicating remaining health floats above an enemy's head, or a white outline highlights that a player is able to manipulate a particular diegetic object, or the route and location of the next objective is visualised with a marker inserted within three-dimensional space, the fictional world of the game collapses together function and fiction, operational possibility and representational veracity. The gameworld is therefore an interface as much as it is a fictional world, prompting Kristine Jørgensen (2013) to call the arising system a 'gameworld interface' – a desktop style environment which combines explicit functionality with representational realism in ways that are indebted to the GUI (a process which I will explore in more detail in Chapter 7).

Videogame consoles function as tools for playing games, but their uses go far beyond this. They often allow their owners to customise apps and access a wealth of streaming media and other internet content, becoming home entertainment media platforms. Plugged into a flatscreen television, the Playstation 4 or the Xbox Series X does not just enable gameplay, but also – with the necessary apps and additions – the viewing of a film on Netflix, immersion in a VR experience, chatting with friends online, and browsing YouTube, among other things.

So now let's save and quit our game, and turn to this television. In the 1970s, Raymond Williams (2003) famously described television as defined by 'flow': an unfolding and ongoing constellation of scheduled content into which the viewer dipped or surfed. But in the twenty-first century the television has, like so much else, become 'smart'. Smart TVs are not just conduits to discrete channels, but have their own operating systems and encourage users to add multiple apps and features. Television programming, as Daniel Chamberlain (2010: 86) states, 'has become just one category of content streamed or stored alongside other types of video, audio, images, and data files, served up by such competing convergent devices as personal computers, set-top boxes, personal portable media players, and mobile phones'. As a result, the television appliance, once defined by a need to 'tune in', turns now into a desktop interface in all but name. Certainly, the average set has a bit less functionality than our computers – it would be challenging to write a document using even the smartest of smart TVs, for instance – but they nonetheless offer the customisable, personalised on-demand experiences of GUI media engagement.

This is about more than those TV shows like *Mosaic* (2018), *Black Mirror: Bandersnatch* (2018), or *Animals on the Loose: A You vs. Wild Movie* (2021), which all solicit viewers to choose plotlines to follow or make decisions on behalf of characters. In fact, the beginning of TV's gooification can be identified earlier in the 'what's on' or 'menu' screens that began appearing from the 1990s. These navigational thresholds, absent from prior television, became necessary as the number of channels grew (Hesmondhalgh and Lotz 2020: 393). They engendered a shift in the design of TV remote controls: a spatialised 'D-pad' (a circular collection of four buttons in the centre of the remote) was now necessary for the user to easily move up and down and forward and back through onscreen menus, rather than just from visible channel to visible channel as in prior remote switching (Benson-Allott 2015: 117). Displaying available programming across an array of channels, these menu screens expanded temporally thanks to the rise of TiVo in the 2000s – material could be found to watch from earlier in the day or week, and programs could be scheduled for recording and later consumption. In her history of the remote control, Caetlin Benson-Allott (2015: 118) describes how these screens (and their accompanying remotes) 'helped viewers approach television as information'. Such menu screens are a bridge towards the streaming platforms of the late 2000s onwards. Merging earlier television programming with the logics of YouTube, Netflix, Amazon Prime, Disney+ and their ilk, interactive broadcast menus offer on-demand presentations rather than access to ongoing, scheduled televisual content, and present this material as a wealth of data to be actively navigated by the viewer.

Moreover, the already fuzzy line between the television set and the computer gets even fuzzier at the level of programming, as, in a telling lexical shift, we now watch a lot of TV on appliances that are not TVs. The TV may have become like a GUI, but streaming platforms render all GUIs into potential televisions. Programming becomes decoupled from device, as users encounter essentially the same interface whatever device they employ to access a given streaming service. Navigating through and watching the content of, say, Disney+ is a highly similar experience whether undertaken on a TV, a phone, a tablet, a laptop, or even a VR headset (albeit possibly with some minor variations depending on technological capacity). The branded platform and (many of) its features migrate fluidly across all these various screens.

Television programming, and the television appliance itself, become entwined with the contemporary computer desktop. If this allows for the interactive TV content mentioned above, it also, less obviously, changes our experiences of both television and media. Apps, as Catherine Johnson (2020: 166) puts it, 'have insinuated themselves into our quotidian television viewing habits', but have done so stealthily, without this shift really being taken note of by scholars or audiences. The interfaces of streaming platforms may be transient screen spaces, designed to be passed through on the way to content, but Johnson (2019: 109) stresses how they play a vital role in organising television viewing. Streaming platforms therefore shape our experience of television not just through the content they make or the algorithms they employ in devising, producing, and advertising this content, but also through the way they organise our access to this and all other content on their platforms.

Johnson (2019: 114, 118) argues that the visual iconography of these interfaces 'is closer to that of a row of shelves or a catalogue' than the typical GUI desktop, and that they offer little opportunity for customisation. While this is true in many senses, these shelves and catalogues are – I would argue – still built on GUI foundations. For instance, these interfaces privilege navigable windows rather than command-line style text. Content is accessed via navigable menus and thumbnails, and organised using the visual impression of objects arrayed in quasi-three-dimensional space. As of 2022, Netflix presents multiple horizontal bands filtered by genre (and by the hidden parameters of its recommendation algorithm), giving an at-a-glance view of a dozen or more pieces of discrete entertainment. When scrolling through these bands resting on a particular thumbnail for more than a split second makes it expand in size, giving the impression it is being lifted out of its surroundings and pulled forward towards the viewer. This thumbnail might then cede to a list of its multiple seasons, which flows in turn into a list of all available episodes. The easy drift through these menus, and the way they visually swipe, maximise, or fade in, spatialises our engagement with the embedded media. TV may become information, an instant access database, but it is one which looks more like a GUI than an Excel sheet.[8]

This quasi-GUI is then personalised through our own interaction with the screen. While any content is playing, I still have instant access to further episodes or alternate audio and subtitle feeds at the touch of a button. All of this accentuates the impression that the chosen material exists alongside a wide array of alternatives (the NowTV app even has a button appear labelled 'watch something else' whenever the user pauses, a statement which sometimes sounds like an earnest plea to level up one's choice of media). And there are as many Netflix interfaces as there are Netflix users – we can all create our own playlists, but, more than this, mysterious algorithms work over a user's viewing history to decide which films and genres are foregrounded, and even which thumbnails are used to advertise them. This latter form of personalisation may be invisible, but it presents a profound difference from pre-streaming television navigation.

The multiple windows of the GUI, meanwhile, can be found in a prominent genre of television programming, one that, quite exceptionally, does not (yet) feature on media platforms like Netflix: live news. From the beginnings of the twenty-four-hour news cycle in the 1980s, to the introduction of the chyron (or ticker) in 2001, news broadcasts have increasingly emphasised the wealth of information they provide. Both a financial trading news channel like Bloomberg and a less specialist news outlet like Al Jazeera will regularly commit only around half of their screen to a program's hosts or the footage of a particular broadcast; the remainder of the screen will be devoted to real-time financial index information, scrolling news updates, sporting scores, weather forecasts, and other data. The ideology of 'liveness' that Jane Feuer (1983) noted was so critical to news programming in the 1980s has been continually expanded through these additional components. The implication is a host of simultaneously unfolding events of which the viewer should apparently be aware. The result – perhaps ironically – is that a typical news channel broadcast now closely resembles a desktop interface

---

8 The DVD menu can be seen as a stepping-stone between TV channel listings and the kind of display seen on Netflix. Containing images for decoration and navigation, DVD selection screens spatialised access to films and television programs in ways that were more familiar to the Netscape or Encyclopaedia Britannica user than the 1990s VCR owner or television viewer.

with multiple programs open, all of which have some purchase on the user's current attention.⁹

Having caught up with the news, let's finish our extended browsing session by watching a film. The preceding discussion of streaming interfaces of course still applies here – few platforms offer only TV, but bedazzle the subscriber with a combination of film, television programming, and sport. But a pre-history of the film as displayed in this way must also take into account DVDs. Supplanting VHS tapes across the late 1990s and early 2000s, DVDs promised better quality sound and image as well as greater access to texts through jump-to-a-scene menus and expanded special features. As Jo Smith (2008: 146) states, this makes them 'neither cinema, television nor database, but an amalgam of all three'. For Smith, DVDs that come loaded with additional making-of content 'scramble the received wisdom of consumer identity', as the imagined consumer being appealed to 'is an assemblage of media categories that include cinema, television, computers and books':

> The technological dimensions of the menu screen (which invokes the similarly embodied logic of computer gaming) make an appeal to the computer user [...]. The TV buff can manufacture a hybrid telecinematic flow by viewing documentary footage, commentaries and behind-the-scenes footage back-to-back, while the high-definition rendering and surround-sound of the DVD production (coupled with immersive home entertainment systems) can absorb the cinephile. (Smith 2008: 139–40)

For Smith, DVDs are therefore a 'hinge condition' to a different kind of media experience. And, subsequent to Smith's writing in 2008, we can see clearly how the format has been a hinge towards digital streaming. This includes those discs which offered access to internet-stored material when played on computers. But even the majority of DVDs which do not provide this feature still – through the use of interactive menus – assertively spatialise their texts as a series of navigable scenes (just as the streaming service does). Indeed, the emphasis on additional content of any kind in the DVD further turns the TV screen from pseudo-cinema to proto-browser.

Outside of DVDs and other home viewing contexts, cultural discourses on cinema often stress not overlap with other media but dissimilarity

---

9 Equally, the desktop interface can be set up to resemble a news broadcast, with stock ticker apps, chyron extensions, and other forms of relentlessly scrolling and updating information about current events.

and qualitative divergence. Filmmakers and industrial agents will fiercely defend cinema's conspicuous uniqueness in the face of this otherwise converging media environment. Whatever cinema is, it is ideally *cinematic*, a term which alludes to a kind of spectacular and immersive verisimilitude. This label then paradoxically filters down in a degraded form to other media. Witness, for instance, videogames or TV shows being praised for their 'cinematic' qualities. Such qualified praise makes claims about these other media as well as about cinema: videogames, this claim subtly asserts, are generally thought to offer lower-quality graphic fidelity, which 'cinematic' offerings overcome. Meanwhile, television programs are considered to offer repetitive or visually uninteresting storytelling, strictures which 'cinematic' examples surmount. This is an extremely simplified model of media affordances, certainly, but it is one which circulates in some form or another in cultural discourse, industrial commentary, and academic discussion.

The existence of cinemas themselves is crucial here. These sites of theatrical exhibition are distinct from other screens for various reasons, among them presumed and enforced audience attention; the screening of material prior to this material's release on other screens; and, of course, sheer size. These screens seem not to be multipurpose in the way that tablets, phones, and computer screens are, and both Barbara Klinger (2006) and Charles Acland (2020) have drawn attention to the importance of technological factors here. Cinemas are separate entities culturally but also technologically, with Acland arguing that cinephilia is bound up with ideas of ideal technical conditions for screenings: '*the secret life of the cinephile is that of the technophile*' (Acland 2020: 275; emphasis in original).

But it is almost inevitable that, whatever the film, it will be seen far more extensively on other screens than those of the cinema (if it ever gets a cinema release at all). These other screens will in turn change the film. As Acland (2020: 274) puts it, mainstream texts today are often a kind of 'Silly Putty': 'produced with paths of media migration in mind, [they are] designed to be stretched and squeezed, giffed and guillotined'. In an era of proliferating platforms for the viewing of cinema, *cinema* (as place, as event, as ideal) becomes more not less important. Films outside the cinema are not denuded or deprived, but rather platform variations, alternatively accessible options with their own affordances (changeable subtitles; skipping, fast-forwarding, and freeze-framing capacities; hyperlinked information and trivia about actors and the production of the text).

Writing about the 'poor images' of gifs, memes, and other low-quality, low-fidelity content which proliferates and circulates online, filmmaker and essayist Hito Steyerl (2009) stresses the relational importance of cinema, which is always what these images are not: 'In the class society of images, cinema takes on the role of the flagship store'. This is a helpful definition for the cultural place of cinema, which is a kind of floating signifier of value and prestige. Moreover, the cinema is, as I have already noted, not just a space of film viewing, but also a site in which live theatre, sports, television, concerts, and a range of other content might be consumed. These screenings of this non-film material will variously borrow from the cultural prestige associated with cinema (exclusivity; immersive spectacle) *and also* the convenience associated with television (cheaper than a concert or theatre ticket; easier than travelling to an overcrowded urban sporting venue). So, while *cinematic* as idea and ideal has industrial and cultural power, it is a relative term, and one with extremely fuzzy edges.

Nonetheless, cinema (as a venue) seems to lack the kind of GUI style interfacing described in relation to videogames, television, and DVD menus. Once we have taken our cinema seat and put away our phones, we may tend toward a non-gooey experience of media immersion. However, there are texts and scenarios which ask viewers to interact. Cinema releases like *App* (2013) and *Late Shift* (2016) prompt audiences to use their smartphones alongside the film screening to make choices and to access further content (Blake 2017). Practices such as hecklevision and bullet-screens arose in the 2010s allowing cinema attendees at specific sites to send text messages which would appear on the screen, concurrently scrolling with dozens of other quips and comments from other live audience members (Dwyer 2017). Relatively marginal at the present time, these examples still indicate how the cinema is not always so cinematic and non-interactive as we might expect.

This tour through videogames, television, and cinema indicates a few of the ways in which GUI aesthetics and functions are crucial to these media formats. Serving different audiences, found in different sites, and with different cultural expectations, these formats are unified in their adoption – whether significantly or more marginally – of desktop interface practices. This functional bleed is complemented by extensive aesthetic bleed at the level of specific media texts themselves. This happens at a range of levels and in a variety of ways, as I hope to demonstrate in the remaining chapters. But for the time being, we turn to a series of texts which have explicitly centred the GUI as a dominant feature of textual expression, and so further show its compatibility and allegiance with other media.

Screen share

The intermedial connections and overlaps described above become most overt in texts which openly adopt the aesthetics of the GUI in other contexts. A growing body of videogames, fiction films, and even documentaries have appropriated the visual and aural elements of the desktop computer. In this lengthy – but by no means exhaustive – section I will explore such texts, indicating not only the way they take up GUI aesthetics and affordances, but also how their existence can teach us more about the GUI's place in screen culture.

The gooey approach taken by the examples below might be labelled 'remediation'. As Jay David Bolter and Richard Grusin (1999: 273) put it, new media refashion prior media forms, adopting and adapting traits of those media which came before. Likewise, 'older' media, in a bid for continued relevance, might seek to adopt traits that personify new media. As such, those texts which employ GUI aesthetics in many ways display remediation in action. While it is certainly the case that newer media forms do take up the conventions of those that preceded them and vice versa, though, the implication of evocation or containment is somewhat limiting in relation to the contemporary, GUI-inflected media landscape. What is interesting about the below texts, and indeed all the texts described in this book, is not that one media 'contains' or is being 'contained in' another. Instead, what we see are much more hybrid forms. In this way, ideas of screen mirroring and screen sharing seem more useful than remediation when thinking about these texts, foregrounding as they do concepts of equivalence and intermingling rather than hierarchy and replacement.

The most mainstream mirroring of GUI may be found in the cinema, and a body of horror filmmaking which takes place entirely on desktops. Films such as *Unfriended* (2014), *Open Windows* (2014), *Unfriended: Dark Web* (2018), *Searching* (2018), *Host* (2020), and *Profile* (2021) all depict complex interpersonal dramas solely through the desktop interface. They literally demonstrate the existence of the GUI in cinema – not as a prop in the diegesis or the subject of a cutaway, but as a replacement for the cinema screen. In a way, this might be seen as a response to the threat cinema seemingly faces from alternative platforms. When seen theatrically, these films enfold cinema's main rival within its own borders, but still assert something *cinematic*. The cinema screen shows its allegiance to the GUI through aesthetic quotation, but also accentuates its difference through attributes of superior image size, surround sound, and a communal viewing situation (this last especially pronounced in the tense and shrieking audiences of horror). Nonetheless, these films indicate how the affordances and possibilities of other narrative media might in fact be amplified through their adoption of the GUI's methods of information delivery, rhetorical appeal, and affective solicitation.

While indebted to the short film *Noah* (2013) – another GUI-based narrative focusing on visual distraction and teenage characters – these films are also in many ways a software update to the found footage filmmaking that became popular in the 2000s thanks to the success of *The Blair Witch Project* (1999) and *Paranormal Activity* (2007). Revising the epistolary novel (which consists of letters between characters, news cuttings, diary entries, and the like), found footage offers the viewer supposedly 'real' material captured by amateur filmmakers on handheld cameras, home security systems, or, increasingly, smartphones. As in horror more generally, there is a reliance on scenes of drawn-out suspense, jump scares, and concealed or ambiguous information, but the diegetic acknowledgement of the act of recording adds even more emphasis here: the apparent 'liveness' and seemingly unedited quality of found footage allows for long passages of inactivity followed by blasts of excitement, and for maddeningly tense uses of off-screen space.

Like earlier found footage cinema, desktop films claim to offer material that has been captured by diegetic media devices. Rather than just hand-held cameras and CCTV, though, the GUI setting allows for an expanded suite of media sources. In *Unfriended*, for instance, the central narrative unfolds via Skype window, as five teenage friends undertake a group call – only for this to be invaded by a spectral sixth attendee. Skype is just one source of narrative information, though. The film unfolds on Blaire's (Shelley Hennig) desktop, and in addition to contributing to the group video conversation, she is also instant messaging, scrolling Facebook, googling, accessing Spotify, and many other things (Figure 1.1a). Initially, this is a trace of her characterisation and her demographic: a digital native, she tends towards constant distraction and stimulation, carrying on multiple conversations and activities simultaneously. In this way the film appeals to spectators whose attention is similarly diverted, those who think little of carrying on three conversations at once thanks to simultaneous use of video calling and instant messaging platforms. But as *Unfriended* goes on, these multiple program windows move from traces of character realism to vital tools in Blaire's frantic investigation into the demonic spirit which seems to be gruesomely killing her friends one by one (Figure 1.1b). Similarly, *Searching* consists of numerous scenes in which protagonist David Kim (John Cho), who is looking for his missing daughter Margot (Michelle La), skips from program to program, simultaneously on a Skype call, cracking passwords, and scrolling message feeds.

38 Gooey Media

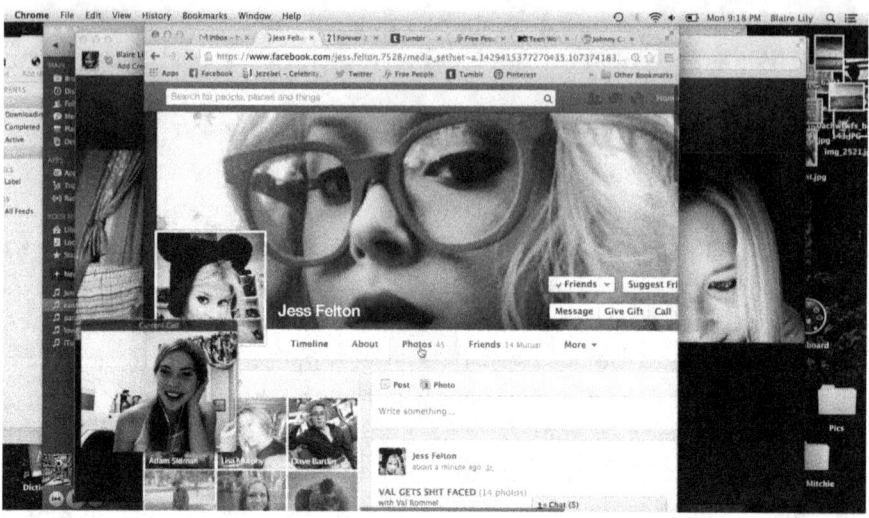

Figure 1.1a The cluttered desktop from *Unfriended* (2013), in which Skype, Spotify playlists, Facebook profiles, background images, and private messages all contribute to story and character information. Frame enlargement from Blu-ray.

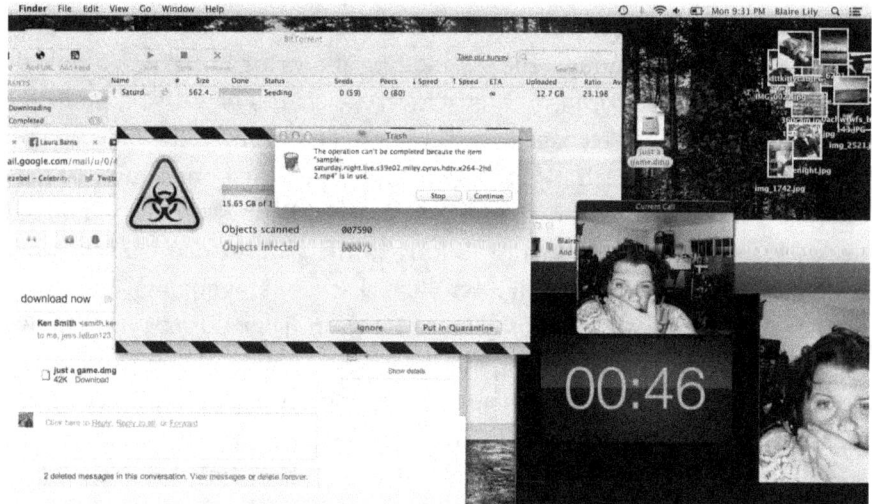

Figure 1.1b Narrative events and their aftermath play out simultaneously across multiple layered program windows in *Unfriended* (2013). Frame enlargement from Blu-ray.

The navigation of the diegetic desktop user controls what film viewers see, as they pull windows to the fore, play and pause embedded videos, mute and unmute audio sources, access files, and track down evidence on search engines. If the diegetically implied camera operators of found footage horror are cinematographers, in desktop horror the protagonist functions more as editor, selecting shots and scenes and handling the flow of information delivery. This is not just about choosing one source then another; rather, the protagonists of these films re-position and re-layer their open windows in accordance with the requirements of the moment. In *Unfriended*, as the conversation among her Skype friends becomes repetitive, Blaire mutes them and hides their faces beneath other program windows, while at other times she resizes Skype to balance it alongside a browser or instant message window. In other films, unwanted incursions are made onto the protagonist's desktop to do this work. Throughout *Open Windows*, the seemingly hapless Nick (Elijah Wood) loses control of his screen as various hackers take control in order to activate programs and reveal information to him. With its evocations of *Rear Window* (1954), this remote access furthers the film's themes of voyeurism and powerlessness. The GUI is both a site of ultimate control (Nick gets access to the life of a starlet he is hopelessly obsessed with) but also of chilling immobility (he can do nothing as she is tortured via webcam).

In their screen-centricity, these films indicate the extent to which the GUI is the hub of social life today, a portal to and enabler of entire biographies. *Searching* begins with a montage compressing the time between Margot's first computer use at age five to her first day of high school. Uploaded videos, calendar entries, highlighted emails, eBay purchases, and Google searches foreground the story of her mother's battle with leukaemia, with the clip art creation of a funeral program informing us of the eventual tragic outcome. This material indexes lives (and deaths) beyond the screen, but the sequence also indicates the extent to which the GUI is central to these lives. That is, it is not just an archive or communication tool, but a very precondition of a networked social existence. With its emphasis on major life events, the nuclear family, and the perseverance of love even in the face of inevitable loss, the opening sequence of *Searching* almost evokes a Facebook ad, as it similarly frames computer use as intrinsic to contemporary socialisation.

The later portions of *Searching* indicate the double-edged nature of the pivotal role of the GUI in life today, with the growing distance between Margot and David catalogued through un-returned calls, un-replied messages, and missed calendar appointments. In similar but darker veins, *Open Windows*, *Unfriended*, *Unfriended: Dark Web*, and *Host* use misogynistic fan sites, online pornography, cyberbullying, and unethical dark web practices as jumping off points for narratives both supernatural and not. In *Open Windows*, Nick's unhealthy adoration of Jill Goddard (Sasha Grey) is both enabled by and expressed through his fan site and his scouring of the web for pictures of her, and then, later in the film, through the non-consensual access to her emails and webcams enabled by the hacker Chord (Neil Maskell). *Unfriended* and *Unfriended: Dark Web* both show how digital communication can facilitate lies, mistrust, anonymity, and ethical flexibility. In such cases, replacing the cinema screen with the desktop works to centre the latter as a key concern of the narrative and thematic world of the text. These films do not just take place on the GUI, they are about the GUI.

The desktop visuality of these films can lead to more than just the overt layering of program windows, or the multi-tasking of the distracted browser. These images are inherently and openly technological, a fact which also allows or encourages the exploitation of new kinds of visual knowledge. In *Unfriended: Dark Web*, the threatening purveyor of dark web entertainments wears some kind of glitch-cloak: when he steps into a webcam's frame, he is seen as a silhouette only, and the image skips and fragments around him. In *Open Windows*, a bag of webcams and motion detectors spilled in a car boot along with a captive Jill allows for the creation of a kind of abstract spatialised composite image of her situation. Visualised as a shifting mass of pictorial shards and wireframe pulses, Jill becomes a kind of posthuman index of digital ubiquity and what we might call the internet unconscious.[10]

In desktop cinema, then, the aesthetic of the GUI is far more than a gimmick. These films reveal how the GUI is not only a window onto particular narratives but a key facilitator of the very issues that lie at the heart of these narratives, as well as a driver of new forms of aesthetic presentation. Much the same is true of some notable short documentaries and video essays which also utilise the GUI. Indeed, if anything the non-fiction format seems an even more appropriate site for this kind of visuality; after pseudo-found footage content, it represents one more step towards our own screen use.

Screen-captured GUI material is commonplace in video essays, a format which has proliferated enormously thanks to the accessibility and affordability not only of editing software but also online archives of clips and other material, as well as the capacity to share essays on sites like YouTube. Video essays might employ voice-over, onscreen narrators, guiding text, or some combination of all of these in tandem with excerpted clips or the essayists own audio-visual material. Capturing the desktop screen, though, allows for

---

10 Similar ideas are put forward by *Cam* (2018), in which the camgirl protagonist has her identity stolen by an ambiguous digital entity whose genesis and actions are never explained.

the absence of more overt forms of argumentation or direction. Likewise, GUI video essays usually foreground the pre-existing nature of their material – they are not about newly recorded interviews or fresh footage, but about unearthing some truth from the flotsam and jetsam of the digital media wash. The choice of search terms, program windows, and the selection of clips within the visually quoted desktop all guide the viewer towards the essay or documentary's central claims, sometimes without any further explicit commentary. In this way, and much like desktop fiction filmmaking, these non-fiction videos do not just employ the GUI as a handy communicative device but position it as *the* central node in today's knowledge and experiential economies.

Early examples include the work of Nick Briz and Camille Henrot, among others (Lee 2016: 218–19). Briz's *Apple Computers* (2013) explores the limitations and ideologies of Apple operating systems, and includes footage of Briz calling the company's helpline, interviewing app developers and artists, and playing new media art on Vimeo. Formatted for internet viewers, it includes embedded hyperlinks to relevant material as and when it is mentioned. This turns the video into a kind of interactive lecture, Briz's quoted desktop ceding to the viewer's own as they follow the threads they are invited to explore. *Grosse Fatigue* (2013), by contrast, is designed for gallery exhibition: Henrot describes how the cornucopia of swiftly opening and closing videos and images requires the large format screen provided by the context of fine art appreciation as opposed to online circulation.[11] For many scholars, *Grosse Fatigue* is somehow post-cinematic. Miriam de Rosa and Catherine Fowler (2019: 293–4) describe how it demonstrates 'the contamination of film with other media', although they too emphasise the *gallery's* role as a site of 'contestation and negotiation, intersection, reference and cross-pollination' rather than the desktop's. Lisa Åkervall (2020: 270) is more explicit that *Grosse Fatigue*'s 'post-cinematic unframing' maps 'a changed relationship to the world and different frame of mind' that has come about in the digital era. What we see here are 'framing, stacking, and layering strategies' that have a 'parasitic reliance on cinematic protocols even as they explore the new technical and aesthetic tactics of contextualisation emerging in contemporary media cultures' (Åkervall 2020: 256).

Kevin B. Lee claims inspiration from Briz and Henrot, among others, in his *Transformers: The Premake* (2014). In this documentary, the desktop is the vehicle for an exploration of the production of the fourth instalment of

---

11 She states this in the interview and promo by Collectif Combo available here: https://vimeo.com/86174818.

a global blockbuster film franchise.[12] The twenty-five-minute video touches on participatory culture, international co-productions, tax incentive location shooting, and geopolitical soft power to provide an overview of the embeddedness of commercial cinema within everyday global lived realities (Figure 1.2a). As an essay about 'amateur-produced images as a form of commodity production', it is highly reflexive and open in its gathering and delivery of images – very few of which come from authorised industrial sources (Lee 2016: 215). Scouring YouTube for footage by fans and pedestrians of the filming of *Transformers: Age of Extinction* (2014) on the streets of Chicago, the essay introduces ideas of fan labour by visibly googling 'crowdsourced movie production' and highlighting relevant portions of the resulting hits. It also brings up related academic sources (such as the website for *Spreadable Media* (2013), a scholarly project by media theorists Henry Jenkins, Sam Ford, and Joshua Green), strengthening its credentials as a piece of research.[13] A text document appears from time to time and is used to make leading notes (for example, 'zero amateur videos found in mainland China'), while Google Maps and Google Earth are used to track filming locations and sites of fan activity, and direct messages show Lee making enquiries to YouTubers about copyrighted footage. Lee even shows himself uploading his own set-adjacent footage to YouTube, and later gives us a glimpse of his own timeline when remixing a media clip of Michael Bay fluffing his lines at a media event launching a new television set (Figure 1.2b).

Through not only the choice but also organisation of visual and sonic material, Lee teases out the connections between Steyerl's 'flagship store' of images and those many other sites in which adjacent content is generated. In the process, and by showing not a single clip from the finished film (but plenty from its marketing), he reveals a variety of media relationships both parasitic and productive. We might think of *Transformers: Age of Extinction* as a discrete text, but this premake uses its desktop format to show how that film is the sum of many more parts. These parts, products of the 'seemingly undifferentiated spiralling networks of digital cultures' that predominate today, all intersect with and depend on the GUI (Åkervall 2020: 272). Lee (2016: 212) thinks of videographic film studies as inevitably bound up with this kind of reflexivity, suggesting that 'the form may have less to reveal about the material it regards than its own act of looking upon the material'. As such, the presence of his desktop – rather than Lee himself as narrator

---

12 *Transformers: The Premake* is available here: https://vimeo.com/94101046.
13 The website is www.spreadablemedia.org.

Figure 1.2a Multiple windows open on a desktop to demonstrate the range of fan videos of the shooting of *Transformers: Age of Extinction* (2014), in *Transformers: The Premake* (2014). Frame enlargement from YouTube.

Figure 1.2b Kevin B. Lee reveals his own editing timeline at the culmination of *Transformers: The Premake* (2014). Frame enlargement from YouTube.

or onscreen presence – is crucial. As much as the documentary is about the production process of a new blockbuster and the engagement and involvement of fans, it is simultaneously – once again – a meta-reflection on the place of the desktop and its functions at the centre of media production, media dissemination, and cultural life more generally.

In another desktop exploration of cinema and its social meaning, Jessica McGoff's *My Mulholland* uses the desktop as a tool to explore her viewing of *Mulholland Drive* (2004) in 2007, when she was thirteen years old (Figure 1.3a). She links this unsettling experience to 'screamer' videos from the same period – in which an innocuous video or game is interrupted by a jump scare – and the unruliness of the nascent internet, a place in which, as she states, shocks lie in wait 'like snakes in the sandbox'.[14] Again, a text file takes the place of a voice-over, and the onscreen typing of this document creates an impression of liveness and discovery, while also providing a kind of meta-monologue (describing her teenage self, McGoff seems to think twice as she re-types the word 'pretentious' to read 'precocious'). Wayback Machine, a tool for accessing archived internet pages, shows what IMDb.com looked like in 2007, and the autobiographical video also employs msn.com pages, YouTube videos, Wikipedia, clips from *Mulholland Drive*, and even webcam footage of McGoff herself as she recreates the shock she experienced watching a screamer a decade and a half earlier (Figure 1.3b).

Mulholland Drive, a film in many senses deeply concerned with cinephilia and the dream of moviegoing (but which itself has fraught media boundaries, beginning its production life as a TV pilot), is convincingly re-interpreted as an allegory of internet culture and the volatility of online discourse (Nochimson 2002). The use of the desktop setting here, as in the case of *Transformers: The Premake*, connects cinema with personal experience, and shows how today this connection takes place through the desktop and the many networked possibilities it offers. More than this, it illustrates how our interface with the interface impacts both media and us in profound ways. This can be through traumatic, hesitant glimpses at an online world which can be gothic and inexplicable. But it can also be through our own processing of this world through active, GUI-enabled engagement. McGoff's essay, no less than Lee's documentary, invites the viewer to undertake their own reflection on internet knowledge and media production, highlighting as both texts do the fact that the necessary tools (Google, YouTube, editing software) are all at the viewer's fingertips, accessible with the click of a button or the swipe of a touchscreen.[15]

---

14 The video essay is available here: https://vimeo.com/426494447.
15 Similarly, viewing these texts in the cinema can be a strange experience. During a scene break in *Searching*, the 'flurry' screensaver associated with some 2010 Mac computers fills the screen for several seconds, offering an encounter between film and desktop which seems more palpable because of its separation from narrative concerns. Here we are, a hundred people sat in the dark, staring at a fifty-foot screensaver.

Screen Mirroring   45

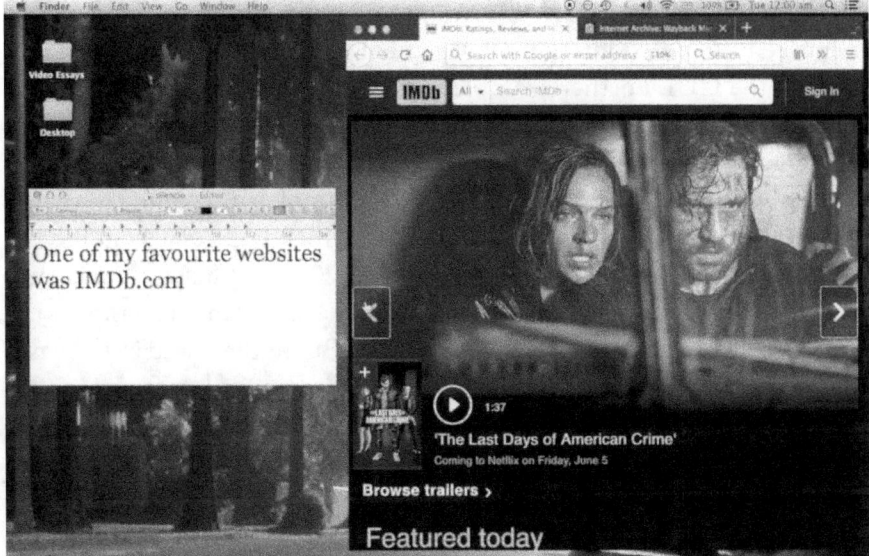

Figure 1.3a Multiple tabs on a mac desktop in Jessica McGoff's *My Mulholland* (2020). Frame enlargement from Vimeo.

Figure 1.3b McGoff includes webcam footage of herself on the desktop in *My Mulholland* (2020). Frame enlargement from Vimeo.

These are just some of the ways in which the wider media environment seems to be exploring its engagement with and relatively recent reliance on the GUI. Further examples which I do not have time to explore in more depth include music videos, such as the official lyric video for Katy Perry's 'Wide Awake', which not only mimics a Facebook timeline but includes actual material from Perry's Facebook fan account (McLaren 2019); web series such as *Content* (2019), which takes place entirely on the protagonist's phone; or even Eva.Stories (2019), an Instagram account staging the imagined social media posts (and accompanying hashtags) of a real-life Holocaust victim (Holmes 2019). But in these and in the cases I have explored, while the desktop may be evoked, its key functions are absent. There is some limited interactivity: we can play and pause, minimise and maximise; *Apple Computers* embeds hyperlinks, and when featured on streaming services or video sharing sites all the other films and videos described might have algorithmically generated lists of related content placed adjacent to their windows, inviting us to click elsewhere. But, since these are videos, we cannot interact with their visualised desktops to anything like the extent to which we would with our own GUI.

Considering the mixed medium nature of these works, this ironically foregrounds issues medium specificity. For digital film theorist Shane Denson (2020b: 28), *Unfriended* 'begs to be seen on a computer's small screen for full effect', because in theatrical settings 'the desktop framing jarringly contrasts with the scale and non-interactivity of the big screen and therefore detracts from the spectator's involvement'. This is an inversion of normal discourses of the cinematic, in which the big screen experience is usually the one celebrated as the most authentic or suitable. Meanwhile, when watching one of these texts via the seemingly preferred format of the GUI, a certain cognitive dissonance can arise, especially if the viewer is distracted by a second screen such as a smartphone. Watching *Apple Computers*, with the video playing within Chrome and my own notes and open files scattered around it on the screen, it was easy for me to confuse my own desktop with Briz's. During *Unfriended* there were moments when I personally attempted to resize windows or re-arrange programs to get a better look at something, before realising that no, this was not *my* desktop, even if it was playing on my MacBook Air. This is very much a feature, not a bug. This actually was, after all, *my* desktop, but it had been hijacked *by* the film, much as a ghost hijacks elements of Blaire's GUI *in* the film.[16]

---

16 *Apple Computers* and *Unfriended* feature no zooming or cropping into the screen; *Noah*, *Open Windows*, and *Transformers: The Premake*, among many others, all by contrast

In this way, these texts all highlight what communication scholar Paul Frosh has usefully described as the desktop's interplay of hermeneutic and operative modes of attention. In the former, users effectively look through the screen, attending to words or text, 'moving beyond the screen surface into the virtual space behind it'; in the latter, by contrast, users 'constantly scan [...] the potential functionality of the objects displayed' (Frosh 2019: 153). Operative attention changes our relation with elements on the screen, making us expect things of them. We shift 'from epistemological relations with texts or images (what do they mean? what knowledge do they impart?) to an interactional focus (how will this text or image respond? what connections to the world does it enable?)' (Frosh 2019: 154). The computer interface contains the potential for hermeneutic modalities (full-screen viewing, pop-ups disabled), but these are embedded choices within a much wider constellation of user-centred, operative functions. The screen of a digital device is personified by interaction, to the extent that even when it is used as a vehicle for a cinematic, televisual, or documentary video, its operative mode is always latently present. Whether we are watching a Marvel TV show on Disney+ or a Béla Tarr film on the Criterion app, and no matter how engrossed we are, the digital screen always promises an infinitude of alternative activities. As Frosh puts it, operative attention makes its existence felt in the gentle pressure of the hand on the mouse, or the eye which tracks the onscreen cursor. '[S]ensorimotor restlessness' is not a sign of boredom, it is a 'system requirement' (Frosh 2019: 154).

If the videos described already make us aware of this restlessness by denying us any recourse to interact, then other participatory media can directly exploit restless interaction. Interactive music videos like Arcade Fire's 'We Used to Wait/The Wilderness Downtown' draw on the user's own data and present them with a personalised GUI scenography across multiple windows (Korsgaard 2013). This approach is even more pronounced in videogames. Mimicking desktop interfaces, immersive sims like *Her Story* (2015), *Sara is Missing* (2016), *Simulacra* (2017), and *Telling Lies* (2019) ask the player to make gameplay choices by navigating program windows and accessing material from hard drives. *Her Story*, for instance, positions the player as an investigator given access to an old laptop, upon which are hundreds of video clips of police interviews concerning a missing person. Meanwhile, *Sara is Missing*,

---

navigate around magnified portions of the desktop for much of their running time. The latter approach implicitly reveals the guiding hand of a filmmaker and a scripted narrative, and creates a subtle gap between the GUI that is the video and the GUI that might be delivering the video.

with which this chapter began, frames itself as the OS of a phone found by the player. Accessing the phone's files, answering messages, and interacting with the digital personal assistant pulls the player into a horror scenario involving witchcraft, viral media, and ethical compromises.

Videogames are normally required to hold representational realism and schematic metaphor in delicate balance. That is, a game's fictional world must be to some extent real-seeming or otherwise predictable, even as our engagement with this world occurs via displaced commands. Bodily physical actions both simple and complex are translated into equivalents that can be undertaken with one or two hands using a keyboard or controller: pushing on a thumb-stick moves a character through space, pressing a button makes a character jump, and so on. Moreover, the contours of these relations must often be spelled out, whether early on or throughout: videogames must tell us when and why to press triangle, square, or spacebar; they must show us how to access and manipulate our inventory, and so on. I will discuss the relationship between representational realism and interactivity in videogames in more detail in Chapters 3 and 7, but for the time being it is only necessary to note how, in games which adopt a GUI or OS aesthetic, issues of functional equivalence effectively disappear. If we know how to navigate a GUI, we know how to navigate the game.

Our exploration of the world of *Sara is Missing* closely matches our navigation of our own smartphone. The game takes over the entirety of the phone's screen, offering no additional border or frame to suggest its fictionality. We click on logos labelled 'email' or 'gallery', we scroll up and down, and we use a keyboard to type our responses to messages (Figures 1.4a–b). There are slight divergences that reveal the gameness of the game: the AI tells us that pressing and holding on a message or photo will allow it to be 'scanned' as evidence, a feature which is somewhat advanced or even science-fictional; and though the game allows us to free type responses to message threads, whatever we choose to type is automatically translated into one of two or three set replies (a necessity given the complex programming and memory required to create a game AI that can reliably interpret free typing). However, even these departures tightly align with everyday smartphone functionality. The translation of the player's message typing even employs a predictive text interface to push the player towards seeing the baked-in responses as their own (and in the process perhaps makes us reflect on the extent to which, in everyday life, our own predictive-enabled replies are pre-ordained by algorithmic prompts).

If the game's fictional world is accessed through an interface which is in complete harmony with the device providing this access, then this

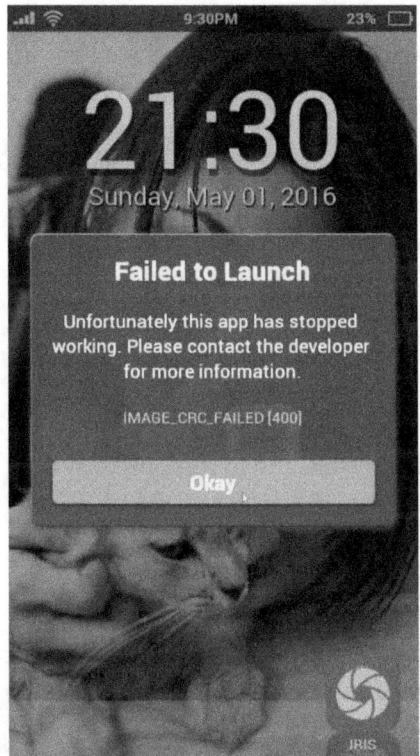 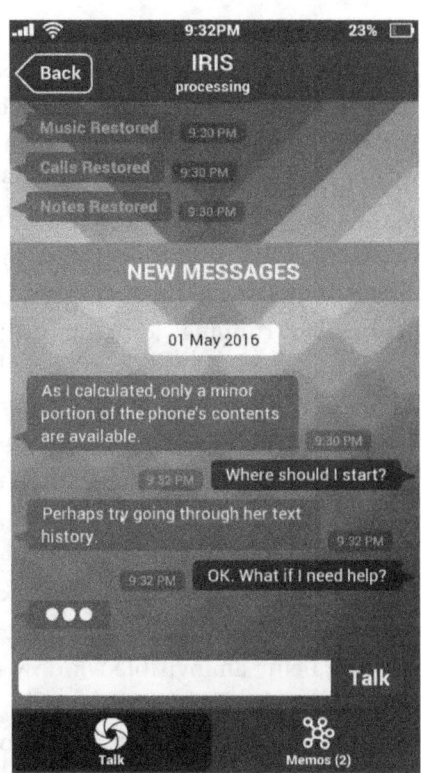

Figures 1.4a and b The player's phone screen is synonymous with the videogame *Sara is Missing* (2016). Frame enlargement from Android gameplay.

correspondence can result in moments in which the player might temporarily forget the interface is a game, and the game an interface. Like my experience watching *Unfriended* on a laptop, the first phone call in *Sara is Missing* was both jolting and engaging, confusing my roles as phone owner and game player. Even downloading the game posed some intriguing ontological slippage. My Android OS cautioned me against installing apps that might be malicious, a warning which seemed prophetic when, as my first in-game action, I restored corrupted system information, and a loud glitch crackled ominously across the screen. Was this the game, or have I just invited a raft of malware to destroy my personal files? Here is the affective charge of found footage, but even more tightly and insidiously programmed into the circuits of media delivery and reception.[17]

---

17 Denson (2020b: 28–30) notes a similar phenomenon in relation to *Unfriended*, which begins with a glitching logo for studio Universal, and so doing suggests to those viewers who have illegally downloaded the film from a torrent site that the file is corrupted.

Games like this bind together operative and hermeneutic modes of attention – to be immersed is to interact, with the constraints placed by videogame designers on this interaction ensuring that gameplay always pushes forward or loops back round to the central mystery or narrative. *Sara is Missing* and its ilk also show the overlap between the GUI and videogameplay of any kind. Videogames are above all technical systems, even though they may often disguise this fact through verisimilitudinous scenography, character depth, or affective appeals. Often adopting the guise of physical actions like running, jumping, driving, or eating, videogames are always just about moving cursors, clicking buttons, and undertaking the cognitive labour of action and reaction. As in the GUI, then, we use screens to access a virtual world, an activity that requires us to balance sources of information through our own agency in relation to the screen, and to respond to system prompts and our own curiosity.

Even though desktop filmmaking and documentaries do not ask for nor allow the same interactivity, they nonetheless similarly testify to the close proximity between the GUI and these other media. Desktop computing, far from being an invisible window, closely maps onto systems of narrative delivery and knowledge enquiry developed in cinema, television, and associated media. This is not a case of one media (film, documentary, videogames) trying to claim relevance or novelty by awkwardly forcing itself into the clothes of another (the GUI). No, the convergence is much more effective and harmonic than that.

If we return to the lawsuit between Apple and Microsoft that resulted in a legal definition of the graphic user interface, we can see how all of the texts described in this section include features that are intrinsic to the GUI. That ruling outlined five features: (1) multiple windows to facilitate user interaction, (2) iconic representation, (3) manipulation of icons, (4) use of menus to save screen space, and (5) opening and closing objects to access information. From *Unfriended* to *My Mulholland* to *Her Story*, these attributes are not only clearly and consistently in evidence, they are relied upon and structurally necessary. Multiple windows provide a rich mise-en-scène which adds to character biography and narrative delivery; drama is created from opening menus and revealing information (or its absence); and the depths of the desktop, the space beneath windows, and the content hidden in folders, all becomes charged with potency and suspicion.

The GUI, the fiction film, the documentary, the videogame: all share the qualities of one another, but not in the sense of derivations or copies, nor of encapsulations or quotations. Rather, we might think of them as a funhouse mirror maze. The source image is unclear, and we encounter a cascade of reflective forms. Or, to return to a metaphor pitched in this book's Introduction, we might consider them multiple program windows on the same desktop, used for different things in different contexts, but collected together in a way that foregrounds functional and aesthetic similarities. Adapting GUI functions to narrative ends, the texts described in this section show how the desktop can function as a vehicle for narrative content *because of* its layered and multiple visual organisation of multi-tasking program windows, not in spite of them. Likewise, the GUI is revealed to be cinematic, televisual, and gamified all at once, elements which do not just manifest in these entertainment texts, but in any desktop interaction.

Conclusion

This chapter has traced some of the connections between the GUI and other media. This work has started to reveal how the desktop interface sits at the centre of today's screen media web. But by foregrounding the GUI I do not intend to suggest that it is the stable hardware upon which the software of other media rely. Rather, the intermingling is much more complex and multi-directional.

Divergent media have changed one another's shape before, of course: the rise of television altered the way in which films were shot (Bordwell 2002: 22), the cultural prestige of cinema influenced the evolving language of videogames (King and Krzywinska 2002), and so on. But in the GUI we are presented with more polyvalent mixing. Discrete media still draw on their particular lineages and the aesthetic tendencies that come with them, and the borders between all these media are still in many ways culturally, industrially, and economically policed. But with the increasing importance of the GUI to all screen media creation, distribution, and reception, it does not take much to see through these borders to a wealth of likenesses and interdependencies.

The influence of the interface has really only been hinted at in this chapter, as the GUI borrows from and bestows upon other media in ways that go beyond technical similarity, or direct cross-medial quotation. The remainder of this book takes these further overlaps as its subject, beginning in the next chapter with a deeper discussion of the GUI's representational realism.

2
Interface Realism

I write this chapter using a MacBook Air. To accomplish this task, arranged on my computer desktop are the following: a Microsoft Word file containing a draft of the chapter; another Word file of notes; an internet browser with multiple tabs; a file management box, with lists of folders in which I can find further chapters, notes, and pdfs; and Spotify, a music player. I have listed these programs in their order of recession – that is, the Word file of the chapter is at the perceptual forefront (apart from the ever-present arrow of the cursor which I move around the desktop) and all the other programs are partly concealed, slid beneath both the chapter file and one another, such that sections of program windows peek out in an overlapping constellation on my 13.3-inch screen. I tell myself that this arrangement is convenient for switching between all these sources of information as and when the need arises: I can easily manipulate all the open programs to change their order and placement, bringing the file management window to the fore and moving the browser to the back, for example. The interleaved approach also allows me to keep a sneaky eye on my emails while engrossed in other tasks.

But this arrangement is by no means fixed. When the need arises, I can reposition all these windows both in space and in perceptual depth – for instance, I can bury the internet browser beneath everything else so that, while it is still present and open, I won't actually see if any new emails appear within its window. During such reshuffling, program windows and the onscreen cursor move fluidly, sliding around the screen with flowing clarity and laser-like precision. This rearranging can also reveal what lies behind all these open windows – namely, an image of Lone Pine Peak, a rock formation in California, captured in the early morning light. Bundled with the OS, this natural scene suggests even more depth – it is a distant landscape photo, after all – but the image itself signifies the very back and limit of the screen's navigable, overlapping space. Moreover, I can get a kind of 'master' view of everything open on the desktop by pressing the 'launchpad' button, at which point this background image drops out of focus as though receding into the far distance and all the currently open windows disappear; sharply defined program icons instead appear to dominate my vision/screen, seemingly in front of and closer to me than everything else.

This description indicates how my desktop, for all its flatness, has depths. Although as a material object it is smooth and two-dimensional, as a perceptual environment it is infinitely layered. This allows the GUI to be, in many ways, bigger than it actually is. Computer screens come in many sizes, from generous monitors (which can be as big as a room or bigger) to small phones, tablets, and smartwatches (as small as an outstretched hand, fist, or even a thumbnail). The screen of the laptop I currently use is slightly smaller than the double-page spread of an average book, yet a dizzying density of digital objects can be squeezed into this space. Illusory layers allow content to overlap, and this in effect provides much more access – albeit partial access – to visual material than might be expected of a mere thirteen inches. My brief clicks and scrolls are helped by 60 Hz screen refresh rates which make navigation a liquescent experience free from judder or visual interruption. All this encourages multi-tasking and creates an information aesthetic steered by ease of access, visual clarity, and manipulable arrangement of virtual objects in deep space.

This chapter focuses on these attributes of the GUI and connects them to the wider environment of screen-based entertainment media. Crucial in what follows will be the concept of resolution: the amount of pixels or other granular detail that can be delivered to viewers. In the context of the GUI, high resolution has allowed for more and more simultaneous program windows: more graphic detail increases the perceptual layers that the user has access to, boosts the legibility of those layers, and makes shuffling between them more effortless. But resolution is a key concern for a wider variety of media than just the desktop interface. In videogames, the greater levels of detail provided by each new console generation, each new game engine, and each new software update all allow the player to navigate the virtual space of the game with more efficacy. Other media like film and television tread an identical path, with cinema chains, television manufacturers, production companies, and creative personnel relentlessly developing ways to create and deliver ever more lucid imagery. Rarely thought of as anything other than intrinsically desirable, developments in resolution across the media landscape nonetheless reveal the gooiness of a specifically GUI version of resolution, and the influence of this GUI resolution on other media.

In relation to videogames, television, and cinema, the stated goal of amplified resolution is invariably realism. Greater pixel counts, higher frame rates, and even added dimensions are often framed, however loosely or unknowingly, around a myth of media teleology that was most influentially described by André Bazin in the middle of the twentieth century. This *myth of total cinema* – and that word myth is crucial – frames changes in cinema technologies as movements towards the alignment of media and IRL perception. Far from just applicable to cinema, though, such a model is applicable to the wider media ecology and its development of graphic density. The higher the resolution, the greater the realism.[1]

But what happens if we consider aspects of contemporary screen resolution in entertainment media not according to realist dictates, but through the lens of the computer desktop? What if instead of sites of observation and entertainment, we read the spaces of our screens (whether used to watch a film, navigate the internet, or write a book) as sites for the management of tasks? Through such a lens, screens can be thought to offer us not the real but rather 'real estate': high-cost parcels of space demanding great financial investment. Amplifications of resolution that occur across digital media – amplifications like higher pixel counts and greater frame rates – enable less the conjuration of reality and more the creation of navigable or pseudo-navigable information spaces. Investments in screen resolution are investments in time, our time. They make the periods during which we attend to a screen – by no means a small fraction of daily life for many – more valuable, which is to say both more enjoyable and more efficient.

To untangle resolution from realism, this chapter will discuss aesthetic developments in GUI layering, the evocation of these in some contemporary entertainment texts, and the frame rates preferred across different media. Continuing some of the work of the last chapter, I will directly consider how a film like *Gravity* (2013) employs features of the desktop interface, and why. I will then compare the way that higher frame refresh rates are framed across the production and reception of cinema, videogames, television, and the GUI; as I will argue, the varying embrace of certain frame counts across these media are an indication of medial boundaries and the multifaceted – and debated – nature of realism in the digital era. First, though, we are required to dig more deeply into technological change and Bazin's mythical model of cinema, and so it here that this chapter begins.

---

[1] This model has subsequently been deployed beyond cinema: witness the discourse proposing virtual reality as a kind of achieved 'total cinema' in the digital era (see Chapter 7).

The myth of total resolution

Bazin wrote extensively about film in the 1940s and 1950s, asking questions about what the art form was for and what it should seek to do. From its earliest days, Bazin argued, cinema sought 'an integral realism, a recreation of the world in its own image' (Bazin 2005b: 21). He saw filmmakers and audiences pushing changes in narrative cinema's technology and language which all sought to seemingly mimic our perception of the world in non-cinematic contexts. Cinema, in this view, was about replicating non-cinematic embodied vision; therefore, what he described as a 'total cinema' would be a cinema that entirely succeeded in this goal, replicating sight and sound in ways that made it indistinct from non-mediated experience.

But what is this 'integral realism'? Bazin's model of total cinema is predicated on the indexical nature of the film image. The photographic image, Bazin (2005a: 14) states, 'is the object itself, the object freed from the conditions of time and space that govern it', and so cinema is 'objectivity in time'. Certain stylistic elements could intensify and expand this connection with reality, namely wide angles, deep focus, and longer takes (Bazin 2005c). These filmmaking choices became cemented as a desirable feature of auteur cinema in the US in the 1940s, thanks to cinematographers such as Gregg Toland, and Bazin's writing on the films of Orson Welles and William Wyler. For Bazin, the images found in films like *Citizen Kane* (1941) and *The Best Years of Our Lives* (1946) allowed the spectator to actively explore the spaces and situations presented. The film could be navigated, and the job of filmmakers was to orchestrate space in such a way that attention was subtly managed rather than tyrannically dictated, with composition and mise-en-scène creating meaning relationally and holistically instead of through the spatial fragmentation of close-ups and edits. Such an approach, Bazin argued, privileged the reality of that which was presented, and spoke to the film camera's unique ability to reproduce this reality (Elsaesser and Hagener 2015: 16).

Bazin's 'myth' is particularly useful as a discursive model explaining how new technologies like widescreen film formats and surround sound – and later digital media – get sold as uncomplicated improvements upon representational media, and also how audiences are led to gauge the success of these improvements through realist readings. Crucially, in calling the realism of total cinema a 'myth', Bazin points to the impossibility of what he also frames as cinema's guiding principle and ontological foundation. This allows his model to open up from a narrowly positivist teleology to the diagnosis of an organising intention (even if this intention is always claiming a teleological form of progress and forward momentum). It's not so much that cinema is growing like a living organism towards some ideal form, but that it is pushed and prodded in particular directions because of wider cultural expectations and presumptions.

Greater levels of resolution are bound up with this apparent goal of reality replication (Bazin 2005b: 21).[2] If resolution names the amount of information in an image, such as the number of pixels, then expansions in this regard make images more 'realistic' through higher levels of detail. Expanding levels of resolution are invariably framed in Bazinian terms, with the myth of total realist representation driving much stylistic and technological innovation and its subsequent wide adoption. Crucial to industrial cycles of planned obsolescence and marketing imperatives, higher resolution capacities are also explained through consumer demand: we get new formats because we apparently demand them (audiences want sharper images or more immersive sound, and technology manufacturers obediently provide).[3]

This perspective casts media evolution as a Darwinian process of successful adaptation to realist imperatives – those formats or technologies that do not seem to function as steps up the ladder towards a total recreation of reality are derided as dead ends or false prophets. These aberrations can, however, remind us that 'realism' is an endlessly moving target, a set of codes and expectations which can be both wildly flexible and stubbornly and unexpectedly intractable despite great financial and creative investment (as we will see later in this chapter).

---

2 This is not necessarily an automatic model for moving-image media. Formalist film theorists who were roughly contemporaneous with Bazin offered a counter-model that saw the artistry and creative potential of cinema in precisely its divergence from embodied vision and realist dictates. Rudolf Arnheim, for instance, provides a long list at the beginning of *Film as Art* (1957: 8–34) outlining the many ways in which film departs from lived experience: it is precisely in the partiality of film's illusory representation Arnheim sees the possibility for artistry and creativity.

3 Requiring large investments by both media industries and solvent consumers, greater levels of resolution, and therefore realism, represent changes that are rarely backwards compatible in a straightforward way. New technologies and systems must be purchased (as well, perhaps, as new copies of recorded media compatible with these new systems). But in the process consumers also come to realise that previous standards were apparently insufficient – VHS seemed fine until the DVD arrived, and so on. Resolution seems therefore to be a way of marking time, of recording media history. Each technological change ticks the clock forward, although we seem to move not in a circular motion but rather in linearly, towards greater realism.

One strategy for mitigating the multifaceted nature of perceived realism is to use numbers. The supposed realism of media can be implied and assessed through its translation into resolution, which can itself be quantified in reassuringly technical and declarative ways. The bigger the number, the higher the resolution, the greater the realism, the better the media. Take, for instance, the growing size of widescreen throughout the 1950s and 60s, and the touted improvements these ever larger and wider images offered over 'more primitive forms of art and verisimilitude' (Acland 2020: 143). Today, digital media provide ample basis for the continuing play of this numbers game, since computational foundations allow quantification to be carefully managed and measured.[4] Digital cameras initially had resolution of a fraction of a megapixel (MP); by the late 1990s 1–2 MP consumer cameras were available; and the iPhone X (released in 2017) has a 12 MP camera on the rear and a 7 MP camera on the front. Blu-ray discs (first released in the late 2000s) offer 1920 × 1080 pixel resolution compared to the 720 × 480 (or 720 × 576) of DVDs; this doubling of data is then compounded with the arrival of 4K and Ultra HD Blu-ray discs (first released in the late 2010s) which offer 3840 × 2160 pixel resolution. The Atari 2600 videogame system, released in 1977, had a resolution of 160 × 192 pixels; the 1994 PlayStation offered up to 640 × 480; and in 2017 the Xbox One X was one of multiple ways gamers could access 4K and HDR content. In addition to these measurements of visual resolution, other technological amplifications that have been highlighted to consumers in a numerical fashion include: colour range (256 shades of possible colour becomes 1024 and beyond); perceptual dimensions (2D becomes 3D and even, in some cinemas, 4DX); frames per second (from 24 to 48 to 60 and beyond); and speakers (Dolby 5.1 becomes 7.1 and Atmos and beyond). There is no point producing material at a resolution that cannot be accessed by a reasonable number of solvent consumers, and so televisions and computer screens accordingly keep pace, and domestic space becomes a site of high-quality media consumption (Klinger 2006: 18).

Does this mean everything is quantifiably more realistic today, since much of our media now has – apparently – higher levels of resolution

---

4 As architect and visual theorist William Mitchell (1982: 6) states, a digital image 'has precisely limited spatial and tonal resolution and contains a fixed amount of information', in contrast to the 'indefinite amount of information' contained in an analogue photograph. It is hard to count infinity, so the former provides more rigorous bases for quantification. The contrast Mitchell makes is often used in industrial and academic discourses to valorise analogue over digital recording, even though the comparison is problematic on many levels, for instance by disregarding the mutability of the digital image thanks to lossy compression – see Manovich 2001: 52–4.

than earlier periods of media history? Not necessarily. While measuring the amount of data contained within a media source has certainly become crucial to the development and commercial positioning of higher resolution technologies, the relationship between these values and human vision is contestable at best.[5] Unlike a digital screen, vision does not have a 'resolution', and there is debate as to whether the human eye is capable of seeing all these added pixels (Vox Creative 2018). The PS4 Pro gaming console advertises 4K capability, but actually uses selective rendering and algorithmic in-filling to provide something a little below this, since studies show that the overall differences to the player will be effectively indistinguishable (Grubb 2016).[6]

We should therefore not automatically equate greater resolution with greater realism. As media theorist Jonathan Sterne (2012) argues, media technologies do not march steadily towards total fidelity (which, as Bazin also knew, is impossible). A 'dream of verisimilitude' (a myth of total media) may be the story that markets new technology to consumers, and it certainly filters through into 'academic and journalistic commentaries on technology', but it is never the whole story (Sterne 2012: 4). Treating media history as 'a quest for definition, immersion, and richness of experience' ignores those moments when higher resolution, better experience, and increased definition have decisively *not* gone hand in hand (Sterne 2012: 4). As a result, Sterne helpfully suggests thinking about media development as a much more complicated negotiation of biological function, technological investment, commercial pressure, and aesthetic remediation. This approach allows any analysis to side-step the cul-de-sac of corroborating claims around realism and verisimilitude. Instead, it offers a way of investigating the constellation of discursive models – industrial, aesthetic, cultural – that all seek in their

---

5 These measurements are at times effectively technobabble, and, as such, are crucial to marketing the otherwise questionable newness of new media products. On this issue in relation to videogame technobabble and technological determinism, see Nicoll and Keogh 2019: 95–6.

6 Nonetheless, calculation of the supposed limits of human perception allows them to be creatively exploited, and indeed colonised as places of capital expenditure. The 2019 4K release of *Apocalypse Now: The Final Cut* (1979) contains a new sound mix of the film employing 'Sensual Sound', a process that claims to deliver sounds 'down to 13Hz' – below the range of human hearing. We might question how something we cannot hear can be an improvement to a film's sound design, but industrial voices attest that such a frequency is within the range experienced as a physical sensation. As director Francis Ford Coppola states, '"Sensual Sound is when you 'feel' the movement of air vibrating everything, including your bones, before you actually hear it"' (Kenny 2019).

own ways to describe what information a particular media or format can or should communicate.

Bazinterface

It is with this model of Sterne's in mind that I would like to turn to the desktop interface, considering its own relationship to these Bazinian ideas. The last chapter addressed the development of the GUI toward a certain kind of 'realism', and we can now see how the deep, layered space of the desktop is connected to these changes. In the move from command-line to graphical user interfaces the computer screen adopted a kind of cinematic representational realism. Indicators of shape and depth are privileged by the GUI, and new operating systems focus on their ever more effective resolution – an evolution towards a more 'realistic' rendering of space and vision.

Indeed, graphical fidelity to contour and nuance quickly become fundamental to this interface, as they worked as markers of aesthetic importance, user-friendliness, and technological innovation. The importance of such verisimilitude is amply indicated by the early design philosophy of Apple. In the early 1980s, Apple engineer Bill Atkinson developed a complex algorithm to handle rounded corners on the computer's screen. As told to Steve Jobs's biographer, Atkinson was initially resistant to undertake such seemingly frivolous and time-consuming work, considering curves to be surplus to the functional requirements of the interface. However, Atkinson was convinced (or coerced) when taken on a tour of the streets around the company's Californian offices by Jobs, throughout which Jobs pointed out the real-world prevalence of rectangles with rounded corners, alighting on everything from street signs to car windows (Isaacson 2015: 119–20). This, apparently, meant that the Apple had to have them – the interface had to mimic the contours found in the real world.

Rarely granted much attention beyond their functional use, these features of the GUI are nonetheless important interventions in the visual culture of the screen. Furthermore, they are only the thin, curved end of the wedge. For instance, GUI developers focus considerable resources on making onscreen buttons into skeuomorphic representations true to their name. Since the 1990s, Windows operating systems have included buttons that are shaded and shaped to appear as protrusions which perceptually depress when clicked upon. More recent versions of Windows add to these elementary depth impressions in a variety of subtle ways: offset shadow effects behind windows (as though these windows were lifted out from their surroundings); the visually complicated suggestion of cylindrical shaping on start bars and menu lists; and even the depiction of file and program windows as hazily translucent, with windows that are 'behind' others perceived as though seen through frosted glass (a system called Windows Aero). Through such developments, the GUI becomes not just layered, but contains perceptibly volumetric forms that have been deliberately and carefully sculpted through visual effects.

This all promotes the myth that the screen is a tactile, material space. But while these features certainly connect the GUI with mythic models of cinematic realism, this is not the whole story, since the GUI is less about absorbed media attention and more about functional use. The real world may be full of rounded corners, but it is also a larger and more enveloping terrain than a computer screen, no matter how big this screen may be.

Since the proliferation of items on a desktop can threaten the sought-for legibility of the interface, high levels of resolution therefore must be tempered with tools that cultivate the GUI as a space not just of Bazinian realism but operational involvement and technical legibility. Yet these tools, which reframe the space of the GUI in distinctive and novel ways, can nonetheless be productively read in these Bazinian ways, as I will now show.

Given a multitude of open windows which might be constantly shifted in size and position by the user, some can disappear beneath others with little indication of their presence or location, leaving the user dragging and dropping windows in a tiresome hunt for a particular program. To counter this, many GUIs employ shortcuts which re-distribute the contents of the screen for brief moments. Windows's 'Flip 3D' button provides an instant visualisation of all open programs by arranging them in a three-dimensional stack, like a rack of vertically stacked papers looked at from above and to the left (Microsoft n.d.). Similarly, Android mobile phone and tablet operating systems contain a shortcut key which sorts open programs into a kind of upright flip book, again using the addition of further depth to help the user navigate their proliferating apps. Like exploded diagrams, these shortcuts reconfigure the arrangement of the screen, mapping its real-time contents and re-spatialising them as inter-locking three-dimensional components. Apple's 'Mission Control' shortcut is comparable, but displays programs in 'a bird's-eye view' format (Apple Inc. 2022). This is a flatter, more linear arrangement than that of normal system use, with no overlaps and much smaller program windows; these windows, meanwhile, illuminate when the cursor moves over them, stressing the capacity for selection when in this control mode. In Mission Control, what was deep and excessively overlapping becomes flatter and more ordered.

These way-finding shortcuts tackle the potentially confusing realist depth of the interface in many cases by adding *more* depth, extending the links between layering, volumetricism, and legibility. Even in the relatively planar Mission Control, both depth and overlaps are retained in diluted or adapted guises: the desktop retains its background image, and there remain the slight suggestions of shadow around the edges of program windows, making them seem to hover above the background. For all their continued emphasis on depth and contour, these shortcut features seem distinctively gooey in their aesthetic and use. This is not a cinematic form a realism, but a computational form of navigation. Nonetheless, as the next section will demonstrate, these shortcuts are one of many aesthetic effects that migrate into other media in both obvious and surprising ways.

Before getting to that, though, I wish to focus a little more on the functionalism of the GUI space, and the relationship of this to mythical ideas of realism. After all, the perceptibly bigger and deeper the screen is, the more all-enveloping it can be for users, becoming a productive, comfortable, alluring environment in which we can multitask for hours. Higher resolution and accentuated verisimilitude in digital graphics production deepen a screen which itself has somewhat limited options for growing larger. Rounded corners, protruding buttons, spatial toggling, and these shortcut reorientation keys all subtly increase the amount of concurrent operations for which the screen can be comfortably used, as well as the immersive pleasure of this experience. They boost the 'real estate' of the screen.

This term is worth paying attention to. In physical space, real estate of course denotes property ownership. It is space rendered as commodity, something owned (and then perhaps leased), the worth of which might be susceptible to market forces but which is often equated with sensible or aspirational capital investment. Owners can capitalise on their real estate through maintenance and further building, which all usually raise the space's original value. If the screen is real estate, then what does this mean? Its parameters of space and investment are slightly different: no matter how well looked after or nurtured, the actual physical screen of a media device is unlikely to increase in value; it will even get used up over time, requiring the purchase of the latest replacement.

But greater levels of resolution *do* amplify what we might consider the *perceptual* value of the screen. Even as device screen size might remain relatively stable from generation to generation, the amount of material that any given screen can communicate can greatly increase if its levels of resolution are heightened, whether this is in the form of more pixels, greater colour range and brightness, or whatever. Investment on the part of manufacturers boosts the value of the limited parcel of virtual space purchased by consumers. Finer grained pixels mean more of them can fit into the same size frame; like adding another floor to a house on a fixed parcel of land, this results in more valuable property. The screen user also benefits as program interaction becomes more intuitive and predictable: as buttons depress, minimising a file or window becomes an activity of pseudo-physical feedback, a small portion of the screen relinquishing to our pressure.

In high-resolution GUIs, more programs can be open and navigated simultaneously, and these windows and sub-windows are designed and arranged in ways that allow users to more easily and swiftly navigate their digital worlds. Realist features like curves and depths make the contents of the screen more haptically graspable, and so more knowable and perceptible on some level. No longer a mathematical wonderland, the screen becomes a habitable environment through its appeal to Bazinian total cinema aesthetics. Abandoning the semiotics of command-line code – a rigid, otherworldly space of technocratic functionalism – the screen adopts instead a broadly recognisable, albeit unusual, space of apparently volumetric objects, softly cast light sources, and smooth shifts in focus. Our engagement with this environment then occurs in what is effectively a wide angle, deep focus single take. The computer user arranges their own mise-en-scène of program windows within an overarching, holistic screen space, and then their attention moves through this as demanded by the imperatives of task management and drifting attention. This is very different to the sequential montage of the command-line, which requires just one program be open at any time.

In this way, the myth of total cinema becomes a myth of total information access and digital navigation, one which is native to the GUI but visible across a range of media. The resolution amplifications of the desktop, while potentially viewable as in realist terms, must also been seen functionally, as a form of real estate investment in the usable space of the GUI. While realistic, the desktop could never be mistaken for reality: habitable only on some imaginative and interactive level, the elements of realism that the GUI adopts must be seen principally as tools for improved user experience and effective task management (including media consumption). Even so, as indicated, these forms of desktop visuality *do* migrate into other media, where they retain, even in their new contexts, this emphasis on function and information navigation.

Workflow cinema

In the early days of screen-based computing, it was unlikely that two-colour, 8-bit graphics would be confused with either the real world or with the photographic imagery of cinema and the electronic imagery of television. But now, program windows and contoured buttons become equivalent to the photographic or photoreal environments of the films, TV shows, and videogames that are themselves accessed using these curve-cornered browsers and haptically cylindrical media players. Pop-up notifications about emails or system updates can become almost indistinct from the media material they may interrupt. As shown in Chapter 1, this allows these other media to explicitly intermingle with the GUI through its direct quotation. More than just these isolated examples, though, the amplifying resolution of the GUI impacts ideas of realism in texts which seem very far from evoking the desktop interface.

Take, for example, split-screen sequences. Cinematically dating back at least to Lois Weber's film *Suspense* (1913), split-screens divide the frame into multiple smaller frames, showing related or concurrent events. But the tenor of recent split-screens place them firmly in the GUI era. Both Aylish Wood and Deborah Tudor alight upon the importance of the films *Timecode* (2000) and *Hulk* (2003) here. In their own differing ways, these films are 'contingent on emergent digital technologies', with *Timecode* benefitting from MiniDV shooting, and *Hulk* from digital editing software (Wood 2007: 77). Tudor claims that in these films the cinematic image 'mimics the appearance of multiple computer windows and resituates the spectator in relationship to on-screen space' (Tudor 2008: 90). Their split-screen effects evoke the desktop in their erosion of any boundaries between shots, as the cinematic frame brings together a constellation of spatial elements that integrate and overlap (Tudor 2008: 95). In *Timecode*, four adjacent, simultaneous screens follow the movements of multiple intersecting characters in real time, placing the burden of navigation upon the viewer for the entirety of the film's ninety-minute running time (although sound modulation is used to guide our attention). Meanwhile, in *Hulk*, shots appear and float through the frame, editing swipes between one panel-like shot and another, and at times the film even 'zooms out' to show up to a dozen discrete shots all overlapping before quickly plunging back into a particular one. Indebted to the panels of its comic book source media, these sequences also rethink cinema as an interface. They draw attention to the technology underlying the film, and its capacity to transform space and time into an array of programs to be visually navigated (Wood 2007: 100;

Tudor 2008: 98).[7] There are even several moments in *Hulk* when the split-screen content of the film is repositioned into or is revealed to be a desktop interface itself, testifying to how this multiple-window aesthetic engenders an overlap between cinema and computer screen.

Tudor calls this an 'array aesthetic', and it is a model that Lisa Purse effectively extends in her own 2018 article on the rise of self-consciously layered composite visuals in contemporary commercial cinema. In digital films in which images freeze or are dissembled, or in which elements of the frame move at divergent temporalities, or in which the viewer is made aware of the layered and artificially conjoined nature of what they see, cinema evokes its kinship with the GUI. For instance, the 'exploded view' action and credit sequences found in *The Matrix* (1999), *Swordfish* (2001), and *Resident Evil: Afterlife* (2010) offer a GUI-style experience through their creation of multiple overlapping digital layers through which the viewer must optically navigate. Other layered composite sequences can be found in *Dredd* (2012), *Oz: The Great and Powerful* (2013), and *Doctor Strange* (2016), all of which offer moments that 'articulate an encounter with a digital interface' in their 'spatially dense and temporally evolving spectacles' (Purse 2018: 159). These arrayed layers and composite visuals seem distant from Bazinian realism, but, as Purse notes, they map closely onto the viewer's visual experience in other contexts. Frozen or slowed-down imagery renders the multiple objects that make up a scene into perceptibly distinct layers. This is a form of 'smoothly articulated analytical visuality' that is, Purse states, directly tied to desktop navigation (Purse 2018: 161).[8]

Evan Calder Williams goes somewhat further in this regard. Coining the term 'shard cinema', he calls attention to scenes from *Constantine* (2005), *Sherlock Holmes: A Game of Shadows* (2011), *Transformers: Dark of the Moon* (2011), *300: Rise of an Empire* (2014), and many others in which surfaces shatter and 'fragments are decelerated to the point of near-arrest, only barely spreading through the air' (Williams 2017: 161). Despite the name, these aren't only cinematic either, but found in videogames like *Max Payne* (2001)

---

7 Such techniques are used both as transitions and to provide the simultaneous appearance of both shot and counter shot. But they also appear more arbitrarily, as when multiple shots of the same event or character all cluster within frame, adding no new information, but providing a general sense of visual excitement.

8 For media philosopher Steven Shaviro (2010: 6), digital media gives birth to 'radically new ways of manufacturing and articulating lived experience'. These texts, with their array aesthetics and exploded views, might then function as 'affective maps' that reveal much about the emotions, cognitive experiences, and dispersed attention of a today's computational media economy.

and *TimeShift* (2007), where they can be key mechanics of gameplay. Such moments, while they function as violent spectacle, also index the computational, desktop-enabled workflows that produce them. VFX imagery, while usually perceptually realistic as a holistic scene, is stitched together from multiple layered components; for Williams, shard sequences revel in returning the worlds of these images into these constituent parts. In doing this, they connect the finished film to its aesthetics of digital production:

> Quite plainly, the finished film looks like the work one does in the [3D graphics and compositing software] program, like when fixing the bevels or rigging of a model – zooming in close, pulling back, rotating around it, letting its motion advance slightly before halting it at any moment to see how the light is hitting it, if the texture effects are working or not, if it is worth looking at. (Williams 2017: 204)

If these sequences erode the gap between Maya viewport and final text, then they are not alone in this. As Chapter 4 will show, VFX breakdowns similarly explode digital imagery in ways that are not separate from but closely intermingle with both desktop use and the aesthetics of finalised effects sequences.

Array aesthetics and shard cinema, then, are names for some of the ways that films and other media can appeal to digital interfaces. Evoking photo editing, street navigation software, and other GUI functions, their images are unthinkable without the tools and aesthetics of the desktop interface. As a result, they offer a more animated, flexible form of cinema than the kind of realism associated with Bazin. These moments are less about a single spatial unity, after all, than about disintegrating space and revealing it to be a series of modular, interlinked components.

But there are nonetheless overlaps between cinematic Bazinian realism and cinematic gooiness. Just as the GUI can be productively explored with recourse to a modified or updated version of the myth of total cinema, so too the realist aspirations of other media can be seen in light of the kind of information aesthetic that the desktop propagates. A good example of this is the blockbuster film *Gravity* (2013), which balances digital spectacle with Bazinian realism in ways indebted to the GUI.

The story follows inexperienced astronaut Dr Ryan Stone (Sandra Bullock) and veteran spacewalker Matt Kowalski (George Clooney). Cast adrift in orbit during a mission to upgrade the Hubble telescope when satellite debris obliterates their shuttle, they must attempt to survive a series of intense action set pieces. The film's principal photography for the most part involved capturing footage of actors Bullock and Clooney within a 'light box' (a cube of LED panels), their faces then composited onto digitally-created bodies within digitally created environments. Numerous extended sequences see these characters drift in orbital space, and consist of what are apparently single takes lasting several minutes, during which the camera is aggressively mobile and operates independent of horizon points and gravitational restrictions. In the thirteen-minute opening shot, for instance, the virtual camera glides in a series of arcs, flowing smoothly from subject to subject. Stable, perspectival space seems to be abandoned in favour of a weightless, actively shifting diegesis: the shuttle, telescope, various moving bodies, and, in the background, a looming planet Earth all constantly change position and orientation. This dynamism palpably intensifies with the arrival of the debris field, as not only the camera but also the shuttle and onscreen characters move around even more wildly. Even so, throughout such sequences, foreground, midground, and background are for the most part all kept in clear, hyper-detailed focus.

Kristen Whissel (2016) proposes that these extended virtual shots reflexively work through ideas of technological perception. For her, *Gravity* is a 'drama of locatability' which uses its aesthetics and exhibition to render states and conditions visible that would otherwise be beyond our optical grasp (Whissel 2016: 235). Like the Hubble, the film adopts technological, computational forms of vision – CG and digital 3D – to immerse us in an extra-planetary location 'associated with technologically-enhanced forms of seeing-in-depth that aid in the production of information and the formation of new modes and means of producing knowledge' (Whissel 2016: 236). But as much as satellites point outwards toward the mysteries of deep space, they also point inwards, towards our personal computing devices. 'Half of North America just lost their Facebook', Kowalski says wryly when the catastrophic cascade of destruction begins, a line highlighting the surprising relationship of the film's spectacular orbital milieu with desktop navigation and the visual experience of social connection it provides.

Mal Ahern (2014) explores the deeper traces of this equivalence, writing that the film is a drama of problem solving apposite for the desktop era. She describes how Stone's body is less a corporeal entity than 'an operational device, a cursor', and argues that the drama of *Gravity* comes not from physical threat exactly but from the management of information and Stone's capacity in this regard (Ahern 2014). Comparing the film to videogames, Ahern stresses the processual (rather than representational) nature of such a link: this isn't the videogame aesthetic of *Gamer* (2009) or *Hardcore Henry* (2015), but something more mundane. 'The kind of work we do watching *Gravity* resembles the work many of us do at our desks every day: we devour and analyze images, at the expense of our bodies', and so Stone's task, like the computer user's, is 'simply to organize the overwhelming flow of visual data she receives through her visor' (Ahern 2014).[9] Ahern's suggestive phrase for *Gravity* is 'workflow cinema', a term which suitably points beyond just videogames to an entire ecology of digital cognitive labour.

We can extend Ahern's suggestion that Stone functions as a cursor in order to draw a series of connections between this character's surroundings and our own computer desktops. The 'disembodied, floating point of view', 'free-floating ubiquity', and 'vastly expanded optical field' that Whissel (2016: 238) detects in the film is as much associated with everyday GUI operation as with a spacewalk. Another weightless environment, the desktop interface is similarly characterised by multiple, sharply defined elements floating in a groundless, pliable digital void. On our GUIs we encounter less shot-countershot editing than flowing single takes, as program windows glide beneath one another, or visibly grow or shrink as we maximise and minimise them. The film's use of deep focus and hyper-detailed computer effects allow us to select points of interest and relevant information and to visually navigate to them with our own foveal targeting as we see fit, just as we might navigate the planar computer screen. Stone and the various vessels she encounters all float discretely within the expanded 3D stereoscopic field of the film like clearly organised desktop paraphernalia.

Meanwhile, the orbital environment of the film evokes less the actual footage of spacewalks disseminated by organisations like NASA – with their locked cameras, partial views, or GoPro wobbliness – than it does the background images that were bundled with many of operating systems in the 2010s. The out-of-the-box background of the 2012 OS X 10.8 (called Mountain Lion) is an image of the Andromeda Galaxy. This glowing galaxy – with its dissipating disc of ethereal blue stars and ambient sense of the majesty of space – sits casually behind the daily task management and entertainment activities of these OS users, quietly asserting that deep space has been brought under our personalised control. *Gravity*'s own backgrounds

---

9 The comparison with videogaming is productive, and goes beyond the aesthetics described here, as the film's narrative construction and screenplay evoke gaming in their structure and mode of address. Stone solves a series of complex puzzles and physical challenges of escalating difficulty; alongside this, first Kowalski and then Stone's own running commentary work to remind the viewer of the constituents of these puzzles and the importance of solving them. This is highly reminiscent of, for instance, *Call of Duty* campaign missions, in which non-playable characters (NPCs) constantly recap goals and dangers over the diegetic radio, keeping the player focused amid the chaotic shootouts.

not only resemble this desktop wallpaper aesthetically through their digital sharpness and colour palette, but also operate in the same manner. Mostly concealed by other elements but seen at moments of task reorientation (on start-up, or when switching program windows), the majesty of space becomes the focus of attention only when Stone takes a fleeting break from her stressful multitasking (her own form of Mission Control).

At each of the three moments the debris field strikes, the horizonless but legible GUI-style space of the film becomes cluttered and dynamically unstable. At these points *Gravity* resembles nothing so much as untidy, disorganised desktop space. As craft shatter and fragment, the layered space of the frame becomes akin to a desktop clogged with too many icons, all overlapping in ways that occlude their meaning and purpose. Clarity of resolution may be maintained, but the haphazard, unpredictable arrangement of all these high-resolution elements threatens successful workflow. Shard cinema tilts from stilled contemplation to frenzied disorder, and space is rendered much harder to navigate for Stone, film viewer, and desktop user alike (Figures 2.1a–c). The pleasure of interface use is placed at risk, and the film's drama comes from Stone's journey from panic to confidence within this environment.

There are moments when the film abandons deep focus and wide angles, but still retains a kind of GUI visuality. Perhaps most telling is a shot in which extreme narrow focus is used to capture a tear drifting away from Stone's face. This occurs at the lowest point in her arc: as the third act

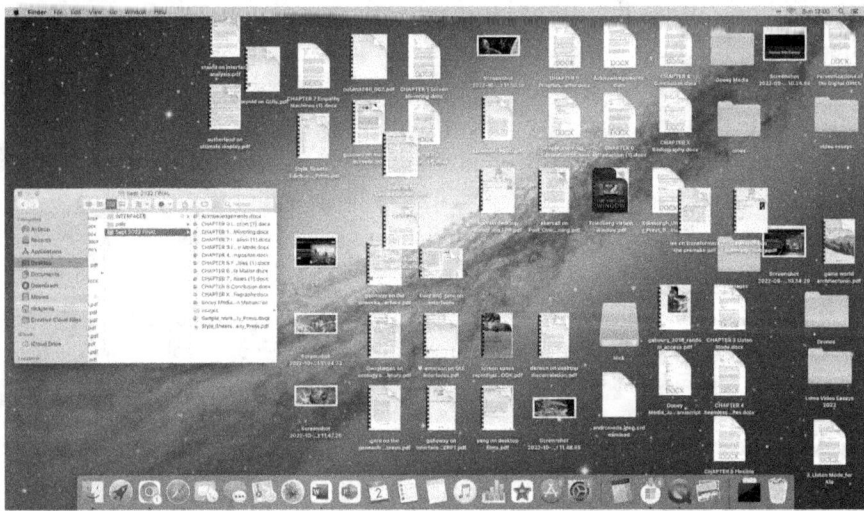

Figure 2.1a A mac desktop cluttered with icons. Frame enlargement of author's own desktop.

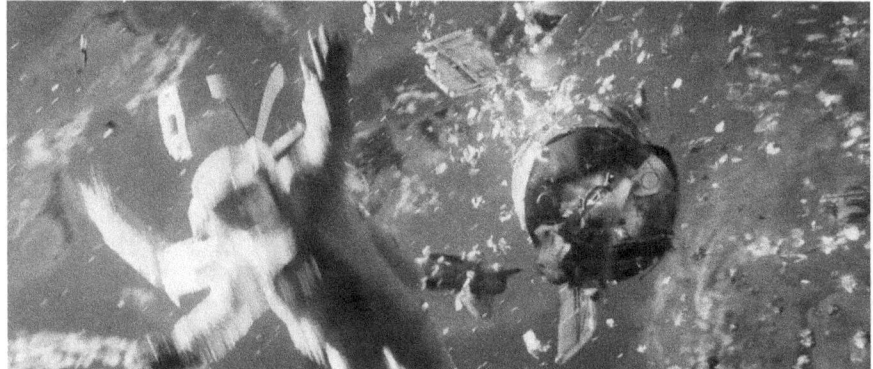

Figure 2.1b *Gravity's* (2013) terrifying orbital mise-en-scène. Frame enlargement from Blu-ray.

Figure 2.1c Stone looks on at the chaos in *Gravity* (2013). Frame enlargement from Blu-ray.

begins, Stone is giving up hope of returning to Earth, preparing instead to freeze to death alone in a space capsule. Just as viewers might notice the globule of grief floating toward us, the film quickly racks focus to it, blurring Stone herself into an amorphous mass and bringing the single hovering tear into sharp clarity; after allowing us a few seconds to contemplate it, the focus shifts back to Stone, and the droplet drifts imperceptibly beyond the edges of the frame. This racked shallow focus strongly resembles that which occurs in Apple's Launchpad, when the computer user seeks access to their array of programs in a decisive, global fashion (Figures 2.2a–c). The tear is a digital production, as is the focal shift, meaning that, like Launchpad, they rely on VFX procedures of easing and motion smoothing that allow focus to alter in a mathematically smooth manner. And, like Launchpad, this moment blurs what has been the functional zone of the image in

Figure 2.2a Stone begins to lose hope in *Gravity* (2013) ... Frame enlargement from Blu-ray.

Figure 2.2b ... and the camera racks focus to a single tear floating in front of her. Frame enlargement from Blu-ray.

order to manifest and literally foreground available operations at a time of operational decision-making. On a Mac, this is a move from the clutter of open programs to the lucid simplicity of shortcut icons; in *Gravity*, it is a shift from the protagonist and her actions to a list of possible alternative procedures – which for Stone now consist of a single icon, the affective tear of surrender.

In these ways, a film invested in spectacular realism but seemingly uninterested in digital interfaces (there are a couple of fleeting command-line CRT monitors, but no other screens) nonetheless draws on visual ideas native to the GUI. *Gravity* is a particularly good example of this intermingling, but other films like *Avatar* (2009) and *Life of Pi* (2012) are comparable. Again, this is not just about the presence of digital environments, but the evocation of weightless, layered space and the implicit equation of the

Figure 2.2c The Launchpad function on a mac computer, revealing application logos and throwing the background heavily out of focus. Frame enlargement of author's own desktop.

characters with navigable cursors. In an article on digital 3D cinema and its aesthetic particulars, Thomas Elsaesser (2013) alights on precisely this aspect of contemporary stereoscopic visuality. 3D experiences like *Avatar*, he argues, are less about Hollywood spectacle than about reflecting on the profusion of digital screens in our lives and the new visual experiences they offer. When he states that they 'introduce[e] the malleability, scalability, fluidity, or curvature of digital images into audiovisual space', by 'doing away with horizons, suspending vanishing points, [and] seamlessly varying distance', he may as well be talking about everyday GUI use rather than extra-terrestrial adventures (Elsaesser 2013: 237). In an early scene, *Avatar* even features a teardrop rack-focus shot much like that found in *Gravity*.

Successful desktop navigation is dependent both upon the legible presentation of information *and* upon our capacity to insert ourselves into this infoscape through touchscreen gestures, keyboard strokes, or the movement of a mouse or trackpad. Film and other pre-recorded audio-visual media do not seem to offer this kind of insertion and interactivity: short of playing, pausing, forwarding, or exiting (if watching on a personal device), we cannot navigate what we see. And yet, the cursor that is the protagonist performs this navigation for us. Our hands and fingers may be still, but through the onscreen characters we can browse, select, and edit. In this workflow cinema, as in array aesthetics and shard cinema, we can see how other media are not as discrete from the desktop interface as might first be assumed, and also how facets of the GUI have become generalisable as methods for organising and processing visual information. In the GUI, multiple windows, overlapping layers, and impressions of interactive optical navigation align with a Bazinian aesthetic of expansive visual terrain to conjure a high resolution, information-rich, realistic virtual space. As the GUI moves toward this verisimilitudinous but hardly photographic form of visual design, it is not surprising that other photorealistic media begin adopting their own versions of the desktop's organisational strategies.

Frames win games …

Gravity's release included a stereoscopic 3D version which was generally praised (see, for example, Hornaday 2013). The dimensional effects of that format accentuate the layered nature of the film's compositions, and potentially amplify its Bazinian spatial richness. Yet this only highlights how the average GUI is not 3D – the alternative spatial experience offered by stereoscopy has historically not been a required value for information navigation in desktop contexts. Equally, streaming services that carry this film will offer the 2D version for viewing on the customer's laptop or phone. While the film *can* be purchased as a 3D Blu-ray, the market for these and 3D-capable televisions is minimal (such that production of the latter almost completely halted in 2016). So while 3D increases the resolution of *Gravity*, it does so in ways that distinguish this resolution as a particularly cinematic experience. This places it at one remove from the GUI screens upon which it will also circulate, and which its other aesthetic features otherwise evoke.[10]

This discrepancy indicates that for all the convergence of elements within the media landscape, and for all that the gooiness of the GUI is central to this process, there remain borders between media, even in terms of resolution and realism. In the remainder of this chapter, I focus not on 3D but on another, at times related format which has been unevenly adopted across the screen media landscape: high frame rate (HFR) display. A consistent yet rarely noticed element of the GUI, HFR is connected to both realism and the layered information space of the computer screen. As such, it would seem to be innately gooey. Yet it has not stuck to other media in ways unanimous or unproblematic. HFR's realism is debated and contested

---

10 One possible reason for the stubborn 2D-ness of the GUI could be 3D's inherent distortion and subversion of visual norms. I discuss these throughout Jones 2020.

in non-desktop contexts, and so it reveals how GUI visuality and digital verisimilitude are subjects of careful negotiation and intense disagreement. When bringing together GUI, videogames, and cinema, there is not always unanimous agreement on what counts as desirable resolution.

First, though, what is HFR? To refer to a 'high' frame rate is to imply a lower standard to which it is being compared. Throughout much the history of moving image media, the normalised rate of frames per second (or fps) has been twenty-four, or something very close to this. This was not always the case: early cinema offered a variety of speeds in terms of both capture and projection, but the widespread adoption of synchronised sound in the 1920s put an end to this multiplicity, as audio systems required more predictable and stable rates of picture flow (Turnock 2013: 33). The standardisation of twenty-four frames per second combined efficiency and aesthetics, allowing expensive film stock to move through the camera gate just fast enough that, when projected back, it could be perceived by audiences without flicker or apparent distortion, but not so fast that stock is being effectively wasted. Television's similar frame rates of twenty-five and thirty frames per second might imply a medial debt to cinema, but are instead the result of a different technological necessity. These rates match the mains frequency of local electrical grids, namely 50 Hz (in most of the world) or 60 Hz (in parts of America and Asia). The power grid frequencies are then halved to get the frame rate, since TV images are interlaced to reduce flicker: each frequency oscillation provides half the vertical scan lines, the immediately following oscillation providing the remaining half. This results in the enculturated, but nationally specific, norms of 25 and 30 fps for television broadcast (Marshall 2019: 4).[11]

'High' frame rates therefore generally name anything above 30 fps – despite the fact that we experience this higher rate many times a day on our GUIs: most computers, laptops, and tablets refresh their content sixty times a second or more, and from 2020 onwards, a variety of smartphones also started adopting these higher refresh rates too (Horwitz 2020).[12] Why are these higher rates common for operating systems, but not for film and

---

11 Tying frame pulsing to electrical grid pulsing was a necessity for two reasons: television sets were more efficient if they aligned with the local power frequency (reducing error and flicker in image presentation), and much TV studio filming used alternating current lamps (linked again to local power supply frequency), meaning that any playback rate that differed from this frequency could produce a stroboscopic effect.

12 These rates allows file-sharing sites to host a selection of 60 fps content, as YouTube has done since 2015.

television? Precisely to assist in operation: the fluidity created by these rates aids task navigation and user experience, ensuring predictable and responsive interaction with the desktop. In 2017, for instance, Apple introduced what they call ProMotion to their higher end iPads, an even higher frame rate that they claim is an improvement to the scrolling experience because it allows for more 'fluid and natural' engagement with the screen, especially when drawing (Apple Inc. 2017).

PC and console videogames take advantage of these higher frame rates by utilising refresh rates of 60 Hz and 144 Hz. (A quick clarification: because there is no interlacing, this means the screen displays of these games refreshes 60 or 144 times per second respectively, and this broadly equates to the frame rate, although fps names the frames produced by the graphics engine of a system and Hz refers to the refresh rate of the display). This is not new: refresh rates of 60 fps were used for videogames like *Pong*, first released in 1972 (Skelly 2009: x), while the 1989 Nintendo GameBoy also offered 60 fps play (Reynolds 2016). These rates provide a flowing gaming experience, and while this no doubt offers affective and aesthetic pleasures, consumer-facing articulation of these systems homes in on performance enhancement, which is related explicitly to the management of spatial data. Many games are predicated, at root, on the navigation of space (Nitsche 2009; Wolf 2011), and so the clarity of these spaces and their contents is crucial to high performance play.

Witness, for instance, a 2020 advertising campaign by technology company Nvidia for their GeForce Graphic Processing Unit (Figure 2.3). Here, frame rates above 60 Hz are linked to superior achievement in online multiplayer gameplay. In their succinct terms: 'frames win games' (Nvidia n.d.). This is not just marketing bluster. The latency present in a 60 Hz (or lower) display means that the appearance of fast-moving objects upon the game screen might lag slightly behind the spatial positioning of the object according to the internal readings of the game system. This could result in a player missing a target despite their well-placed shot, as they have been provided visual information concerning their enemy's position which was milliseconds out-of-date by their display technology.

And, invariably, these consumer-facing discourses around higher frame rates and their advantages for gamers *do* concentrate on gunplay, and the militarised, projectile-weapon-based combat of the first-person shooter, or FPS genre.[13] These games require demanding levels of player precision, and their online versions foster a culture that rewards high performance play.

---

13   See, for instance, the examples in Claypool and Claypool 2006.

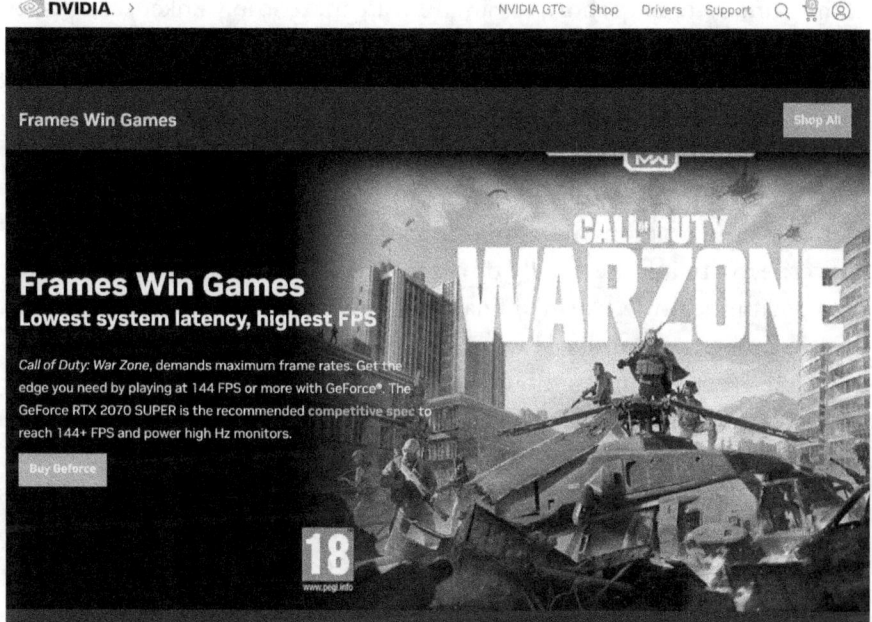

Figure 2.3 The website for Nvidia's 'Frames Win Games' advertising campaign. From Nvidia, n.d.

Consisting of doorways from which an enemy might emerge, crannies into which a player may conceal themselves, walls upon which to bounce a grenade, or alleys in which to find containers of strategic material, space in these games is a source of anxiety and possibility, a field of potential action. If Pasi Väliaho (2014: 33) describes the gaming experience of the *Call of Duty* (2003 – ongoing) franchise as primarily about 'moving around in and exploring a virtual environment', then Alexander Galloway (2006: 63) more specifically proposes that in such games any kind of vision fundamentally requires 'actionable' spaces.

Clarity of visual space becomes synonymous with activity and agency. Exploration in shooters like *Call of Duty* and *Gears of War* (2006 – ongoing) consists of stealthily tracking NPCs, shielding oneself from gunfire, or blasting through a narrow corridor of action littered with possible cover points. The player's ability to quickly scan, interpret, and move through a space made unpredictable by possible enemy activity is as vital as their trigger reflexes or their wider strategic approach. A single shot can be the difference between victory and ignominy. If frames do indeed win games, then the committed player is required to invest in technology that will allow the visual outputs their display to sync as closely as possible to the internal state of the game system. In short, fps and FPS are inextricably linked, as a player must get their system's fps performance up to the highest spec in order to maximise their own FPS performance.

The importance of infinitesimal temporal intervals in FPS gaming contexts resembles that of the world of financial trading. Banking may seem far away from the discourses and technology of HFR, but with its suggestively similar acronym, high frequency trading (HFT) is comparably concerned with infinitesimally timed responses to changes in digital data. An algorithmically led form of financial speculation in which the analysis, decision, purchase, and sale of securities occurs in a matter of milliseconds, HFT exploits micro divergences between markets before these are digitally updated and eradicated. Successful HFT depends on being faster than one's competitors – even if this advantage is at an almost quantum scale, and enacted by algorithms rather than human beings (Lewis 2014: 9–10). Vast sums of money are accordingly spent on infrastructure that can intercept trading information literally a fraction of a second before competitors. For instance, between 2010 and 2015, Hibernia Networks, a telecommunications company, spent upwards of $300m on a communications cable between Canada, the UK, and Ireland that would shave a mere six milliseconds off trading times for financial firms (Williams 2011).

As in the case of the higher refresh rates of competitive videogaming, winning in HFT is a matter of investing heavily in resources that provide more fine-grained access to a complex system of spatial and numerical relations. Tellingly, companies such as Nvidia provide tools for both domains. 'Acquire targets faster, act quicker, and increase aim precision through a revolutionary suite of technologies' states the Nvidia GeForce GPU marketing blurb in the 'Frames Win Games' campaign (Nvidia n.d.), words that might equally be deployed to sell the very same company's A100 GPU, which can be used for HFT analytics (Xenon n.d.).

In relation to gaming, smoother image flow amplifies the palpability of space, as well as the digital screen user's sense of possible engagement with it. This, in turn, amplifies the potential efficacy of this engagement. The kinetic information of high frame rates goes hand in hand with high resolution rendering, all of which is vital to the committed navigation of competitive terrain. In this, videogames adopt and extend the task management of the GUI generally, putting the additional frames to use in a similar way. This is normalised to such an extent that, for many gamers, what might in other contexts be called HFR is just regular FR.

... Not films

One of these other contexts is cinema, a media in which HFR refuses to become a standard. This is despite a long history of attempts to make it so. In the early 1980s, special effects designer and director Douglas Trumbull developed a 60 fps recording and exhibition system called Showscan, advertising it as more real than its slower cinematic competitors (Turnock 2013: 38–9). But rather than launch the era of HFR cinema, this was just the first of its many commercial and financial failures. Trumbull's experiments in the 1970s and 1980s were never widely adopted, and in the digital era only a few films have been viewable in the format, and only under very specific conditions. The *Hobbit* trilogy of films (2012, 2013, 2014) were significant HFR releases, running at 48 fps, but available cinema screenings in the format decreased with each subsequent instalment thanks to negative audience reaction (Swift 2014). Shortly thereafter, *Billy Lynn's Long Halftime Walk* (2012) and *Gemini Man* (2019) were filmed at 120 fps and made available in both 120 fps and 60 fps versions, but again were more commonly available in 24 fps.[14] They were also both likewise commercial and critical disappointments, neither recouping their production and marketing budgets.[15] If earlier periods of HFR were aberrations in screen frame rates, rolled out before desktops and their fluid 60 Hz images were common, then these later films were by contrast released in an era of widespread HFR screen use outside of the cinema. Why, then, were they similarly unsuccessful?

Julie Turnock describes how the smoothness of HFR removes what might be thought of as a perceptual pane of glass that exists between spectator and media. The interface, it seems, is so successful that it entirely disappears. As a result, the viewer is given seemingly immediate access to 'a high definition, participatory illusion of 3-D space' (Turnock 2013: 38).[16] In this way HFR

---

14 Not all cinemas could maintain the higher resolution attributes of these films. In the case of *Billy Lynn* and *Gemini Man*, only a handful of cinemas worldwide could maintain the 120 fps HFR and 8K resolution of the shooting process. See Setoodeh and Lang 2016; Patches 2019.

15 This is perhaps particularly notable in the latter's case: a Will Smith action blockbuster produced by super-producer Jerry Bruckheimer, *Gemini Man* made $140m globally; released six months later, *Bad Boys for Life* (2020), a similar Will Smith star vehicle (in which he also faces off against an illegitimate son) made over $400m (although it is admittedly part of a long-running franchise).

16 This removal can undermine spectator pleasure as much as it might be able to reinforce it, and in this vein Turnock shows how different media have different criteria of realism, resulting in audience displeasure when these categories are blurred (as

appeals to increased presence and immersion, and in its cinematic guises is often equated with increased verisimilitude, or at least the intention of such. Trumbull, for instance, claimed that 60 fps was biologically closer to human perception (Turnock 2013: 38), while ancillary marketing material for *Billy Lynn* proposes that the technology gives the viewer access to the titular protagonist's experience in the same manner as virtual reality media (Rotten Tomatoes Coming Soon 2016).

But critics disagreed, with frequent comments that the use of HFR did not meet the apparently realist goals stated by the filmmakers in these instances. An empirical reception study on HFR in *The Hobbit* by Carolyn Michelle et al. reveals how a significant number of viewers 'experienced [HFR] as unconvincing and distracting, and as undermining suspension of disbelief' (Michelle et al. 2017: 230). In a typical piece on *Billy Lynn*, meanwhile, Jackson McHenry (2016) describes it as 'a better film' in the lower frame rate, since at 120 fps the staggering array of detail in each shot becomes distracting, and classical elements of film grammar like cuts and fades become overly noticeable. If frames win games, then they apparently lose films.

How can we more carefully explain this apparent dissatisfaction? The participation that HFR seems to offer has in cinematic contexts been associated with realist models which code participation as presence. But this model never quite fits. Realism, participation, presence, and resolution are not all tied together in mutually reinforcing ways, and their relationship to 'the cinematic' is not as straightforward as might first be expected. HFR therefore reveals the extent to which the concepts 'realism' and even 'cinema' are highly contingent and historically constructed (Turnock 2013; Michelle et al. 2017). In Todd Jurgess's (2017: 11) words, in both the use of HFR and the responses to it, 'the seeming one-way street tying increased referential fidelity to quantifiable optimization seems to be put into question'. Amplification of resolution does not, in this instance, equal greater immersion. Indeed, quite the opposite.

Turnock (2013: 47) concludes from her study of the format that HFR as it is used in mainstream commercial cinema often 'strips the footage of much of the sheen of its "cinematographic" effect, removing much of its expensive production value that has come to separate its look from that of television or videogames'. As a result, she states that HFR offers an 'aesthetic of digital convergence' (Turnock 2013: 31). Here, then, cinema's overlap

---

when big-budget HFR cinema looks disconcertingly similar to soap opera television broadcasts). See also Michelle et al. 2015.

with the GUI and videogames becomes an apparent hindrance rather than an advantageous intersection. HFR reveals common ground normally concealed or underplayed, threatening the distinction (both culturally and qualitatively) of cinema as a discrete media form. The increase in resolution offered by HFR's additional frames results in a fluidly unfolding series of images that does not seem to match the grammar of the medium in which it is being employed. The molten smoothness of 48, 60, or 120 frames per second is unremarkable when our cursor is gliding across a screen, or our avatar navigates a digitally generated gamespace, but it becomes abnormal in a cinematic context.

Indeed, if it shares kinship with any media, cinematic HFR can be aligned with television, its aesthetic often termed a 'soap opera effect' (Turnock 2013: 43). This is a reference to the slightly higher frame-rates of TV, in particular programs recorded on videotape with studio lighting. Despite offering only a few more frames per second than film, the recording equipment and the interlacing of frames in these 25 and 30 fps broadcasts generate a subtly different visual aesthetic, characterised by smoothness and a kind of flat plasticity. As a label, 'soap opera effect' also conveniently points to the perceived cheapness or artificiality that detractors identify in the HFR format. A technology of exhibition designed to be a pinnacle of expensive cinematic spectacle gets tarred with the brush of its seeming exact opposite: disposable daytime TV.

The comparison with TV soap opera also draws HFR into debates around the motion smoothing settings found on many digital television sets. Interpolating additional frames in order to remove judder and motion blur, motion smoothing (which goes by many different names depending on brand) is often activated in the default settings of many LCD TVs. This fluid imagery is highly contentious, the subject of much vitriol from self-certified media connoisseurs. The scale of this ill-feeling can be found in message boards, memes and comment threads, but is perhaps best portrayed in a video made by actor Tom Cruise and writer-director-producer Christopher McQuarrie in 2018. As the key creative professionals of *Mission: Impossible – Fallout* (2018), they implore viewers of that film's Blu-ray to experience this film – and all films – 'to the fullest possible effect' (Page Six 2018). 'To that end we'd like to take a moment of your time to talk to you about video interpolation', says Cruise, as though he were a TV evangelist, or a door-to-door salesperson. McQuarrie continues, defining interpolation, or motion smoothing, as 'a digital effect on most high-definition televisions', intended to 'reduce motion blurring in sporting events'. 'The unfortunate side effect', Cruise chimes in, a palpable note of disappointment creeping into his voice, 'is that it makes most movies look like they were shot on high-speed video rather than film'. They go on to describe how difficult it is to turn off this setting, but urge viewers to make the effort.

The tone of this somewhat bizarre short clip is that of a public service announcement, imploring savvy and cinephiliac TV owners to rid themselves of the plague of this misguided technological liability. A loud shot fired in a propaganda war contesting what consumers should expect films watched at home to look like, the video exposes a strange fissure in the relationship between major electronics companies and the Hollywood film industry (personified by major global brand and super-producer Cruise). Interpolation is not the same as HFR. It might be considered 'fake' HFR, although this categorisation is unhelpfully qualitative.[17] Unlike HFR, it uses algorithmic interpretation to create frames that were not originally present. Nonetheless, the aesthetic is highly similar, and for all the evocations of realism by some commentators, both HFR and interpolation get widely criticised for providing a kind of molten and artificial digital clarity. In Cruise and McQuarrie's video, interpolation – a conspicuously HFR-like digital effect – is conceived by industry insiders to be a betrayal of the artistic labour of all those involved on a production, watching it tantamount to a cinematic crime.[18]

Whether native (in the case of films like *The Hobbit*) or interpolated (in HD TV sets), higher frame rates do not seem to fit the visual language of film as it is conceived by most viewers and commentators, or at least those with a platform to air their beliefs. This is not (just) a case of troubled and thus frustrated expectations. Filmmakers shooting in HFR have for the most part adapted aspects of their aesthetic approach to align with the sharper, more spatially assertive visual signature of the format. After all, there seems little point in stepping beyond conventional frame rates if other aspects of filmmaking practice are going to conceal all that extra detail. HFR seems to encourage the cinematic depiction of space in ways that are as hyper-clear as videogames and bring into play the same kinds of GUI visuality earlier

---

17 The same problematic qualitative presumptions beset discussion of post-converted 3D content, which can be condemned in some sectors as 'fake' 3D (Kushigemachi 2020).
18 Partly, this is a repeat and symptom of the film-v-digital debate: despite the existence of earlier high frame cinema, motion smoothing is a quintessentially digital phenomenon. As Matthew Hockenberry and Jason LaRiviere (2020: 114) describe, interpolation is part of a digital platform ecology, and asking home viewers to turn it off 'is a futile request. Like modern televisions, streaming services like Twitch and YouTube expect pure digital signals at the highest frame rates, pure digital production for pure digital playback – the output of digital devices intended as the inputs for yet another digital device.'

identified in *Gravity*. This further moves these films into the orbit of the desktop, albeit in apparently less productive ways than that orbital thriller.

Gemini Man, for instance, uses wide angles and deep focus, as well as many takes that are reasonably lengthy for the contemporary action genre (with around 1200 shots across a two-hour running time, the film has a relatively languorous average shot length of roughly five seconds). Combined with the regular use of long- or mid-shot scales (in which most or all of an actor's body will be in shot), the result is a wealth of high-resolution detail at every moment. In HFR this detail is retained and continually visible even when the camera or elements of the onscreen environment are in rapid motion.[19] For instance, during a chase scene in Cartagena in which Will Smith's protagonist Henry Brogan evades an attacker (a clone of his younger self, known in the film as Junior) the camera rarely moves closer than a mid-shot, and only very occasionally throws elements of the background out of focus. As Brogan runs through apartment blocks and rides a motorcycle down tight streets, his surroundings – which would normally become to some extent blurred or hazy thanks to the speed of the camera's movement – remain sharply distinct.

This is what grants HFR its liquid or velvety quality, the impression that imagery is flowing rather than unspooling. The same is true of the three *Hobbit* films, which similarly utilise wide angles and deep focus for many shots. Certainly, close ups and shallow focal planes appear regularly, but the use of the HFR 3D format has encouraged the filmmakers to again place their characters within highly legible (albeit in the case of Middle Earth, sometimes digitally manufactured) spaces. The most pronounced – and in some sectors mocked – example of this is to be found in the second film, *The Desolation of Smaug* (2013), in which the protagonists escape pursuers by riding barrels through white water rapids. In HFR these images are unsettlingly clear, creating a piercing impression of overwhelming and unattractive lucidity. In tandem with bluescreen shooting and oddly metrical action beats, HFR changes the river from a natural environment to a level in a platform videogame.

---

19 As stated, feature-length HFR film content is difficult to source. As of 2021, the *Hobbit* films have not been released in HFR for home viewing; *Billy Lynn* received a 4K release which included a 60 fps copy but, due to technological limitations, this was on a separate disc to the 3D version (which itself ran at 24/25 fps); while the highest spec of *Gemini Man* is a 3D Blu-ray (2K, 24/25 fps). As a result, I will openly state here the singular conditions of my viewing when undertaking this analysis (I saw the film in 2K 60 fps 3D, at the Odeon Cinema in Leeds, UK, in 2019). This means this analysis does not benefit from ideal repeated viewing, and the closer scrutiny this brings.

Aesthetic effects like focal blur and even movement judder implicitly emphasise how the screen is an intentional arrangement of compositional elements that each have relative value and importance; in their absence, everything is important. As journalist Alissa Wilkinson states of *Gemini Man*'s HFR, 'with everything in focus in the frame, it's hard to know what to look at', and she goes on to suggest that a result of this clarity is that 'artistry has been ripped out of the visual essence of cinema' (Wilkinson 2019). In HFR cinema, images are so highly legible that they become – paradoxically – less clear to many viewers, as they lack some standardised cinematic strategies for directing attention. The removal of 'artistry' – the guiding visual hand of focal contrast, or the subtler effects often found in 24 fps shooting like backgrounds becoming blurred in moving shots while central figures remain sharp – results in a space of unremitting presence and even urgency.

But if this is felt by some to be un-cinematic, it is, as we have seen, very familiar to videogames, particularly first and third person shooters. Space in these HFR films is made more comprehensible, even palpable through the absence of spatial distortion or blurring at moments of movement. This is a legibility inherited from (or at least processed through) the experience of videogames that themselves depict intense, participatory environments. Watching Brogan navigate Cartagena or Bilbo navigate Middle Earth is in many ways like directing Private First Class Joseph Allen through the streets of a terrorist-controlled shanty town in Rio de Janeiro in *Call of Duty: Modern Warfare 2* (2009): space is not just highly perceptible but relentlessly and insistently *perceived*, an ever-moving field of detailed distractions and strategic possibilities. In either case, HFR and deep, sharp focus amplify our cognizance of the environment, endowing it with a sense of potential or implied actionability.

This is, as indicated, not so different from the way in which the GUI uses high frame rates to provide navigational assistance. Apple's addition of ProMotion on iPads claims to let viewers continue reading even as they incessantly scroll feeds and program windows, words and images becoming not staccato pulses but flowing interactive reams. The sinuous refresh rates of the interactive screen are intrinsic to its very interaction, amplifying our haptic orientation with virtual content. HFR cinema seems to make a comparable promise of interactivity and navigation, but this promise is unfulfilled. If HFR removes the pane of glass between player and videogame, then it does this not for purposes of greater realism or immersive 'presence', exactly, but to improve the operational usability of the representational system, improving less gameplay *experience* than gameplay *efficacy*. Videogame HFR shares this intention with GUI HFR. But if we likewise perceive the spaces of HFR films as sites of possibility in which we have some kind of agency, then they fail to manifest as such. Unlike videogaming and desktop use, the cinema viewer cannot actively navigate these virtual worlds. So, for all that HFR cinema seeks to conjure a space as immersive and agential as those other screens, the result is failed interactivity rather than successful realism.

Conclusion

In its development and its technological updates, the GUI treads a Bazinian line towards a kind of total representational world, a rich and enthralling virtual space of user navigation. Resolution is crucial here, but not because it is synonymous with realism. As the screen's resolution expands so do the simultaneous or near-simultaneous uses to which it can be put. Collapsing many activities into this small but incredibly dense patch of real estate lessens the need for the screen user's gaze to move beyond the bounds of this rectangle. This increases productivity – or, indeed, the sheer range of procrastinating micro-activities in which a screen user can engage at any one time.

The GUI proffers a particular form of realism, one which seeks to adhere to ideas of depth, shape, shadow, translucency, and contouring drawn from the real world, but which also enables specifically and intrinsically digital forms of task management. This interface realism brings the aesthetic of the screen itself – its windows, buttons, objects, and the way they overlap and interact – into alignment with the media texts it is used to access. One result of this convergence is the screen sharing explored in Chapter 1, in which texts like *Unfriended* and *Sara is Missing* adopt the GUI as a mode of presentation even within the context of other media. Here, though, I have tried to show how this correspondence runs deeper than these overt quotations. For all its digital spectacle, *Gravity* is assertively 'realistic', and its affective charge is linked to the convincing quality of its orbital mise-en-scène, but this does not preclude this film and others from entering into correspondence with the GUI.

If resolution, realism, and interaction are composited together by the digital screen ecology, then HFR indicates how they nonetheless all remain subtly different elements. The result is a debate across film, television, and videogame stakeholders. Natively HFR, the GUI is rarely thought of this way; on the other hand, videogames are openly described as benefitting from the equation of resolution with information and improved interactivity; an echo of this alliance then appears in cinema, where the absence of interaction confounds the hyper-fluid three-dimensional visuals of higher frame rates. All this testifies to the ongoing cultural and functional differences between these media, something I do not wish to ignore even amongst my claims of medial gooiness and cross-pollination, claims to which this book will now return in the form of a sonic corrective to the visual emphasis so far.

3
Listen Mode

'Oh' appears on screen eight times in eight different fonts, each one superimposed over the other, at the same time as the word is sung over and over, in a light and fruity vocal, by singer-songwriter Charli XCX. A tone in the background, like in inverted cymbal crash, grows and takes us into the start of the song proper, as Charli sings about the thrill of getting calls from her crush. Like a karaoke video, the lyrics continue to appear on screen at the same time as they are sung. But unlike karaoke, they manifest in a staggering array of fonts, and they pulse and stretch to correspond with the aural qualities and inflections of their vocal articulation. At times they become completely illegible, a mass of neon globules and baffling superimposition. After the first chorus – in which Charli describes how her boy's unique ringtone is the only one she knows – pop trio Kero Kero Bonito arrive into the song and ruminate on how a ringtone 'could be anything', even a 'barking dog' or a 'revved engine'. The key, as they sing, is that the noise must capture the user's attention. Each line of this verse is plastered across the screen: the word 'ringtone' dominates in a chunky 1970s font, purple outlined with orange, beating like a heart with the rhythm of the song; subsequent lines appear over this, with 'dog' and 'engine' accompanied by low-resolution images of these things.

This is the lyric video for the song 'ringtone (remix)' by the experimental hyperpop duo 100 gecs (2020a). Available on YouTube, this extremely lo-fi video relies on a tight intermingling of image and sound – and little else. As a lyric video rather than a more traditional or official music video, it prioritises the words of the song, and seems to have very little production value (a single talented individual might have put it together in an afternoon using After Effects). But this does not mean it is sparse, simplistic, or that the relationship of the visuals to the music is purely that of semantic illustration. Rather, the bubble-gum baroque designs on display articulate the aural qualities of the voice, key, rhythm, timbre, and pitch of each particular moment of the song in peculiar but tightly bonded ways. Like the titular ringtone, the look of these lyrics could be anything, as long as they visually map onto the sonic attributes of the sung word or accompanying instrumentation in some way, and as long as they solicit our interest. Visuals and soundtrack are bound to one another – with the word 'bound' used advisedly, implying as it does not only obligation and constraint, but also opportunism and typicality (as we will see, this binding is bound to happen in a gooey editing environment). As musicologist Laura McLaren sums up of lyric videos generally, 'there is more to discover in the deceptively simple format of words on a screen accompanying a song' (McLaren 2019: 163).

McLaren's comment is true of digital media soundtracks more generally, which seem deceptively simple in the manner that they 'accompany' the images of today's cinema, videogames, television, and more (and these images are themselves much more widely discussed in scholarly work). But there is indeed much to discover in relation to the GUI and media soundscapes. The last two chapters have asserted that the graphic elements of the GUI, rather than being neutral, are in fact defining features of the broader visual media environment today. If this is the case, then is the same true of the soundscapes created by the desktop interface? I will argue here that yes, we should indeed listen for echoes of the GUI's approach to sound design in other media. Just as the graphic attributes of the desktop are profoundly entwined with other media like films, television, videogames, apps, and so on, so too the sonic environment that accompanies the computer screen synchronises with those found in other digital texts. Listening to these links will reveal a significant – albeit subtle and nuanced – shift in the GUI era in the way that audio functions in relation to imagery, and vice versa. As I will claim, the soundtrack of the desktop and the soundtracks of the media that are enabled by and heard through this desktop must be listened to in concert.

In many ways, the history of screen sound harmonises with that of screen imagery. In either case, the amplification of representational fidelity is foregrounded. As I described in Chapter 2, Bazin's myth of total resolution is a useful way of thinking about the sought-for, but ultimately unattainable, idea of pure fidelity and immersion that structures our thinking about changes in the media landscape. Across media, sound, like image, becomes more complex and layered in ways that are directly tied to the concept of realism. Increasingly crowded soundtracks, the ability to place sounds such that they seem to surround the viewer and originate from distinct spatial areas, and the broadening of dynamic range (the difference between the loudest and quietest sounds a system can produce) are all ways in which the sonic qualities of screen media have claimed to become more verisimilitudinous.

These features are closely connected to digital technology.¹ The use of digital editing and audio mixing software allows and encourages the adoption of highly layered and even spatialised soundtracks, as well as the manipulation of the sonic qualities of all sound elements. Editing programs like Final Cut, Adobe Premiere, and iMovie support sedimented and highly dense soundscapes by enabling users to create and populate dozens of audio tracks (compared with sometimes just two or three image tracks). Pro Tools, a digital audio workstation by Avid, facilitates the adjustment of sound clips in highly variable and modular ways, while videogame engines and plug-ins like Wwise and a FMOD allow for similarly crowded soundtracks and highly nuanced articulation of sounds according to player movement and activity.

Significantly, all these tools offer a highly convenient visual coding of sound – discrete labels for audio clips and the bins that contain them; the placing of these on visual timelines upon which minute changes can be made by moving elements forward or backward a fraction of position; waveforms that can be tweaked through drop-down boxes or small up and down nudges to onscreen levels.² This is facilitated, of course, by the use of the GUI. To design sound for today's screen entertainment landscape is to spend a lot of time at a desktop. More than this, and just as is the case with imagery, the convergence of audio design and GUI practice leads to overlaps in aesthetics and approach. It also leads to image and sound being linked in a particular manner. As this chapter will aim to show through a discussion of various soundscapes (including that of blockbuster cinema, triple-A videogames, and, finally, lyric videos) the sonic space of the GUI – in which aural notifications are linked to visible onscreen alerts – can be found across the wider media landscape. Contemporary 'blended' soundtracks and so-called 'ultrafield' sound design offer a tightly synchronised but highly malleable binding of audio and visual elements from moment to moment: whether interactive or not, the soundtracks of digital media function as navigational aids and synchronised notifications. While it is unconventional to think about audioscapes as overlapping with and connected to GUI aesthetics in this way, I will hope to convince the reader that it is at least a helpful thought exercise for better understanding the relationship of sound and image in gooey media.

---

1 That said, in his work on Dolby Surround Sound in cinema, Mark Kerins (2011: 6) is keen to note that while high-quality, multi-channel soundtracks may have become an industrial standard in the digital era, they are nonetheless not intrinsically or natively digital, and pre-dated widespread use of this technology by some decades.

2 I am grateful to Alessandro Altavilla for pointing this out.

Ping

One way to consider the sound of the GUI is to explore the codecs, formats, and compressions through which it delivers sound to us. Jonathan Sterne's *MP3: The Meaning of a Format* (2012) shows how that apparently invisible coding format in fact profoundly shapes our experience of recorded music in the twenty-first century. From its inception in the 1990s to its massive adoption thanks to the music streaming service Napster to its current incarnation as enculturated standard, MP3 has become central to digital listening. Sterne's book reveals how the format's development shapes the kinds of audio it provides and the kind of listener it assumes: by discarding certain data in order to allow smaller file sizes, MP3 makes judgements about what people want to hear and how and whether they can hear it. The result is that a seemingly utilitarian format 'carries within it practical and philosophical understandings of what it means to communicate, what it means to listen or speak, how the mind's ear works, and what it means to make music' (Sterne 2012: 2). In short, the MP3 encodes cultural practices of listening as much as it does audio data.

Unlike Sterne, though, this chapter will not consider issues like lossy compression and the influence of specific media formats upon the properties of media delivery. To do so would be to march to a slightly different beat than the other work undertaken in *Gooey Media*. Certainly, codecs *do* shape our experience of digital media in profound ways, something also effectively demonstrated by Rosa Menkman (2010; 2011), Anne Pasek (2017), Shane Denson (2020a), and others. But the organisation and implementation of sound within the desktop environment is just as important, and in many respects picks up on the imperatives of both realism and functionality discussed in prior chapters.

That said, attending to the way in which other media sonically mirror the GUI's soundscape perhaps poses even more of a challenge than identifying visual connections. As scholar of film sound Mark Kerins states:

> Aural analysis is an inherently more difficult and more subjective endeavour than image-based analysis. The transient nature of sound itself, the fact that a soundtrack can include multiple elements at one time, and the lack of standard vocabulary for describing sounds all make it impossible to neatly break down soundtracks into the aural equivalent of shot lists common to image-based analysis. (Kerins 2010: 202–3)

I am inclined to agree, although I must also acknowledge that my own background is in visual not aural analysis. After all, the sound scholars

I engage with below certainly tackle the challenges that Kerins notes admirably (including, of course, Kerins himself). Their work demonstrates that detailed exploration of audio elements is just as possible and fruitful as that of visual composition.

So, with these challenges in mind, what does the GUI sound like? Before we jump to the software, we might consider hardware and machinery. On the one hand, for all that the cultural myth of digital immateriality implies an invisible and silent cloud of particles and bits, computer infrastructure actually makes a lot of noise: fans must whir, hard drives must hum, and disc drives must spin. If a computer is struggling for any reason, these otherwise almost soothing sounds can produce a grim anxiety, as whirs turn to clunks, and spins become staccato, rasping jerks.

But if we listen beyond these noises and focus instead just on the screen, then silence would seem to be a defining feature. The aural desktop is, after all, a neutral ground over which the sounds of any particular media can claim dominance when cued up. Of these, multiple sources can be active at any one time, and the user controls which tabs or programs are muted and which are not, selecting a particular audio feed (a Netflix show; a YouTube clip; a Soundcloud recording; a Skype call; a Steam game), or letting numerous media sound out simultaneously if they seek sonic cacophony. Depending on settings, media might be interrupted by or interleaved with notifications – the pings, beeps, chimes, and rings that tell a user they have email, are the subject of social media activity, or should pay urgent attention to a breaking news story.

Let's focus on one of these pings, the first we hear in fact. The Mac start-up noise tends to be a rich, slightly descending multi-note chord evoking a deep exhalation, while a Windows machine tends to greet users with a more ornate, melodic passage with a rising refrain (although these are undergoing constant revision as key pieces of branding architecture).[3] So ubiquitous as to be almost unheard, these seconds-long musical numbers are nonetheless precision-engineered and carefully calibrated (the start-up chimes of Windows 95 were composed by avant-garde musician Brian Eno).

This is just the start of the symphony that these machines can offer. Specific, highly designed sounds alert the user to incoming emails, the need to install updates, and the unfortunate event of a program crash, among

---

3   These are available in many forms on YouTube, for example Apple Explained 2017; and Apple Explained 2020.

other things.[4] These are examples of sonification: the communication of information via sound, information which has gone through some process of translation or codification in order to make it aural. Such sounds are called 'intentional', because they have been explicitly designed, rather than being incidental synchronic events (Walker and Ness 2011: 9–11). That is, the sound of a car engine may communicate information to its user, but these sounds are specifically related to the object's material functioning – the engine makes noise because it has to in order to move the car. By contrast, the ping of a microwave or the chime of a computer start-up have been explicitly designed to be communicative: they are additive and not intrinsic.

The GUI, then, is a place in which audio cues provide auxiliary information in an intentional and designed fashion. Users are given updates regarding program use and system functionality through visual signals like pop-up boxes and spinning wheels of death, but these are often accompanied by an auditory layer which reinforces that visual information. Sound and image are tightly related: a message notification *ding* comes with a glimpse at the message via an onscreen bubble; the Skype ringtone prompts part of that program to appear in front of any others currently open. Smartphones may not always light up when messages are received, but in most modes they will make some kind of noise (whether a chime or a vibration), and the user will be shown the message or a portion of this communication when illuminating the screen.

In many cases these cues are exactly that – they cue a response from the user. The sound of an email notification pulls us to check our messages, a beeping alarm begs to be switched off, and a start-up noise solicits our hands to take their position over keyboard, mouse, and trackpad, ready for action. GUIs contain these noises because they help orient us, and they direct our activity by encouraging specific reactions. In this they seem quite unlike the soundscapes of screen entertainment media like television and cinema, which create rich diegetic worlds in ways that the viewer is not necessarily designed to notice moment to moment, but rather encouraged to enjoy as part of an unfolding fiction.

That said, this brief description of the GUI's audio environment does find an overt echo in some of the key mainstream media products of the digital age. With their emphasis on constant lush orchestration and the sonic interplay of complex layers of sound effects and the voicework of multiple actors,

---

4 Different sounds are associated with different brands and, of course, there is significant work undertaken to ensure that these are perceived as appropriately rich or luxurious by the consumer (Lageat et al. 2003).

superhero films, for instance, might sound very different to desktops. But in these films sound similarly functions as an anchoring point or a sonified unit of data, especially during frenetic action, during which it helps viewer navigation. Supervising Marvel Cinematic Universe sound editor Shannon Mills describes how her work involves being a 'walking encyclopaedia' of sounds that have appeared in the many films that make up the franchise (Walden 2019). She also indicates how these sounds all converge in the climactic scenes of team-up films: when the Avengers assemble, they do so not only visually but also sonically. During a fight in *Captain America: Civil War* (2016) that features a dozen MCU superheroes attacking one another, each hero has a sonic signature, in many cases featured and developed within their own films and associated with powers or weaponry. Scarlet Witch conjures magic with a pulsing, liquidy throb; Captain America's shield makes a deep, throbbing metallic thud; Spider-Man shoots webs from his wrists with a tensile squirt; Black Panther's vibranium claws scratch and slash with a high-pitched slice; and Iron Man's palm-based repulsors link a brief charge-up chime with a subsequent explosive scorch in a nimble one-two sonic punch. These sounds play alongside each character's onscreen appearance, and so orient viewers during crowded sequences like this. Quick cuts and hand-held camerawork might visually confuse similar-looking characters like Iron Man and War Machine, or the Winter Soldier and Hawkeye, but these audio signatures establish and maintain distinctions. As characters pair off to engage in specific combat scenarios, these sounds then create a series of duets. Not only signifying who is fighting who, they even sonically depict who is winning – an interrupted sound effect is a sure sign of a character losing the upper hand, as when the charge-up sound of Iron Man's repulsors is followed not by the expected explosive scorch but by a splutter and a clang as his suit is disabled by a rogue Ant-Man.[5]

This quick example (to which I will return below) shows how the functional soundscape of the GUI might be playing in conceptual harmony with the ambient, richly textured sonic worlds of those media we use it to access. In either case, the audio and the visual are bound together. While this might seem an obvious statement, it draws our attention to the importance of both confluence and orientation. These are not soundtracks which accompany visual content like a chaperone, but which address us like a tour guide: they

---

5 Much the same statements could be made of one of Disney's other cross-media mega-franchises: the sound effects of *Star Wars* function as unifying threads throughout films, television programs, and videogames. It simply would not be a Star War if lightsabers, laser blasters, or droids did not make the noises so closely associated with them.

tell us what, in the visual barrage of either our desktop or a crowded action scene, is most salient to our visual navigation and more general perceptual attention.

This act of guiding is greatly aided by developments in dynamic range. Naming the potential to simultaneously play high-pitched and low-pitched sounds, or very loud and very quiet sounds, in ways that keep them all distinct and which avoid audio masking, dynamic range is central to contemporary digital soundscapes (Kerins 2015: 54–5). It allows these soundtracks to be used to effectively point to multiple image elements simultaneously using multiple soundtrack elements. As a result, these media texts can keep various audio sources in play simultaneously, much like the numerous program windows and browser tabs that populate the visual field of the typical desktop.

Through their focus on notifications, interactivity, and guidance, the sounds of the GUI might be thought to function much the same way as the soundscape of a videogame. Videogame theorist Kristine Jørgensen (2013: 5) argues that both the visual and aural cues of a game work to generate a 'gameworld interface' through which relevant information is provided to the player. This interface combines many different orders of information, from the realistic to the operational to the purely functional. The sonic worlds of videogames, while they may at times be highly realistic, always function to inform the player about changes in the game state. Whether it is the sound of a character's breathing as they run out of stamina, the background music which cues up possible danger, or the short pings which might accompany selections on a menu screen, videogames use audio not only to develop the diegesis but also to provide extensive and constant feedback.

However much the soundtrack of a game might be 'cinematic' – which is to say, broadly realistic, perceptually immersive, sonically rich, and tonally consistent – it is also therefore accomplishing other tasks of notification and feedback in subtle ways. As Jørgensen (2011: 93) states, 'When sounds work functionally in the sense of providing gameplay-relevant information to the player, it must be seen as part of the user interface of a game.' Understanding gameplay demands an appreciation of how this is shaped by audio cues as much as visual ones.

As such, videogames are a good place to listen more carefully for the ways in which the aural qualities of the GUI combine with other media. To demonstrate this, we could consider an iconic videogame like *Super Mario Bros.* (1985), in which clearly delineated sound effects accompany Mario's actions (a 'bwoop' when he jumps; a staccato juddering glug when he shrinks). But I would like to consider a more recent game, and one which asserts the kind of representational credibility found in many contemporary photorealistic blockbusters. *The Last of Us Part II*, a triple-A title released in 2020, might seem a long way from the cartoonishness and simplicity of *Super Mario Bros.*'s sound effects. Yet the detailed description that follows will, I hope, give some indication of the way that the layered soundscape of this kind of 'cinematic' game is equally working to provide detailed information to the player in regimented, predictable ways. This will establish crucial ideas of interaction and what has been called 'transdiegetic' sound, ideas which I will then consider in relation to other screen media before connecting them to the GUI.

Gooey listening

The Last of Us Part II is a third-person action-adventure game involving exploration and resource scavenging in a post-apocalyptic world, punctuated by combat with zombies and rival human gangs. Roughly halfway through the game, the player's initial avatar, Ellie, exits a tense encounter in a Seattle subway. Picking up my game at this section, as Ellie I begin making my way through an overgrown urban park. An eerie silence is perhaps only noticeable in hindsight. Crickets chirp persistently around me, and there is the pervasive crashing and rolling of a distant flooded river. More occasional are the faint sounds of birds and frogs, and the cracks and snaps of twigs which more clearly emanate from the overgrown park in front of me. I push forward on the left analogue stick of my controller to navigate Ellie into this wild space, the sound of her weary footsteps accompanying the visual movement of the character and confirming my agency.

A whistle sings out as I reach a slight step in the leafy terrain, but this cry blends with the surrounding animal noises to the extent that, while I notice it, I do not register it as important or anomalous. A musical cue triggered by my forward movement beyond a certain part of the park terrain – a rising, high-pitched string note – is also fluid and subtle enough not to be directly discerned at first play. However, this apprehensive sound soon accompanies the much more striking visual revelation of a dead body hanging from a lamppost. As I instinctively manoeuvre Ellie closer to this body there is another whistle, this one more urgent. It's a signal, I realise, too late, and immediately after this a loud disturbance of air is heard rustling past me, chased by the whoosh of an arrow, the latter stopping violently with a thump as it hits Ellie in the shoulder. A thud and a crash follow as Ellie falls, the wind knocked out of both her and me by this sudden ambush.

A quick time event or QTE (a portion of gameplay in which the camera is locked, with only minimal button prompts for the player) asks me to press R1 to extract the arrow from my shoulder, an action which understandably triggers some anguished grunting from Ellie, as well as a sharp, splintered hissing noise which gives sonic shape to the pain she expresses. Realising I am in trouble ('what the fuck', Ellie mutters, as though concurring with my grave assessment), I turn and jump for the cover provided by overgrown ferns. A hollow, smooth rumble imposes itself, clearly separate from other elements of the soundscape, and though it seems to be rising quickly towards a crescendo, I manage to interrupt its flow by dropping Ellie to her belly to hide in the undergrowth. The rumble cuts off with a small echo as I do so: it is, as I know by now from my many hours of gameplay up to this point, the sound of non-player characters (NPCs) catching a glimpse of me; or rather, it is the sound that cues me to the fact that they are *about to* locate me. If I hide before this sound reaches its apex then I am safe; if I don't, it climaxes in an echoing beat, and I am immediately attacked.

The hunt now on, I stalk the undergrowth. I move Ellie at a crouch when I can because it is slightly faster, but when that triggers the rumble of growing NPC awareness I drop to my stomach and crawl instead. A slow, drawn out, gruellingly relentless thudding musical march escorts my arduous movement. Its low pitch and dark resonance accentuate the tension and Ellie's crouched desperation, and it also blends fluidly with the squelching of mud and Ellie's frantic but quiet breathing. The whistling continues, as the NPCs signal one another and search for me. This reminds me that I am prey, but also, through the way it echoes around the trees, gives me some clue as to the position of my enemies. Even better for locating them, though, is the game's 'listen mode': I press and hold R1, and a dropping swooshing noise compliments the desaturation of colour from the image and the slight reframing of the view to a tighter angle. In this mode, nearby enemies are highlighted with a glowing white light, the implication seeming to be that Ellie's ears function as a kind of sonar, articulating the position of moving bodies outside of her line of sight.

Getting the drop on one of these enemies, I sneak up behind her and press square, triggering a melee attack. The sound of my axe slamming into the enemy's shoulder is gruesome, realistically evoking the tearing of flesh by a dull, heavy, but ferociously swung weapon. Even more unpleasant is the gurgling death rattle the enemy emits as she crumples to the floor, a horrific noise which is nonetheless not heard by the other NPCs thanks to the stealth of my attack. Moving to my next target behind cover, I press the left arrow to bring up my inventory, then press it again to select my rifle. Each press is accompanied by a modest clicking sound from the game's soundtrack (but also not audible to enemies, it seems), and in barely a second Ellie has pulled the weapon from her backpack, an action complemented by a quiet clatter as she gets a grip on it. Standing, I take aim and shoot the NPC in the back: pressing the trigger initiates not only an ear-splitting blast, but also, instantly after, a blood-curdling scream. This scream is longer than expected, leading me to think I have only wounded my prey, and so I waste another two shots unnecessarily – the first bullet had, I now realise, torn off a limb, and the NPC was just dying in a particularly agonising way.

This death itself cues up a vocal from another nearby NPC, who cries in horror 'oh god, no!' Other NPCs signal that they now know where I am: 'she's over there!' one of them yells; 'caught you!' shouts another. I do not see the arrows that they loose in my direction, but I hear them whooshing around me, slamming into trees, and – alas – thwacking into my body, another violent sound matched with an equally violent camera jolt and a yelp from Ellie. Injured again, I hide once more and select a medkit from my inventory. Applying it takes a few seconds, during which there is the sound of bandages being wrapped. I know the process is finished not only when the bar in the bottom corner of my screen fills up with reassuring blue but also when Ellie mutters 'okay' in a satisfied and determined way. Yet this action has allowed my enemies to get closer, and a bass-heavy thump explodes in my ears as I am shot, eradicating most of the health I just recouped. There is nothing for it but to run, and Ellie's footsteps join the arrows, gunfire, and enemy yells to generate a climaxing cacophony of threat and action. Inevitably, Ellie is killed, emitting dire screams as her head is caved in by an axe-wielding NPC. A short sonic crescendo also rises and strikes me with almost physical force as the screen cuts from gory death to black screen, audio echoes of the butchery fading quickly in the bereft void.

Collision boxes

This segment of gameplay took around two minutes, and such a detailed sketch hopefully indicates not only the range of audio cues at work in even the smallest passage of a typical triple-A title, but also the variety of ways in which they shape gameplay. Audio cues are crucial in expanding the experiential depth of a videogame, and they also anchor its represented actions, providing 'the pixels a sense of physicality', imbuing them with weight, materiality, tactility (Jørgensen 2017: 72). More than this, videogame soundtracks are dynamic: they react to player input, and prompt particular actions. In this way, they join up with the GUI.

As Jørgensen (2017: 72) describes, videogame sound 'gives the player in-depth understanding of the gameworld as a living ecosystem, and provides information with direct impact on the players' choice of actions and their playstyle'. This is achieved in large part through 'collision boxes': invisible bubbles connected to spaces and characters which trigger audio effects when the player crosses their borders. Unknown to the player (but visible to the videogame designer using Unity, Unreal, or a similar engine), the world of the game is a kind of sonic minefield in which each movement threatens to loose forth some change in the audio environment.[6] Like the use of editing timelines to organise highly layered digital soundtracks, this is another spatialisation of media sound which has been enabled by GUI use and the 3D virtual programming environments of contemporary videogame engines.

In this vein, Karen Collins (2013) draws attention to the interactive nature of all videogame sound. Whether directly responding to player input (shooting a gun activates the sound of a gunshot) or 'adaptive' (the music changing to indicate a shift in the game state, as when enemies are near, or when a player crosses the threshold of a collision box), the audio cues of a game are not like those of a film or a television show – they respond moment to moment to player input, seemingly appealing to and demanding a more active listener than these other media. The player's agency in prompting specific sounds both intentionally and unintentionally can even be thought to turn any videogame player into a musician, one who is both creating sound and listening intently for audio cues to help structure their own play. Sociologist Graeme Kirkpatrick (2011: 101) is one of several scholars who make this connection, suggesting that a lot of contemporary gaming 'is well described as music and sound wrought from a score that presents physical challenges to a player'. Plenty of videogames are explicitly about this kind of explicitly audio-centred play – rhythmic games like *Rez* (2001), *Vib-Ribbon* (2004), *Thumper* (2016), *Metal: Hellsinger* (2022), and Kirkpatrick's example of *Elektroplankton* (2006) – but any game that

---

6 These cues are not even necessarily stable and repeatable, as they can automatically adapt pitch, timbre, volume, and more according to player location, facing direction, and other factors, while sound synthesis and procedural generation programs allow for the creation of new sounds on-the-fly from pre-existing conditions. Once again, I am indebted to Alessandro Altavilla here, in particular for the image of the soundscape as a minefield of collision boxes.

has any kind of interactive soundscape (which is in effect most of them) is played both as game and as instrument.

The Last of Us Part II is typical in the way it deploys sound in tandem with visual information to help players navigate their environment and accomplish a range of necessary tasks (including crafting, scavenging, and combat). It is also typical in the way it contours those sounds around its broader stylistic attributes in order to retain overall aesthetic coherence.[7] We cue up certain sounds through our actions, and though we may do so for functional purposes, we nonetheless create a rich symphony of interactive and adaptive audio stings. More than this, the passage of play described above indicates the extent to which the game's audio cues strike a balance between verisimilitudinous and purely or schematically informational, and indeed how the two have been productively combined.

This negotiation of realism and what we might call operationalism is perhaps most obvious in the visual attributes of videogames, in the form of menus and the delivery of other baldly functional data in the player's optical field. That is, the sometimes richly detailed worlds of videogames do not stop when a menu screen is accessed, and these menus seek consistent aesthetic attributes with the rest of the game. For instance, in *The Last of Us Part II* the crafting and menu screens complement the game's dour tone and stripped back look, employing simple diagrams, a monochromatic palette, and unfussy visual markers of selection and task completion (Figure 3.1).[8] Likewise, other operational features such as ammo counters, maps, and enemy health bars, hover uncertainly between diegesis and data: even though they are clearly informational additions to the cinematically realistic world of this and other games, these overlain fragments nonetheless seek visual harmony with this world.

The same is true of videogame sound. Distinctions between what we might think of as a non-diegetic, informational ping and a diegetically convincing depiction of an audio action can become very hazy in games like *The Last of Us Part II*. This aids a particular form of player immersion. The result is a sonic balance between cinematic verisimilitude and GUI interactivity, something

---

7 The foregoing description even indicates how the soundscape propagates the thematic concerns of the game. NPCs may often suffer violent death in many games, but here the lingering screams that accompany a slow death and, in particular, the cries of shock, anguish, and disgust from other enemies underscores *The Last of Us Part II*'s broader attention to futile cycles of vengeance and related moral murkiness.
8 In some videogames, such screens can be diegetically motivated, taking the form of a hand-held journal which is brought into view, obscuring the rest of the screen, as in 2019's *Metro: Exodus*.

Figure 3.1 The crafting menu from *The Last of Us Part 2* (2019). Frame enlargement from PS4 gameplay.

hopefully indicated by the foregoing description. But we can dig deeper by looking at a particular gameplay mechanism, such as the act of crafting.

There are a limited number of resource types in *The Last of Us Part II*. To collect them, players must be close to the item in question and press a button, rather than just wander into their collision box (as is the case with, for instance, ammo pick-ups in many *Call of Duty* games). Each resource type makes a different noise when picked up – a piece of blade sounds like a knife unsheathing against metal; grabbing alcohol sounds like a glass bottle half-full of liquid being swilled around. This is representationally convincing: these are broadly speaking the sounds one would expect when picking up each of these objects. But there is no attempt to alter the timbre of these sounds depending on context, location, or the specific amount of resources gathered at any particular moment (which can vary quite a bit). This may be a consequence of processing power and other software affordances, but the result is that such cues strongly align with desktop notification pings. Yes, the sounds are 'accurate' on some level, but they are also generalised enough to be instantly and predictably recognisable. This aural consistency also endows these acts of appropriation with a clarity that is particularly important in high-intensity moments of gameplay. The player charges at full speed through an environment as they are attacked by enemies, mashing the triangle button to gather whatever scraps they can get to aid their fight; the sound of this resource collection then lingers a few fractions of a second longer than the brief visual prompt showing the presence of the resource.

This subtly but crucially helps the player perceptually register that they now have bottled water, blades, or whatever.

When there are enough of these resources to craft an item, a spanner-click noise accompanies the fleeting appearance of a small spanner logo in the lower right-hand portion of the screen. Again, the rising 'click' noise here is designed to evoke the mechanical manipulation of some object or other, and so gestures towards verisimilitude. But this sound functions only to inform the player that crafting is possible, not that Ellie is engaging in any act of engineering at that moment. It signifies opportunity, rather than mapping onto a visual action being undertaken then and there.

Finally, when crafting takes place, we hear the same sound regardless of the item being crafted. A health kit, a Molotov cocktail, and an arrow all prompt the same granular surge and metallic shuffling noise. This cue gestures to the *idea* of crafting more than it seeks to represent the creation of a specific chosen object. The act is even augmented by a very non-diegetic 'ping' once crafting is done, a sound more redolent of receiving a text message or completing a download. This ping would seem to be redundant, but it further aids the player in knowing – in tandem with multiple other visual and sonic cues – that their freshly crafted item is ready to use. This redundancy might be crucial if a Molotov is being hastily assembled as a terrifying zombie bears down on us.

The sounds of crafting, then, indicate the extent to which the soundscape of *The Last of Us Part II* fluidly blends the diegetic and the seemingly non-diegetic. The same is true of other mechanics in the game, and indeed in many other games: diegetic and non-diegetic are combined in order to adhere to the imperatives of both perceptual immersion and lucid interactivity. Jørgensen goes so far as to suggest that the selfsameness of these two elements of a videogame's soundscape make any distinction between them unhelpful. After all, since the 'concepts of diegetic and non-diegetic are developed with traditional media in mind', they cannot be uncritically transferred to games, where sound has 'a double status in which it provides usability information to the player at the same time as it has been stylized to fit the depicted fictional world' (Jørgensen 2011: 79). She accordingly proposes the term 'transdiegetic' to describe the game-specific way in which sounds can be both world-embedded and extra-textual: 'transdiegetic sounds merge game system information with the gameworld and create a frame of reference that has usability value at the same time as it upholds the sense of presence in the gameworld' (Jørgensen 2011: 85).

This term is useful in describing audio cues, like those listed above, which sit uncertainly between a game's representational reality and its status as a computational system that must feed its user relevant information. Such cues highlight the way game audio functions as a series of notifications and confirmations, a layer of vital feedback aiding navigation of the screen's visual contents. As mentioned, this is not just limited to crafting: Ellie's muttering helps inform me of her status (certain lines of dialogue indicate that processes have been completed, whether a combat encounter or the application of a bandage); the sound of shells sliding into place assures me that the system has picked up my frenzied input to reload my weapon without my eyes having to focus on either my ammo counter or the arms of my avatar as the reloading animation is performed; the musical score changes pitch, timbre, and rhythm when I wander into enemy territory and hostile NPCs begin spawning, telling me almost subliminally that the dominant mode of gameplay has changed from exploration to combat.

Like their visual counterparts, such audio cues combine what might be considered diegetic and non-diegetic elements in ways that are difficult to unpick. Is the smooth rising rumble that occurs when Ellie is about to be spotted by an NPC a diegetic sound (the blood rushing to Ellie's ears as her adrenaline surges, perhaps) or a non-diegetic soundtrack element (a ping)? Is the urgent hiss that accompanies the prompt to remove an arrow embedded in our shoulder an odd materialisation of the sound of an arrowhead slipping through flesh, or is it a more gestural signal of bodily emergency? Ultimately, it does not really matter – these transdiegetic sounds suit the tone of the game, build out its world, and inform me of required inputs (look out for the NPC!) as well as of the result of inputs just made (yes, the gun is now loaded).

This combination of diegetic sound and notification ping is nothing new. As Tim Summers states in his history of videogame music:

> The square wave tones used in [1972's] *Pong* are very simple: one pitch for the ball hitting the bat, another for striking the wall (an octave lower), and a distorted version of the lower tone for when a point is scored. This musical sound sits at the boundary between sound effect and music – undeniably pitched, but synchronized to the on-screen action in a way more similar to a sound effect. (Summers 2017: 140)

Collins (2013: 3) agrees, suggesting that in many videogames 'we might question whether we are hearing sound effects, voice, ambience, or music' at any given moment. As a result of this blurriness, she argues that 'sound design in some genres of games is much closer to slapstick comedy and cartoons than it is to most live-action Hollywood films, with music more intimately tied to action, rhythm, and movement and stylized in ways that are often not intended to be realistic' (Collins 2013: 3). For her, synchronisation and responsiveness across all forms of videogame audio inevitably override other factors like ambience, consistency, or realism. But the mixing is often more nuanced than this might imply, with a balance found between notifications and these atmospheric and aesthetic effects. So, even a videogame privileging the highly realistic creation of space and characters (as *The Last of Us Part II* does) will still frequently combine the representational and the functional on its soundtrack.

If a blending together of score, sound effects, and notifications has always been part of videogames, then it is increasingly being applied in other media as well. Despite Collins's statement, films, television programs, and other non-interactive forms now often take a similarly blended approach to their sonic environments. As shown by music scholar Danijela Kulezic-Wilson, the once disparate elements of musical score, ambient sound, diegetic music, and sound effects have converged or blended in the twenty-first century. This, she states, 'relativize[s] the boundary between scoring and sound design and subvert[s] long-established hierarchical relationships between dialogue, music, and sound effects, challenging modes of perception shaped by classical soundtrack practices' (Kulezic-Wilson 2019: 3). The examples Kulezic-Wilson discusses are specifically those which confront certain dominant narrative and ideological conventions, being arthouse, auteur, or avant-garde cinema. However, her points hold true for a wider range of texts. Take, for instance, the inclusion of heavy breathing in the orchestral scores for films like *King Arthur: Legend of the Sword* (2017) and *Shadow in the Cloud* (2020). Deployed at moments of high action and drama, the urgent inhalation and exhalation, mixed with percussive instrumentation, confuses music, sound effects, and actor vocal performance in highly affective ways.

This blending is partly thanks to technological changes. As mentioned, electronic and digital sound recording and editing allow for far greater dynamic range and so encourage more complex sound patterning in contemporary audio mixes (Kerins 2015: 54–5). Kulezic-Wilson (2019: 6) points out that the rise of digital workstations in the 1990s allowed musical software to be used for processing not just music 'but also dialogue and sound effects', while the digital sampling found in popular genres like hip-hop and dubstep 'spread the idea that any kind of noise or speech can potentially be regarded as music'. In this environment, where 'every sound can be perceived as inherently musical', it is possible for *all* sounds to be used musically (Kulezic-Wilson 2019: 16). The result is a distinctly musical approach to the overall soundtrack of a media text, a holistic audio design in which all elements of the sound mix can do duty for one another and borrow each other's codes and possibilities.

In videogames, the design of such blended audio can be as closely tied to player experience and emotive feedback as it can be to ideas of realism. If the player functions as a kind of musician, triggering a range of sounds from effects to music to ambience, then they seek to play beautifully, avoiding bum notes. Simple actions like collecting resources or crafting items make noises that are carefully calibrated by sound designers to be enjoyable: the player should want to prompt these noises whenever they can (Polygon 2020). By contrast, deaths and other setbacks sound like interruptions, suspensions of rhythm and flow. The rising rumble of NPC awareness in *The Last of Us Part II* is not a pleasant sound, but a hollow and tense one; this further disincentivises the player from (inadvertently) letting the cue reach its zenith (when the NPC gains clear view of Ellie's position and attacks). Effective and successful gameplay often sounds as enjoyable as it feels, and indeed the two are tightly linked. As if to stress this, a mini-game throughout *The Last of Us Part II* asks the player to strum a guitar, turning their gameplay into a literal musical performance.

In all these ways, then, videogames create blended soundscapes that orient and direct, even as they might also seek to generate realism and atmosphere. Their inherently interactive audio cues provide information to the player while also maintaining immersion in the representational fiction presented by the game. To do this, videogames actively combine the kinds of sonification found in audio notifications with the sorts of verisimilitudinous and diegetically motivated soundscapes present in other media such as cinema and television. Their sound cues also work affectively, the design of each one shaped by the subtle emotional impact it can have on players, an impact that motivates (or de-motivates) certain gameplay activities. We can see clear connections here with the GUI as it has been explored so far in this book. Realism is an important factor driving aesthetic design but is balanced with functionality and the delivery of information regarding the state of the technical system and the user's involvement with this system. Layered, complex soundscapes (consisting of music, voice acting, sound effects, and atmospheres) orient and direct our activity as much as they contribute to the creation of a believable representational environment.

In sync

In *The Last of Us Part II*, as in all videogames, synchronisation is crucial: in order for audio to provide effective feedback, it must align with player input and visual information. In this last section, I will expand on this concept of synchronisation, and connect it to some discussions of contemporary audio-visual style. A vast majority of media sync up their sound and image tracks, after all, even if they might offer moments of dissonance within those aligned sensory inputs. And yet, as I will suggest, the specific kind of interactive syncing at work in both videogames and the GUI can in fact also be heard across films, television, and other media forms. The relationship between soundtrack and image is, therefore, subtly changing in the desktop era.

This shift in audio-visual practice is connected to broader transformations in media aesthetics. Carol Vernallis and Amy Herzog describe some of these changes and their technological bases in the introduction to their *Handbook of Sound and Image in Digital Media* (2013). As they propose, 'New forms of sound compression, 5.1 surround-sound, Pro-Tools, Avid editing, computer-generated imagery (CGI), digital intermediate color and image processing, previsualisation, high-speed information data transfer and data storage' all contribute to 'a painterly, capture oriented aesthetic' which predominates across various media today (Vernallis and Herzog 2013: 2). That is, the digital capture and editing of both sound and image result in their being bound together in new ways, ways that are linked with a kind of high-speed media intensification.

Indeed, formalist film theorist David Bordwell refers to contemporary mainstream style as tending towards 'intensified continuity': an amplification of classical systems for organising screen space and narrative in which shots are closer, cuts more numerous, and style more mannered and reflexive (Bordwell 2002). Essentially, intensified continuity turns up the metaphorical volume on what continuity editing has always done. Focusing on the visual side, Bordwell's model can nonetheless also be heard at work in soundscapes, and has been applied in this manner by other scholars, all of whom are helpful here.

Jeff Smith (2013: 335), for instance, describes how 'contemporary sound designers and mixers have developed a set of strategies for the soundtrack comparable to the changes in visual style that Bordwell identifies as central to intensified continuity', and argues that these align with those visual strategies 'insofar as they function similarly to heighten the affective, sensory, and phenomenological dimensions of contemporary film style'. To demonstrate this, Smith compares the sound design of the 1974 film *The Taking of Pelham 123* with its 2009 remake. He shows how the latter provides a wider array of aural effects, has a 'sharper' and busier audiofield, and increases impressions of spatialisation through audio cues. Particularly intriguing are the nondiegetic sound effects in the more recent version, with 'whooshes', beats, pulses, DJ scratch sounds, and expressive re-mixing of train sound effects responding to and underscoring visual details of camerawork and editing. These noises therefore bind image and soundscape together more concretely, while also amplifying the self-consciousness of the film's overall style (Smith 2013: 346).

Vernallis and Steven Shaviro each go further than Bordwell and Smith. Across several pieces, Vernallis (2013; 2014; 2017) suggests that this kind of style is not just about intensification, but about the creation of new relationships between sound and image, relationships which are enabled by the foregrounding of sound. We are, she claims, 'in the midst of an international style that has heightened sonic and visual features', one shaped by digital technology and a globalised popular culture, and which asserts powerful affective experiences of swirl, flow, and ungrounding (Vernallis 2013: 4). Shaviro agrees, with his book *Post Cinematic Affect* (2010) being a particularly influential mapping of this territory. As he argues, digital technologies of sound and image production alter the media we encounter through their creation of new affordances and new networks of distribution, meaning that they feel different to that which came before (Shaviro 2010: 2). Digital editing systems both expensive and free allow ever-more fine-grained control of visual and aural elements, as individual frames and pixels can be tweaked in order to adhere to a larger formal aesthetic pattern. Meanwhile, the circulation of clips, programs, and films online – where they share space with user-generated material – changes our relationship to them, and places more emphasis on ephemeral spectacle.

Shaviro is emblematic in calling this a kind of 'post-cinema', a fundamental shift in moving images (and their sounds) that occurs as cinema as it was once conceived of and thought about fades into silence (see also Denson and Leyda 2016). Whether we agree with this eschatological framing, it is clear that things have changed in significant ways. As I will shortly indicate, this is partly evidence of the intermingling of cinema and other media with the GUI. But there is another crucial track to this argument.

Vernallis argues that the peculiar affect generated by contemporary media and their audio-visual effects can be traced back to, and understood through, the music video and its development as a simultaneously discrete and inter-medial form. She notes how, since their inception in the 1970s, music videos have offered audio-visual choreography beyond just onscreen dancers, with their editing, mise-en-scène, and cinematography responding to the musicality of the content, and therefore all contributing to our perception of the song (Vernallis 2017). Different kinds of cutting and different kinds of images can make a song sound different by underlining different parts of instrumentation, rhythm, or tone. More than this, music videos privilege moment-to-moment sensation in their aesthetics, entwining and feeding this sensation with the sonic features of their audio tracks. Vernallis (2013: 11–13) calls this an 'intensified audiovisual aesthetic' – a pulse or wave which affectively carries us along with it.

While the music video is the potential origin point of this aesthetic, it has migrated far beyond this form. Music videos themselves are increasingly fluid and difficult to define as such, with their parameters placed under strain by such novel phenomenon as music videos that feature no music at all (Korsgaard 2017). They also bleed across the media landscape. Barbara London (2010: 59) even proposes that 'the music video has become the signature form of all media – migrating away from MTV toward YouTube and scaled down to iPhones', to which we might also add cinema, television, and videogames. In the digital media ecology, platforms and genres interpenetrate, and user-generated mashups and mainstream content all trade in speed, flexibility, and rhythm in newly convergent ways.

At the simplest end of this scale, cutting on the beat is easier in a digital editing environment. More intricately, digital intermediate colour manipulation can flare or shimmer a particular frame or part-frame in order to draw out a soundtrack element. If this can create fractal or prismatic patternings rather than the linear continuity of classical cinema, then it is easy to condemn such a style as incoherent; or, indeed, to dismiss the texts employing this style as 'music videos' no matter what else they might be (Vernallis 2014).[9] But this is insufficient, given that from YouTube to TikTok, indie game to Triple-A title, television show to blockbuster film, we can see and hear this form of audiovisuality in action. Digital modulation and polyphony occur visually and sonically, weaving a tapestry which is more like a feedback loop. To make sense of today's 'media swirl' we must therefore think beyond ideas of continuity and intensification and address new audio-visual relations and their consequences across all kinds of media (Vernallis 2013: 3).

---

9 Vernallis (2014) addresses some of these objections in her piece on *Transformers: Age of Extinction* (2014), in which she describes how the de-emphasising of continuity allows the film to use each element in the frame and on the soundtrack as 'pliant material in the service of musicality and speed'. If for her Bay's films excel in the 'intangibles' of movement, sound, and line, then in discussing all this Vernallis's writing itself echoes and reverberates with unexpected rhythms, fragmentary sentiment, and affective evocation. Nonetheless, or rather precisely because of this, Vernallis's work on the audiovisuality of screen entertainment in the digital era is invaluable in drawing attention to new relationships between sound and image, and a new kind of musicality in which 'everything is bound together'.

As already indicated, the way that both desktop interfaces and videogames bind together visual and sonic information (and the way they do so for particularly navigational ends) is instructive here. But the ping of an email notification seems a very long way from these ideas of rhythmic media flow, doesn't it? And if we are just talking about the linking of audio and pictorial information, then hasn't this always been the dominant approach taken by screen media since at least the large-scale establishing of synchronised sound technologies in the 1930s? Certainly, synchronisation seems unremarkable – whatever we are watching, we expect dialogue spoken by characters to match up to the movements of their mouths, and sound effects to occur simultaneously with their visual sources. Even the audio-visual feedback tapestry just described might be heard as one more example of quite straightforward (albeit now highly nuanced) synchronisation. So, beyond production contexts and the use of software to create and edit the sounds and images of media texts, what is it about this contemporary audio-visuality which might make it indebted to the GUI?

Crucial, I believe, is the way that synchronisation is linked to navigation. Films like *Captain America: Civil War*, as indicated, use sound cues help orient viewers during large-scale action scenes. But this is just one of the more overt ways in which sonification is used for perceptual nudging and shoving in the increasingly complex visual field of digital media. Mark Kerins's discussion of the 'ultrafield' is helpful here. Drawing on the writing of Michel Chion (1994: 150), Kerins argues in *Beyond Dolby (Stereo)* (2011) that technical changes in the production and delivery of soundtracks have changed not only the relationship between sound and screen, but also the evocation of space by and through both sound and image. As Kerins describes, in mono and stereo mixes of the early and mid-twentieth century, a combination of technical capacity and creative conventions meant that audio had to emanate from the screen and direct attention towards it. Moreover, soundtracks could not be too cluttered due to dangers of masking and legibility. Dolby Stereo and similar surround sound technologies of the 1970s and 1980s changed this, allowing for immersive spatial environments that extended *beyond* the screen, what Chion (1994) called 'superfields'. But in the digital era of the 1990s onwards, the provision of multi-track soundscapes, high-fidelity audio recording, and expanded dynamic range all allow for a richer, more spatially varied sonic environment: the 'ultrafield' (Kerins 2010: 66). This ultrafield does not generate a constant, coherent screen-centric space in the manner of earlier Dolby soundscapes. Instead, it 'allows for a *shifting* aural environment that functions in *dialogue* with the visual one' (Kerins 2010: 92; emphasis in original). While the superfield is 'passive, continuous, and stable', the ultrafield is 'active, jumpy, and constantly shifting' (Kerins 2010: 91). In it, the 'multi-channel sound space shifts with each cut to keep itself oriented to the image track', and so 'the *sonic* space changes to match the *visual* one onscreen' (Kerins 2010: 92). As a result, sonic space is being continuously reoriented alongside visual cutting.

The move from superfield to ultrafield is, in effect, the move from a sonic space that creates coherence across cuts and through which the viewer's eye is carefully guided, to a sonified space of notifications in which audio responds to each and every separate image and its contents (Kerins 2010: 95).[10] The former creates the feeling of an immersive diegetic environment, while the latter yanks the viewer/listener into the audio-perceptual centre implied by the image. We might distil this as the difference between soundtracking a scene and soundtracking a shot. There are many places we can hear this in action. One of Kerins's key examples is the opening sequence of *Saving Private Ryan* (1998), in which aural and visual information match even when shots and perspectives are changing rapidly (Kerins 2010: 97). But to focus on this prominent and lauded sequence perhaps implies that the ultrafield is always a site of chaos, or a brief incursion of sonic disarray into a film's audio terrain. Instead, I want to stress the presence of the ultrafield across a broader swathe of media.

To do this, let's initially take a listen to a much briefer, less frenzied, and certainly less written-about scene near the start of *Aeon Flux* (2005), an adaptation of a dystopian animated TV show. In this sequence, lasting only a minute or so, the title character breaks into a surveillance database via the roof. After entering, she ties a rope across a set of bars near the ceiling, and rappels towards a wide pool in the floor in which dozens of surveillant images shimmer, each one the result of a liquid drop of surveillance data. Like the rest of the film, the sequence is rapidly cut, but each shot nonetheless carries with it its own audio data. Whenever there is a close-up of a rope or hands we aggressively hear the tactile sounds of material, skin, and straining muscle. The sound of the surveillance files – which seems to echo loudly around the room – only manifests when we cut to a wide shot, despite the scene having been set inside this space for several seconds already (that is, we only hear them when we see them). While the sequence overall does

---

10 Applying this model to videogames, Kerins (2013) notes that ultrafield aesthetics assist in navigation thanks to their spatialised positioning of sound around the player, and that this placement is (normally) untroubled by cuts. He also, quite pertinently, describes in passing how spatialised sound cues will often be linked to visual cues in order to help orient players in particularly cacophonic moments.

certainly have a particular and consistent sonic ambience, this is a bed beneath a much more responsive set of cues, cues which are anchored to each shot and each movement and which serve to keep the scene in the 'continual present' (Kerins 2010: 121). Further amplifying this continual present is the use of the kind of nondiegetic sound effects described above by Smith: everything whooshes or pulses audibly as it glides past or around the camera, creating an enveloping and sonorous soundscape which nonetheless resonates with the pace of the cutting and the visual qualities of each shot.

This continual present becomes even more notable in the action sequences of recent cinema. Take, for instance, a series of shots from a car chase in the Netflix production *6 Underground* (2019). Over the course of just 35 seconds (between 0.07.07 and 0.07.42 as it streams on Netflix in 2022) – during which the protagonists attempt to outdrive a motorcycling assailant – the soundscape varies wildly. At times it offers hyper-clear Foley with little else, at others a throbbing barrage of techno score, at others an overlapping chorus of frenzied voices. Many objects we glimpse in each fleeting shot get sonic signage: the keys hanging in the car ignition jangle softly but with utter clarity when they fill the frame; the motorcyclist's gun clicks metallically as it gets drawn; each car fleetingly sweeping past in wider shots honks a horn or screeches its tyres in exact time with its appearance. Gunshots sound different from shot to shot, responding to the placement and proximity of the weapon in the frame. As the camera sweeps speedily through a series of architectural arches, each one loudly 'whooshes' by us, a noise that pulses in rhythm with Lorne Balfe's percussive synth score during these seconds. Moments of slow motion are emphasised by deep drawn-out bass notes that come and go in an instant. An extreme close-up of a hero's glancing eye is accompanied by a soft but urgent exhalation, a breath sound which might be diegetically emanating from the character or part of the score – not that it matters. When the motorcycle crashes, the sound is less of a single collision than three or four smaller impacts all hastily happening one after another, each demarcated by a few frames of tinkling glass and a sliver of silence either side; such a soundtrack gives this crescendo of mini-climaxes a reverberating, ricocheting finality … until, a few quips later, we're right back to the action.

For Shaviro (2010: 80), in the digital era 'sound operates overtly rather than covertly', and we can certainly see this in evidence in such examples of the ultrafield in action. This does not mean that sound draws attention *away* from images. Rather, sound amplifies and reverberates moment-to-moment visual information. While one of the earliest things that a budding editor will learn is the importance of capturing room tone and how a consistent audio bed is vital for stitching together the different shots of any given scene, in these examples, and in the ultrafield in general, we hear a reinstatement of shot-by-shot sonic specificity, albeit one that is polished and purposeful. Whether we call it intensified continuity, post-cinema, or a new audio-visual aesthetics, contemporary media generally uses faster shots, closer framings, and more splintered spaces. This allows or demands soundscapes which foreground shot details rather than scene consistencies. This is partly why contemporary texts of this sort seems to so closely resemble their own advertising. After all, whether they promote films, TV, videogames, or other material, contemporary trailers are not about creating a consistent visual or sonic environment of diegetic immersion, but about shot-by-shot thrills and sensation: the pinnacle of the ultrafield in action.[11]

The ultrafield, by privileging the contents of each shot on the soundtrack, is a kind of inversion of lyric videos, and can certainly be thought to function according to the same dictates. Lyric videos, as hinted at in the beginning of this chapter, are typical products of a GUI era, and not just because they have flourished alongside user-generated video sharing sites like YouTube, nor just because they can be created by the most amateur of editors with access to an MP3, a few images, and the cross-fade button. More than this, lyric videos exemplify the kinds of gooey audio aesthetics I have been discussing because of the constrained but potentially highly creative connections they make between audio and visual content. They must show the words of the featured song at proscribed times, with just a sentence or two visible at once. But while they might, as a result, seem very similar to karaoke aids, they are much more expressive than this, and are a useful way of further revealing how the preceding ideas of interactive audio, blended soundtracks, and ultrafields all cluster together in relation to the GUI.

As Laura McLaren argues, lyric videos are highly distinctive. They 'create fictional worlds', and 'explore a range of audiovisual effects' in idiosyncratic

---

11 Trailers stack visual and aural sensation for the purposes of a kind of visceral crescendo. Like the sequences described from *Aeon Flux* and *6 Underground*, they will create soundscapes that move fluidly (or joltingly) between a variety of affective states, with changes in tone and location occurring every few seconds, accompanied by shifting musical and sonic patterns (whether needle drops, rising score, or bathetically interruptive moments of character dialogue). These are frequently choreographed around moments of sublime grandeur or terror, pinnacles that were invariably marked in the 2010s by deep, droning 'bwah' or 'braam' sounds (Shirr 2017). For a further discussion of the sonic attributes of contemporary action trailers, see Watts 2021.

ways (McLaren 2019: 171, 176). On the one hand distinct from official music videos (they are released separately, and usually augment a more ornate and expensive official video), lyric videos nonetheless similarly generate visuals that respond to and embellish the tone, theme, and musicality of their songs. This is not just about font choice, but about when words appear on screen, their size and positioning, and how they interact with backgrounds or any other visual content. As McLaren (2019: 172) states, the 'use of colors, textures, and movement offers artists the ability to create a physical world, imitate another world, or create an aesthetic world within the lyric video setting'. These procedures can be exceedingly complex.

The early example of Prince's 1987 'Sign O' the Times' video (itself the song's official music video), for instance, uses a range of fonts and effects, with words receding, slowly scrolling, and crowding or pulsing around the screen in order to match the singer's inflection and cadence (see McLaren 2019: 164). The more recent lyric video for 'Roar' by Katy Perry, meanwhile, depicts the lyrics as messages in a WhatsApp exchange, with liberal use of emojis instead of written words (Figure 3.2). Unlike the official video (which features Perry living in a jungle after a plane crash, surviving tigers, elephants, and leopard print bikinis), the lyric video creates a kind of meta-performance of the song's empowering content, framing the lyrics as reassurances within a group chat being accessed by a young woman throughout her day. If the WhatsApp mise-en-scène evokes the desktop texts explored in Chapter 1, then the musicality of the video is visually highlighted in the way the various emojis pulse to the song's beat, and in the way the background of the WhatsApp group morphs and changes colour in line with the choral climaxes.[12]

In such cases, we are offered affective, rhythmic experiences rather than narrative ones, with visual elements choreographed to the music in ways that go beyond just lyrical content. The use of 'kinetic typography' allows these words to 'do wonderful and interesting things in digital space', not only entertaining the eye but creating new understandings of these words and elements of their vocality (Kuhn 2021). In such cases, onscreen words do not just illustrate, they express and synchronise. If music videos both 'visualise music' and 'musicalize vision', as Mathias Bonde Korsgaard (2013: 502) suggests, then here we can see how this is the case even when pretty much the only vision on offer is typographical. In the lyric video, the words *are* the music video, and so the fluid stylistic changes and orchestrations of

---

12 I am indebted to Laura McLaren for bringing Katy Perry's various lyric videos to my attention.

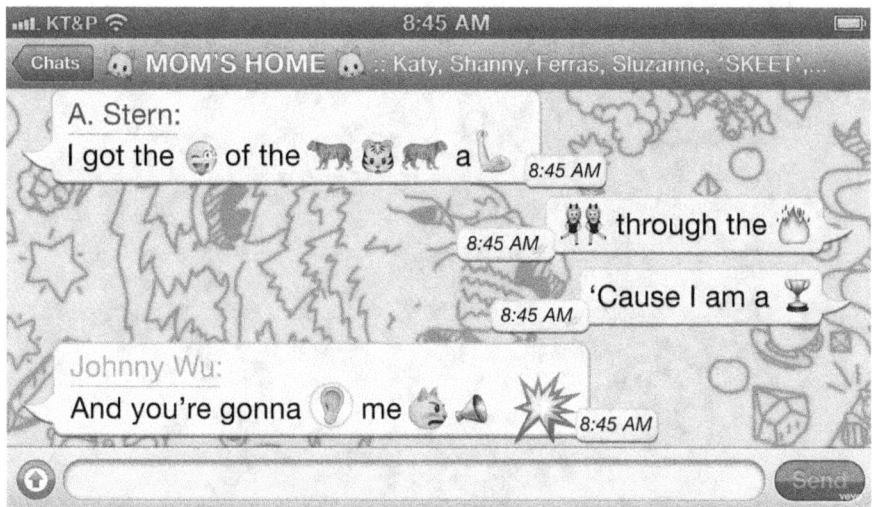

Figure 3.2 A WhatsApp group message chat is the setting of the lyric video for Katy Perry's 'Roar' (2013). Frame enlargement from YouTube.

these words allows them to express the kind of audio-visuality that Vernallis has identified both in music videos and across the wider media ecology.

This audiovisuality reaches what might be considered a limit case in examples like the 'ringtone' lyric video with which I opened this chapter, and which pushes the inherent audio-visual responsiveness of the form beyond the imperatives of lyrical elucidation. As stated, for the song's intro Charli XCX softly and briefly sings the word 'oh' eight times, and each 'oh' is illustrated on screen, superimposed over the last in a new colour and font, some of them also swivelling or pulsing in time with the shifting notes of Charli's singing. This sets the pattern for the video, which uses an array of typography, some of it almost unreadable, and which resembles a WordArt experiment gone horribly awry. A few images also appear, such as a ferocious dog when Kero Kero Bonito sing that a ringtone could be a 'barking dog', but these too testify to the cut-and-paste nature of the video: searching for this exact generic term on Google quickly identifies the picture, which is a Getty Images stock photo (Figure 3.3).[13]

The aesthetic of the 'ringtone (remix)' lyric video is adjacent to what Nick Douglas (2014) has called 'internet ugly', an aesthetic of mussed, pixelated, carefully unpolished material, one which is often deployed for memes, web comics, and gifs. This look points to speedy production and dissemination and to a kind of amateur authenticity. For Douglas (2014: 315) it even 'best

---

13 And which has accordingly been used to illustrate news reports, such as Anon. 2016.

Figure 3.3 The chaotic but carefully orchestrated visual field of the 100 gecs 'ringtone' lyric video, including an internet-sourced image of a 'barking dog'. Frame enlargement from YouTube.

defines the internet against all other media'; 'ringtone' evokes this ugly aesthetic, but in a studied and careful way. One YouTube comment on the video reads simply 'graphic design is my passion', a sly bit of internet humour pointing to the generic parameters of the cut-and-paste, rococo style which is very precisely deployed in this video. This aesthetic, after all, fits the hyperpop sound of 100 gecs, and closely aligns with the more mainstream Charli XCX's late 2010s/early 2020s synth style, which combines heartfelt earnestness with overt auto-tuning and videogame electronica (all perhaps most widely heard in her single 'Boys' from 2017). The lyric video highlights the pop kitsch, techno juiciness, and teetering instability of the remix.

It also, and no less importantly, joins up with the song's lyrical content. A slightly unhinged sketch of romance in the digital age, 'ringtone' describes how relationships play out through phone lines and message threads (Mapes 2020). It highlights how the customisation of a ringtone is the quintessence of romance: what says 'I love you' more than a personalised and unique audio ping whenever your partner contacts you? If ringtones can, as the lyrics state, be 'whatever captures/your attention', then the same is true of the visual design of the lyrics in this video, which capture attention through garish colours and a constantly altering typographical mise-en-scène.[14] The customisation

---

14 Far less ostentatious is the aggressively low-fi official video, which depicts 100 gecs (Dylan Brady and Laura Les) avoiding the camera's gaze and despondently

of the sonic notification of a phone call is related to the kinetic typography engendered by digital space – but the video's anarchy undermines any claims of clarity and comfort. In its later stages the song edges towards mania, with Charli wishing she could no longer hear the titular ringtone, which haunts her much like Edgar Allan Poe's tell-tale heart. The lyric video's audiovisuality accordingly expresses this descent, with fonts and superimposition occluding legibility, making a mockery of the once reassuring sound of a lover's phone call. This is still synchronisation, and it still orients us, but in an affective manner no less frenzied and responsive than the *6 Underground* car chase.

Indexing its GUI production through these digital audio aesthetics and internet ugly visual style, this lyric video is not itself interactive (barring its pausing and playing, or the multitude of links that may appear around it when viewed on a platform like YouTube). Nonetheless, like other examples of the form, it places intriguing emphasis on synchronised audiovisuality. In this genre, the tight matching of sound and image creates a navigable world in which visual and sonic aesthetics seem imbricated with one another. Onscreen lyrics provide information about and augment our understanding of a song, most obviously by allowing us (normally) to sing along, but also more deeply through their typographical alignment with and embellishment of auditory and conceptual attributes. As in the ultrafield, what we see and what we hear rely on one another in newly delineated ways. The order of priority may have seemingly switched – with the visual field here markedly responsive to the shifting audio space of a song's lyrics, its sonic qualities of timbre, pitch, rhythm, and the way in which words are sung – but nonetheless what we witness is a musicalisation of vision as much as it is a visualisation of music.

Conclusion

The graphic user interface is an overwhelmingly visual space, one in which sound seems at first listen to operate as minimal, occasional reinforcement.

---

dancing – shuffling, really – in poorly seen domestic spaces (100 gecs 2020b). Listed as a '{VISUALISER}' on YouTube, this clip has had several million views, and is clearly positioned as the official video (in contrast to the lyric video, which is labelled on YouTube as such). In it, Brady and Les hold cheap cut-outs over their faces of whichever singer is audible at any moment, a technique which similarly highlights but deconstructs ideas of synchronisation and legibility: we may see Charli XCX as she sings, yet this is just a paper visage, not the singer herself.

Just as going full screen on the visuals of a piece of media removes the traces of the desktop, so too the audio of selected media can override any other GUI audio and fill in the blank sonic space that it seems to offer by default. And yet, just as embedding videos within a multitude of program windows and surrounding them with links all changes how they look and how they are treated by viewers, so too the audio ecology of the desktop alters the way media soundscapes are heard and designed.

I have argued here that we can best perceive this by paying close attention to the idea of synchronisation. Not every desktop activity comes with an attendant sound, but those sounds that are heard call on the user to undertake a particular action in relation to the visual desktop – click to answer that Skype call, click to read that email, click to turn off that auto-playing ad. As described in Chapter 1, Frosh has identified an operative attention in GUI use in which the functionality of the desktop is always being latently perceived (Frosh 2019: 154). This is augmented by the 'pings' of alerts, notifications, and updates, which are operative in nature. This operationality can make itself literally felt in other media when these pings intrude on our viewing of Netflix, playing of a videogame, or browsing of YouTube. But in this chapter I have considered more formal, and much more subtle echoes of these pings and beeps, tracing how an aesthetic of synchronised alerts – clearly audible in the transdiegetic interactive soundtracks of videogames – has also seeped into the ultrafields of narrative cinema, and the audiovisuality of lyric videos. In all these cases, image and audio are tightly in sync, not in the sense that audio might seem to slavishly follow the leads of visuals (as might have been the case in earlier periods of audio-visual production), but rather in the sense that both provide overlapping, augmenting, and sometimes redundant information for the navigation of a media text.

These soundtracks are frequently composite entities, consisting of many individual tracks (sometimes several dozen). The rise of object-oriented audio engineering (such as Dolby Atmos) then allows sound designers and composers to place and move specific sound objects within the listening environment. Such developments may be framed as an amplification in the immersive capacities of cinema (Sergi 2013), but they might equally be thought of as expanding the navigational nature of media soundscapes. In any case, this aggregate sonic ecology – the soundtrack as a collection of highly synchronised individual events, all of which align thanks to digital mixing – is a marker of desktop processes. Indeed, whether object-oriented or not, these digital soundtracks resemble VFX images, which are similarly constructed from multiple highly malleable elements. Such images – or rather, their destruction and reconstruction – are the subject of the next chapter.

4

Seamless Composites

On an airfield in France in 1918, a group of desperate soldiers run through the open doors of a large aircraft hanger. As they emerge, the hanger begins to explode behind them, blasts of flame and debris flaring up in the doorway. But this exciting scene from a blockbuster Hollywood film is rudely interrupted – the image slows and then freezes, before detaching from the edges of our viewing screen. The now-mobile film frame swings to the side, so we view it as a parallelogram within an otherwise blank void. Multiple other parallelograms quickly manifest in a line in front of the original, each one containing different pieces of that first image. Before we have a chance to digest this carved-up series, the numerous slices re-converge into a single plane, and this plane swings back to once more occupy the entire frame of the video we are watching. The soldiers resume their running, albeit with an even greater fireball behind them, a fireball which we now understand – albeit only quite dimly and generally – to be at least partly the product of digital visual effects work.

Generated using programs like Autodesk 3ds Max, Maya, Adobe After Effects, and NUKE, the digital effects of contemporary cinema and television are most often outsourced to effects companies rather than made by the production personnel of a given film or show. Larger media productions will contract a range of companies to complete the many hundreds of visual effects shots, insertions, and clean-ups required by today's digital media ecology of spectacle. Described above is a brief moment from a short video by the effects and post-production studio Universal Production Partners (UPP), showcasing their work on the major blockbuster film *Wonder Woman* (2017). It is available on the company's website, where it is listed as a 'Showreel' (UPP n.d.), and also on YouTube, where it was re-posted in 2018 by the FilmIsNow Movie Bloopers and Extras account under the title 'Wonder Woman – VFX Breakdown by UPP'. In the former context, it advertises UPP's technical capacities to prospective clients; in the latter, it is likely to be encountered by a more general audience (including fans of the film and those broadly interested in visual effects spectacle). It is a typical example of this kind of video, many hundreds or thousands of which circulate on video sharing sites (with the most viewed inevitably being those that are connected to high-profile releases like *Wonder Woman*).

These kinds of videos are all about VFX, and, as creations of the desktop, VFX are themselves inherently gooey. Intriguingly, Aylish Wood (2007) even considers them to be interfaces in and of themselves. For her, the combination of digital VFX elements with pro-filmic content (i.e., that which is captured with cameras on set, using actors and material props) in films like *Wonder Woman* provide visual 'encounters' in which viewers see the negotiation of physical material and computational constructs (Wood 2007: 4). Dynamically distributing our attention across these two fields, the composite VFX image enacts our own interface with digital systems beyond specific media. After all, our own lives increasingly sit between digital worlds and corporeal ones, between virtuality and actuality. Similarly emphasising the gooiness of VFX, albeit in a different way, Bob Rehak argues that these sorts of images hold together the various strands and epochs of transmedia franchises like *Star Trek* (b. 1966) and *Star Wars* (b. 1977). In these brands, VFX images play 'crucial, productive roles both within individual textual "homes" and across media platforms, creating and expanding the storyworlds and characters around which our systems of blockbuster entertainment – not just movies, but television, videogames, comics, and other materials – are increasingly organized' (Rehak 2018: 2–3). VFX, like other special effects, are a kind of glue, a connective tissue across the many proliferating properties of today's expansive media universes.

But this chapter is not about VFX generally, it is about VFX breakdowns. Why unpick this seemingly marginal form of VFX re-distribution and exposition, rather than the source texts themselves? VFX breakdowns might to greater or lesser extents be accurate expressions of the features and processes of digital effects production, but fidelity is not quite my focus here. Whether or not these breakdowns provide 'true' or 'useful' information regarding the creation of effects for a specific film is presently less important than the way in which, taken together, they promote a coherent and powerful vision of what digital effects are and how they work.

If VFX breakdowns function as advertisements for specific media companies and specific media products, then I argue that they also advertise a particular set of ideas regarding the creation and nature of digital effects imagery, one which aligns with the gooey aesthetics already touched on in Chapters 1 and 2. Breakdowns show composite elements overlapping and recombining fluidly in ways that point towards a screen culture of multitasking and swiping, of disaggregate assemblage and representational fidelity. Idealising digital imagery as a series of highly malleable layered spatial elements all available and editable at the touch of a button, breakdowns manifest the way that GUI practices and aesthetics have informed wider imaginations about digital media, and images in general, in the twenty-first century. In this, they are connected to and extend the 'array aesthetics' and 'exploded views' that Deborah Tudor (2008) and Lisa Purse (2018) have identified within narrative media themselves (see Chapter 2).

And breakdowns are hardly niche – the ILM breakdown for *The Avengers* (2012) that I discuss below has been watched over 7 million times on YouTube as of 2022. As such, it is necessary to understand what kind of vision of effects production is being so widely propagated in these videos, and what disappears into their blind spots. Breakdowns, for instance, omit contexts beyond the interface, and so imply that to understand the production of these images there is no need to see the VFX worker at their desk or sitting in a meeting or undertaking repetitive coding tasks (Jones 2023b). Breakdowns also render somewhat invisible the more granular operations of the software programs that are being employed by these artists. The result is less an understanding of Maya, Nuke, or even the broader techniques of, say, texture mapping, and more a sense of autonomous digital assembly. This depiction is indebted to, and itself influences, a wider range of digital media.

Breakdowns therefore show us much about gooey screen aesthetics, and in this chapter I explore them as a useful – but mostly unremarked upon – site in which GUI visuality and functionality has informed wider perceptions of digital imagery and their associated production processes. To do so, I provide my own breakdown of the breakdown, using several examples to identify consistent features of the form. I then trace how the visual logic of the breakdown, itself indebted to the GUI, manifests in finished screen media both past and present, and describe some of the consequences of this imagination for our ideas of digital imagery. But before getting to these issues, we need to briefly contextualise breakdowns within the longer history of digital effects in cinema.

Asset management

Digital images and sounds became increasingly pervasive in entertainment media throughout the twentieth century. Shortly after the computer began its ascent to become a mainstay of corporate, military, and governmental life in the 1940s, it was employed to create elements of popular texts.

Electronic circuits were used by Bebe and Louis Barron to generate the soundtrack of *Forbidden Planet* (1956), and a military computer was used by John Whitney to craft elements of the opening sequence of *Vertigo* (1958) for titles designer Saul Bass (McCormack 2013). The influence of computers then becomes much more pronounced with the mainstreaming of the GUI from the 1980s onwards, leading to the current prevalence of digital visual effects within narrative screen entertainment, especially commercial material with high budgets.

Yet digital effects have long been conceptually bracketed out from the rest of a production. These, after all, are 'special' effects, requiring greater or at least different forms of effort to manufacture than the rest of the media text of which they form a part. As a result, digital effects are often framed through the lenses of medial and temporal difference: the long history of celluloid film gets contrasted with the newness of the digital, the physical work of shooting contrasted with the computerised key-tapping of digital effect creation, and so on. Moreover, despite being conceived, developed, and revised throughout an entire production, digital effects get associated with post-production: once the work of planning and shooting has finished, the effects artists step in.

This is no clearer than in the case of special edition re-releases of films like *Star Wars* (1977; re-released 1997) and its immediate sequels, or *E.T. the Extra-Terrestrial* (1982; re-released 2002). Here, digital material has been layered into the older texts: computer-generated creatures (some of them visible only as massive legs stomping in front of the frame) in *Star Wars*, and the changing of guns to walkie-talkies in the hands of federal agents in *E.T.* While such additions and alterations can shift the meanings and aesthetics of scenes in ways that some audiences find troubling, what is most pertinent here is that these revisions accentuate the gap between shooting – including practical effects – and the digital work of post-production. For all the seamless integration of the two forms of material, the digital components become something that happens *after* the film is made, their inclusion still possible even many decades after the original period of shooting and editing.

In these instances, a film – say, *Star Wars* – as it was originally made becomes another piece of raw material within a VFX program. Celluloid film, digitally scanned, becomes an element within a VFX programmer's toolkit. But if the twenty-year temporal gap between the original release of *Star Wars* and its VFX-heavy special edition suggests distinct stages, then this is no longer the case. In films made since the late 1990s, any lines separating GUI VFX and film production are much blurrier. Effectively all screen media now involve a desktop interface in their production, from editing to colour grading to sound design. Adding VFX simply requires that some or all material be imported into the relevant digital effects software package. The footage from *Wonder Woman* may have initially been captured on 35 mm film using Arriflex cameras, but it has been digitised in order to layer in further explosive effects, effects which are carefully arranged to create a realistic composite. Once shot, the film goes into the GUI and comes out changed.

The work of VFX production relies upon complex, algorithmic programming, and so at times requires proficiency in coding and programming languages like Python or Maya Embedded Language (and large-budgeted productions can involve the writing of new software additions or packages, further swelling the demand for such command-line skills). As Chapter 2 showed, though, the GUI creates a virtual, tactile space behind which this coded ontology can be concealed. The VFX artist uses a viewport in which they can tweak, zoom, rotate, and recombine material, and various dropdown menus and plug-ins allow them to alter parameters or add information without going into the code itself. As a result of these features, the image of the text itself becomes a kind of desktop interface for the visual effects artist, who rearranges elements according to the requirements of narrative, expressivity, and spectacle. This is much like the way we rearrange elements of our own desktop according to our preferred aesthetics and the functions to which it is being currently put. But this description threatens to create a timeline in which VFX always take place after shooting, and this is no longer accurate. Pre-visualisation, or 'previz', has become a common tool of pre-production since the early 1990s. Replacing or augmenting other techniques such as storyboards or rough edits of clips drawn from other media, key special effects sequences and now entire films are often effectively premade as digital animatics. These then function as templates to guide shooting and digital effects production. Far more rudimentary than the VFX of a finished film, these moving storyboards nonetheless rely on similar or identical software like Maya.[1]

As Rehak (2018: 82) points out, previz is just one of a large range of preproduction materials that only intermittently receive public attention, despite being central in shaping a finished media text. For Holly Willis

---

1 Brad Alexander of previz company HALON describes how the work undertaken for actions sequences in *Star Wars: Episode VII – The Force Awakens* (2015) used Maya and After Effects (in Hogg 2016). Meanwhile, on *Replicas* (2018), the software iClone was used for previz and the animation of final components such as interface screens and a climactic onscreen robot (Seymour 2019).

(2016: 47), the significance of previz means that 'the entire workflow of traditional filmmaking gets turned inside out', as the linear sequence of filmmaking is 'reimagined'. Industry discourse and prestige may still emphasise writers, directors, and cinematographers, but the shot designers of previz material have more influence on a text than usually acknowledged (and indeed these designers are rarely acknowledged at all). As blueprints, digital animatics shape the way shots are composed, edited, and even conceived. Crucially, they introduce a computational flexibility and fluidity to these shots, or at least the latent potential for this fluidity. This, as I will later discuss, has important consequences for the aesthetics of the final texts.

Whether found in cinema, television, advertising, videogames, or elsewhere, digital effects imagery is always an amalgamation of diverse assets, and the product of multiple iterations and passes over time. In their final form within finished media, these images do not often wish us to perceive this composite, iterative nature. To do so would be to imply that the effect is rudimentary, badly executed, or just generally ineffective. It must look finished, complete, and a holistic part of the final text. As an ancillary form, though, the VFX breakdown reveals not only the existence of digital effects (showing us that this dinosaur, or that vehicle, or that explosion, was, in fact, added digitally in post) but also divulges some of the elements and layers of which these effects consist. As their name suggests, breakdowns deconstruct the unified whole that is the more widely circulating finished image, unpicking the seams of these normally seamless composites. They rely on a rather narrow range of methods for visualising this procedure, all of which assert that the digital special effect is a layered, three-dimensional space, and that it is assembled within and by a kind of autonomous digital universe.

Breaking down the breakdown

VFX breakdowns focus not on the particulars of filming but on the processes involved in the generation and perfection of CG content, displaying the creation of digital locations, characters, and set pieces. They often focus on the apparent procedures required to make these 'perceptually realistic', to use Stephen Prince's (1996) term for the convincing integration of digital elements with profilmic space. They are several minutes in length and consist of a range of shots from their primary media product. These shots are variously frozen, deconstructed, and reassembled, and are often shown without narrative or thematic grounding, a decontextualisation that is usually furthered by the soundtrack, which usually consists of music taken from the primary text's orchestral score rather than the diegetic sound effects or dialogue that might accompany any given shot in its final form.

To demonstrate the common approaches adopted by the vast majority of VFX breakdowns, I will discuss a small but representative survey: El Ranchito's overview of their work for an episode of *Game of Thrones* (2011–19), ILM's breakdown for mega-hit *The Avengers* (2012), UPP's above-described breakdown for the superhero film *Wonder Woman*, CGF Studio's reel for sci-fi action film *Shanghai Fortress* (2019), and Zero FX's demonstration of their work on a scene from *Little Women* (2019).[2] All are available on YouTube or Vimeo, as well as in many cases on the websites of the relevant companies. Drawn from film and television, large blockbusters and smaller dramas, and made by established effects company powerhouses and boutique effects studios, these breakdowns are nonetheless very similar, and analysis of them therefore allows us to identify consistent aesthetic approaches.[3] These strategies might be perceived differently by those with different levels of knowledge regarding VFX production. In what follows, though, I focus not on the specific VFX details revealed by this content, but rather on the visual attributes and their rhetorical (rather than technical) assertions.

First, and perhaps most overtly, breakdowns stress the blended, composite nature of digital effects. They employ strategies which indicate that many effects shots are amalgamations of location-based footage, green screen capture, and CG material. These include showing these elements discretely before then revealing their consolidation, or vice versa. For instance, the breakdown for the *Game of Thrones* episode 'Hardhome' focuses on select moments from the episode's climactic battle between humans and zombies, including a composite shot of an enemy's head being crushed beneath a hero's boot. Footage of an actor playing the ill-fated undead is followed by a digital model of the same, then a rubber-headed physical prop, and finally

---

2 These videos are listed in this book's bibliography under the name of the respective VFX company. For possible convenience, I will also provide the links here: El Ranchito's *Game of Thrones* (2011–19) breakdown: <https://vimeo.com/132571771>; ILM's *The Avengers* (2012) breakdown: <https://www.youtube.com/watch?v=MnQLjZSX7xM>; UPP's *Wonder Woman* (2017) breakdown: <https://www.youtube.com/watch?v=5PX2GrxSY3o>; CGF Studio's *Shanghai Fortress* (2019) breakdown: <https://www.youtube.com/watch?v=6i90oYtHyY4>; Zero FX's *Little Women* (2019) breakdown: <https://www.zerovfx.com/video/little-women>.

3 VFX breakdowns are available for some videogames, focusing on either the creation of cinematics (see, for instance, FilmIsNow Bloopers and Extras 2021) or real-time reactive environmental effects (see, for instance, Control Remedy 2020).

a foot crushing a head full of black goo on a green screen stage. Displayed one after another in quick succession, the breakdown provides no contextualising information for this material – it is up to the viewer to note how the various aspects of each element are then manifested to some extent in the final shot, barely two seconds in length, which is shown as the culmination of this short passage. We are presumed to be savvy enough to understand that no actor actually lost their head, and that the gooey ball being squished on a green floor is not some separate, unrelated activity, but a visual detail which will be plucked from its inappropriately coloured background and composited into the more picturesque surroundings of Westeros.[4]

Similar moments are found in many breakdowns, which show imagery which is distinct in a variety of ways (location shot and green screen; pro-filmic and digital), doing so sequentially and speedily to indicate the amalgamation of this material in the finished shot. Through this focus on blending, breakdowns moreover demonstrate how on-set footage is embedded into a virtual world. In the *Wonder Woman* breakdown by UPP, we are shown footage of two actors strolling back and forth on a green screen; this content is then shrunk within the frame (like a minimised program window) and spatially embedded within a digitally created castle to the point that the actors – originally captured in full frame – are barely visible behind the ramparts. Similarly, in ILM's video for their work on *The Avengers*, a famous shot from the film is featured in which the titular heroes assemble in a battle-ravaged New York City. Shot on a green screen stage, this pro-filmic content again shrinks in the frame in order to take its place amongst a wider, digitally generated scenography.

These moments show photographic material being placed within a VFX shot in a seemingly straightforward manner – footage is implicitly dragged, dropped, and resized. But at other times, VFX breakdowns imply that more rigorous procedures of schematic mapping are needed for footage to be combined. The breakdown for 'Hardhome' shows a complex orange mesh covering a fence in the background of a handheld shot, indicating that the precise dimensions of this structure need to be interpreted by the VFX program in order for the surrounding effects work to take place (a process called rotomation). Zero FX, meanwhile, in a rare example of explanatory text, place the phrase 'LIDAR scan of environment' onscreen as the photographic plate of a country lane and lake from *Little Women* is replaced by its digital double

---

4   Of the VFX breakdowns listed above, all but the *Shanghai Fortress* breakdown describe comparable blending procedures, although even in that breakdown the city skyline appears to be a relatively unedited photographic reference plate.

Figure 4.1a An outdoors scene from *Little Women* (2019) … Frame enlargement from Zero, n.d.

Figure 4.1b … fades into a LIDAR scan of this environment in the VFX breakdown for the film. Frame enlargement from Zero, n.d.

(this virtual surrogate, as is normal for breakdowns, is noticeable as such thanks to its monochromatic, rudimentary visual quality, an aesthetic that I will explore in more detail in Chapter 6) (Figures 4.1a–b). These moments suggest that sometimes some form of scanning and contour plotting needs to occur before photographic content can successfully sit alongside digital elements.

Even more complex processes of blending are implied by other means. Elsewhere in ILM's *Avengers* breakdown a virtual camera moves smoothly through a pre-textured model of New York: buildings are clean white, the sky an abstract black. Large reflective spheres drop from the sky like rain, coming to rest on the edges of buildings and between skyscrapers. We infer that these bubbles represent photographic visual information because visual detail starts bleeding out from them over the nearby buildings, filling up the white surfaces with photo-real coating (Figure 4.2). This is the breakdown's way of communicating that ILM effects artists visited New York's rooftops and took hundreds of 360° photographs of the skyline, using this information to create textured skeins that were wrapped over the digital model of the city – although this process of visual data capture and re-interpretation is not presented explicitly (Robertson 2012).

If VFX indicated to be the products of blending and layering, then they are also shown to be the result of numerous iterations. To demonstrate their work on *Shanghai Fortress*, CGF freeze a shot of an enormous cannon rising from the Huangpu River. The breakdown then zooms out, showing the film frame at an angle within a black void, revealing the multiple layers of 2D water splash which are built up onto this model. Each layer of splash is contained within a blue-outlined box which slides into the perspective of the final shot, this perspective articulated by a wireframe model of a camera and its point of view (a wireframe which resembles an Albertian diagram of vision) (Figure 4.3). This shift of perspective away from and at a diagonal from the image is a common strategy – for instance, as described at the beginning of this chapter, it occurs in the *Wonder Woman* breakdown, where the multiple angled layers exhibit layers of fire, smoke, and other atmospherics (Figure 4.4); it also occurs in the 'Hardhome' breakdown to show the

Figure 4.2 A rudimentary model of New York has detail added to it through a rain of spherical camera data in the VFX breakdown for *The Avengers* (2012) (Industrial Light and Magic, 2013). Frame enlargement from YouTube.

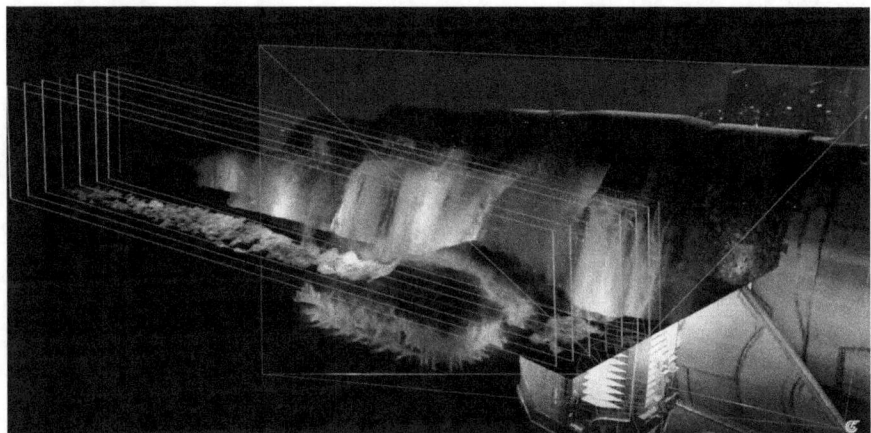

Figure 4.3 The VFX breakdown for *Shanghai Fortress* (2019) swings out from the final image to show layers arrayed in front of it in three-dimensional space (CGF, 2019). Frame enlargement from YouTube.

Figure 4.4 The VFX breakdown for *Wonder Woman* (2017) undertakes a similar manoeuvre, showing layers of detail making up an explosion (UPP, n.d.). Frame enlargement from YouTube.

fragments of digital ice that accompany the dismemberment of a zombie (Figure 4.5). Such 'swing-out' shots display the multiple tiers of information that apparently comprise the final VFX shot.

Another strategy for showing all the sedimented elements, colours, textures, and atmospheric effects of composite shots is to swipe through these

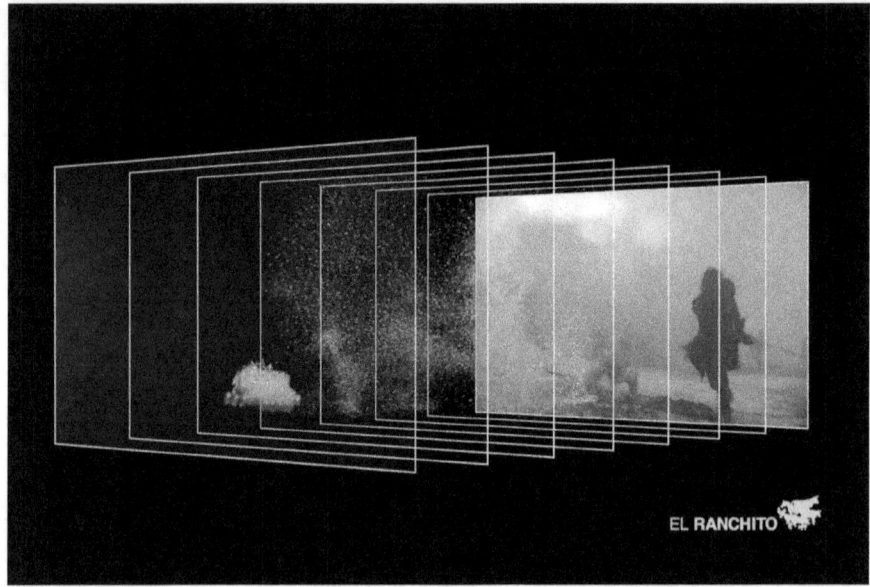

Figure 4.5 And, once again, in the VFX breakdown for 'Hardhome' (El Ranchito Imagen Digital, 2015). Frame enlargement from YouTube.

layers in quick succession. For example, Zero VFX indicate that an ice-skating scene in *Little Women* involved layering digital elements like the lake surface, snowy backgrounds, and water splash onto the captured footage by sequentially wiping these elements away from the image. In this way the breakdown effectively 'digs' through digital deposits to uncover the unaugmented profilmic content beneath. Even more layers are shown in several moments of the 'Hardhome' breakdown, with green screen footage, distant objects like trees and figures, a layer of mist, a layer of snow, a layer of fire effects, and other material all swiping by in quick succession. Similarly, in *Shanghai Fortress*, extremely quick wipe transitions (each lasting less than a second) show tiers of water, light effects, and mist that cover the aforementioned cannon as it breaches the river's surface, and then, in an identical process, illustrate the many components that make up the massive explosion caused by the cannon's subsequent firing. At times, elements strangely vanish after one swipe, only to return with the next – a cabin in the 'Hardhome' encampment appears as a digital model, then disappears while ground-snow is added, then reappears with the next swipe, now on fire.

If the digital effect is made up of many layers (as these moments imply), then these layers seem to be generated through multiple passes, with the use of wipes suggesting the application of different kinds of effects software or expertise in the successive stages of a shot's creation. In this way, the process of digital effects manufacture is discursively asserted as being highly iterative. CGI looks like it consists of a series of passes or plug-ins, each of which deposits new details. This sensation is imparted even as the precise names, nature, and uses of these tools is left entirely unremarked upon. When circulating as a promo tool to industry insiders the precise software in use at any moment may be a given, but to wider audiences accessing this material via YouTube or Blu-ray features these kinds of details are likely a mystery. All that less specialist viewers are left with is the general impression that a steady build-up of subdivided digital activities ultimately amplifies the believability and perceptual realism of the digital parts of the image and the smoothness with which they interlock with photographic material.

Even if a shot is shown to be an entirely digital creation, a process of compositing and – crucially – *assembly* is still demonstrated. For instance, in the *Avengers* breakdown, ILM asserts the sheer number of pieces involved in the creation of the film's enormous helicarrier. A shot of this vehicle from the finished film is excerpted, but is quickly halted and put into reverse. The background disappears, and the helicarrier quickly disassembles itself, hundreds of constituent pieces flying out of the frame in multiple directions. These pieces then return in a more leisurely fashion, locking into place upon the 3D skeleton of the carrier like parts of an Airfix model, with the virtual camera drifting in an arc around this spectacular re-composition. Similarly, the *Shanghai Fortress* breakdown takes us inside the cannon to indicate how its barrel consists of hundreds of individual mirrored pieces mounted on mechanisms that shift their angle and direction. One of these mechanisms is pulled out and isolated, the workings of its mirror apparatus performed with a helpful shard of light bouncing through a black void, before this individual component is placed back inside the cannon, the breakdown then showing the panels moving in tandem to generate a virtual laser beam which sweeps through the cylinder.

If these moments resemble anything, it is a demonstrator or engineer removing part of complicated apparatus, showing this part to us separately or allowing us to handle it with our own hands, then reinserting this piece into its proper place and turning the apparatus on. Digital models are in this way 'exploded' in the fashion of engineering construction diagrams, with an emphasis on the many interlocking pieces that make up the final, apparently singular article. In this way, the digital creations of the final image are shown to require building just like a physical structure would. And if digital models seem itemised – consisting of interlocking parts that balance co-dependent forces – then this works to further stress their realism, their three-dimensional depth and weight.

While their soundtracks normally consist of soaring music cues, breakdowns occasionally employ audio cues to further proclaim the (disingenuous) physicality of such moments of de- and re-assembly. Many pieces of the ILM helicarrier audibly click into place in the *Avengers* breakdown, making sounds of different pitches and tones depending on the scale of the component in question. Other parts of the model appear within the structure as spontaneous manifestations, and these emit a kind of sucking or slurping noise, as though being poured in from another realm. Pre-finalised digital material is similarly granted materiality by CGF in their *Shanghai Fortress* breakdown: in the first shot, a virtual camera moves from an image of the titular city's skyline and into the Huangpu River; as it does so, the surface of the water folds back as though it consists of dozens of carpet-like rolls of digital wrapping, and this spooling is accompanied by a swooshing noise. All such sounds are of course additions for this promotional material. Digital cogs do not click and digital surfaces are not textured rolls of audibly rustling fabric, and they only make these sounds if programmed to do so or if, as is much more likely, such audio effects are added as a supplementary soundtrack during the editing of the VFX breakdown.

While these diagrammatic explosions and idiosyncratic sound effects grant digital models an implied physicality, the VFX breakdown also emphasises at every stage the immaterial ease with which CG scenography can be navigated. Yes, these are apparently material and tangible objects (or collections of objects), but the processes of gravity-defying, non-violent dismantling that we witness simultaneously accentuate their weightless fluidity, their virtual flexibility.

This is personified by the digital fly-through. As already indicated, the camera of the VFX breakdown is often freed from the framing of the final film or television show, instead moving gracefully under, over, around, and sometimes directly into the digital models and environments presented. For instance, the *Wonder Woman* breakdown begins with a virtual reverse tracking shot through an untextured digital model of Piccadilly Circus; as we sweep backwards, layers of detail accumulate, and as the virtual camera comes to rest a few hundred feet from where it began, profilmic footage of the film's stars materialises into this digital terrain (Figures 4.6a–c). A digital fly-through in the *Little Women* breakdown similarly moves in a fluid, computer-generated arc from one shot of the final film on one side of a lake to another shot on the other side. This move shows how Zero VFX have interpreted the 2D pictorial content provided by two separate location shots as fundamentally spatial data, as two points on an implied line, a line which can only be articulated by digital interpolation. Two shots from separate

Figures 4.6a, b and c The VFX breakdown for *Wonder Woman* (2017) begins in a rudimentary Piccadilly Circus (a), pulling back as layers and detail accumulate (b), with the final position (and shot) barely showing the initial space (c) (UPP, n.d.). Frame enlargement from YouTube.

angles become windows on a reconstituted, digital space, through which the virtual camera glides. The same approach is taken with digital characters, with models of, for instance, the head and body of superhero Hulk being frozen, rotated, and zoomed into in the *Avengers* breakdown (Figure 4.7).

Figure 4.7 The various iterations making up the character of the Hulk and their relationship to facial capture data drawn from actor Mark Ruffalo are all demonstrated simultaneously in the VFX breakdown for *The Avengers* (2012) (Industrial Light and Magic, 2013). Frame enlargement from YouTube.

All this swooping communicates an impression of comprehensiveness, and of the spatial veracity of these digital models. We see this content from every conceivable angle, and so are taught that these are not 2D animations designed solely for the frames in which they will feature, but rather three-dimensional objects with consistent measurements and movements that have been 'captured' by a virtual camera. While pre-digital effects work may have relied on two-dimensional illusions of three-dimensional space – think of matte paintings, rear projection, or visual animation drawn onto the frame itself – the constant motion of the virtual camera in VFX breakdowns stresses the spatial nature of CGI.

Digital graphics scholar Jacob Gaboury (2015) describes how digitally generated imagery relies upon the construction of discrete computational objects, objects which are then rendered in ways that precisely conceal some of the detail that they inherently have within themselves (i.e., the other side of a digital prop, the back of digital character's head). In these fly-throughs and swoops, the VFX breakdown rediscovers this detail, taking us into the 'hidden surfaces' of these models (Gaboury 2015: 51–2). Indeed, in line with Gaboury's arguments, in VFX breakdowns the digitally generated material is implicitly *more spatial* than its photographic counterparts in these breakdowns: 2D footage of actors and sets is shown being mapped with wireframes and rotomotion in order to volumise it in a way that aligns with the natively spatial contours of the digital material. Processes of layering then either flesh out the detail of these three-dimensional elements in the case of texture maps, or fill up empty space as in the case of environment atmospherics like water spray, smoke, or snow.

Like the wealth of individual components, these layers are shown to be abundant. Rapid editing stresses the sheer amount of digital artefacts and textures and the investment of fine, even convoluted detail. The wipe-by addition of layers in particular stresses the large number of iterations needed to achieve a perceptually realistic image. At times, the accretion of elements and finessing of pictorial content reach what the amateur spectator might consider absurd heights, as the extent of the layering, compositing, and atmospherics seems to occlude rather than sharpen the final product. As stated, the *Wonder Woman* breakdown begins with the virtual camera gliding through Piccadilly Circus: it moves over a digital model of Shaftesbury Memorial Fountain, tracking back as layers of detail, colour, and texture are added. And yet in the final shot as featured in the film the London tourist attraction is barely visible in the background above the heads of the extras, and it resembles more a 2D backdrop than a 3D spatial simulation – indeed, it is so far back in the shot, this is all it needs to or could resemble. Meanwhile, there are so many modular pieces to the explosion featured in the breakdown for *Shanghai Fortress* that some of them seem to disappear completely beneath others. Effects company CGF advertise the atomic-style clouds, swelling orange bubbles, and shiny spark-like flecks that they have gone to the trouble of embedding within the detonation, but in the final rendered shot they all but vanish beneath a glaze of burning white light.

Finally, it is worth stressing again that all these swoops, deconstructions, and reassemblies happen at high speed. From the many pieces of footage and digital material included in some shots, to the multiple layers that wipe across the frame, to the swing-out shots or virtual cameras that glide around models and digital sets – everything moves exceedingly quickly. The absence of voice-over or any other indication of the specific processes, software programs, or individuals involved helps maintain this pace. The overriding impression is of a giddy ride through a three-dimensional digital space in which the layers and pieces of VFX are arrayed for our glancing appreciation.

Narrow viewports

This breakdown of the breakdown reveals several things. First, VFX breakdowns propose an innate spatiality to the digital effect and to digital imagery in general. Second, combining as they do multiple elements (whether these include digital and pro-filmic sources or just multiple digital sources), breakdowns assert the inherently composite character of these images and of digital spaces and objects. And third, the accretion of many layers – each of which moves the effect from abstract virtual object to verisimilitudinous piece of mise-en-scène – declares the process of effects production to be iterative and effectively teleological (there are no errors, only the accumulation of perceptually realistic detail).

These features are not limited to breakdowns though, but rather bleed across and inform the representations and use of VFX in other contexts, and even larger ideas of digital space. In this way, breakdowns are fascinating hinge points in the digital media ecology. They perform imaginations of both VFX production and the nature of screen media in the era of the GUI. Before expanding on these connections, though, it is necessary to mention what the breakdown doesn't show.

First, for all their seeming revelations about process, breakdowns strip away the times, spaces, bodies, and decisions involved in the work of VFX. As a result, they minimise our awareness of the very labour that they purport to track. This is in line with some other ancillary material related to contemporary media production. As Chuck Tryon (2009: 18) states, making of supplements tends to 'obscure the work of below-the-line laborers and, quite often, mask the fact that digital media have led to the increased use of non-union labor, often on a part-time basis'. And yet in other, non-breakdown making-of supplements we do often glimpse a wider labour force, whether this is named talent (interviews with directors, actors, effects technicians, or stunt choreographers) or unnamed individuals who are informally glimpsed on set (the gaffers, riggers, caterers, personal assistants, and so on who might walk through the background of an on-set interview with a star). In the VFX breakdown, by contrast, we see no sign of people, and most tellingly the worker whose labour is directly producing and manipulating the images we are seeing disappears. This is because the breakdown stays resolutely locked on the screen, omitting the desks, offices, and company structures that work to produce these images. As a result, and as we have seen, the work is shown effectively completing itself (see Jones 2023a).

Moreover, breakdowns limit their visual content to the material that programming produces, and in this way they shun the act of programming itself. Software like Maya provides its users with a wealth of windows and drop-down panels full of numerical values, as well as a central viewport which shows the image resulting from these calculations and adjustments (Figure 4.8). Animators can tweak images by changing values in the many menus, toolboxes, sliders, and selectors. But they can also zoom into and rotate the contents of this viewport at will, undertaking direct manipulation

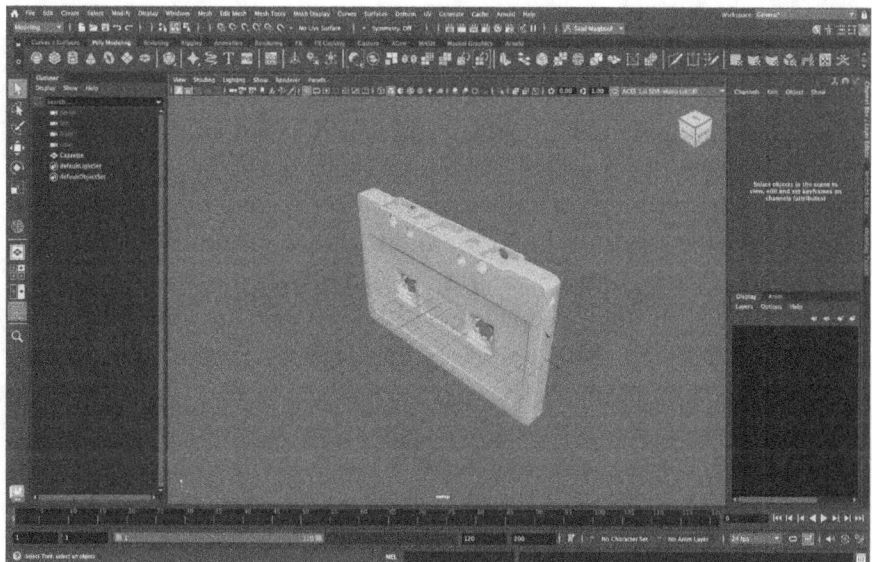

Figure 4.8 A typical Maya viewport with a central viewport and numerous surrounding panels. Frame enlargement courtesy of Saad Maqbool.

using a mouse, touchscreen, or stylus, and the breakdown favours a kind of surrogate performance of this direct approach, entirely eschewing windows and drop-down menus.

This aligns with how animators themselves often think about their work. In a detailed study of Autodesk Maya and its users, Aylish Wood (2015) interviewed a diverse group of effects artists about their working processes using the program. She summarises how they tend to consider the viewport a welcome opportunity to see 'digital entities in three-dimensional space' as they use it to spin digital objects around, scrutinising them as they float in an abstract void (Wood 2015: 322–3). She also notes a preference for tools that allow these artists to engage directly with the resulting digital creation, rather than with the code or numerical values that contribute to that creation. Plugins are sought which provide a 'heightened impression of access to the [digital] model', and so displace 'the process of negotiation with an algorithm' behind more direct forms of manipulation (Wood 2015: 323–4). Wood undertook this study in the early 2010s, but this tendency is nothing new: Manovich (2001: 80) describes how PowerAnimator (a digital animating tool of the 1990s) foregrounded spatial navigability, with 'each window, regardless of whether it displays a 3-D model, a graph, or even plain text, contain[ing] Dolly, Track, and Zoom buttons'. For animators, the command line and drop-down menu are repeatedly snubbed in favour of representational elements that offer a haptic encounter with the digital model.

It might not be shocking that this is replicated in the VFX breakdown: the algorithmic access provided by programming windows speaks to the laborious, time-consuming processes of VFX production which cannot possibly be covered in a three-minute video, and which would fail to excite many viewers. And yet the omission is still important, as it wrests the process of effects production away from the calculative tweaks and tool-based adjustments that are essential to it. Furthermore, this displacement of programming for direct manipulation accords with the GUI's focus on virtual space, and its provision of what Wendy Chun (2011: 63) calls 'participatory structures' rather than commands. VFX are framed by the breakdown as inherently representational, a collection of assets that are easily tweakable and changeable, digital *objects* rather than digital *code*. By presenting none of its material as algorithm, the breakdown only breaks down so far, showing only the equivalent of the viewport, and a rather narrow one at that.

The breakdown in history

Why does any of this matter in the context of the GUI, or the wider visual culture of which it forms a part? The VFX breakdown would seem to be a marginal media form, a niche display of a much commented upon but little understood element of digital media production. And yet, as indicated, the strategies the breakdown adopts place it into dialogue with a range of other media, both historical and contemporary. While the latter are our key focus here, the former deserve a quick mention for their intriguing links and aesthetic echoes.

For instance, we can discern connections between breakdowns and seventeenth-century peepshows and tunnel books. These amusements used overlapping flats to create dense and subtly stereoscopic compositions through recessive miniature corridors in which each paper wing adds new visual information. Such an approach is highly evocative of the VFX breakdown's own depictions of layering, in which a similarly accretive environment of finely detailed tiers is represented. Rather than a single image or a conventional space, visual material is revealed to be a kind of optical illusion. If this might be thought a tangential connection, then the peepshow's emphasis on the revelation of delightful secrets is perhaps suggestive. As Lynda Nead (2005: 138) states, the 'special appeal of the peepshow was that, unlike other forms of public amusement, it offered the viewer a private pleasure; a glimpse of a closed, hidden scene and the possibility of seeing secrets'. The breakdown might not offer voyeurism exactly, but it similarly promises tantalising revelations that go beyond the surface of the final text.

Meanwhile, the dissection of the VFX image into component parts which are arrayed next to one another suggests several experiments in late nineteenth-century photography and animation, experiments which are written into the lore of pre-cinema history. Optical toys like zoetropes, mutoscopes, and phenakistoscopes arrayed multiple images in ways that showed their viewers both the individual fragments and their amalgamation – usually through spinning a handle – as a single, moving composite. Such toys allowed movement to be petrified and unstitched, a process which revealed its dynamics. Going further in this regard were the locomotion studies of Eadweard Muybridge in the 1880s and 1890s, in which the scientist famously anatomised the movement of animals and people and displayed these as sequences of photographs. Similar work was also undertaken by Etienne-Jules Marey and Lilian and Frank Gilbreth. Marey's chronophotography used multiple exposure techniques to reveal the composite pieces of seemingly fluid actions within a single image (a bird's smooth flight, a worker's hammering at an anvil). The Gilbreths' time and motion studies, meanwhile, captured similar temporal processes in such a way that they could be frozen and reconceived as three-dimensional diagrams. Indeed, the Gilbreths even used long exposure photography and flashing marker dots, turning the simple folding of a handkerchief into a twirling ribbon of pulsing arcs; when these patterns were printed as a stereocard or built as a sculpture, they could then be scrutinised as spatial objects (Cresswell 2006: 98–101).

In all these instances, the unfolding flow of material action is frozen and somehow spatialised for contemplation. The resulting interplay between 3D and 2D and between stillness and movement expose the otherwise unseen through the creation of smoothly navigable spaces, whether this be the sculptures of the Gilbreths, the pages of Muybridge books, or the paper sleeves of a zoetrope. In contrast to these frozen composites, the VFX breakdown seems to be relentlessly on the move. But through its rapid editing and sweeping virtual camera, it nonetheless evinces the same composite methodology, the same assertion that time and space need visual dissection to reveal their truths. Are those moments when the VFX image freezes and is pulled apart into its many layers not the contemporary equivalent of stopping a zoetrope in order to observe the many individual images that only moments before created a fluid sense of animated movement?

The connection with Muybridge moreover implicates the VFX breakdown within Lev Manovich's (2001: 298) widely cited proposal that in the digital era, cinema has returned to its pre-cinematic roots in animation.

After all, breakdowns celebrate the various CG animation techniques that make up apparently photographic final material. They show how a singular image in the digital era might actually be an accumulation of many separate pieces. Just as, for Manovich, cinema is more about the assembly of elements within a bricolage than about a kind of Bazinian holism of time and space, so too the breakdown announces with a flourish how that which presents in a final text as a spatio-temporal unity is in fact a seamless unification of diverse animated pieces.

In these ways, we can see how the VFX breakdown is aligned with visual histories of both scientific rationality *and* optical illusion. These historical connections indicate how the VFX breakdown is concerned less with showing a *process* of production, and more about *unravelling* something discovered in the wild, about catching the VFX shot in the act. It is seemingly the gaze of a scientist or engineer, wresting apart the final shot to reveal its inner workings. The spectacle they offer is bound up with a particularly quantifying form of visuality, one which unpacks, explodes, and dissects (Jones 2013).

In the case of the breakdown, this seizure does not allow for careful inspection, as it does in the work of Muybridge or Marey. Instead, there is a dazzling impression of multiform activity, the specific contours of which will remain effectively a mystery to all but industry insiders perched with the pause button at hand. In this, breakdowns move away from the purview of the scientist and into that of the illusionist. Breakdowns create miniature, dense worlds of spatial artifice. They show a trick in action, then spin it around or halt its motion so viewers can understand how it gains its illusory power.[5] The evocation of zoetropes and peepshows, then, reveals the breakdown's appeal to delightful deception.

Media (dis)assemble

What of contemporary media, though? The breakdown may be a distinct, ancillary form, but, like its vertical associations with earlier visual culture and optical illusions, it also connects horizontally to wider array of contemporary media. In this way the seeming marginality of the breakdown belies the way it adopts and widely inspires a range of approaches for depicting digital images and for navigating digital space.

We might begin by noting the way the breakdown is often evoked in another somewhat ancillary form, the opening and closing credits sequences

---

5 On peepshows, miniaturisation, and mastery, see Stewart 1993.

of popular cinema. Across the 2010s and beyond there has been an increasing tendency for these sequences to provide a breakdown-like exploration of digital models and textures. *Pacific Rim* (2013), *The Avengers, Shanghai Fortress, Black Panther* (2018), and many others all seize the opportunity offered by their non-diegetic credit sequences to prepare viewers for, or remind them of, the digital spectacle of the main narratives. Virtual cameras swoop around digital creations and composites while the names of the production crew float in 3D space, or are even embedded within these models as yet another spatially composited layer. As in the breakdown, these models are isolated from any surroundings, floating in some abstract space for non-narrative contemplation, and are observed by a camera unmoored from spatial constraint (Figure 4.9).

Lisa Purse (2018) notes that this stylistic trend might be motivated as much by logistics as it is by creative agency. Such sequences, she proposes, 'become popular in part because of the pragmatic sharing of 3D modelling assets between a film's visual effects vendors and its credit sequence designers to help speed the credit sequence along' (Purse 2018: 162). Since the effect already exists as a malleable spatial element because of its creation using software like Maya, why not get more screen-time out of this work by revelling in the effect's contours and detailing in a credit sequence? In a linked manner, the Blu-ray disc for *The Avengers* features a wireframe schematic of the aforementioned helicarrier as the introduction to its menu screen. Seemingly incidental, this confluence nonetheless links together

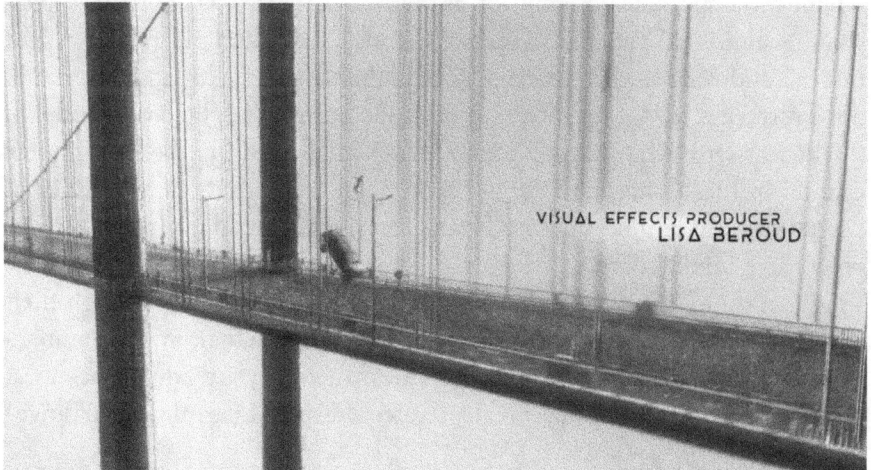

Figure 4.9 In the credit sequence of *Black Panther* (2018) the names of production personnel fly around digital models of the key vehicles and action of the film. Frame enlargement from Disney+.

two forms of expanded, spatialised access: that of a VFX breakdown-style roaming around a digital model, and that of the databased textual navigation offered by the 'jump-to-a-scene' menus of DVD and Blu-ray discs.

Beyond the non-diegetic bookmarks of credit sequences and disc menus, these digital models can also frequently appear within a film's diegesis. Several scenes of *Shanghai Fortress* are set within a military installation, and a detailed holographic representation of the cannon is often visible on a conference table here, observed by various personnel. As in the VFX breakdown, the cannon is rotated, enlarged, and minimised by unseen hands during any given scene.[6] Similar holograms appear in many other contemporary blockbusters, where their ethereally glowing forms may be the subject of direct attention or just incidental mise-en-scène (see Jones 2020: 97–100). In either case, these holograms represent a graphically stripped-down vision of the more verisimilitudinous VFX found across the rest of a film's running time.

Including digital models and breakdown-style flythroughs within credit sequences, mise-en-scène, or even para-textual Blu-ray navigational screens would all seem to call attention to the virtual nature of these elements as they appear elsewhere in these films. Surely seeing the helicarrier on a disc's navigation screen works to detach the vehicle from the photographic reality of *The Avengers*, marking it out as a digital effect in ways that run counter to all the work that has gone into making it perceptually realistic? Likewise, seeing the grandstanding cannon in *Shanghai Fortress* as a diegetic piece of computer software must make its appearance on the film's profilmic Shanghai skyline more suspect? Possibly not, as these appearances can work to emphasise the additional qualities of texture, atmospherics, and perceptual weight that are endowed to the diegetically 'real' digital effect. Not all viewers will opt to watch a VFX breakdown, but by including the schematic model of the helicarrier on the Blu-ray of *The Avengers* or featuring the holographic cannon in the background of scenes in *Shanghai Fortress*, the qualities of photographic verisimilitude and layered detailing granted the 'real' narrative objects are implicitly revealed through direct contrast. These broken-down VFX therefore offer a breakdown form of visuality not only through their stripping back of textures and atmosphere, but also via their implied emphasis on the value of these additional qualities when they are 'added back in' at moments of more perceptually realistic effects display. Like mini-breakdowns

---

6 In line with Purse's comments, the holographic cannon may be the same digital asset as the fully detailed CGF model, although the interface tables and panels were handled by a different effects vendor, Territory Studio (see Territory Studio 2019).

hovering at the edge of the text, they potentially allow audiences to marvel at the elsewhere-depicted 'finished' effect.

Credit sequences, disc menus, and even diegetic holo-tables present relatively segregated sites of visual spectacle. A more prominent – and perhaps more significant – overlap between breakdown visuality and finished texts can be found in the use of virtual camera movements in both, and the way such camera movements evoke a kind of posthuman approach to space. Much written-about virtual shots in films like *Fight Club* (1999) and *Panic Room* (2002) cut trajectories through walls, human skin, and coffee pot handles in ways that mimic and lay the groundwork for the swooping digital gaze of the breakdown. These shots, especially in their most fantastical guise, are often used to communicate mastery of space, or to reveal and glamorise the workings of complex technology (and indeed the mastery of space shown by the long take digital composite shot is itself a form of mastery). When the protagonists of *Sucker Punch* (2011) take on a squad of armed robots in a train carriage, a two-minute shot darts and ricochets around the space like a projectile as the onscreen action switches fluidly in and out of slow-motion. In *The Fast and the Furious* (2001), viewers are provided photographic footage of an actor behind the wheel, before then being sucked into a digital rendering of various parts of the vehicle's engine as the virtual camera sweeps through the chassis, then ejected from the exhaust port as the once-again photographic car now screeches away.[7] Taking cues from the bullet-time effect of *The Matrix* (1999), the image becomes spatialised and the camera ostentatiously probes the (digital) depths and layers therein.

For William Brown (2013), these are examples of how digital cinema apparently rejects cutting, favouring instead the creation of navigable spaces.[8] But such shots must also be seen as evidence of digital VFX in the pre-production of these texts. As indicated, digital previz has become

---

7 More grounded long takes in films like *Children of Men* (2006) and television shows like *Daredevil* (2015–18) and *Game of Thrones* no less rely upon digital post-production to composite the various elements that invariably make up what is apparently a single in-camera take.

8 Twenty-first century film, Brown (2013: 103) argues, 'has shifted from being a temporal depiction of space (one analogue frame, then another, revealing a space over time via cuts), to being a spatial depiction of time (different digital/digitized elements forming a harmonious whole within the frame, without the need to cut)'. This is not only a case of changing film language, but of a deeper shift to a posthumanist vernacular: a kind of non-anthropocentric thinking, an expression of a digital logic in which all spaces and objects are granted equivalent status by the dematerialising flow of the virtual camera (see also Crockett 2009; Ayers 2019).

increasingly important for the planning and execution of production and post-production activity. In these animatics, a virtual camera captures a virtual space; the affordances of this virtuality can then influence the kinds of shots that are conceived and that are then captured and rendered for the final cut. Indeed, the related process 'techviz' allows previz data around virtual camera movement and lenses to then be exported into physical shooting set-ups and final VFX composites (Willis 2016: 45; Insider 2021). The space of the viewport, with its rotations, plunges, swipes, and unbroken 'takes', guides the space of the finished text, just as it guides the spaces of the breakdown.

These digital long takes, moreover, connect contemporary cinema with videogames. As Matthias Stork (2013) argues, shots like the one described above from *Sucker Punch* 'emulate the video game's use of post-cinematic space' in their adoption of a 'machinic gaze' which explores a 'computerized spatial construct'.[9] Whether in first or third person perspective, or as a god-like presence hovering above large swathes of territory, a videogame player is usually endowed with the ability to dynamically investigate the digital spaces provided by a game, and of course many games tend toward long stretches of uninterrupted 'shots' as opposed to cutting.

But, as ever, this is not simply a case of one kind of media (film) borrowing from another (videogames). The digital long takes found in cinema employ the same or similar software programs as those shaping videogame navigation, so it is inevitable that they resemble one another. In either case, space – and the objects within it – are computerised in the sense that they are imported into or generated by programs like Maya, where working with them involves rotating and zooming, potentially in a continuous, 'unbroken' fashion.

The 'machinic gaze' that Stork identifies is, then, a digital animator's gaze. The computerised perception of this gaze is found in the flowing, fluid shots of the VFX breakdown as much as in the cinematic digital long take and also the uninterrupted visual unfolding of videogame play. In all cases, the digitisation of space allows its disclosure as a series of layers or elements through which an individual (whether player or camera) can navigate at ease.

Videogames also echo the aesthetic features of the breakdown in less obvious ways. Many games allow players to move perspective within the game world – on console controllers for the various iterations of the

---

9 Holly Willis (2016: 141) emphasises the 'first-person shooter' aesthetic of films less oriented around digital spectacle, such as *Birdman* (2014) and *Elephant* (2003).

PlayStation, the left analogue stick is usually employed to move the virtual camera alone, while the right stick moves the onscreen avatar. But players can also increasingly switch to 'photo mode', in which the virtual viewpoint becomes more than just a tool for gameplay. Offered in games like *The Last of Us* (2014), *Shadow of the Tomb Raider* (2018), *Forza Horizon 4* (2018), and many others, photo mode allows players to appreciate the dense visual detail of the game while its contents are paused. By selecting photo mode, the player is able not only to freeze the game world for contemplation, but can also manoeuvre their perspective through this stilled scenography, tilting, zooming, tracking, and panning in order to grab an image (which can then be shared on social media). While the 'shots' that result from photo modes can be thought of as a new genre of photography (Zylinska 2020), what most concerns us here is the way that visual exploration is unmoored from the onscreen avatar and the demands of instrumental gameplay, becoming instead a way of navigating the digital composite and revealing its extensive detailing in the manner of a VFX breakdown.[10]

Furthermore, many games offer access to interactive digital models in ways that are ancillary to gameplay, and which resemble a kind of artefactual photo mode. Completing parts of videogames like *Spider-Man* (2018) or *Resident Evil 2* (2019), for instance, rewards the player with digital objects, characters, and concept art. These are displayed in abstract space within a sub-menu, and players are encouraged to rotate and zoom into these artefacts. As with photo mode, players become less participants in a game's fiction, and more surrogate animators, exploring the contents of the game-world within viewports.

These experiences highlight how videogame cameras and features can work to bridge animator and user. Photo modes and artefact rewards offer players a surrogate experience of programming digital space, one shorn of further program windows and drop-down menus. In such cases we become proxy digital designers. This can involve exploring the assets and textures of the virtual world of the game for moments of beauty, or even for weak points in the visual simulation. Or it can have more ambitious creative ends, as in the case of 'machinima', in which non-interactive stories are generated from captured videogame material. Essentially a prosumer version of previz which creates not blueprints but final texts, in machinima the videogame itself becomes a shooting stage, a camera, and an editing room. This makes its status as a discrete media format hard to define: as Jenna Ng puts it, machinima is 'less a discrete, distinguishable media form

---

10 Further discussion on videogame photography can be found in Rizov 2021.

than a fluid *dialogue* of and between media – reproducing them, translating them, merging them, subverting them' (Ng 2013: xiv; emphasis in original). Moreover, as with previz, the GUI-based nature of machinima allows for a certain kind of visual language. As machinima practitioner Chris Burke (2013: 33) states, the abstract topologies of games 'allow us [as machinima designers] a far more plastic and manipulable approach to spatial and temporal aspects of our creations therein'. That is, machinima, while potentially including the shot-reverse shot editing and balanced compositions associated with classical filmmaking practices, also often takes advantage of the sweeping virtual camera and ethereal non-materiality of the mise-en-scène of its source game(s).

A fast, sweeping virtual camera which reveals the many elements and details of a digital creation is, then, a facet of digital image-making more broadly, with the planning of imagery, the content of finished entertainments, and the style of behind-the-scenes revelations similarly emphasising layering, virtual navigation, spatial access, and even a posthuman visual consciousness. This is a two-way street: the breakdown adopts the language of digital image-making in order to demonstrate the workings of digital image-making; meanwhile, the visual aesthetic of digital effect production bleeds across into the aesthetic of finalised digital media products themselves.

A short moment from *The Avengers* effectively demonstrates how all this works in action. In the extended climax of the film, a long take shows the various members of the titular superhero team working to one another's mutual benefit even though they are dispersed across mid-town Manhattan, each taking on different alien invaders. We swoop from an airborne Black Widow to the street-level combat of Captain America to the rooftop archery of Hawkeye via the aerial acrobatics of Iron Man, before settling on the brutal pugilism of Hulk and Thor. Narratively, the forty-second shot is a bravura display of the Avengers working together as a team. But how was it designed, and what does this have to do with VFX breakdowns and GUI visuality?

The shot, like the rest of the finale, was previsualised by Third Floor, a VFX company who describe themselves as 'the world's leading visualization studio', and who work on film, television, videogames, VR, and commercials (Third Floor n.d.). The final version is assembled from numerous separate greenscreen shots (of actors Scarlett Johansson, Chris Evans, Jeremy Renner, and Chris Hemsworth, among others) and a wealth of VFX imagery, and is presented as though it is an unbroken single take captured by an extremely mobile camera. Third Floor previsualisation supervisor Nick

Markel describes how in the sequence 'It was important creatively to keep all the Avengers involved and not feel like we were leaving any one character for too long', a statement suggesting that this previz team were endowed with a certain degree of agency over the shot's particulars (Seymour 2012). Likewise, the company's postvisualisation supervisor Gerardo Ramirez describes how the team 'first previsualised the shot to help map out the choreography. Once the elements were filmed, we were tasked with combining them into one continuous shot' (Seymour 2012). The shot is conceived and built in ways native to the GUI, which are intended to serve this thematic idea of coherence and assembled continuity.

In the ILM breakdown for the film, this shot is then highlighted. The initial frame of Black Widow is shown being assembled from composites (Johansson, digital models, backgrounds), then the shot plays as it does in the film for a few seconds, until Iron Man reaches Captain America on Park Avenue Viaduct. At this point, the shot is frozen, and the expository breakdown camera becomes unmoored from the film's finished virtual camera shot. Like a videogame's photo mode, the VFX breakdown camera sweeps up and away from the protagonists, moving fluidly around the surrounding buildings; unlike photo mode, it shows their undergirding digital wireframes, and swipes through the addition of textures and atmospherics such as smoke. Having established the scale of layers that cluster around but are not the subject of the action, the virtual camera of the breakdown swings quickly back down to street level, re-adopting the finished shot as Captain America undertakes a flying kick.[11]

Previz, final film, and VFX breakdown therefore all effectively overlap. The ILM VFX breakdown seeks in familiar ways to testify to the detail of the effects – it reveals the digital ontology of the buildings, and the veracity of the three-dimensional digital model of New York. But the way in which the breakdown does this crucially extends work that is already being undertaken by the choreography of the virtual camera shot as it appears in the final film. That is, the exposé of the breakdown and the spectacle of the finished film adopt highly comparable aesthetic registers, and even do so for similar rhetorical ends. As conceived and designed at previz, this long take narratively celebrates the way the separate

---

11 It is worth noting that the PS4 videogame *Marvel's Avengers* (2020) offers players exactly this kind of photo mode, allowing players to interrupt Captain America's demonstration that he hasn't missed leg day in order to explore frozen combat and its surrounding environs (although the game's narrative does not directly take in the New York battle depicted in the film).

superheroes have overcome their squabbles and now work together as the titular team. If the highly mobile camera of the finished film unites their diverse but coordinated fighting efforts, then likewise ILM's breakdown gestures towards the fragmented nature of the pieces that make up the shot's contents and how these come together triumphantly in the final, seamless render. In both cases, digital unification is applauded through the depiction of its constituent parts, and their linking through smooth virtual camera moves. From previz and techviz, to location shooting and VFX generation, to final rendition, this shot and its ancillary exposition announce not only the dazzling possibilities of digital effects, but also how these effects grant finished texts the mobility and virtuality of the viewport. The film may offer us verisimilitudinous, diegetic spectacle, but the nature of its presentation is deeply indebted to the GUI that has been used to produce this spectacle.

Conclusion

The kind of digital conglomeration that breakdowns describe is inherently gooey. As we have seen, the contemporary computer desktop is a layered, hyper-detailed site of interactive, spatial elements. It can contain multiple open programs, as well as potentially dozens of icons and even additional navigational information and prompts at its edges. All of this material is organised in depth, overlapping in a manner which is user directed, and which implies coherence and the opportunity for effective management. The above discussion reveals how the VFX breakdown therefore interprets the digital effects image as a GUI of sorts, as it imports the visual logic of the viewport from programs like Maya. Viewers vicariously experience the visuality of the effects worker, with rotating, zooming shots confirming the complexity and completeness of the digital scene, and iterative layering indicating how shots are built from multiple passes.

In proposing that the VFX image is a synthesis of multiple programs and processes which align in perfect harmony, breakdowns are almost a dream of desktop multitasking. Like the Apple Mission Control function described in Chapter 2, breakdowns split apart a complex environment of digital programs, showing their mutual co-presence. Swing-out shots show multiple image planes arrayed off-centre in a manner visually identical to Windows' Flip 3D shortcut (Figure 4.10). And even the most rudimentary green and blue screen shooting – common since the 1990s for productions

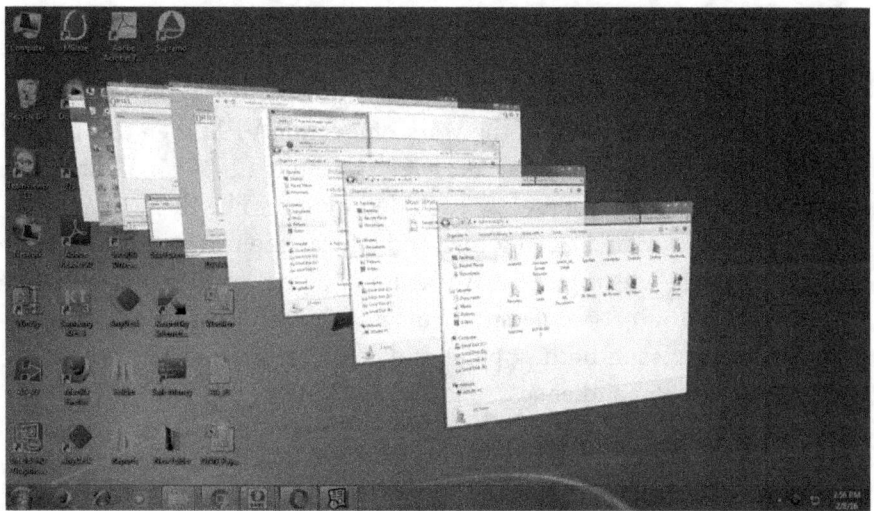

Figure 4.10 Windows' Flip 3D program window shortcut resembles the swing-out shots of figures 4.3, 4.4, and 4.5 (Sanjiv Creation, 2016). Frame enlargement from YouTube.

both expensive and not – is built on the premise that surroundings can be swapped out as needed, an idea also familiar from the GUI, with its customisable desktop background images. As such, a vicarious breakdown-style experience can be recreated by the GUI user simply by tapping shortcut keys, cycling through backgrounds, and altering the textures, colours, and positioning of program windows.

Moreover, breakdowns encourage us to be familiar and comfortable with the composited and flexible nature of digital images and our active engagement with them. As Purse (2018: 158) describes, the viewer of a breakdown, even if they do not work for ILM or UPP, are nonetheless likely to be familiar with 'synthesising and navigating [...] thickly stacked and complexly choreographed digital layers', and with 'oscillat[ing] between two-dimensional and three-dimensional perspectives' – because they do this every day on their phones and laptops. The filters and editing tools of popular photo sharing software, the digital compositing of apps like Face Changer, the multiple spatial perspectives offered by Google Maps (see Chapter 5), and the ability to resize, re-colour, and re-texture programs and other desktop elements all similarly render digital images sites of depth and perspectival multiplicity (Purse 2018: 158–9).

For all its gooiness, though, the breakdown simultaneously removes traces of the actual, much lengthier GUI-assisted labour that has produced these images. As I discuss in more detail elsewhere, breakdowns show nothing of the processes of VFX production beyond those that occur within a viewport, and their features of speed and iterative teleology work to create an impression of VFX production as effectively automatic, flawless, and almost instantaneous (Jones 2023a). If this erases VFX workers from displays of the work of creating VFX, then this is a far from inconsequential omission. As Hye Jean Chung (2017: 10) states, the wealth of information apparently provided by texts like this can actually work to elide the political, economic, and ethical implications of such production cultures. This is particularly acute in digital contexts, as 'the predominant rhetoric of seamlessness, magic, and automation attached to digital technologies in both popular and scholarly discourses encourages the tendency in film audiences, scholars, and industry specialists to disregard multiple stages of creative labor in film production pipelines' (Chung 2017: 1–2).

Far from just a niche 'making of' format, then, the VFX breakdown is a key expression and propagator of ideas about digital images and their manufacture in the GUI age. They tell us as much about how digital effects are *conceptualised* as they do about how a particular effects shot was *achieved*, if not considerably more. Their encapsulation of GUI visuality also makes this visuality more discernible in the aesthetics of other media like films, videogames, and machinima, as they operate as a kind of hinge or node connecting the formal features of contemporary digital texts with the GUI that produces and houses them. Their dreams of flexibility and customisation can even be detected in depictions of contemporary urbanism, the subject of the next chapter.

5
Graphic Urban Interface

We float above a sprawling yet strangely cramped metropolis. A dense collection of city blocks, factories, and leisure facilities stop suddenly at the edges of endless green fields, while a beautiful blue ocean runs along one side. Each of the buildings of this city has a specific, delineated function, which we can reveal by clicking on them. The residential skyscrapers – named things like 'Wilkins Plaza' and 'Gomez Lofts' – come with a caption and an emoji indicating how happy (or not) their occupants are. The population of 'Pitts Place' are displeased with their proximity to a factory ('A factory near my home! Why!?' they exclaim), and this is pulling down the overall satisfaction rating of the city. As unelected but all-powerful mayor, we resolve to do something about this, selecting the offending factory and dragging it several blocks away from the Pitts. Dropped into this new spot, it immediately resumes production of 'seeds' and 'chemicals', both of which will be ready in a couple of minutes. Pitts Place seems mollified, but to make our general populace even chirpier, we open up a menu of possible parks that can be built, dragging and dropping what is listed as a 'Row of Trees' into the gap vacated by the factory. Doing so temporarily turns the city into a mass of 3D vertical bars, each one visually telling us the level of satisfaction felt by every city block. Once dropped into position, the trees do their job, boosting all the adjacent happiness bars towards the sky, and adding to the overall contentment that the fictional populace feel about our mayoralty.

Just another day in Flexiville, the city I have created using the mobile videogame *SimCity: BuildIt* (2014). This game is just one of a host of cities that can be accessed using a GUI, but the malleability of its represented urban space is in many ways indicative of the kinds of newly flexible urban environments that can be imagined in the age of the desktop interface. Today's cities overlap with screens in many ways. Cities are sites of screen production, dissemination, reception and infrastructure. Images of their skylines and neighbourhoods circulate widely on screens in the form of films, television programs, videogames, apps, websites, and more. Their coordinates and contents also form the underpinning datasets of enormous simulations of the kind built and maintained by Google: interactive maps which are not only instrumental in getting us from a to b, but through which we also perceive and interpret our surroundings. Cities may be places that we live in, visit, and move through, but they are also things seen on and understood through our screens, where fictional cities – like SimCity's Flexiville – share space with existing urban realities – like the Google Map I squint at to get myself to an unfamiliar part of town.

This chapter begins to widen the purview of this book by thinking about the material consequences of GUI aesthetics on urban space. So, while I will consider textual representations of space and how they have been shaped by the rise of the computer desktop, I will also address the way this desktop changes space itself. After all, if the GUI provides perceptual access to the info-space of the computer, then it also provides access to other physical spaces, from the imagined spaces of fictional media to the concrete spaces visualised by Google Street View and similar programs.

The ability of screen technology to change space can be traced in various ways. As key elements of post-industrial life and entertainment, screens and screen images mobilise transformations in the layout of the contemporary city, contributing to new landscapes of signification (Gospidini 2006). Computation has concretely reshaped many urban centres thanks to the creation (and at times failure) of tech clusters: geographical zones which have powerful knock-on effects in the form gentrification, speculation, and social dislocation (Graham and Guy 2002). Digital advertising hoardings and information boards, meanwhile, literally embed the GUI within the urban environment: no major intersection is complete without a large-scale LED billboard or several, and smaller elements of urban infrastructure like bus stops are in many cities are now equipped with interactive screens (Jones 2019). And, on a global scale, infrastructures of screen media production and distribution – not to mention the creation of the screens themselves and their supporting technologies – has contributed to the ongoing climate crisis, literally restructuring the ecology of the planet (Maxwell and Miller 2012).

Instead of these points of interest, though, in this chapter I will focus on representations of urban environments that are found *within* GUI screens. I will consider how these representations have had knock-on effects on these environments themselves, and will argue that the dominant urbanism envisioned in the era of the GUI takes on new dimensions: the contemporary, gooey city is endowed with the perceptual qualities of radical personalisation and a particularly digital form of interactivity. Physical space, as a result, becomes a kind of extension of the GUI (a theme which will continue into Chapter 6, on programmable matter).

The first half of this chapter will show how screen entertainments viewed and produced using the desktop interface import aspects of this interface into how they think about their depictions of built space. That is, the use of the GUI to design and navigate built space allows our ideas of space to take on the flexible, composite attributes of the GUI itself. As Wendy Chun puts it, computers

> create a new dynamic reality: the files they offer us are more alive; the text that appears on their screens invites manipulation, addition, animation. Rather than stable text on paper, computers offer information that is flexible, programmable, transmissible, and ever-changing. (Chun 2011: 57)

This mutable desktop environment fuses with and extends the imagination of urban form as similarly programmable and virtual. Far from solely a feature of fictional texts, though, this imagination also changes the way we navigate cities themselves. As the second half of the chapter will show, interfaces like Google Street View and Google Earth present the city as a space of customised routes and personalised recommendations, a tourist's view of a filtered city. As a result, urban space becomes an urban interface, or a graphic urban interface: a site of layered, customisable data and haptic spatial interaction.

Altered urbanism

Before we reach our desired destination and discuss how the GUI changes our portrayals, understandings, and navigations of built space, we must take a few detours. Our course must be plotted first through some historical ideas of urban space as they have been described in Marxist spatial theory; then we must alight on the depiction of bricolage or composite spaces through cinematic editing; our penultimate stop-off takes in the sights of the recursive spaces of videogames; and our final waystation then considers the importance of screens to the navigation of urban space today. This itinerary provides the necessary contexts for us to take a closer look at the customisable interface-space in which we find ourselves in the era of the GUI.

We begin by stepping back in time. While cities in many ways change organically, haphazardly, and unexpectedly, top-down spatial management projects seeking to restructure the urban environment according to master plans have nonetheless been common since the industrial revolution. The razing of Paris by Baron Haussmann in the 1850s and 1860s was undertaken to impose more orderly geometry and to counteract the city's chaotic evolution up to that point. Le Corbusier's influential 1930 proposal of a 'radiant city' of super-skyscrapers and endless highways disregarded any existing urban reality. Robert Moses showed utter indifference to the reality of New York City and its inhabitants when cutting a 'meat ax' through the Bronx in the 1950s (Berman 1983: 294). And at the same time Moses was wielding his axe, the from-scratch design and construction of Brasília envisioned a modernist utopian capital fit for a newly prosperous Brazil. All such plans dismissed entrenched, historically contingent materiality, treating space instead as a void or an endlessly malleable substance.

Key moments in the history of modernity, these examples speak to an imagination of urban restructuring that remains prevalent today. This is an imagination of space as a site not of embedded meaning and contestation, but of flexible creation and re-creation by a sovereign power. This is to imagine space as 'abstract space' in the words of Marxist philosopher and spatial theorist Henri Lefebvre (1991: 229–91). Thinking of space in this fashion allows for its contents to be endlessly reshuffled, a process of 'creative destruction' in which space is simultaneously invested in and demolished to make room for new investments (Harvey 1990: 16–18, 106–7; Harvey 2006). The urban environment is less a site of organic processes than one of programmable actions and outcomes.

The imagination of abstract space is part of a larger 'restructuring of geographical space' that has occurred on a global scale from the 1960s onwards (Smith 1984: 1). Thanks to the ascendency of *laissez-faire* free market ideologies that emphasise privatisation and self-sufficiency, both cities and people are now required to continually adapt at short notice to the needs of an ever-capricious market, as they compete in a globalised arena for apparently limited resources. Such restructuring, by its nature, presumes malleability: as economic geographer David Harvey (1989: 256) describes, post-industrial capital accumulation is 'marked by a startling flexibility with respect to labor processes, labor markets, products, and patterns of consumption'.

This concept of flexibility recurs in readings of the contemporary city and geographical labour practices, and is crucial to theories and practices of neoliberalism. If neoliberalism as an economic theory asserts entrepreneurial self-investment and the malleability of individuals living within its dictates (as well as those caught in its inescapable web), then it likewise demands the same of space – at least conceptually. Urban theorist Edward Soja (2001: 42) argues that the 'postmetropolis' that has arisen in recent decades is often viewed by economic geographers 'primarily as an expression of a new regime of capitalist accumulation that is more flexibly organized than the rigid, hierarchical, mass production/mass consumption systems of the postwar era'. Likewise, for geographer Giuseppe Dematteis, the post-1970s city is a less stable, more responsive and malleable entity that that which preceded it. A given city is now only '*one* possible, deliberate construction: a local geographical order born out of the turbulence of global flows and with which it must interact in order to continue to exist' (Dematteis 2001: 113; emphasis in original).

The city is not only more flexible in itself, but must also actively communicate this flexibility in order to successfully participate in global markets of labour and capital investment. No longer a static product of historical process, the contemporary city is a dynamic 'product of self-organization', an 'asset' of 'risk capital to be ventured in global competition' (Dematteis 2001: 118). Witness cities in Europe and the US that lost manufacturing or port industries in the 1970s and aimed to demonstrate their flexibility and adaptability by pivoting to other sectors such as finance capital or the service industries. Baltimore, London, Bilbao, and others sought to enter alternative global marketplaces, shifting their use of land, buildings, and even people accordingly – often resulting in considerable social and economic strain. Relatedly, much discussed processes of gentrification in these and other cities reveal how the industries, economics and demographics of an urban area can profoundly and quickly change.[1]

These then, are real restructurings of lived space. Yet such material changes rely upon an underlying *imagination* of the city that believes it can be altered in this way: you need to conceive of urban space as flexible in order to treat and advertise it as such. As labour markets, production economies and consumption practices are seen to be endowed with new-found mobility in the post-industrial era, so too space and the city undergo conceptual alterations. As a result, it is necessary to think of contemporary urban flexibility as both material and conceptual, or what Jonathan Raban (1974) terms both 'hard' and 'soft'. We might think of this in terms of ware – the concrete lived reality and design of space is the hardware,

---

[1] Such changes adhere to neoliberal demands (an area contains more global businesses and receives more capital investment) but can disenfranchise local communities (increases in rents and the cost of living may displace once stable communities), among other negative effects (Gospodini 2006: 326).

while the software is the way in which this is conceptually framed. Here, software is not simply dependent on the dictates of hardware. Rather, the two mutually intertwine and shape one another's development and possibilities: pinned to certain forms of functionality, software will engender change in hardware to enable this functionality.

Today's urban software, or conceptual urban imagination, is tightly bound up with the desktop interface. Certainly, contemporary urbanism inherits from earlier periods the idea that cities can be carefully and intentionally designed and managed. But it revises this with some crucial software updates: namely, the assertion that cities can transform at the merest swipe of a touchscreen, and that the city is a kind of collection of composite elements from which an individual can pick and choose. Further consideration of this territory is still a little way down the road for us in this chapter, however. Before that, we must take another diversion, through non-interactive moving-image media. The act of audio-visual editing, as we will now see, plays a crucial role in inculcating an urban fabric that is open to acts of remixing. Initially undertaken through the cut, this remixing is now possible and even common within a single composite shot.

Personal space

Cinematic cities have long been virtual, hybrid constructs. An establishing shot of a particular skyline can give way to a scene that was shot in a completely different city. A chase scene – or any involving movement – can use the continuity of bodies leaving and entering the frame to unify vastly disparate locations (Jones 2015: 49–54). In the 1920s, Soviet filmmaker Lev Kuleshov fashioned a single urban space from scenes shot in Moscow (with Gogol's monument and the Moscow embankment visible) and Washington (establishing footage of the White House). Playing continuity editing against itself to unify that which was disparate, he called this 'creative geography' (Kuleshov 1974: 52). This composite urban production underlines the fluidity, virtuality, and produced nature of cinematic space – for all the emphasis on continuity in mainstream editing practices, the very act of producing or representing spatiotemporal cohesion is itself an act of creation, a hybridisation of time and space.

Normally, such composite cities are less visible as such. The contemporary TV show set in New York but filmed for the most part in Vancouver does not wish its viewers to be cognisant of this production reality.

However, cities that noticeably and palpably blend distinct urban realities have become much more common in recent years. Take, for instance, Christopher Nolan's *Batman* films (2005, 2008, 2012), which utilised extensive location shooting in a range of global cities – including Hong Kong, London, New York, and Chicago – to fashion a notably contemporary and pointedly hybrid Gotham City.[2] Somewhat more pronounced is the counter-factual deployment of iconic cityscapes across the *Transformers* franchise (2007, 2009, 2011, 2014, 2016). On the one hand, these films evince geographical authenticity – extended sequences occur in tourist landmarks (the Pyramids) and urban centres (Chicago, Hong Kong). On the other hand, the global production and assembly of action sequences from production footage taken within a range of urban centres results in multiple spatial anomalies. The fourth film, *Transformers: Age of Extinction* (2014), can make Hong Kong a crucial setting for its third act for the purposes of transnational box office appeal, but it can also bulk these Asian sequences out with footage filmed in US cities that offer generous tax rebates like Chicago and Detroit. What is surprising is that the skylines of the latter remain visible in many shots. That the Willis Tower is clearly visible in the background of a battle supposedly taking place in Kowloon Bay speaks less to shoddy continuity or lazy filmmaking, than to the idea asserted by these films that geographical veracity is much less important than spectacle.

Indeed, during a large-scale battle between alien robots in central Chicago in *Transformers: Dark of the Moon* (2011), Beijing's CCTV Headquarters can be glimpsed in the background. There is little reason for this structure to appear in an otherwise highly localised sequence, employing (and naming) as this sequence does Chicago landmarks like Trump Tower, Willis Tower, and Lake Michigan. CCTV Headquarters is an icon in and of itself, part of Beijing's wider embrace of cutting-edge architectural projects of global renown. Its presence is not accidental, as the shot was not filmed in Beijing, but is in fact a digital effects shot, the contents of which are programmable in their entirety. The building therefore appears to have been intentionally added, a way of making the environment as spectacularly recombinant as the titular Transformers themselves (an idea and sequence to which I will return in the next chapter).

---

2 Film and literary scholar Jarrad Cogle (2014) further notes how the blended, flexible approach to Gotham in these films impacts its intended mapping of a social reality. While they attempt a convincing articulation of contemporary urban space and the problems that plague it (wealth disparity, criminal gang culture, alienation), this simply cannot hold when the real-world coordinates of this space keep changing.

Even more direct remixing can be found in *Her* (2013) and *Big Hero 6* (2014), films which create their science-fictional urban spaces from a combination of US and Asian cities, and foreground impossible amalgamations. *Her* blends Los Angeles and Shanghai without motive or explanation in order to conjure a future US metropolis of pedestrian possibility, while *Big Hero 6* goes so far as to name its location San Fransokyo, a city with the geography of San Francisco but Japanese mise-en-scène (the Golden Gate Bridge is adorned with torii-style detailing). In neither case is this mere decoration. As Lawrence Webb (2016) argues, the setting of *Her* responds to utopian dreams about Los Angeles and US cities more generally, rendering the city a site of romantic possibility and successful globalisation. Meanwhile, *Big Hero 6*, with its Asian protagonists and soft anime stylings, aims to build a bricolage bridge between the Marvel brand and Asian consumers. The setting of San Fransokyo even also makes an appearance in the videogame *Kingdom Hearts III* (2019), in which the characters of the film team up with those from a variety of other properties owned by Disney (the central character can team up with Goofy, Buzz Lightyear, and Jack Sparrow, among many others).

Spatial flexibility is also common to videogames. Videogame environments can, after all, be considered 'recursive spaces', sites produced through the alignment of player, software, and hardware. As Aylish Wood (2012: 93) describes when she proposes this model of analysis, 'the gamer is both embedded within a space defined by the organization of objects, and also creating that space at one and the same time by altering the organization of objects'. When playing videogames, space is not just something we find ourselves in, but something actively produced through our movement and interaction with the game's technical system. In moving our avatar down the left path or the right path, we prompt the game's programming to render that path in particular, and so we take part in the materialisation of the screened world. Space is thus recursive in the sense that it is continually reconfigured by the interaction of gamer and game.

In videogames, then, we find an expansion of the idea that space can be user-generated and user-compliant, a site of continual feedback and potential manipulation. This comes to the foreground in particular texts. The archetypal early game *Tetris* (1984) demands spatial management on the part of the player, and requires her to perceive space as inherently changeable: screen territory must be altered from one state (occupied) to another (unoccupied) by creating horizontal lines that are entirely filled with blocks (which then disappear to provide more space). The more recent

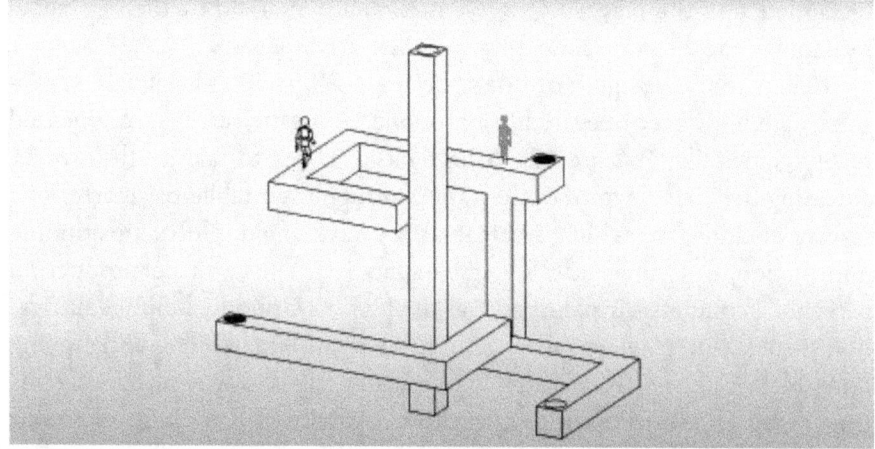

Figure 5.1 The player of *Echochrome* (2008) manipulates space in order to keep a constantly strolling figure from falling. Frame enlargement from PS4 gameplay.

Echochrome (2008) asks the player to rotate an abstract, Escher-esque structure in order to keep a walking stick-figure from falling into the void. Gaps in the schematic structure onscreen must be blocked so that the figure can walk smoothly behind them, or a ledge must be placed below the figure to catch it if it drops (Figure 5.1). *Manifold Garden* (2019) and *Maquette* (2020), meanwhile, place the first-person player within their fractal settings, where they must solve spatial puzzles that are literally recursive – infinite topological regressions in the former, and Matryoshka doll nested spaces in the latter.

In these games, every interaction with the gameworld takes the overt form of manipulating this world. Recursion is therefore easy to detect, since it is distilled into an explicit gameplay mechanic. Harder to discern in more conventional games, spatial feedback nonetheless remains a foundational pillar of all videogameplay (Wood 2012: 100–2). In first-person action-adventure *Dishonored* (2012), for instance, the player's actions – and their relative morality – results in the presence or absence of plague rats in the central setting of Dunwall, a steampunk metropolis. Gameplay here generates spatial features, even if the architecture of Dunwall itself remains fixed no matter what the player does (Zonaga and Carter 2019). In the third-person shooter *Control* (2018), meanwhile, a malevolent transdimensional force has infected a Brutalist government building, and gameplay involves solving puzzles and killing enemies to 'cleanse' these areas. Deformed, bulbous protrusions of concrete shift and slide back on themselves around the player's avatar when they initiate a certain command. These institutional spaces return to more recognisable architectural formations as they are reclaimed, and the player's progress is explicitly marked by their personal reshapings of otherwise alienating and alien-ated spaces.

Thanks to the ubiquity of smartphones, GPS, and Wi-Fi signals, videogames are no longer relegated to immobile, domestic screens. Augmented reality games like *Pokémon GO* (2016) ask players to take to the streets, accessing the virtual world of the game through their tablet or smartphone screen, an interface which amalgamates camera feed, global positioning information, and game code. Recursive space is not just a virtual production here, but a concrete-virtual hybrid, as the player's embodied mobile navigation shapes gameplay: we create gamespace by walking around and moving our tablet or phone. This is a trace of a wider trend in which the screen is considered an access point to a wealth of spatialised data invisible to our non-augmented eyes (Jones 2020: 102). It is also evidence of the increasing capacity for cities themselves to be composite creations of embodied movement and digital navigation. After all, whether chasing Pokémon or the bus, we increasingly rely on smartphone screens to traverse urban space.

Nanna Verhoeff proposes that such screens make our navigation of urban space into a form of 'performative cartography' (Verhoeff 2012: 13). This is a new regime of vision, one foregrounding navigation and all its interactive possibilities. Like the gamer's 'recursive' space, we simultaneously move and create our spatial reality. Mobile devices free their users from geographical limitations (although Wi-Fi signal may still be a factor), allowing them to navigate the city in a way that is enriched with personalised material. This might take the form of soundtracking one's walk through a Spotify playlist, consulting maps, searching for local recommendations, or observing the city itself through the screen (for instance to take a picture, or activate some form of augmented reality). Of course, the reality we seek to create is always a more user-friendly one. If the city we experience becomes more convenient and personalised thanks to our screens, then alongside this the city itself as an entity becomes more flexible, at least to those of us with access to these devices and their programs of personalisation.

Screening source code

The waypoints covered so far have charted our route to the involvement of the GUI in contemporary perceptions of the city. A great deal of spatial theory and city planning all imagines flexibility as an urban ideal, and this flexibility is remediated in the editing and amalgamation of moving-image media. Videogames and street exploration software then build on this by rendering urban spaces highly customisable, recursive at an individual level. This digitally flexible imagination then finds potent expression in a range of mainstream media material (the focus of this section), as well as in the way the city is presented in Google's suite of navigation technologies (the focus of the next). These texts and programs present a malleable, user-centric urban fabric which shares many attributes with those GUIs upon which these cities are viewed.

Let us begin with *Inception*, a 2010 blockbuster. A critical and commercial success, this film's central narrative conceit is a machine that allows characters to enter the dreams of others, a machine used by the film's protagonist Cobb (Leonardo DiCaprio) and his team to both steal secrets and plant ideas. Having established early on that dreams can be built and occupied, the film expands upon this by suggesting that dreamspaces can be transformed at will by the dreamer. Noteworthy scenes show Cobb explaining these rules to prospective dream architect Ariadne (Elliot Page) on the streets of Paris. This Paris, we find out part-way through the sequence, is itself actually a dreamspace, inhabited by the dreaming consciousnesses of Cobb and Ariadne. Once Ariadne gets over the shock of its verisimilitude (she initially did not know she was dreaming), she is given a tutorial by Cobb on how to manipulate her surroundings. Applying these lessons, she looks carefully down the length of rue Cesar Franck, at which point the end of the road begins arcing upwards and folding towards to sky, coming to rest, inverted, on the other half of the city. She and Cobb step up onto the angled street and nonchalantly continue their tour, with Ariadne subsequently generating a footbridge over Avenue du Président Kennedy from thin air, then playing idly with a series of chunky infinity mirrors she manifests on the pont de Bir-Hakeim.[3]

Inception is, on the surface, an aggressively analogue film. Its writer-director-producer, Christopher Nolan, is known to prefer film rather than digital cameras and uses extensive practical visual effects. *Inception*'s mise-en-scène features a few mobile phones but almost no computer technology of any sort – the machine used to send the characters to sleep has no screen interface, and paper models and white boards are improbably used to design the dream worlds rather than, say, videogame engines and CAD software. Such absences might seem to disavow the desktop's role in the

---

3 An important precursor to *Inception* is *Dark City*, a dystopian science fiction from 1998 in which malevolent aliens have abducted a portion of the population in order to discover the meaning of the human soul. This involves creating a city that floats unmoored through the galaxy, the architecture of which shifts and re-mixes in order to stage different scenarios.

film's flexible urban imagination – is the statement not being made that is avowedly not a digital process?

Perhaps – but this is something of a feint. *Inception* claims to be at least in part about dreams and the possibilities they offer for psychic spatial expressionism, but its spatial imagination is indebted instead to our experience of the computer interface.[4] The film shows a literally mobile city, one which the master planner can instantaneously reshape without the delay of planning permissions, land purchases, contract negotiations, or material destruction and construction.

Ariadne – named to evoke the Greek myth of the labyrinth that can only be navigated thanks to an eponymous thread – tests her spatial control by folding the very ground she walks on, then by manifesting and tweaking public space. These are not exactly acts of imaginative creation, but of rejigging – existing material is subjected to radical rearrangement and repurposing. Ariadne claims later that the spaces of real life might no longer be enough for her after the heady experience of dreamspaces, but this is probably not because the latter are aesthetically divergent from the former (since in the film they are often identical). Rather, it seems to be because dreamspaces offer her more creative freedom and control, allowing the repositioning of city blocks like so many program windows. Why ever leave the labyrinth, if your thread can change its very structure to your liking?

To think of urban space as something that can be personalised according to our preferences is to think of it through the lens of a GUI or an augmented reality display: as a site of personalised access and visual customisation. Similarly, when they find themselves in deep 'limbo' dreamspace, Cobb and his wife Mal (Marion Cotillard) embed the highly personal and historical within a corporate expanse, placing a series of out-of-place suburban houses and rural cottages in the middle of an urban plaza, and fashioning a Frank Lloyd Wright-style rural bungalow *within* a modernist skyscraper. As Cobb explains to Ariadne, while in the real world it would be necessary to choose to live in either a Mies van der Rohe glass-and-steel structure or a rural idyll, in this dream world both spaces can be impossibly conflated.[5] This is

---

4 As I argue elsewhere, these dreamspaces are also indebted to a mall-like consumerist imagination of corporate space – an imagination not unrelated to their connection with the GUI (Jones 2015: 107–15; see also Goss 1993).
5 These comments highlight the audacious double standard of Cobb and Mal's architectural and planning ideology: seeing the value of memory, history and personalisation, they have nonetheless built a city purposefully lacking these (except in their own private enclave).

the freedom of the GUI – a desktop space of personal remixing, of endless copying and pasting.

Another cinematic blockbuster, *Doctor Strange* (2016), admits – at least partially – to the digital basis of this imagination. In this superhero film, egotistical surgeon Dr Stephen Strange (Benedict Cumberbatch) learns the mysterious, supernatural ways of a group of ancient sorcerers who protect Earth. The film may explain its dazzling urban effects as magic, but magic and digital effects are often equated (Jones 2023a). The plot involves several trips into a 'mirror dimension' where space is rendered highly, catastrophically malleable. This conceit, much like *Inception*'s dreams, allows the film to visualise fantastical spatial alterations in urban centres. In London, the neoclassical architecture around Whitehall becomes a series of enormous grinding gears, and a slowly curving street is turned on its side to become a rolling conveyor belt. In New York, city blocks bend and become vortices, and duplicated skylines bear down from all sides of the frame (Figure 5.2). These changes, like Ariadne's, are enacted by characters who have inordinate spatial agency, who can wave their hands and change the very gravity and corporeality of their surroundings.

It is therefore no surprise that Strange's mentor The Ancient One (Tilda Swinton) describes the paranormal sorcery that she teaches as playing with the 'source code that shapes reality'. The world is again akin to a digital construct, one which can be tweaked by master programmers, those who can access the black box of the representational simulation and alter the source script. And indeed, source code is an apt metaphor here. In *Programmed*

Figure 5.2 New York is easily modified and duplicated by the sorcerers of *Doctor Strange* (2016). Frame enlargement from Disney+.

Visions (2011), Wendy Chun describes how such code is shaped by its executability. The code is not just an instruction, but the very foundations of the program to which it is linked. As such, it is connected to governmentality: source code 'is executable because it embodies the power of the executive, the power of enforcement that has traditionally – even within classic neoliberal logic – been the provenance of government' (Chun 2011: 27). This is about more than just having the authority to issue directives. Source code is ontologically foundational, the basis of the reality of the program. It must be *enacted* in order for a system to run, and so, as Chun (2011: 29) puts it, it is a command that brooks no opposition and requires no consensus, a 'conflation of instruction and result'. This programmability provides the programmer with a kind of sovereign power.

Knowing the code provides an individual with an 'x-ray vision' of a system's internal workings, and the implied – if not always actualised – power to alter this system at will (Chun 2011: 53). As Chun describes, this makes source code into a kind of 'sourcery', a magical incantation that changes reality. This is a dream(scape) or mirror (dimension) of governmentality in which the authority of the empowered individual is absolute, and neither material reality nor urban populations offer any friction. Chun connects this power to command-line logic (the code in source code), but while this is a framework that the Ancient One repeats in dialogue, nonetheless the transformations in *Doctor Strange* are achieved not through abstract and coded language, but rather a haptic engagement. The characters of *Inception* and *Doctor Strange* do not need to get to grips with programming languages or their metaphorical equivalents since the cities themselves allow for their direct editing by those with the right skills (or perhaps just the right interface). Buildings are stretched, resized and repositioned according to the user's whim. Just as VFX breakdowns promised to provide access to structures of digital labour and coding that were actually absent from their speedy, autonomous images, so too *Inception* and *Doctor Strange* offer a metaphor of tinkering that leaves the actual source code of these changes black-boxed. Like GUI users, all Strange and Ariadne have to do is point and click.

Procedural rhetoric and spatial flexibility

The desktop cities that these films depict are, in line with Anne Friedberg's (2006: 232) description of the GUI, 'gravity defying space[s]'. Simultaneously up and down, characters walk on streets which are now inverted and run up the sides of buildings, while structures overlap in ways that evoke not the perspectival cues of embodied vision but the overlapping of several program windows or the visual sorting of a shortcut key. Cities are turned into Maya-like viewports, sites for the user to rotate, inspect, and instantaneously tweak to better suit their needs. Supervillain Kaecilius (Mads Mikkelsen) has only to reach out his hands and twist them in the air, and the world around him reacts to these haptic commands as though he navigates an interface using a mouse or touchscreen. When he slams the side of a skyscraper, the structure does not buckle or break; instead, a rippling wave rolls across the length of the building in manner that evokes less any actual physical substance and more a computerised rendering of fluid dynamics, or an expanded version of Apple's slow genie effect (in which windows resize in supple slow motion), or those moments in VFX breakdowns when materials are isolated and their dynamic properties demonstrated in isolation (the crashing of a wave; the blossoming of an explosion). Meanwhile, Ariadne idly asks 'what happens when you start messing with the physics of it all?', as though she is tweaking the programmable collision dynamics and material attributes of CG objects via direct manipulation, just to see what that will do to the live running of a simulation.

This points us beyond these cinematic texts to another medium in which urban flexibility is not just visualised for a viewer but enacted by a player. Many videogames ask their users to not only navigate a recursive space but to also actively shape and re-shape their surroundings in a manner reminiscent of Ariadne's tinkering, and of GUI use generally. Games like *Minecraft* (2009) and *No Man's Sky* (2016) procedurally generate enormous environments which the player then explores and adapts by mining for resources and building increasingly ambitious structures. This is not just about navigation through a world or solving spatial puzzles, but about making active and extensive adaptations to the environment – everything from collecting wood in order to make a fire, to constructing complex semi-automated factories that produce precious materials, to working with other players to assemble highly detailed replications of other media worlds (Morris 2017).

Top-down strategy games which ask the player to manage land use and population activity are perhaps the most overt expression of the kind of desktop urbanism explored in this chapter. Designed by Will Wright and first released in 1989, *SimCity* games are a key example of the form, allowing the player to administer a range of infrastructural processes in a growing metropolis. The initial games proved so popular that they spawned a raft of related content, including a videogame which outstripped *SimCity* in popularity, *The Sims* (which replaced cities with domestic spaces and micromanagement). Visually, *SimCity* games pull back to give the player an aerial view of the urban space that is the focus of their gameplay activity. In early iterations of the franchise, this view is directly from above, in the manner of a map, and operation of the city was undertaken using extensive sidebars. However, over time and various iterations and releases for multiple platforms the game format has shifted to an isometric projection view, through and into which the player can zoom and rotate. Direct manipulation of elements within this map also become as important to gameplay than the use of drop-down menus, if not more so.

Somewhat typical of the franchise is *SimCity: BuildIt*, a mobile and tablet app released in 2014 and free to download (albeit with extensive microtransactions). The player begins with a blank parcel of land, upon which they are encouraged to construct roads, factories, power plants, residential zones, and other buildings. They can zoom and rotate the arising three-dimensional urban zone using touchscreen gestures, selecting building projects from subpanels and placing them into desired areas. When doing this, a green glow indicates that the intended structure will fit, in which case the player can 'drop' their selection, which will immediately start being built (with an attendant sound of ground being broken and the immediate appearance of cranes). On the other hand, a red outline notifies the player that they must choose somewhere else (perhaps because there is not sufficient room at the current site). The simple interface scales up as the player balances the various needs of the growing populace – and indeed, growth is the name of the game, with the player tempted by the new buildings, biomes, and resources that can be unlocked with larger and larger cities.

While other franchise entries have attempted to integrate some aspect of mixed-use land use and development (Kolson 1996: 43), this is not the case in *BuildIt*, where parcels of land support one building, and this building has one use. For all this monomania, once chosen these sites themselves are not fixed – unlike some *SimCity* releases for PCs, the smartphone and tablet app *BuildIt* allows and even encourages players to instantly move any building in order to maximise the productivity and pleasure of your citizens. A vocal minority complaining about living next to a factory? Simply select the industrial structure with your finger and drag it further away. This process of relocation will have no effect on the factory's productivity, as long as you connect the factory once again to the rest of your urban fabric with roads and power lines.

These are games of effective spatial management, and all entries in the *SimCity* franchise are merciless in the way that they prompt the player to maximise the value of land, resources, and citizenry. Simoleons, the in-game currency, are used to build spaces which then earn the player more Simoleons.

The happier and more numerous your city's populace, the more Simoleons you receive in 'taxes'. SimCities must relentlessly expand and upgrade – not to do so is to fail your hypothetical population and the game (Kłosiński 2016: 136). If this administrative balancing act sounds stressful (and it is), the game is at pains to render fictional urban management a pleasurable experience. Like other popular mobile games such as *Angry Birds* (2009) and *Fruit Ninja* (2010), *BuildIt* places great emphasis on haptic screen swiping and direct manipulation and provides positive reinforcement when these are undertaken. Grateful messages from citizens appear above their homes when they are happy, trails of glowing gold twinkle from city hall to your coffers to indicate the collection of tax income, and there is a flurry of triumphant music and sparkling graphics when the player 'levels up'.

This gameplay encodes the kind of neoliberal spatial flexibility described above within what can be called *SimCity*'s procedural rhetoric. As put forward by videogame theorist and philosopher Ian Bogost (2010: 3), 'procedural rhetoric' is a way of describing how the mechanics and tasks of a system convince their users of certain ideological presumptions and inculcate certain psychological habits. For Bogost, videogames are therefore 'persuasive' in the way they make suppositions about systems, and about the way the player interacts with those systems. The gameplay universe of *SimCity* prompts the creation of more and more densely packed skyscrapers, as these make the most Simoleons out of the space available (and Simoleans = happy Sims = more investment = player progress through levelling up). The franchise therefore proposes that only particular kinds of urban form – namely, commercial, high-density developments, with a smattering of parks and privatised leisure provisions – can successfully flourish and reward their investors. The higher the literal skyscrapers, the higher the status bars of citizen satisfaction (as long as all requirements of leisure, education, industry, and so on are also being successfully balanced).

These processes of gentrification have no discontents. In *BuildIt* in particular, Sims are not affronted by continuous rezoning and tweaking – they only become angry if they must continue to live near a garbage dump, or without a local fire station. Since they will leave en masse if their needs are not met, the player mayor must move buildings around to ensure satisfaction. Urban flexibility is a system requirement: in the early portions of the game, the player can only afford small fire and police stations; as the population grows, these must be upgraded, but also often moved to ensure they provide the necessary coverage (multiple stations are needed depending on the size of the city). In the case of these and other system-designed problems, spatial repositioning and repurposing are always a viable solution, and sometimes even the only solution. The 'creative destruction' diagnosed by Harvey as a consequence of the neoliberal city is here itself repositioned from by-product to the name of the game.

The sovereign power granted to a SimCity mayor means that social services can even be switched off or not built in the first place, since they are not state guaranteed elements of urban infrastructure but mayoral choices to appease a dissatisfied consumer-citizenry (Kłosiński 2016: 138).[6] One of the earliest problems to be encountered in any *SimCity* game is the balancing of loss-making public services like fire stations and water utilities (which are among the first things to be demanded by your fledgling population) with the more attractive activities of generating profit and expanding real estate. Creating mechanisms that ensure basic human rights regarding safety and housing are here self-interested manoeuvres, necessary expenditures to be undertaken on the way to more personal enrichment during the player's endless term in office. Daniel Dooghan (2019) therefore argues that sandbox games of this sort function as 'apologetics of neoliberalism'. Emphasising the creative possibilities of spatial personalisation on increasingly grand scales, and allowing for the constant remodelling of one's freely given surroundings, *SimCity*, *Minecraft*, and their ilk encourage the player to read the world of the game as a place 'full of resources to be consumed, without concern for ownership or equity, where technological superiority becomes justification for action, and individual labor is always fairly rewarded' (Dooghan 2019: 71).

Appearing on desktops, SimCities offer a desktop-like space of access and personalisation. Chun (2011: 8) describes how GUIs seek to create empowered and powerful users, subjects who are 'driven to know, driven to map, to zoom in and out, to manipulate, and to act'. *SimCity* demands this manipulation and action, and in incarnations like *BuildIt* it encourages the player to zoom and click as ways of getting to know their city better, and to milk further resources from it. Asking the player to become a spatial programmer, it places them in the same role as Ariadne and Kaecilius. In *Inception* and *Doctor Strange*, after all, characters act like SimCity mayors, flexibly altering their surroundings with pinches and swipes. These changes manifest with similar instantaneity, occurring without the expenditure of any more effort than the waving of a hand. Conjured without resistance or accident, these decisions, once made, can even be overturned with little consequence by further haptic reprogramming. *Inception*, *Doctor Strange* and *BuildIt*

---

6 Although neglecting such public services does impede the growth of the city and the options open to the player.

therefore engage in the same sorcery as VFX breakdowns, turning difficult, time-consuming, and resource-intensive processes into immediate conjurations. One striking shot in *Inception* shows Cobb and Mal in limbo building and demolishing sandcastles, structures which simultaneously manifest as enormous skyscrapers in the distance behind them, while wide shots show hundreds of miles of identikit skyscrapers, generated by the couple merely for the sake of it, their own out-of-control SimCity.

Where do you want to go today?

In the texts described above, the city becomes a program to be written and re-written, a game to be played. The films imagine spatial programmers at work, and the videogames prompt us to ourselves become programmers of space. If the cities being programmed in these cases are virtual and representational, the same functionality nonetheless creeps into the real world. Thanks to our use of the GUI and its urban navigation tools, movements through concrete, lived surroundings can adopt these same qualities of flexibility and customisation, at least in terms of our experience and expectations of space.

This is most clear in the case of Google's suite of locative apps. Consisting of Google Maps, Google Street View, and Google Earth, these tools allow us to program our itineraries through urban space in highly personalised ways, plotting routes, finding destinations, and warning us of transportation snarl ups. Often feeling incidental, they are significant aspects of contemporary GUI use: the company claims that Maps alone has more than a billion users (Glasgow 2020). Many of the desktop media explored in Chapter 1, meanwhile, employ one of these apps – or a non-branded equivalent – in some way: *Transformers: The Premake* plots the geographical sites of filming locations on a map of Chicago, while *Open Windows* uses maps and real-time vehicle tracking to flesh out a car chase seen only through dashcams and webcams.

The various apps and technologies in Google's storehouse were all originally developed with slightly different functionalities and emphases – historically, thanks to its release prior to the widespread adoption of smartphones, Earth is more associated with virtual tourism and spectacle than with wayfinding, for instance – but in many ways they are indistinguishable to users now.[7] Whatever the program, location data is inputted by the user in

---

7 Earth may offer its own suite of further cartographies in the form of under-ocean, telescopic, and Lunar and Martian data, but Maps allows users to select satellite and 3D

the form of a postal code, the name of a landmark, typed GPS coordinates, or the self-registered geolocation of the device being used. This triggers the visual display of that space, in the form of an aerial, isometric, or street level view, and this can often be rendered as either schematic or verisimilitudinous, or some combination thereof. Navigation is then possible by clicking and dragging a cursor or swiping and pinching a touch screen. Users can also turn on various forms of annotation, which will then appear embedded or as logos or pop-ups upon the displayed map.

The simplicity of the interface belies the complex material histories of these technologies. While they are now consumer products and conveniences, these apps initially arose through military research and development: the Global Positioning System upon which they rely was launched by the US military in the 1970s, and although increasingly opened up to civilian use under the presidencies of Ronald Raegan and Bill Clinton, this satellite infrastructure remains under the control of the US Department of Defence and US Space Force (Schroeer 2000). Meanwhile, the specific technology now known as Google Earth started life inside a data company called Keyhole, which was bought by a CIA-funded venture capital firm in 2003, at which point the geospatial technology was used to plan elements of the invasion and subsequent occupation of Iraq (Levine 2018). Google acquired Keyhole the following year, and Keyhole's founder, John Hanke, would soon lead Google's maps division before later founding Niantic, a software company that emerged from Google and which created and released *Pokémon GO*, a game in which Google's mapping software is fundamental (Zuboff 2019: 117).

The navigation these GUI apps offer seems to be a far cry from the flexibility envisioned in *Inception*, *Doctor Strange* and *SimCity*. For all their military lineage, Google's (m)apps principally seem like nothing more than the straightforward migration of physical, paper-based maps onto the GUI screen. More convenient than a cumbersome, multiply folded A2 sheet, they perform much the same function as this analogue counterpart, showing users how to get from a to b. Yet, of course, their placement within the graphic user interface, along with their reliance upon the network connectivity that is today synonymous with such interfaces, means that quite different representational and navigational operations are in play. Maps is much more than just a collection of maps, Street View is more than simply a series of street views, and Earth is much less grounded than it might first

---

views that are effectively the same as those offered by Earth, and Street View (sometimes) automatically shifts into the aerial views of Earth if the user zooms out enough.

appear, and in all instances space is endowed with a gooiness that marks out these technologies from any analogue precursors or equivalents.

To get a sense of this, let's start with an aerial view. In the case of the kinds of god's-eye-view images of terrain that these apps provide, what the Google user sees is not a live or recent photograph, captured by a camera. Instead, they navigate a holistic globe generated from many years of satellite and aircraft imagery. This is a sutured, digital creation which allows for fluid movement and features consistently cloudless skies. It can take the form of a 2D plane or a 3D model: in the latter, the images of buildings and geographical features are mapped onto volumetric forms, which allows for motion parallax during aerial movement, creating less a map and more a model. From this sky-view, users can switch to Street View by selecting a small icon of a person (known as 'Pegman') from the bottom right corner of the screen and dropping it onto any highlighted street; this changes the visual field to a ground level perspective, at which point users can again navigate around the selected area through clicks or swipes. This Street View content is another composite creation, an amalgamation of photographic material captured by fleets of Google cars and other vehicles.

The navigation provided by these tools comes with its own visual quirks. The photographic composites of Street View are for the most part highly detailed, offering sharp resolution and a wide focal plane (although some fish-eye distortions can arise). If this seems a promisingly Bazinian totalised recreation of space, then this dream is thwarted somewhat when this material warps and spasms as the user darts perceptually down the road: despite the investments made by Google to create software providing smooth transitions across different 360° photographs and between map and photograph, at such moments the countless individual photographic plates can nonetheless become perceptible as discrete units between which one skips (Hoelzl and Marie 2014: 265).[8]

The cities pictured, meanwhile, are distinctive in other ways. Images may depict cities in which everyday activity is taking place – with pedestrians on the pavements and cars on the roads – but this activity is frozen and captured sometimes in odd configurations, and the people have no faces because these have been algorithmically blurred out as a concession

---

8 These transitions are very much like the (very frustrating) movement controls in VR games like *Doom VFR* (2017) in which spatial navigation is achieved by targeting a nearby area and pressing a button, at which point the player 'teleports' through space. In both cases, the virtual environment promises total access and navigation, but provides a series of embedded positions rather than the possibility of flowing movement.

to privacy concerns. These are lived cities, then, but populated with anonymous and static entities who are meant to be ignored in favour of the terrain and features of location. Aerial views, meanwhile, show pavements shorn of people, and very few cars in the act of travel, these elements also having been algorithmically scrubbed. The result is a quasi-post-apocalyptic terrain, as though the facial blurring operation that began in Street View has extended into an unthinkable rendition of local populations and their physical traces. This subtraction is at times only half complete, as glimpsed vehicles shimmer translucently when the automated compositing software has not quite managed to remove them from the scene.

There is a radical novelty to the spatial experience these tools provide, especially in their mobile incarnations. Thanks to smartphone GPS data, users are provided real-time information about where they are within the observed map. This alters our relationship with our surroundings: unlike an analogue map, we always know (Wi-Fi signal allowing) exactly where we are in a digital projection. This, along with the visual capacity to move down streets and toggle effortlessly between map and street views, allows digital maps to become 'tours' as much as 'maps' – a distinction foregrounded by French sociologist Michel de Certeau in the context of the verbal delivery of spatial knowledge. A 'map', he points out, schematically describes the placement of space as a fact ('room x is next to room y'), whereas a 'tour' articulates movements and embodied relations ('you go through room x to reach room y') (de Certeau 1984: 119).[9] The latter outlines for the listener a series of actions rather than providing a fixed image of space. So while analogue maps are always maps in that they show the layout of space, digital maps offer both this layout and an imagined, lived itinerary which can be customised by the user.

These Google tours are then made even more personal through their interactivity. When navigating Street View, our clicks, drags, and swipes move us from location to location, and even if we happen to be observing the schematic aerial diagram of Google Maps there is the tendency to avoid leaving this image as it is initially presented. Why just look at a static slice, when we can do so much more? The edges, corners, and sidebars of the program window contain prompts to a wealth of tasks: plus and minus boxes for zooming; thumbnails of alternative visual presentations (such as a terrain map or virtual Street View composite showing particular environmental features); icons of cyclists and cars to remind us we could change the proposed vehicle of a hypothetical journey we are plotting; even tabs

---

9 In this passage, de Certeau draws on Linde and Labov 1975.

prompting us to search for takeaways or to 'explore' our local area ... We are not only always made aware of where exactly we are, but are also insistently reminded that we could harvest more information about this locality or even navigate elsewhere with ease.

This returns us to Frosh's definition of operative attention described in Chapter 1, and the inevitable 'sensorimotor restlessness' of GUI media navigation (Frosh 2019: 154). The focus in these apps is on interaction, not (just) observation. *Is* there a takeaway nearby? *Has* this side alley been photographed for Street View? *Can* I fly inside this local landmark? Asking these questions of the system allows users to engage with it in ways that create an impression of control. We bend space to our will as we reveal the features necessary to us in the moment: street names, local businesses, points of nearby interest. The city is sorted and remixed into only what we need it to be, and even the strangers we share it with are blurred or extracted. As Chun (2011: 62–3) states of GUIs generally but with specific reference to Google Earth, the desktop is framed as empowering through its emphasis on direct manipulation: users who can enact visible changes in represented screen content feel more enjoyment and confidence. The more such features these tools provide, the more power the user seems to be granted. These GUI maps create a directly manipulable (representation of the) city, offering users experiences of extra agency and customisation within lived space.

The representational realism offered by many of these apps then extends aspects of this spatial mastery. Schematics are available, but great effort has been expended in also crafting a photorealistic world to which we can also toggle, and through which we can vicariously travel. If the amplifying realism of the desktop traced in Chapter 2 seeks to make the screen a habitable environment, then Google's touristic maps show the extent to which this has been successful. The street is imported into the screen in the form of photographs and 3D composites, and then this street can be treated like a screen, as so many layers and possible program functions, all of which can be manipulated by the user.[10]

---

10 Augmented reality games like the aforementioned *Pokémon GO* then perform this intermingling through their own hybrid interfaces. This videogame extends the hugely popular *Pokémon* franchise into the real world, prompting players to navigate their physical surroundings in order to search for and take part in digital fictions embedded at certain GPS coordinates. These fictions are presented as spatially embedded in the physical world when seen through the cameras of personal devices like smartphones. Users encounter Caterpies on their doorsteps, Stantlers in the train station, Jigglypuffs in the town square, and perhaps even a Magikarp while they relieve themselves in the office bathroom. The presence of such strange creatures transforms the city into a space

The adaptability of the navigational images provided by Google's suite of mapping programs therefore grants the user something of the power conferred upon Ariadne, Kaecilius, and the SimCity mayor. The lived city is placed in the hands of the individual user, and they can re-tool it to their preferences. Certain features can be highlighted at the click of a button, altering the user's perception of their surroundings – which effectively alters these surroundings themselves. Selecting 'bars and pubs nearby' turns the city into a site of easy consumer pleasure; switching to traffic navigation allows the user to see which roads are congested, and so re-route themselves and maximise the efficiency of their personal urban experience. City structures themselves may not have the flexibility imagined by *Inception*, *Doctor Strange*, and the *SimCity* franchise, but the city as perceived by the user becomes a form of recursive space, an environment actively generated by the interface of user, software, and hardware.

As we have seen, Verhoeff proposes that the mobile cartography of smartphone navigation changes the way we see the city. A closer look at Google's maps reveals how the films and videogames explored earlier in this chapter trace such changes, and re-code them as spectacular entertainment. And all of these – functional app, blockbuster film, mobile videogame – are indebted to the affordances and experiences enabled by the GUI.

If we operate the maps provided by Google, and so feel a sense of mastery as we render the city flexible and customisable, then it is important to note in closing that we are equally ourselves operated upon by these maps. Google's mapping software takes aim at us, targeting users with its own customised ads and algorithmically personalised suggestions (Hoelzl and Marie 2014: 267). At times convenient, at times creepy, this seemingly benevolent surveillance is by now an expected part of any app of this sort. But these useful, entertaining, tailored maps are integral parts of a larger system of data capture and commodification which is dependent on GUI use.

Shoshana Zuboff (2019: 8) calls this surveillance capitalism, a new but enormously powerful mode of capital production that 'unilaterally claims human experience as free raw material for translation into behavioural data'. In Zuboff's (2019: 9) reading, Google is the master of this new market form, a pioneer in the reimagining of digital connectivity from an implicitly pro-social, democratising opportunity to a relentlessly commercial phenomenon. Google's many archiving procedures – from indexing the web

---

of magical, unusual sights, and gives the player privileged access to this world. Thanks to mobile screens, the lived city is rendered into a gamespace.

to scanning books to photographing physical streets – are undertaken not out of some beneficent impulse to bring knowledge to all, but for the chance to sell advertisers data about the way in which users access these massive, interlinked archives.

This relies on a presumption of access and entitlement: as with Google's other endeavours, Maps, Street View, and Earth presume their raw material to be an unclaimed resource, virgin territory in which they can plant a digital flag. Just as the company began scanning millions of books and making them available online without first establishing the legality of doing so (Hillis et al. 2013: 146–8), so too their mapping technologies act as if all public space is fair game for capture, using a variety of vehicles to harvest visual data without contacting national, corporate, or individual agents for permission and without announcing the undertaking of this act of data collection. As Zuboff outlines, this is an intentional strategy to normalise such conduct, creating subtly different expectations of ownership and privacy for the online archives of the twenty-first century.

Google's (m)apps provide searchable simulations that are created through the amalgamation and algorithmic processing of GPS information, publicly available infrastructure documentation, and images captured both by Google's many vehicles and uploaded without charge by its many users. These simulations are valuable on their own terms: they make the Google platform more attractive and useful, and so boost its value as real estate for advertisers. More than this, though, such simulations function as part of Google's wider project of capturing 'behavioural surplus', Zuboff's term for data regarding our movements, our musings, and even – thanks in part through the work of subsidiaries like DeepMind – our thoughts. Merging these spatial simulations with the real-time tracking data of millions of Google-enabled smartphones provides staggeringly comprehensive information not only about how we move but also how we plan and modify our travel arrangements, and the relationship between those sites we visit virtually and those we journey to in person. This data in turn allows Google to intervene in our behaviour, prodding us this way or that, usually to steer us to some commodity or another. In Zuboff's words, the ambition of the company becomes *'no longer [...] only about routes, but about routing'* (Zuboff 2019: 152; emphasis in original). Control of the map allows advertising to occur flawlessly, invisibly, and in a way that literally points the docile user in the direction of the commodity being sold, regardless of this user's other intentions. The tour of de Certeau – 'you go left at the coffee shop' – becomes a consumerist imperative: 'you go left and into the coffee shop'.

This fits what Zuboff sees as surveillance capitalism's cycle of dispossession: corporate agents claim ownership of that which was previously unthinkable as a capitalist product (our social relations and their particular tenor and flow; our tiny hesitations and unthought detours on our commute to work), then build programs which shape future actions through recommendations or through the content of seemingly neutral embedded information. This, for Zuboff, is a market that trades in behavioural futures, and it reveals prediction to be the first step in lucrative coercion and control. With this model in mind, the smartphone map user becomes less the empowered mayor of a flexibly neoliberal city, and more an Ariadne whose thread ties her invisibly to a corporate maze.

Conclusion

If there is a final piece in this puzzle of flexible urban imaginations, it is an acrylonitrile butadiene styrene polymer one. Lego, an unerringly successful global brand which has even overtaken companies like Amazon and Google in the late 2010s in terms of brand strength and reputation (Mazzarella and Hains 2019: 2), offers its own dream of urban customisation. Consisting of innumerable types of brick, Lego encourages its users to recombine pieces in an endless number of ways. Nonetheless, it is frequently sold in themed sets, the most notable for present purposes being that of Lego City. This collection, available since 2005, includes a range of infrastructural elements found in the modern city, such as emergency services (police stations, fire engines), transportation facilities (trains, auto repair shops) and consumer destinations (a donut shop). The theme communicates an idea of urban life as consumerist and scientifically ambitious – space shuttle and ocean exploration sets sit alongside ski resorts – while also benefitting from extremely well-resourced public safety organisations (the police force is equipped with drones and planes).[11] Lego's inherent logic of possibility generates an urban space that is simultaneously stable in its limited referents – police, fire, transport, construction, downtown – but also highly, fundamentally flexible in its particulars – any building can be swapped for another, and, in being played on carpets or kitchen tables, individual structures are unlikely to have fixed geographical placements. The brand itself has even increasingly moved into urban planning contexts: workshops and art installations have provided

---

11 This aligns with some of the core services that need to be rendered in a SimCity, as police and fire stations are crucial for growing one's Sim population in this game.

members of the public with piles of bricks to design the cities they would like to live in, while MIT's Department of Urban Studies and Planning have employed Lego alongside augmented reality to render the modelling of complex urban change more tactile and intuitive (Gillies 2014; Poon 2015).

The Lego Movie (2014) further celebrates the urban fluidity offered by this toy. Early on, the film explores the kind of city created by such sets – a city both literally assembled through the toy pieces, and ideologically generated through the assertions made by such sets about what constitutes successful urban space. The protagonist Emmet (Chris Pratt) wakes up in a small, modular apartment, with all his entertainment, food, and hygiene needs catered for (he even celebrates these in a running monologue). Strolling into the sunny street to go to work, he greets his neighbours and purchases a $37 coffee from a corporate cafe, expressing delight at the eye-watering price. All around him, the Lego city pulses with automotive movement, its populace singing the film's theme song 'Everything is Awesome'. And indeed, everything *is* awesome in this represented urban space: mindless pop tunes and overpriced coffee can be enjoyed in abundance, traffic moves swiftly, and everyone knows their neighbours by name.

The villain of the film, President Business (Will Ferrell), is a corporate leader who is horrified by the potential for creativity and self-expression inherent in Lego bricks, and seeks to glue all his Lego domain together, including the urban centre Bricksburg. He is opposed by a group of 'master builders', renegades who choose to forsake instructions of any kind. The plot's conflict between order and chaos, fixity and flexibility, generally valorises the latter – towards the end of the film, a meta-textual turn takes us out of the animated Lego world we have been watching, revealing it to be the property of a live-action middle-aged bureaucrat. This man wrestles with his creatively minded young son about the value and use of Lego, with the former demanding methodical organisation, and the latter favouring anarchic reinvention. But President/Lord/Father Business soon learns the error of his ways, and joins his son in a free play session in which the creative, rather than prescriptive possibilities of the toy are embraced. As an extension of an enormously popular toy franchise, then, the film affirms the toy's value as a creative tool: Lego sets may be sold on the basis that the pieces build a certain vehicle or building, and may contain instructions to this end, but the consumer has the power to reject these prescriptions, and make (and remake) whatever they choose. Despite the villain Business's desire for fixity, constant spatial restructuring is sketched as a key element of urban life. In the animated world, Emmet and a large crowd of blue-collar workers are gainfully employed demolishing and remaking entire neighbourhoods apparently for the sake of it. In light of this, glue is framed not only as a threat to the creative potential of individual creative play, but also as a danger to the everyday pulsing life of the metropolis and its highly profitable processes of creative destruction. The toy, whether presented in the film, played with by consumers, or employed as a tool by university urban planning departments, always encodes urban space as a site of endless recombination, and devoid of history and fixity.

This makes Lego an apt metaphor for the gooification of urban life (and the proliferation of Lego videogames, many connected to major transmedia brands, only underlines this suitability). The flexible cities of films, games, television programs, toys, and apps, all not only *reflect* a GUI-inflected imagination of urban form, then, but *actively participate in and help constitute* an urban ideal of literal and metaphorical flexibility. The cities and buildings discussed here disregard the material restrictions and messy complexities of urban form, and instead bestow physical structures with the instant flexibility and personalisation of the GUI. This gooiness conceives of space as a blank slate filled with programmable objects, and such objects will be the subject of the next chapter.

6

Programming Matter

Deep inside the Chicago headquarters of technology company Kinetic Solutions Incorporated (KSI) is a top-secret military wing. During a tour of this facility, the company's supercilious CEO Joshua Joyce (Stanley Tucci) exhibits the 'quantum leap' that he believes will give KSI the edge on all global competitors. 'It's the Holy Grail: Transformium', an associate (James Bachman) calls it, which Joyce jumps in to explain is a catchy, focus-grouped and trademarked moniker. What is so special about this substance? It is 'programmable matter', and now that KSI have 'mapped' its 'genome' they can control it as they see fit. To demonstrate this, Joyce lifts a small white ball from the table in front of him; the ball begins to float above his hand, before suddenly disassembling into a seemingly weightless, endlessly squirming cloud of small white cubes and intersecting geometric lines. 'Sensual, almost', Joyce comments as this cloud moves with sinuous elegance in the space between his hands. 'Do you like music?' he then asks, and the undulation of cubes suddenly coheres in his outstretched hand as a Beats Pill, a brand of portable Bluetooth speaker. 'Perhaps something a little more violent?' he prompts, and the substance morphs into a handgun.

This sequence takes place halfway through *Transformers: Age of Extinction*, a 2014 blockbuster. The subject of Kevin B. Lee's *Premake* video essay discussed in Chapter 1, the film is either a barrage of nonsensical and offensive spectacle or a trace of the 'reinvention of cinema in the age of polymorphous and ubiquitous screen culture', depending on who you ask (Koepnick 2018: 19). Indeed, it may well be both. This sequence, and the sub-plot it kick-starts involving an army of KSI-produced robot soldiers hijacked by the consciousness of franchise master-villain Megatron, indicates the film's own preoccupations with polymorphism. The enormous robot aliens of the series are heavy and machinic: they wreak palpable physical destruction and emit mechanical clunks and whirrs. But they are also light and digital, products of VFX work which, for all the perceptual realism in play, can seem disconnected from all physical surroundings. They shapeshift fluidly, impossibly, hypnotically, and fling themselves through space in inconceivable ways. Like Joyce's programmable matter – which can shift in the blink of an eye from consumer entertainment commodity to functioning weapon – Transformers are manifestations of digital possibility made narratively material.

This idea of digital matter has a long history, one closely connected to the interface. In 1965, Ivan Sutherland offered a prescient discussion of the 'ultimate display', a computer interface which would not only be kinesthetic and highly responsive to user input, but which would not even be confined by the boundaries of a screen:

> The ultimate display would, of course, be a room within which the computer can control the existence of matter. A chair displayed in such a room would be good enough to sit in. Handcuffs displayed in such a room would be confining, and a bullet displayed in such a room would be fatal. (Sutherland 1965)

A key – albeit brief – text in the archaeology of the contemporary GUI, Sutherland's proposal manifests in *Age of Extinction* and elsewhere, and in this chapter I explore several discourses and media texts which imagine the screen and its aesthetics and possibilities spilling out into material reality in exactly this way. Building on the last chapter's discussion of the ways in which GUI functionality intersects with ideas about built space today, I here consider various expressions of digitally generated objects and spaces, as well as the deeper conception of digitally generated materiality itself.

The desktop interface impacts material space partly through the new capacities of computational design it offers. Simply put, structures can be conceived and built which were not possible prior to GUI programming. Complex algorithmic modelling has become increasingly prominent in architectural discourse and practice, and this form of design often claims to imbue material substance with the liveliness and pliability of a desktop program. Architecture itself becomes an ultimate display, a manifestation of digital possibility. There is even a particular aesthetic to all this, and it is one that we have glancingly encountered before, in Chapter 4's discussion of VFX breakdowns. In those videos, the computational quality of images and elements is revealed in part through the polished-pebble quality they exhibit before any textures or other features of perceptual realism are layered in. If added textures are in some contexts called 'skins', then the sculptural, unadorned shapes beneath them might be the muscle and bone of digital imagery. A visual mode associated with the unfinished workflow of a virtual object as it might appear in a program like Maya or Houdini, this aesthetic migrates far beyond such confines. As I will show, it has become associated with programmable digital objects generally, especially those of contemporary architecture. Yet for all that its use in architectural contexts might imply fixity and stability, this polymer style is also wedded to an idea(l) of flux both within and beyond building design.

As hinted at by *Age of Extinction*, manifestations of digital materiality take the form of fractal, undulating, thrillingly unpredictable (but ultimately controllable) substances. The sensuality of this materialised code lies in its delicate receptiveness to gesture and environment. This is a dream of digital pliancy. But, as a dream, it is a kind of vapourware. More investment opportunity than tangible artefact, programmable matter is, like the visions of urban flexibility shown in the previous chapter, more of a guiding principle and conceptual belief than a material possibility. As such, it is fitting that Transformium is introduced in the form of a product demo.[1] Similarly, some of this chapter's later objects of analysis are buildings which have never been built and were never intended to be. Nonetheless, these visions of screen interactivity and GUI functionality have serious material consequences.

Animate form

Like it has on many other fields, digital technology has had a profound impact on architectural practice. At the planning stage, computer-aided design (CAD) tools are used to sketch, prototype, and visualise all forms of building, from bus stations to skyscrapers. Computer-aided manufacturing (CAM), which automates elements of fabrication and construction, can then be used to translate these and other designs into material reality. As a result, it becomes easier and cheaper to design and build complex structures. Digital affordances and workflows allow for finer detail and topological troubleshooting. But this new complexity is not just quantitative. Computer-aided architecture enables structures that could not have been designed or built without the use of digital media. The most noteworthy

---

[1] Transformium may not be real, but many brands 'demo'd' or otherwise displayed in the film are, including the Beats Pill. So clumsy was this product placement that the film received the dubious award of 'Worst Product Placement' in 2015 from Brandcameo (Han 2015). We also later glimpse Transformium being used by a KSI employee to create a toy of Rainbow Dash, a character from the *My Little Pony* franchise (b. 1981) – a brand, like *Transformers*, owned by Hasbro.

buildings in this regard are often iconic, or seek to be. They perform their digital ontology through fractal, organic, or mathematical forms that often sit conspicuously amongst buildings that hew to more traditional design and construction methods.

Major figures such as Zaha Hadid, Rem Koolhaas, and Frank Gehry are synonymous with this kind of work, with their hotels, urban towers, transportation hubs, and museums in many cases employing and advertising digital methods of planning and construction. One of the most significant examples of this is the Guggenheim Museum Bilbao, by Gehry. Completed in 1997, it is a compound accumulation of stacked contoured ribbons, all shimmering silver as they reflect (and reflect back upon) the water of the harbour in which the museum sits (Figure 6.1). Architect and theorist Branko Kolarevic calls it an Eiffel Tower for the Information Age: 'the best known example' of this kind of architecture, and one that 'captures the zeitgeist of the digital information revolution, whose consequences for the building industry are likely to be on a scale similar to those of the industrial revolution' (Kolarevic 2003: 3). What are these consequences? Kolarevic provides a hype-filled overview:

> In the conceptual realm, computational, digital architectures of topological, non-Euclidean geometric space, kinetic and dynamic systems, and genetic algorithms, are supplanting technological architectures. [...] The generative and creative potential of digital

Figure 6.1 The Guggenheim Museum Bilbao, designed by Frank Gehry. Photograph by Jeremy Jones.

media, together with manufacturing advances already attained in automotive, aerospace and shipbuilding industries, is opening up new dimensions in architectural design. (Kolarevic 2003: 3)

The result is buildings like Gehry's Guggenheim, the Sage Music Centre in Gateshead by Norman Foster, the City of Culture of Galicia in Santiago de Compostela by Peter Eisenman, the CCTV Headquarters building by Rem Koolhaas and the 'Bird's Nest' Olympic Stadium by Herzog and de Meuron (both in Beijing). In all these cases, designers draw on abstract mathematics, biochemistry, and space exploration to launch an architecture of the future.[2]

If the most visible and hyped examples of digital architecture are these kinds of iconic, fractal structures, then it is necessary to note that these are far from the only manifestations of computational architectural design. As the editor of *The Digital Turn in Architecture 1992–2012* points out, 'Building a multistorey car park these days typically involves more digital technologies than were available to Frank Gehry's office for the design of the Guggenheim Bilbao in the early 1990s' (Carpo 2013a: 8). Equally, the software used in such design processes – whether for Olympic stadiums or car parks – is not unique to architects, but also employed by VFX houses and videogame designers. Maya is as crucial for parametric building design as it is to the fractal reshapings of urban space witnessed in *Inception* (see Fordham 2010: 48) and *Doctor Strange* (see Seymour 2016), not to mention the interactive cities that can be found in videogames like *Mirror's Edge Catalyst* (2016), *Watch Dogs 2* (2016), and innumerable others.[3] Such multipurpose application is to be expected: architects, digital effects artists, and videogame developers all undertake similar tasks. They design buildings and other spatial elements which will be occupied or otherwise inhabited (whether by a physical individual, a gameplayer, or footage of an actor), and to do this they move from 3D schematic to much more detailed final render (whether a completed digital effects shot, a verisimilitudinous gamespace, or a material structure).

The most notable genre of digital building design – both materially and conceptually – is probably parametric architecture. Involving procedural

---

2 These buildings are discussed (and celebrated) in Jencks 2005.
3 A lead architect at Hadid's architectural firm has written the foreword to a book celebrating Maya's usefulness for parametric building design (Wirz 2014). Other packages for this purpose are available (such as Dessault Systèmes's CATIA), some of which do not have Maya's emphasis on moving-image rendering and real-world texturing. For a full account of the use of Maya in creating animations, see Wood 2015.

algorithmic generation at the design phase, parametric architecture was a kind of response to postmodern and deconstructionist architectural styles that stressed contradiction and difference. Parametricism claims the kineticism, organicism, and technological futurism that Kolarevic outlines in relation to digital building design, performing these in its distinctive visual aesthetic. This aesthetic, meanwhile, is perhaps somewhat counterintuitive: parametricism's execution of digital logic is not connected to the coordinates of linear binary logic, or even the mess of cyberpunk, but instead to the infinite regression of the curve. As the previous chapter indicated, earlier modernist architecture focused on rectilinear order at sometimes massive scales (as in the case of the work of Le Corbusier or Robert Moses); in the twenty-first century, the computer enables a curvilinear style, a planned disorder of unpredictable but functionable generative growth.

Before exploring the visual qualities of this style (and connecting this to the GUIs that facilitate these designs), it is necessary to consider in some detail the origins of parametricism, and the foundational suppositions that lie at its core. This work builds on the previous chapter's discussion of flexibility, and will, I hope, further indicate how the pliability and programmability of digital objects has become a kind of imagined material reality thanks to the increasing ubiquity of the desktop interface.

If Transformium is the fictional 'Holy Grail' of programmable matter, then the writing of parametric architect Greg Lynn is the real-world bible of digital materiality. His 1993 essay 'Architectural Curvilinearity' (2013) traces architecture's discovery of the formal spatial logic of folds, fluidity, and a kind of heterogeneous adaptability. His later book *Animate Form* (1999) – which outlines the projects of his own firm FORM – then makes the embrace of computation much more explicit. In it, he draws distinctions between earlier presumptions around architecture – namely that it is associated with permanence, usefulness, typology, procession, and verticality – and those which he feels should now predominate in a digital era (Lynn 1999: 13). Those old-fashioned 'statics', as he calls them, can now be replaced by architecture which responds to flow and motion, and which uses CAD tools to create shapes expressing 'the mathematics of the topological medium' (Lynn 2013: 18).

Throughout *Animate Form*, Lynn describes how important topology is to this architecture. Increasingly central to geographers and philosophers across the 2000s and 2010s, topological theory speaks to both segmentation and connection, to the experience of space as a divided and compartmentalised on the one hand, but also as a network of connections that reinforce, overcome, and reshape on the other. Cultural geographer Anna Secor's summary is useful here:

> The basic insight of the field of topology is that some spatial problems depend not on the exact shapes of the objects involved but on the ways that they are put together, on their continuities and cuts. [...] Topologically speaking, a space is not defined by the distances between points that characterize it when it is in a fixed state but rather by the characteristics that it maintains in the process of distortion and transformation. (Secor 2013: 431)[4]

Dependent on both movement and the imagination, topology is essentially the bending of space, the way it can fold and loop even as it remains essentially (that is, mathematically) the same (Secor 2013: 435–6). Topological space is innately compound: a series of possible variations from a set of parameters. As Lynn himself states,

> One of the first principles of topological entities is that because they are defined with calculus they take the shape of multiplicity; meaning they are not composed of discrete points but rather, they are composed of a continuous stream of relative values. (Lynn 1999: 20)

Topology is not exclusively digital, but the two are highly related (a relationship Lynn celebrates). Any topographical architecture relies on the mathematical modelling of non-uniform rational B-splines, or NURBS (Lynn 1999: 20–3). Simply put, these are curves which respond to fixed control points; move the control points, and the curve changes in responsive ways. Included in all standard CAD software packages, NURBS allow for fluid, sinuous structures to be easily planned and manipulated. As Kolarevic states, NURBS 'make the heterogenous, yet coherent forms of the topological architectures computationally possible and their construction attainable', and he argues that such topological programming 'opens up a universe where essentially curvilinear forms are not stable but may undergo variations, giving rise to new possibilities, i.e., the emergent form' (Kolarevic 2001: 118–19).

This is not just about the specific possibilities of NURBS, but also their metaphoric potential. Thanks to their focus on flexibility and

---

4 Topology is also significant to Gilles Deleuze and Giorgio Agamben and those human geographers and social scientists that have used their methodologies to analyse space and experience. This work is outside my purview here.

transformation, new media scholar Lev Manovich, writing with Jeremy Douglass, suggests that NURBS emerge 'as the new language for the globalized networked word [sic] where the only constant is rapid change', (Manovich and Douglass 2011: 319). NURBS and their smooth curves may have established an aesthetics of continuity and complexity in architecture, but they seem to speak to larger changes in the imagination of spatial form and even the workings of economics, culture, and politics in a globalised, digital era.

Topological thinking and NURBS allow for the development and flourishing of parametric architecture. Parametric equations permit consistent parameters to be combined with a wide array of more variable conditions. In mathematics these equations often express curves and undulating lines and shapes, and so, in the case of computer-aided design, parametric equations are used to effectively program complex, rippling structures.

Lynn was and is far from the only architect thinking, working, and writing about these ideas, but his descriptions and approach are nonetheless formative for this whole architectural school. As he frames it, from the beginning of the 1990s designers began to extensively explore the possibilities of non-rigid, dynamic buildings, structures which encode pliancy as a central, advantageous value, and use this feature as a way to connect with, but not overwhelm, their surroundings. This is welcome, granting buildings as it does a newfound elasticity which enables amplified complexity, but also internal stability: 'Pliancy allows architecture to become involved in complexity through flexibility. [...] Pliancy implies first an internal flexibility and second a dependence on external forces for self-definition' (Lynn 2013: 30). Informed by the philosopher Gilles Deleuze, Lynn describes folded, viscous buildings which can yield to stress but not buckle. This, he asserts in quite telling language, is not 'flaccidity', but rather 'a cunning submissiveness that is capable of bending rather than breaking' (Lynn 2013: 34).

The resulting buildings (whether built, planned, or only alluded to) accord with Lynn's animosity towards the static. Although the resulting structures are, in most cases, literally static (they are buildings after all), they often appear otherwise. Whether evoking ribbons, blobs, or fractal geometry, the impression of movement is implied or somehow performed, a movement not mechanical but organic. Just as biological organisms evolve in response to environmental conditions, so too these structures can be programmed on the computer screen to effectively 'grow' in certain ways. Algorithms in this context produce quasi-organic arrangements of structural complexity, and the look of these buildings announces this digital ontology. For parametric or generative architecture to be appreciated as such, it must bear visual traces of its growth in just such a computational petri dish. Witness the notable designs and facades of buildings like the Guggenheim Bilbao or the Guangzhou Opera House, with their impossible bulges, folds, and fractal cross-hatching. In these structures, architects seem to want to display the unification of pure informational mathematics with concrete spatial structure (Parisi 2013: xvii).[5]

Lynn was accurate in proposing that this would become a major trend in large-scale architecture, with the work of 'starchitects' like Gehry, Hadid, and Koolhaas defined by their deployment of viscous, folded, or elastic-looking structures. Surprisingly, though, Lynn makes little reference in his 1993 essay to computers actually doing the work of design. The focus is on philosophy and result, rather than the nitty-gritty of programming (an absence familiar from VFX breakdowns). However, he does imply this missing step when he offers an intriguing comparison between the design of built space and the use of digital technology in screen media entertainment. In the late 1980s and early 1990s, the digital 'morph' effect which smoothly transforms one object or figure into another was becoming increasingly popular, used prominently in films like *Willow* (1988) and the music video for Michael Jackson's 'Black or White' (1991). For Lynn, this morph is a suitable point of comparison with architectural curvilinearity: in either case, computer software is employed to construct intermediate figures between two fixed points, which allows for the generation of a bending, blending, bleeding composite which is innately pliant.

If this asserted connection between a fleeting special effect and an architectural style may be something of (ahem) a stretch, then a more convincing link is perhaps drawn by Lynn when he connects the metallic, perceptually fluxing buildings of Frank Gehry (like the Bilbao Guggenheim) with the villainous T-1000 from *Terminator 2: Judgment Day* (1991) (Figure 6.2). Both, in Lynn's words, 'exchange fixed co-ordinates for dynamic relations across surfaces' (Lynn 2013: 37–8). As such, they create flexible forms in which previous understandings of substance and categorisation lose meaning. If in the 'liquid mercury man' of the science-fiction film this unruliness is the source of horror, then in buildings like those of Gehry and Shoei Yoh

---

5 This prompt to connect building and digital process is noted by Lev Manovich (2012) when he lists the Guggenheim Bilbao (along with the first issue of *Wallpaper* magazine in 1996 and the opening of boutique design store Collete in Paris in 1997) as part of a shift towards a design experience aesthetic in the late 1990s, of which the 1998 iMac was the most significant example.

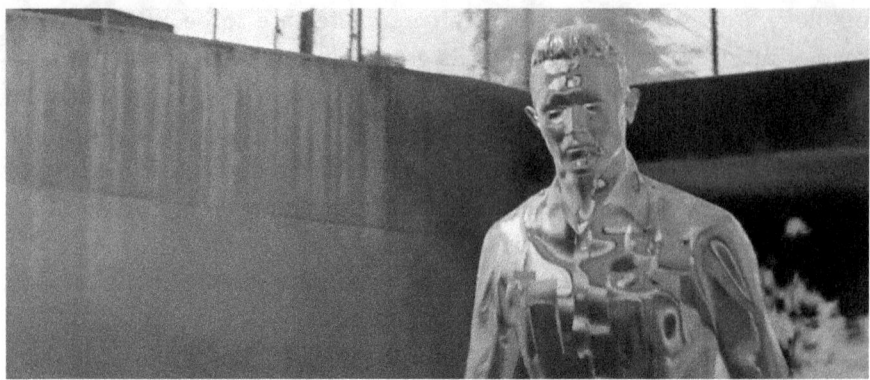

Figure 6.2 The fluxing, metallic form of the T-1000 from *Terminator 2: Judgement Day* (1991). Frame enlargement from Blu-ray.

it bespeaks adjustable accommodation and welcome spatial responsiveness (Lynn 2013: 38).

Although the examples Lynn draws on are from the early era of digital effects cinema, we might note that the ability of computational tools to calculate what he calls 'interstitial figures between fixed figures' has only grown in importance (Lynn 2013: 38). Keyframing is central to VFX production and animation generally, allowing animators to determine parameters and let software fill in the gaps; define the states a and f, and the software generates b, c, d, and e. For instance, a user of Maya can set the start and end point of a digital object or a lighting set-up, and the software will fill in the frames that move it from one to the other. Such computational pliancy is also fundamental to the contemporary motion smoothing and televisual image interpolation technologies discussed in Chapter 2, in which the frames of a given media become boundaries between which a space is found so that it can be filled with algorithmically generated additional content. Finally, the fluid navigations that VFX breakdowns undertake through their layers of digital composites express a similar curvilinear logic of flowing visual matter, an expression of 'heterogenous yet continuous' forms (Lynn 2013: 38). All these examples are about the algorithmic generation of in-betweens, the curving spaces between points that can be authored by computational process.

Lynn's writing is therefore in close conversation with wider developments in digital culture, particularly those tied to the visual qualities of the GUI. Since his conception of space is influenced not just by general computational possibility, but also by the specific tools and functions of the desktop, it is not surprising that architectural structures which announce their reliance on this desktop are to him – and all those that follow in his footsteps – the most significant in today's spatial ecology.

Parametric structures express digital screen experience through the way in which, like a digital model within a Maya program window or a VFX breakdown, they seem to demand the sort of scrutiny that can only be provided by screen rotation and zooming. Their digital topography makes their exact dimensions hard or impossible to grasp from a single angle. Their folds and contortions express the malleability of a digital model and its latent flexibility even in material, built form. If the Guggenheim Bilbao and the Walt Disney Concert Hall look like the shapeshifting T-1000, then this suggests they might morph into something else at any moment. We seem to be catching them in a kind of fluid state between transformations (an effect accentuated in these structures by their reflecting scales). With its sharper, straighter lines and enormous scale, a skyscraper like Rem Koolhaas's CCTV Headquarters would seem to offer more fixity. But the folding, Moebius strip-style design still encourages us to see the building as a temporary or arbitrary arrangement of parts, just one possible output condition of inputted parameters.

Before turning more extensively to media texts and their expression of this logic, it is helpful by way of closing this section to consider a much less known instance of parametric architectural thinking. In the late 1990s, Lynn employed parametric tools to create Embryologic House (1997–2001), a series of potential dwelling spaces.[6] Control points for size and shape were fixed, and then the CAD software MicroStation was used to explore the endless possible configurations that would adhere to this basic geometry (Shubert 2009). This data was imported into Maya and used to generate digital models (Carpo 2013b). The result is a range of unique domestic spaces that combine consistent principles of size and layout with subtle conditional differences (unique curving walls and spatial arrangements). Never built at full scale (and intended as a purely conceptual project), Embryologic House shows Lynn's belief that algorithmic digital processes can allow for individuality in mass production. The conveyor belt cedes ground to the topological algorithm, the project manifesting the multiplicity that can be achieved from a single set of defined structural parameters: as the title indicates, this is effectively a single house, topologically disassembled.

What does Embryologic House look like? As might be expected, it offers fluid, curving structures, each house a kind of programmed blob.

---

6 Also sometimes called Embryological House.

The presentation of these ephemeral structures, moreover, celebrates the digital nature of their design. The speculative dwellings appear in displays of the project as a combination of polished white bulges and binding polymer meshwork; they are ethereal bubbles or pebbles, resembling a rotatable CAD model in a viewport window more than a physical structure one might find on an urban street. They are then arranged as a series against an abstract black background, an endless but linked series, a constellation of scientifically derived slices. Early in *Animate Form*, Lynn (1999: 11) comments that prior discussions of motion in architecture have relied upon a cinematic model, 'where the multiplication and sequencing of static snapshots simulates movement'. Although he complains that this eliminates motion and force from our understanding of buildings, in the static array of Embryologic House as it appears as a pdf or a page in a printed book we see exactly this kind of sequencing. In lieu of a navigable CAD model, we are shown snapshots of a space from another (digital) world.

The result evokes not so much an architectural blueprint as the locomotive photography of Eadweard Muybridge, in which the movement of people and animals is captured and dissected as a series of discrete moments. Here, what is arrayed for the viewer is not the physical world but digital process, the fragments of a galloping algorithm. This presentation, as well as the serial concept of Embryologic House itself (with its infinite variations on a stable topology), emphasises the multiplicity of genealogically networked outputs of which the work consists. As such, it points to the presence of software and parametric equations in their visual production. This is not about using the computer as a tool to find the right design for the problem at hand, but about announcing the presence of computing as the very condition of design itself.

Transforming Packard

Having established at some length the coordinates of topological design processes, it is now time to turn to some media objects which offer their own computational variations on this theme. The previous chapter showed how the contemporary city can now be imagined as a customisable terrain, a digital environment to be re-coded at will. The same is true of structures within the city, which might not only be products of desktop software but physical manifestations of its logic. Iconic structures – actually built concert halls, galleries, and business headquarters – all loudly announce their parametricism in their curvilinear aesthetic, their folding and diaphanous shapes. And these buildings are bound up with broader ideas of urban flexibility. The Guggenheim Bilbao has lent its name to the so-called 'Bilbao effect', whereby striking architecture is used to reinvigorate struggling post-industrial cities by inserting these spaces (or representations of them) into a global image economy, boosting tourism and regional investment (Plaza and Haarich 2015). If these structures perform pliancy in their aesthetic of undulation, then they also claim to render the city itself more pliant, more open to reactive change. As shown in the last chapter, from a neoliberal perspective, this is to be welcomed: cities can refashion themselves according to touristic whims and the desires of corporate investment.

Successful flexibility is equated with algorithmic computation, and with the preservation of a kind of digital ontology even after the translation from Maya to real world. Buildings may have previously been inert structures which only moved when built or demolished, but thanks to the rhetoric of parametric architecture they can now be conceptually endowed with pliancy and digital responsiveness. Through the application of generative algorithms, NURBS, and announcements of fluid suppleness, the architects of these structures seem to have gained access to the source code that shapes the reality. Like the sorcerers of *Doctor Strange* and the architects of *Inception* they use this access to fold and contort built space in ways that assign it the gooey logic of the computer interface. Buildings and the cities in which they sit become SimCities, flexible forms expressing the parameters of digital code.

If parametric architecture is an eruption of effectively alien digital pliancy into our world, then this allows me to return to those building-sized entities the Transformers, and the various films in which they wreak havoc. Is this a spurious connection? Both parametric architecture and the Autobots rely on digital software for their contemporary design and execution. Apart from the related toys, Transformers may remain bound within the screen, but then so does much of Lynn's architecture, which is digitally prototyped but never built. Or, mostly never built: along with images of digital models, the pages of *Animate Form* contain photographs of stereolithography prototypes of Lynn's designs. These table-top structures might be grown-up tools but they could also be playsets for children young and old to stage battles between their plastic Transformers figures. Yet parametric architecture is serious business, a major shift in thinking about and creating built space. What does this have to do with Transformer toys and the seemingly disposable commercial blockbusters they have been adapted into?

As I mentioned briefly in the previous chapter, *Transformers: Dark of the Moon* features Koolhaas's CCTV Headquarters, but relocates it to Chicago.

188 Gooey Media

Battling Decepticons, an airborne Optimus Prime becomes entangled in the wires of a series of cranes arrayed around what is apparently a still-under-construction CCTV Headquarters on the edges of Chicago's Grant Park (Figures 6.3a–b). While its appearance is fleeting, the geographical pliancy demonstrated here is of a piece not only with ideas of urban flexibility but also those of parametric architecture. Koolhaas's structure seems to be a temporary arrangement of folding parts, an intermittent figure in-between more traditional or visually comprehensible compositions. Shown to be equally at home in the Midwestern US as it is in Northern China, the building's use here points to the importance of iconic parametric structures for advertising cities within a global image economy. But its presence also troubles the very concept of urban specificity. This moment renders Chicago a city in flux – and not just because it is currently being demolished from the inside-out by Decepticons. This is again the logic of a SimCity, since in those games players can be as incongruous as filmmakers and place an Eiffel

Figures 6.3a and b During a Chicago-based battle in *Transformers: Dark of the Moon* (2011), the CCTV Building briefly dominates the skyline (in the right-hand side of (a) and the background of (b)). Frame enlargements from Blu-ray.

Tower next to an Empire State Building and a Bird's Nest Stadium, all in the middle of a desert or open green fields.

That the CCTV building ensnares Optimus is something of a surprise, since the two share some fundamental qualities. Transformers, as their name suggests, can change from one state to another – most often, a vehicle such as a car or a helicopter becomes an anthropomorphic titan laden with weaponry. In their toy figurine incarnation, these transformations are bulky and somewhat obvious. Large pieces of chassis rotate or unfold to become legs and arms, a head swivels out from a bonnet, and the resulting character – for all their manipulable limbs – is still recognisable as an adapted car, helicopter, or whatever. But in the film franchise these conversions occur in an almost incomprehensible whirl, an effect which severs many of the links between the two states. Thousands of unique mechanisms and gears move simultaneously, splinters of material speedily rotate and coalesce, and only the vaguest impressions of the colour and shape of the original vehicle remain.

Film studies scholars have noted the significance of these images. Connecting them to ideas of neo-baroque imagery, Bruce Bennett describes how, in these shots, we see an 'architectural complexity of visual detail', with the 'fractally dense CGI animation' of the robotic figures being 'far too visually intricate to comprehend at a glance' (Bennett 2015; see also Ndalianis 2004). In his book on director Michael Bay, Lutz Koepnick (2018: 43) calls the Transformers 'exemplars of unfettered becoming', and proposes that if we 'are unable to tell exactly how the parts of one shape metamorphose into that of another', then this is because these beings are all about swift and constant acclimation to a barrage of external threat. Lisa Purse (2013: 9) connects this to ideas of digital difference, suggesting that for all their perceptual realism, the Transformers appear 'constructed from a different order of images' than their surroundings. The viewer 'is left not with a compelling sense of how these machines transform but instead with a general impression of change' (Purse 2015).[7] This is entirely appropriate, allowing the transformations of the titular characters to embody ideas of digital imagery and the visualisation of computation. The 'unreadability of their metamorphoses signal[s] the extent of their potential', as 'the digital's ability to alter and originate [is] offered as a metaphor for the Autobots' own powers of transformation' (Purse 2013: 9). Shane Denson concurs, suggesting that the robots are sites of digital process and possibility: 'It is the processual flow and speed of algorithmic processing that is put on display here, and indeed

---

7 Purse here draws on Mark Bould's (2008) review in the journal *Science Fiction Film and Television*.

put into effect as the images are played back on our computational devices' (Denson 2020a: 42; emphasis in original). For Koepnick (2018: 43), this makes them icons of flow, masters of pliancy and adaptability, while for Leon Gurevitch (2016: 289), the industrial and digital nature of the transformations makes them signifiers of 'contemporary cinema's capacity to utilize, master, and redeploy the language of contemporary industrial production'.

So, before we are even introduced to Transformium in the fourth franchise entry, these scholars point us towards the links between Transformers, parametric architecture, and the desktop. The shapeshifting activities of these aliens evokes less the blocky clicks and joints of the plastic toys upon which they are originally based than they do the mercury undulations of the T-1000 or the Guggenheim Bilbao. The bewildering jumble of matter visualised in such moments is a marker of the power of digital generation to endow all matter with flexibility, and so functions as a further manifestation of Lynn's dreams of algorithmic (re)vitalisation.

When we do get to Joyce's product demo in *Age of Extinction*, it is perhaps not as transformative as he claims – we have already seen digital technology imbue matter with programmable life throughout the preceding films, just as we have seen versions of this vivification in a wider array of contemporary cinema, and just as we also encounter it in the parametric architecture which sprouts up within or globs onto our urban environments. In all these cases, raw matter is imagined as inherently, endlessly, thrillingly flexible, and this flexibility is dependent on its being conceived of as a fundamentally digital substance. Transformium moves in ways directly related to particle animation software tutorials for programs like Houdini. If we pause the film, it could as easily be a holographic prototype of a new parametric building which Joyce balances between his outstretched hands (Figure 6.4).

Ideas of programmable matter may bleed into the environment in examples like the relocation of CCTV Headquarters in *Dark of the Moon* and in the transformations of the robots themselves throughout the franchise, but at other moments a marked contrast is created between lively matter and inert space. This is an expected part of the action film, which demolishes more than it builds, and which frequently depicts characters at odds with hostile surroundings (Jones 2015). Koepnick (2018: 78) describes how in the *Transformers* films, as in all the films of their director Michael Bay, 'space is never safe, never considered a bulwark against the entropy of time'. For the heroes of these films, he proposes, 'architecture is what needs to be obliterated to create space for human action and heroism' (Koepnick 2018: 79). In action, the human and robot characters of these films tear through their

Figure 6.4 The flexible matter Transformium is demonstrated in *Transformers: Age of Extinction* (2014). Frame enlargement from Blu-ray.

environments, shattering glass and blasting through walls. They do not bend or code like Ariadne and Strange do; they annihilate.

This seems counter to ideas of fluid transformation. Yet the combination of physical space and digital elements stages a pertinent confrontation between algorithmic liveliness and modernist immobility. Whether ancient ruins surrounding the Pyramids, the rooftops of Hong Kong, or the streets of a rundown Texas town, throughout the *Transformers* franchise digital entities are shown bringing outsize life and energy to their surroundings. Entities constructed from baroque visual effects clamber up the side of buildings, occupy intersections, and take greedy hold of city skylines. The collision between material space and digital design is rendered violent and damaging by the generic frameworks of the films, but it is the same clash found in discourses of parametric design. In either case, different orders of imagery intersect in ways that are guided by ideas of spectacle, regeneration, and digital flexibility.

This comes into particular focus in the treatment of the Packard Plant in Detroit by both Lynn and the *Transformers* films. The largest city in Michigan, Detroit is a notable site of post-industrial struggle. A 'manufacturing powerhouse' of the 1970s, the collapse of the auto industry and other factors led to decaying infrastructure and the creation of 'landscapes of abandonment and ruin' in the city (Andersson and Webb 2019: 6). One of these landscapes of abandonment is the Packard Plant, a large-scale automobile factory designed in the early 1900s by noted industrial architect Albert Khan. The forty-acre plant suffered severe disrepair once it was vacated by the Packard Motor Car Company in the late 1950s and then by the remainder of its tenants in the 1990s. It is continually threatened with renovation (or demolition) but remains a stubbornly inert and mostly unproductive presence on Detroit's east side.

It is, however, frequently visited by our alien titans. To manage their ballooning budgets, the *Transformers* films take advantage of the tax rebates offered by particular shooting territories (in which state agencies effectively refund a percentage of expenditure made in-territory during filming or post-production). Michigan offered generous incentives of this sort throughout the early 2010s, leading to considerable portions of the franchise being shot there (along with numerous other blockbusters – Hinds n.d.).[8] A visually striking terrain of graffiti and rubble, the Packard Plant has been employed as a backdrop in sequences in *Transformers: Dark of the Moon*, *Transformers: Age of Extinction*, and *Transformers: The Last Knight* (2016).

The plant does not play itself in any of the films, though, and is instead used to portray various US cities, some of which have been decimated by the war between Autobots and Decepticons, and others which just seem to be victims of post-industrial decay. In *Dark of the Moon*, characters trying to break into an alien-occupied Chicago make their way through the plant's landscape, with the production's addition of elevated trains (some of which have crashed to the ground) testifying to the scene's supposed proximity to the Windy City. In *Age of Extinction*, the location is downtown Paris, Texas, through which protagonists frenetically drive, pursued by villainous private military contractors. In *The Last Knight* we are once again in part of Chicago, this city now quarantined thanks to the presence of alien activity. In each case, foot and car chases propel us through the plant, and Transformers smash through its walls and tussle across its rooftops. Sparks fly, the ground is torn by explosions, and the already damaged landscape is augmented with additional rubble and wreckage. If all this suggests that the location might as well be anywhere, then online promotional videos in which filmmakers and marketers alike make much of the joys of shooting in the Packard Plant somewhat counters this. 'The Packard Plant was amazing', enthuses star Mark Wahlberg in a clip advertising the home entertainment release of *The Last Knight*, while elsewhere in the video director of photography Dominic Sela celebrates the authenticity of the site (Paramount Movies 2017).

These *Transformers* films bring vehicular movement and attention back to a site once renowned for it, but now abandoned. More than this, by placing digital graphics – in the diegetic form of pliable sentient machines – among the ruined landscape of the Packard Plant, these sequences strangely perform the claims made by parametric architects in relation to their own

---

8 Information on the Michigan film industry's incentives program in the 2010s can be found in Elliott 2019.

digital creations. In either case, digital animation once more makes this a space worth looking at within neoliberal cultural networks.

The plant has also been subject to other parametric incursions, at least in demo form. Exhibited at the US Pavilion of the 2016 Venice Architecture Biennale, the 'Center for Fulfillment, Knowledge, and Innovation' by Greg Lynn imagined Packard brought back to life as an urban hub of business and education. This could be achieved, the presentation asserted, through the application of Lynn's usual algorithmic methods of building design. Like much of Lynn's other work, this was a purely conceptual project which was never intended to be actually built. The display consisted of a model with augmented reality (AR) components and a video, all of which outlined architectural additions which turn the plant into a site of human inhabitation and economic activity. These additions take the form of bulging masses and protuberances arrayed across the roof and bleeding down the walls of existing plant buildings; curving, trypophobic meshworks which appeal to the organic and which could only be programmed at this scale by parametric means. In the video we are also shown interior passageways added to the inside of the still-remaining plant, these ovoid-shaped corridors splitting and conjoining like veins.

The resulting structure is described in the accompanying promotional video as a factory of 'things and ideas', an (unwieldy) combination of drone manufacturing plant, university campus, consumer plaza, and food court (Framestore 2016).[9] In the presentation material, the additions to the plant are polished white and notably solely structural (all the spaces are vacant and there are no people visualised here) (Figure 6.5). Nonetheless, the idea of circulation is central – in Lynn's words, the proposed edifice 'is predicated on contemporary mobility and the design vocabulary of curving, twisting and folding volumes driven by the intelligent movement of autonomous forklifts, delivery trucks and drones' (AWN 2016).

Even without showing any occupants, the promo video accentuates this with its depiction of swarming particle clouds, and cameras that glide fluidly whether they are real or digital (the former consisting of drone footage of the decrepit plant as it existed in 2016, the latter virtual arcs through either wireframe schematics of the proposed parametric structure or its polymerised render) (Figure 6.6).

The project was undertaken in collaboration with Framestore, a VFX company who have also worked on major commercial blockbusters (they were one of the effects houses responsible for the film *Gravity*). That company's creative director, Ben West (who describes himself as both

---

9 Since 2021, this video has been taken down from Vimeo, where I originally viewed it.

Figure 6.5 The proposal for the Center for Fulfilment, Knowledge, and Innovation depicts parametric digital structures glomming onto the Packard Plant (Framestore, 2016). Frame enlargements from Vimeo.

Figure 6.6 Physical and virtual cameras glide through the Packard Plant and its digital additions (Framestore, 2016). Frame enlargements from Vimeo.

an animator and an architect), has stated that he is interested in bringing Framestore's expertise to new mediums, including that of lived space itself: 'Framestore is about extending and integrating screens into the landscape so content isn't "seen" on a screen rather it's part of the environment as an architectural statement' (AWN 2016). In the Packard redesign, the plant becomes a kind of screen, or at least is claimed as a site in which screen and physical space can merge. The display at the Biennale invited visitors not only to look at a 3D printed physical model and the video promo, but also to wear Microsoft HoloLens glasses through which the model was supplemented with moving holograms. The proposed space is an amalgam of physical foundation and digital revivification, the logic of the latter foregrounded to such an extent that it seemingly cannot be represented in material space alone. That is, the ephemeral nature of HoloLens depiction places the building's parametric design even deeper within a computational space and aesthetic, rather than the material world of built structures.[10]

---

10 AR was even employed at the design stage, and Lynn has spoken enthusiastically of its potential to aid the development of ambitious architectural projects and even 'revolutionise construction' (Frearson 2016).

The promo emblazons the word 'transformation' across the screen at one point, and even begins with the claim that the Centre is based on the smooth circulation of 'products, people and robots' (Framestore 2016) (Figure 6.7). As such, it is perhaps no surprise that the subsequent images – in which Lynn's polymer meshes have been grafted onto photographic plates of the plant itself – resemble those found in *Transformers* films. In both cases products, people, and robots circulate freely in, on, around, and through the Packard Plant, penetrating its depths, erupting through walls, and almost parasitically glomming onto its edges (Figure 6.8). The Transformers perform the pliancy beloved by Lynn, changing from sleek cars to anthropomorphic titans and back again, and even reassembling themselves when they are dismantled. They are not quite in harmony with their surroundings, though, with the contrast between the photographic plates of the plant and the dynamic, flowing digital elements that have been grafted onto them suggesting not the sympathetic reformation of an industrial ruin,

Figure 6.7 The proposal for the Center for Fulfilment, Knowledge, and Innovation centres ideas of transformation and robotic circulation among post-industrial ruins (Framestore, 2016). Frame enlargements from Vimeo.

Figure 6.8 A Transformer leaps across the rooves of the Packard Plant in *Transformers: Age of Extinction* (2014). Frame enlargement from Blu-ray.

but its colonisation by invading, alien entities. (And indeed, the Hollywood production soon moved on from Michigan, smoothly circulating around the globe to spend its money elsewhere).

The digital elements performing all this motion have in either case been produced by leading visual effects companies. The robots in the films are the work of VFX companies such as ILM, Base FX, and Digital Domain, while the Biennale, as stated, was a collaboration between Lynn's firm and Framestore. A VFX breakdown for Chinese company Base FX's work on *Age of Extinction* employs familiar swing-out shots and iterative layering to show how digital effects have been inserted into the shell of the existing structure (FilmIsNow Movie Bloopers and Extras 2017). As with Lynn's project, Packard becomes a stable point from which digital excursions depart. And in both cases, these digital elements are themselves a strange combination of the perceptually realistic and the topologically complex. Embedded within the space of the plant in a realistic fashion, they nonetheless could never be mistaken for anything other than the product of VFX animation software. (Moreover, just as visitors to the Biennale must put on HoloLens glasses to see the extent of the digital resuscitation of this failed space, so too viewers of the blockbuster films must don 3D glasses to experience the full scale of the VFX spectacle that is bringing explosive life to these surroundings).

So, if Frank Gehry and the T-1000 were in dialogue in the early 1990s, then here we can see how this conversation has continued apace. A Biennale project and the action sequences of a critically panned blockbuster franchise may circulate in very different contexts and appeal to different sets of viewers, but they nonetheless make similar claims about digital technology and its potential relationship with the material world. Whether crass mainstream blockbuster or prestigious avant-garde architectural demo, the Packard Plant becomes a site in which digital technologies can visually perform a revitalisation of what was previously (and in fact, as of 2022, still is) a ruin. The application of software and fractal digital composites transforms built space into seductive, pliant spectacle.

In the demo, parametric architecture is framed as a solution to the problem of post-industrial decay, bringing not only new functionality (factory floors, food courts) but also the touristic appeal of iconic architectural spectacle. The regeneration offered by *Transformers* might by contrast primarily be that of incessant visual activity for consumption by a global audience, but shooting at the plant also brings vital economic investment into the state, as highlighted in the aforementioned paratextual video about *The Last Knight*'s use of the location. These films may transform space in a subtler manner than the literal folds and substitutions of the cityscapes of *Inception* and *BuildIt*, but such Packard showcases still likewise proclaim that computational image-making can bring the flexibility of the desktop and its space-making software to bear on otherwise inert urban form.

Polymer visions

For all the overlaps between the Biennale promo and the *Transformers* films, there is one notable difference in their depictions of digital incursion. Lynn's additional components may be presented as spatially embedded within the real site in the manner of a composite visual effect, but they also remain visibly separate from the Packard Plant thanks to their polished white texture. Unlike the Transformers who do battle within and upon its shattered shell, the proposed Center for Fulfillment, Knowledge, and Innovation does not adopt many visual cues that would allow it to persuasively occupy the same space and time as the Plant. This added architecture instead resembles the half-way point of a VFX breakdown, a glimpse into the pellucid polymer-like structures buried beneath the verisimilitudinous textures of the final digital composite.

This is not accidental. It is, as I will outline in this final section of this chapter, a central aspect of the imagination of programmable matter. The Transformers, for all their outlandishness and their encapsulation of a 'different order of images', nonetheless seek the 'illusion of indexicality' through the 'performance of photographicness' (Purse 2013: 7). This is standard practice for the majority of these kinds of VFX: as indicated in Chapter 4, the idea is to create digital elements that are spectacular but nonetheless anchored in the perceptual coordinates of the real world, with textures, grain, and dirt to match. The parametric models described earlier in this chapter do in some small ways adhere to this logic. The presence of shading and light diffusion helps observers understand their complex spatial dimensions, and the digital models have a haptic quality, a sense that their smooth surfaces could be touched or clasped. But the widely circulated images of parametric and topological architecture also announce their gap from the real. For example, the final presentation images of Embryologic House, as noted above, not only lack spatial context, but also retain visual attributes of their computerised rendering, using block colours and one-point light sources. They are also often devoid of texture – or rather, they adopt a different kind of texture, one which seems alien to lived space or natural or even traditionally manufactured objects, and which instead evokes a digital shell or a sci-fi plastic casing.

This is far from unique to Lynn's work. A 2009 special issue of the journal *Architectural Design* tackles the issue of digital cities, with editor Neil Leach's introduction asserting the importance of both 'standard drafting packages' and 'generative design tools' for urban design (Leach 2009: 8). The articles that follow offer various views on the usefulness of algorithmic, parametric, and topological urban design, all of them richly illustrated. Many of these images expound a digital urban imaginary that is sleek, modular, quasi-organic, and fractal. There is nary a brick in sight, and few panes of glass; instead, the same monotype polymer predominates. These cities are rendered as a smooth material that curves and undulates but has no significant texture or grain, refracts no light, and exists in an abstract universe untroubled by atmosphere.[11]

Such features are, of course, elements of the design process, traces of the digital genesis of these buildings. But these features often then carry over into the actual construction of parametric architecture too. An analogue architectural plan drawn using pencil and paper might offer a two-tone, rigidly geometric interpretation of a proposed structure, but when completed this physical space will be conferred with the textures of brick, steel, concrete. On the other hand, parametric structures overwhelmingly retain some aspects of their polymer aesthetic as they migrate from the PC to the plaza. For instance, Zaha Hadid's Guangzhou Opera House is a dyad of enormous latticed pebbles, making prospective renders of its untextured CAD model almost indistinguishable from photographs of the final structure.

This particular look is made more overt when operating in direct contrast to other approaches. The roof of the western concourse of London's King's Cross train station by John McAslan and partners – a parametric-aided design addition consisting of a kind of a meshwork funnel and canopy – retains the white matte featureless finish of its computer render. This polymer aesthetic of the newer work is then especially noticeable because the curving extension is attached to the rectilinear brickwork of the original Grade I building (Figure 6.9) (John McAslan + Partners, n.d.). This is a familiar contrast: in Lynn and Framestore's proposal for the Packard Plant, the century-old ruin remains visible as an element of a larger composite that includes significant digital elements. Like the King's Cross extension, the Center for Fulfillment, Knowledge,

---

11 To further corroborate the otherworldliness of this look, Leach himself, among his various other teaching duties, works with NASA exploring methods for the creation of habitats on the Moon and Mars.

Figure 6.9 London King's Cross Train Station redevelopment by John McAslan and Partners. Photograph by Jeremy Jones.

and Innovation, if it had been built, would likely appear as it does in the promo, with lustreless, smoothly plastic surfaces intersecting the modernist brickwork.

Such contrasts allow these parametric buildings to assert a new digital ontology even outside the bounds of the desktop interface. It is as though the buildings seek to function as their own VFX breakdowns, peeling away layers of atmosphere and texture. Of course, this confluence is not surprising since the same software is, as already noted, used for both cinematic VFX and architectural design. In neither case is this the *application* of a particular kind of look, but rather the divulging of a digital structural reality. The polymeresque model is always there, it's just normally concealed through additions which seek to bring what we see closer to *our* understanding of reality.

This aesthetic, once identified, can be found everywhere. In *Fast Forward: The Future(s) of Cinematic Arts* (2016), Holly Willis begins a chapter on new paradigms of world building in the digital era with a short summary of a LIDAR scan by creative studio ScanLAB. This process uses pulsing lasers to scan distances between objects for the creation of 3D models, and it manufactures familiar imagery:

> Gliding through the woods, trees diaphanous and white, the forest apparitional and eidolic rather than solid and sturdy, more intimation than image: here in a disembodied traversal we witness the alluring power of an aesthetic of detection and tracing. (2016: 43)

Although Willis's focus is primarily on storytelling, her words seem an effective description of the kind of imagery I am focusing on here. 'Eidolic' – meaning vivid but also spectral or apparitional – is an apt term for the perfected yet otherworldly look of these polymer structures. As Willis suggests, these images are often accompanied by gliding virtual cameras, and their digital fluidity and viscosity gives them an alluring quality. LIDAR scans are significant examples of this form, as they translate the physical world – with all its grain and multi-materiality – into a homogenous, navigable model contained within a software viewport.[12]

This eidolic aesthetic reappears in other contexts in order to proclaim either the programmable, digital nature of the matter being depicted, or to point more generally to ideas of artificial rather than natural spaces and entities. As in VFX breakdowns or even our brief glimpses of Transformium, this polymerised spectacle signifies access to some deeper structure, as we encounter not a finished object but the more pliant expression of modifiable source code.

In *SimCity: BuildIt*, for instance, the user's city is relatively detailed, with a range of colours and building materials (brick, stone, glass, concrete) for different structures; the weather even changes frequently, bathing the streets and skyscrapers in numerous colours and atmospheres. Yet when the player chooses to create a new structure, or to move an existing one, the gameworld shifts register. As the selection is initiated, the city and surrounding land change to polished white – shadows are still visible in their most elemental form, but the people and traffic disappear, as does any hint of weather (Figure 6.10). The switch signals to the player that they are seeing through the representational features of the world to its underlying structure. As with parametric illustrations, the city becomes a site of possibility. When a building is (re)placed, the world returns to representational normality. The stripping away of detail indicates that this is a space to be programmed according to player preference rather than an existing reality to be dealt with as it is encountered.

---

12 Available in many different guises, some LIDAR creates highly colourful images in which the spectrum is used to indicate distance, while other systems produce the kinds of white polymer model described here.

Figure 6.10 In *SimCity BuildIt* (2014), the world turns polished white when the player explores possible spatial additions or rearrangements (EA, n.d.). Frame enlargement from demo.

In *Mirror's Edge* (2008) and its sequel *Catalyst*, meanwhile, the city through which the player undertakes parkour consistently adopts an intentionally sparse and clearly CAD-inspired aesthetic. In these videogames, courier Faith fights against an oppressive state infrastructure of seemingly benign surveillance. While it may narratively be a dystopia, the setting is not crowded or oppressive or dark in the manner of, say, *Blade Runner*'s (1982) Los Angeles. Named in the second game as the City of Glass, this space is instead almost explicitly utopian – a sun-drenched corporate conurbation of skyscrapers, billboards, and building sites (Figure 6.11). It evokes the glossy visualisations that appear on advertising hoardings around construction projects in the contemporary city, images which aesthetically charge urban space with ideas of spectacle, function and relaxation, and which 'invit[e] passing pedestrians, passengers and drivers to pause and experience their high-end design, lovely weather, pretty planting, gorgeous lighting and leisured lifestyle' (Rose et al. 2016: 105). But in the City of Glass, much like in these advertising hoardings, the polish is somewhat overdetermined. In Faith's world there is no greenery or foliage at all, and most surfaces are sterile white, with relatively few pronounced

202 Gooey Media

Figure 6.11 The City of Glass from *Mirror's Edge* (2008), a sparse and CAD-inspired terrain. Frame enlargement from PS3 gameplay.

textures. Indeed, the city resembles a *BuildIt* city mid-modification, with stripped down aspects of representational fidelity. The dialogue frames this as a perverse fall from grace: the city used to be dirty and alive, but now it is scrubbed clean and hollowed out, and the game prompts us to 'equate the cleanliness of the shimmering city with filthy corruption' (Ciccoricco 2012: 270).

Visually striking, this is also central to the gameplay of the franchise. These are games about parkour, a practice which, as many scholars have noted, originates in and propagates the re-embodiment of otherwise alienating urban spaces (Daskalaki et al. 2008; Atkinson 2009). Obstacles are re-interpreted as physical challenges and opportunities, as free-runners scale walls, rooftops, and other spaces that are not designed for pedestrian use. To help provide this experience to the player, the *Mirror's Edge* games colour certain minor architectural features of the City of Glass red rather than white, directing us to the possibility of interacting with them. Termed 'runner's vision', this allows the player to easily identify pipes, ledges, and walls that might be grabbed or jumped to. Navigating the city is thus a question of reading its (colour) coding, and since the games mandate (and reward) constant movement, this legibility is crucial to a player's sense of flow and achievement. Movement energises the city and repossesses the experience of it from the oppressive authorities and their spatial control (the villainous mayor also owns a major construction company). Embracing parkour's association with challenges to urban alienation and the uniformity of corporatised landscapes, *Mirror's Edge* and its sequel create a city which is an architectural concept rather than a real place. This throws the counter-cultural struggle of the player-protagonist Faith and her compatriots into relief. They see the 'truth' of the city, which expresses itself not via the standard cues of darkness, grime, and alienating modernist concrete, but rather through cues of a particularly twenty-first-century kind of urban dispossession: those of polymer spectacle and digital unreality.[13]

Some other texts more directly address the nonhuman implications of these kinds of images. *NieR: Automata* (2017), an open world game, is set many centuries after humanity has evacuated planet Earth. In comparison to the natural (albeit apocalyptically devastated) world where most gameplay occurs, there are portions in which the player enters a strange location called the Copied City. Constellations of white cuboid shapes, described by one character as crystallised silicon and carbon, roughly take the form of streets and buildings. This environment, it transpires, has been constructed by a sentient android in a futile attempt to better understand his absent human creators: unvarnished and seemingly unfinished, the polymer look here underscores the atemporal, nonhuman nature of this space. These qualities are later amplified in the Tower, a level near the end of the game with a similar design, in which massive globules and splinters of polymer edifices float unmoored through spatiotemporal ether (Figure 6.12). Such locations adopt not only the structure of parametric architecture – with their quasi-sublime fractal patterns and swarm-like configurations – but also the aesthetic of parametric building proposals.[14] The Tower would fit perfectly among the pages of Lynn's *Animate Form*, or Leach's edited issue of *Architectural Design*.

These spaces are perhaps redolent of the 'technofuturist' aesthetic that Michele Pierson outlined in relation to computer generated imagery of

---

13 The implicit critique offered by the games through their evocation of these kinds of urban visualisations can only go so far, though: in *Catalyst*, the shift to an open-world grants the player access to a map of the city. Providing waypoints and additional tasks, this separate screen becomes central to gameplay. This navigable, player-oriented map is only marginally different from Faith's representational world, though; it is a hollowed out schematic of a hollowed out city. In adopting the visual attributes of a parametric, eidolic aesthetic, the game allows the logic – and appeal – of programmable space to subtly reassert itself.
14 The stripped down, antigrav quality of these spaces also connects with the hacking mini-game within *NieR: Automata*. This is narratively situated within the consciousnesses of the android protagonists, and so further accentuates the digital nature of this angular, monochromatic, textureless spatial imagination.

Figure 6.12 The Tower from *NieR: Automata* (2017), a nonhuman environment of digital polymers crystallised, rudimentary structures. Frame enlargement from PS4 gameplay.

the early-to-mid-1990s. In her widely cited *Special Effects: Still in Search of Wonder* (2002), Pierson articulates two approaches to CG visuality in cinema, essentially split along representational lines. 'Simulationist' work sought to 'exhibit the photorealistic capabilities of contemporary digital imaging systems', and so aimed to realistically embed itself within a profilmic cinematic reality. Technofuturist images, by contrast, offer 'a hyperreal, electronic aesthetic' – it's not that they 'fail' at cinematic realism, but that they seek something else, something that carries traces of its digital ontology in its cinematic presentation (Pierson 2002: 101).

But the polymers described in this section are not a simple return to the look of the effects of *Terminator 2*, *Virtuosity* (1995) or new media art of the early 1990s. In the era of widely circulating VFX breakdowns and parametric design, the 'technofuturist' and artificial quality of these more recent images operates as both opposition *and* incorporation of more perceptually realistic and representationally fleshed-out content. Eidolic images are conceived of as the bones beneath their more photographically convincing, fleshed out equivalents. When photorealistic textures can be selected at the click of a drop-down menu, their absence highlights the unfinished, still-computational, and so often still-flexible attributes of that which is rendered as smooth white polymer. Evoking the creations of 3D printing, this aesthetic is the real and imagined skeleton of digital objects, even those that have made their way beyond the screen. Like parametric architectural models, the appearance of the aesthetic indicates connections with software and the viewport. Polymer polish becomes a signifier of the programmability of the matter at hand.

Tellingly, the examples of the eidolic aesthetic described here tend to the inhuman, chilling, even grotesque. *SimCity* may celebrate flexibility in its polymerised moments, but the City of Glass, the Copied City, and the Tower are not sites of warm humanity. CAD visuality here weds the seeming liveliness of programmable matter to an alienating otherness. In this way these texts balance the dreams and product demos of a gooey world with a more critical perspective than might be found in architectural discourse. Responding to the content if not the spirit of Sutherland's proposal, these are manifestations of digital handcuffs that are indeed materially confining.

Conclusion

Indebted to digital technology and the GUI, discourses of parametric architecture claim that it can, on some level, imbue built space with the flexibility of the desktop interface. Aligned with the fashionable currents of big data, tech solutionism, and genetic mapping, these buildings advertise the eruption of digital algorithmic complexity into our physical world. In line with the name of Joyce's company in *Age of Extinction*, these are indeed kinetic solutions: they enliven matter and they animate form. In the process they retroactively render other matter and form inert, heavy, stolid. Like the digital effects they are, these buildings declare their capacity to make the world more spectacular through general impressions of change and fluidity.

Their visual aesthetic embodies this. They retain elements of their CAD drafting even when they are materially built (as only a few of them are), and so allege their separate ontological status. Such visual idiosyncrasy highlights their closer kinship with the abstract void of digital navigation windows than with the historical sites in which they might actually, eventually be found. Their polymer spectacle advertises their origins in source code, and their topological shapes exhort us to zoom and rotate, pinch, and swipe, rather than stroll through or inhabit.

This is about more than just buildings. Parametricism speaks to a conception of matter itself as magically acquiescent to human agency. As in the case of 3D printing, the material world becomes an extension of the GUI. If we can create things on the desktop screen at the click of a button, and if we can then continually adjust these creations on the fly with new spatial, physical, and textural values, then why not in the real world?

Once again, though, this gooey imagination has some troubling consequences. Architecture critic Rowan Moore points out that parametric architecture creates buildings that tend to be isolated, expensive, and resistant to interpretive or unplanned uses (Moore 2016). This is far from the fluidity and environmental responsiveness they promise. It is also why relatively few of these buildings – especially the most baroque and spectacular of them – are actually constructed, despite widely circulating as a contemporary architectural paradigm.

These structures also perform a by now familiar erasure of labour. Parametric architecture – with its evocations of genetics, organic evolution, and cascading morphogenetic processes – may use the computer to rhetorically imbue inert structural matter with life, but, as Konstantina Kalfa (2015) argues, the computational 'life' which digital processing apparently conjures overrides and replaces the life (in the form of labour time) required by actual human beings to assemble such structures. As she puts it, the contemporary architectural paradigm

> creates a spell-binding illusion, a magic, acting upon both the field of conception and the field of production of architecture. By ascribing signs of life to the new computational tools and materials, it aligns itself with the age-old deception of capitalism, that lies in hiding that part of human labor which leads to surplus value, or, in its extreme, in hiding the very fact that only *human* labor can be the producer of surplus value. (Kalfa 2015: 321; emphasis in original)

As a 'spell', parametric architecture is an ideological device that removes people, cultures, nations, and environments from the creation of built space (Kalfa 2015: 317). It conjures up a world of labourless production, of 3D printed buildings erected at the push of a button.

This ignores the fact that such buildings at present require complex 'bespoke production chains', making them extremely expensive (Claypool, n.d.). Also disregarded are the labourers and construction economies that would be put out of work by this technological dream, as well as the actual, material, highly 'dirty' labour of 3D printing and its social, economic, and environmental footprints (Kalfa 2015: 318). We have encountered these elisions before, of course, in the way VFX breakdowns framed (or rather, did not frame) the labour of the VFX artist. Similarly, here the computer and the customisable instantaneity of the GUI allow the existence of economic, social, and ecological realities to be sidestepped, as the chanting of the parametric spell magics away the real city along with the material production required to produce and maintain it (not to mention those actual biological events that populate it and rely on their surroundings for nurture and sustenance).

While programmable matter and parametric architecture may seem a relatively far cry from an analysis of the cross-medial aesthetics of the desktop interface, I hope I have shown in this chapter how the former are reliant upon, even grow out of the latter. There is no such thing as Transformium, but there are software packages that allow for digital matter to be played with in similar ways. These packages and their affordances have changed the way that built space, and even matter itself, are imagined today. The next chapter in some ways continues this focus on space, addressing one of the most hyped media forms of the GUI age, virtual reality.

7

Empathy Machines

I am both at my desk and in a Jordanian refugee camp. An apparatus embraces the upper part of my head, slightly weighing down on my skull. I am able to visually explore the mediated space in which I find myself: a small, sparse, windowless room. The walls here have the sheen of light plastic material; slim mattresses are arranged on the floor; a CRT television is propped in a corner beneath a single shelf; a clothes hamper and a couple of mirrors are the only other furniture. I hear the voice of a young girl and look around to find the source – she sits on the floor, talking to me in a language I don't understand. Her voice is tinny and echoes, a marker of inexpensive audio recording equipment and the poor acoustics of this prefabricated space. But an English translation of her words begins speaking above this in the mix, and this other voice is much closer and richer, reverberating around my skull thanks to the in-ear headphones that accompany my PS4 virtual reality rig.

Through this voice-over, the girl introduces herself as Sidra. She tells me that she is from Syria, but has lived here in the Zaatari camp in Jordan for the last year and a half. I am at her eye-level, seemingly sitting across from her, sharing space on the Persian rug. As I settle in to hear more, my vision darkens – a fade through black takes me to the same room, but later, and I presume that the other children of various ages suddenly in this space are the family Sidra is currently describing. Unlike Sidra in those earlier moments, her siblings gather themselves to leave without acknowledging my presence at all, a snub which seems aligned to my new position, which is higher than them, looking down (probably the height of an average standing adult). Over the following seven minutes I am granted a tour of the refugee camp, oriented by the translated voice-over. Routines of school, cooking, sports, videogaming, fitness, and eating are shown in such a way that I am placed firmly at their centre, albeit for the most part as an unacknowledged observer. At the end of this tour, Sidra comments that she feels she has been here long enough, and would like to leave. As I take off the VR headset, onscreen text tells me of the scale of the refugee crisis facing the world.

VR promises to transport us to another time and place. Placing the helmet over our eyes, filling our ears with headphones, we seem to be physically and temporally emplaced within the world represented by the media content we have cued up. The audio and visual components of this mediated world are highly responsive to our own bodily movement – we can look around, crane our necks, glance at something we hear just out of view. We can, it appears, actually experience another space, whether this is a Jordanian refugee camp, a haunted house, an underwater shark cage, a cartoony office, or wherever.

The interface here seems to offer something more than those of laptop, computer, or television screens. VR apparently provides not the hermeneutic attention described by Paul Frosh in Chapter 1, but something more engaging, more immersive. Hermeneutic attention involves looking beyond the surface of the screen and reading the unfolding media content for meaning and significance. This mode of looking is 'based on the interpretive and perceptual practices of either "taking in" informational content (for instance, textual reading), or "immersion in" a representational schema' (Frosh 2019: 153), and might be activated or sought by any kind of screen. VR is often called immersive, and its success in plunging the user into representational worlds seems to make it a medium apart from other screens.

If we accept the claims of perceptual conveyance that circulate around VR, then it is a significant break from the GUI. Not only is VR highly medium specific (that is, for VR to be VR it must not be viewed on a cinema screen, laptop, or TV, but rather through a head-mounted apparatus), it also offers a kind of quasi-physical transportation. Here is the 'total cinema' imagined in Chapter 2, achieved. But if this is the contemporary *promise* of VR, then we should not necessarily believe it to be a promise that the medium can keep. Virtual reality still requires screens to deliver its representations, even if these screens are extremely close to us, and so seem to surround us. The experiences it presents are therefore still screened, and so should be considered in the context of other screen media and devices, rather than hived off as somehow separate.

As such, VR is a fitting topic for the last major chapter of this book, demonstrating as it does that the ideas explored so far concerning the GUI are still, surprisingly, relevant in this immersive, hyped media form that seems in many ways so far from the desktop interface. Indeed, attention to the gooiness of VR might be all the more important given the myths of unmediated mediation that circulate so powerfully around these headsets.

To do this work, I focus for the most part on so-called 'immersive journalism', a growing body of texts in which urgent social stories are reported on and disseminated using VR. As in the example of *Clouds over Sidra* (2015) described above, spectators are perceptually placed within politically potent scenarios (illegal border crossings, refugee camps, breadlines) and so apparently gain empathetic knowledge of such scenarios in ways that would not be possible on a fixed, non-immersive screen. But the ethical frameworks applied to such scenarios must be qualified through closer attention to the screens of VR, and ethical critiques of the format reveal its material and social realities in useful ways. Moreover, while the screens of a VR headset may seem very different from those already encountered in these pages, the mode of engagement they offer and the ideas of immersion they promise all appeal to familiar models of GUI-related interactivity.

This chapter seeks to reveal all this through an appeal to theories of videogame space, and the way such space instrumentalises our relationship with our surroundings. In such a proposed model, digital environments are defined less by realism and more by GUI-style functionality and manipulability, resulting in significant consequences for how we think about VR. Before getting to all that though, it is necessary to provide some further definitions around VR itself.

Getting to VR

If the history of the GUI proper begins with Ivan Sutherland's discussion of the 'ultimate display' in 1965 and Douglas Engelbart's 'mother of all demos' in 1968, then these reference points are equally central to the history of virtual reality (Chan 2014: 25). As we have seen, by imagining the computer as a spatial site of data, the GUI allowed this data to be thought of as immersive. Sutherland extended this idea in his experiments into head-mounted 3D displays in 1968, and further work in the 1970s and 1980s at places like MIT's media lab and the University of North Carolina at Chapel Hill fleshed out the concept of an all-enveloping digital interface environment (Hillis 1999: 9–17).

In the late 1980s and 90s, VR would make a series of significant appearances in popular culture. Science-fiction books like William Gibson's *Neuromancer* (1986), mainstream films like *The Lawnmower Man* (1992), *Disclosure* (1994), and *Virtuosity* (1995), television series like *Wild Palms* (1993) and *Star Trek: The Next Generation* (1987–94), and the popular journalism of countless *Wired* magazine articles and Howard Rheingold's book *Virtual Reality* (1991) all framed the technology as a key element of our digital future. Across these texts, VR offered dreams of immersion in a digital network, contributed to cyberpunk explorations of identity and the human soul, and was implicitly but persistently positioned as an inevitable way to access to growing informational dataspace of the then-nascent consumer internet. But outside of these texts VR was relatively invisible at this time.

Various issues prevented the actual uptake of the technology beyond rather narrow scientific and art gallery circles. Headsets were heavy, the computing power necessary was expensive and relatively cumbersome, and the precise everyday use of the medium was still up for grabs. Was it for consumer entertainment? To organise files in the industrial workplace? To undertake current edge scientific research? For art projects? For porn? VR held promise, but it seemed a poor alternative to what was in many ways an equivalent form of digital access – after all, as a way of gaining admittance to the world of networked possibility that was being propagated by the movement of the personal computer into the domestic environment, the GUI was intuitive, simple, and affordable in ways that VR simply was not. Why bother with a headset and gloves when you can just use a CRT monitor? The GUI made the computer representational and enabled intuitive navigation of this representation, but it did so in ways that appealed to the familiar screen-based codes of cinema and television, rather than the novel amalgam of theatrical, panoramic, and stereoscopic protocols offered by VR.

Since the 2010s, though, virtual reality has become much more firmly established, both as an entertainment form and as a tool for a variety of instrumental ends. Devices and add-ons like the Oculus Rift, HTC Vive, and PlayStation VR headsets position the medium as part of the devoted media technophile's necessary kit. Much cheaper alternatives like Google Cardboard also allow smartphone users to play around with the experience without making large financial commitments. Commercial VR content is also now widely available for download or free to stream online, with VR games having been released for major consoles (Crecente 2018). Meanwhile, at film festivals and in art galleries it is not unusual to find a VR offering among other visual material. VR also continues to be employed operationally: it is used to aid surgical procedures and for medical training (Barad 2019), to assist in the design and selling of architectural projects (de Klerk et al. 2019), and to treat post-traumatic stress disorder in the US military (Friedrich 2016).

Broadly speaking, VR experiences can be classified in two ways: entirely digital creations, or those which are generated from camera feeds. In the consumer sphere, the former are most closely aligned with VR videogames, while the latter usually emphasise spatial placement in some exciting or unexpected real-world environment. There is some disagreement as to whether the latter should be called VR at all, with the phrase 360° video being preferred, since no interactivity (beyond that of moving one's head) is usually offered.

In either case, content is accessible on various platforms, including those that are not, technically, VR. For instance, *Resident Evil 7: Biohazard* (2017) is a flagship title for the PSVR rig, but was also a popular game on Windows, Xbox, and even the handheld Nintendo Switch (although this last was only available in Japan). This first-person game involves exploring gothic environments, gathering resources, solving object-based puzzles, and killing enemies. In VR, its oppressive sense of atmosphere may be amplified for some – with turns of the head offering maybe more immersion than gentle pushes on the right thumbstick – but the space of the game is identical across formats (as is the gameplay).

Meanwhile, platforms such as YouTube allow 360° content to be viewed on computer, tablet, and laptop screens, although for the 'full' VR experience a phone must be used in tandem with a headset of some sort. When viewed on non-VR screens, these videos require the user to click and drag with a mouse or swipe their fingers in order to move the viewpoint being offered, an awkward proxy for head and neck motility. Yes, these videos can be watched without any of this interaction, but this is often unfulfilling, since 360° content creators usually embrace the titular dimensions of the format and place material of interest all around the central perspective of the spherical camera rig. If watching *Clouds Over Sidra* on YouTube in its 360° version rather than a VR headset, the viewer will immediately have to click and drag to find the titular character sitting behind them.

The existence of VR content outside of the VR apparatus threatens to make the definition of this media form somewhat uncertain. As such, it is important to ask what it is that makes VR distinctive, what it is we mean conceptually and technically when we refer to 'VR'. This may seem like a clean enough question to answer, with headsets and ideas of immersion and envelopment ready at hand, but before rushing to classify VR in this way, we need to get a little dirty.

Dirtying up the faceless interface

In *Always Already New: Media, History, and the Data of Culture* (2006), media historian Lisa Gitelman thinks of media not as discrete objects that can be studied in relative isolation, but as murky constellations of cultural, social, and technological norms and expectations. To define media this way, she states, 'keeps things muddy', and this is a necessary precondition for more comprehensive analyses of the work that media do (Gitelman 2006: 7). So, what we might think of as a particular media form includes not just the apparatus or associated media texts, but 'a vast clutter of normative rules and default conditions, which gather and adhere like a nebulous array around a technological nucleus' (Gitelman 2006: 7).

For instance, cinema is not just films: it is a kind of space, a form of spectatorship, a release window, an industry (with affiliated industries), and more. But it's even muddier than this. The norms of a particular type of media may be distinctive, but they are not necessarily unique, nor are they fundamental. The space of the cinema is also used for screening sporting events and concerts; the practice of sitting in the dark with strangers and watching entertainment is shared with theatre; exclusive release windows are found in videogaming platforms and even hardback books; the film industry is dependent on and overlaps with the industries of television, advertising, software, and so on. Likewise, the definition of cinema does not stipulate a set number of essential criteria, but rather a fluid and impressionistic array of possible cinematic qualities. An advert with big stars and an auteur director which is screened before a theatrical presentation of a film probably isn't itself cinema; a straight-to-streaming film made on an iPhone with a miniscule budget probably is. Moreover, these criteria and practices are flexible over time: 'Although they possess extraordinary inertia, norms and standards can and do change, because they are expressive of changeable social, economic, and material relationships' (Gitelman 2006: 8).

So, with this in mind, what is the technological nucleus of VR? And what are the rules and conditions that gather around this not quite stable centre? The phrase virtual reality might feasibly be applied in a range of contexts, including to *any* experience of digital navigation, but it is culturally and industrially understood today as, at the very least, a 360° environment in which some ocular agency is granted to the user (the word spectator seems altogether too passive) and which usually involves a dedicated apparatus. As such, as much as its pre-history involves cinema and the computer, we should also look to the panorama and the stereoscope as precursors (Grau 2004; Ng 2021: 114–23). The former were large-scale installations popular in the late-eighteenth and nineteenth centuries which completely surrounded viewers and encouraged them to look around them at the fullness of the represented scene, while the latter were individual media devices popular in the second half of the nineteenth century which allowed individuals to view stereoscopic content (Jones 2020: 19–24). For all its novelty, the immersive promise of VR was equally made (and, for many, fulfilled) by these earlier media.

In relation to its contemporary digital form, technology writer Adam Greenfield's definition of VR is indicative of wider understandings of this medium:

> VR is an immersive experience, and accordingly requires the use of a head-mounted apparatus that isolates its wearer from the rest of the visible world. Once ensconced inside, the user is psychically present in a thoroughly self-contained, fully rendered environment, and for the most part interacts there with things that do not exist on the outside. (Greenfield 2017: 65)

Based on this, the apparent affordances of VR are isolation, ocular agency, and media envelopment. But a definition of the technology is not quite so straightforward. VR headsets and the content of VR media experiences have changed extensively over the last several decades, and while these affordances have endured as presumed ideals, they are not vital prerequisites.

We can see this if we return to YouTube, where on the VR homepage the platform lists four ways in which users can watch VR material, from high-end headsets and their cardboard derivations to unadorned mobile phones or computer screens. VR here is less a label for a technology and more a concept of media production and delivery which can be quite variable. That said, the website is clear that 'some experiences are more immersive than others', and only one of these types of experience is listed as allowing the user to 'become completely immersed' (YouTube n.d.). So, while the YouTube platform contains many 360° videos listed as VR which can be explored in a number of ways, a subtle distinction is drawn between the properly immersive reception of this material using headsets and other seemingly diluted equivalents.

If the VR YouTube page balances accessibility with immersion, then it also reveals the importance of the latter term. The label VR usually points to the delivery of media via an apparatus which is almost contiguous with the user's body, involving in its ideal state extremely proximate screens a few centimetres from the eyes, the use of headphones, and in some cases additional navigation and interactive possibilities enabled by hand-held controllers. This equipmental nucleus, to use Gitelman's term, is sustained by and itself engenders and propagates an idea that media texts and their worlds are (or can be) spatially extensive, and that insertion into them is somehow desirable. Unlike phones, tablets, computers, and even cinemas, the screen of VR is not something we contemplate as an object in the world, surrounded by other objects (our hands, a keyboard, the living room, emergency exit signs). Instead, its extreme proximity results in its seeming eradication *as* a screen. The frame separating screen and world seems to disappear, merging the two (Ng 2021: 109). We do not see the interface, only the media it contains.

For all that other technologies like panoramas, stereoscopes, and cinema (especially large-format screens and 3D) have sought to engulf the perceptual field of their viewers and obscure any awareness of the planarity of their content, VR appears a quantum leap in this regard. Placed alongside VR, other screens seem retroactively screen-y, becoming just possible points of visual attention within a wider visual field (even if this field can be mostly obscured by darkness). By placing its screens in extreme proximity to the user, VR seems to efface any separation between the two (Jones 2018).

Proximity is only part of the equation, though, and goes hand in hand with sensorimotor responsiveness. For VR to be VR, it has to react to our physical movements. VR users navigate the virtual space in which they find themselves by moving their head, as well as, in some cases, their body (albeit usually within a restricted area). Gyroscopes, accelerometers, room cameras, and sensors track the physical shifts of a user's body, translating them into changes in screen content. Screen refresh rates of 60 Hz and above mean that in many VR systems image movement is perceived without lag or latency: if one moves one's head, the visual field needs to move synchronously (even a fraction of a second's delay can result in nausea and optical confusion). All of this is then aided by stereoscopic presentation – in many VR experiences and applications, either twinned screens or a single split-screen provide slightly divergent views, and this binocular disparity mobilises stereoscopic perception.

This is not just about vision. Unlike communal screen media such as cinema and television, VR depends upon the use of headphones, whether over- or in-ear. This kind of sonic proximity may be fairly standard since the wide cultural adoption of the Walkman and other personal music devices from the 1980s onwards, but VR sound is distinctive in the way that it usually reacts, like the images, to the user's movement. Binaural audio uses data from the headset to change the quality of sounds in response to the user's repositioning, not just surrounding the user with spatially placed sounds, but moving these sounds around with high levels of fidelity to environmental conditions and human physiology (Bible 2016). If a user turns to look at the source of a sound coming from their left, binaural audio techniques don't simply move that sound from the left to the front of the user's audio field, but shift its qualities of timbre and echo to replicate this new auricle positioning.

The result of all this is total perceptual envelopment. In the words of Pasi Väliaho (2014: 74–5), 'there is no distinction in virtual reality between screens and how subjects intuit themselves in space as dynamic, kinetic, affective beings; no distinction, to put it in neuroscientific terms, between the image and the brain's simulation of its surroundings'. Partly as a result of this overlap between image and brain, VR is considered by many to provide a kind of unmediated mediation. Literary scholar Marie-Laure Ryan sums up such claims, and indicates how they seem to work to subtract the technological apparatus in its entirety:

> In its ideal implementation, VR is not merely another step toward transparency that will be 'remediated' by future media, but a synthesis of all media that will represent the end of media history. [...] The 'virtual reality effect' is the denial of the role of hardware and software (bits, pixels, and binary codes) in the production of what the user experiences as unmediated presence. [... In VR,] computers [...] serve as pure media – as largely hollow channels for the circulation of information. (Ryan 2015: 42–3)

VR is then positioned in familiar terms – it is the achievement of the myth total cinema, a media experience that seems unmediated, images 'that *become* rather than *represent* the real' (Wasson 2007: 85; emphasis added).

Is VR a faceless interface? The envelopment and the affective centring that the medium allow (and demand) seem to be very far from the desktop. The GUI provides users with perceptual access to the computer's functions, using representational features, high resolution graphics, layering, and customisation to enable this access. In providing a similar kind of access to the interior worlds of representational media, VR seems on the surface to eradicate the interface (outside of its compulsory employment when cuing up chosen media and putting on the headset). Even though it overwhelmingly relies on production tools of algorithmic image stitching, a digital screen apparatus, and extensive internet bandwidth, VR nonetheless seems to offer something quite separate from standard computer use. Our GUIs are sites of media multiplicity, but VR necessitates a media monomania, its prominent manifestations today requiring a total commitment to an enveloping single world (we cannot even check our phones when wearing a headset).

If these are the technological affordances and ideal imaginations of VR, then it is worth considering how they play out in specific examples of the format in the consumer sphere. In short, what are some of the aesthetic consequences of this apparently unmediated mediation? I will now take up this question, discussing various examples of VR content, before then focusing on the most culturally prestigious form of VR, immersive journalism. Immersive journalism leans into the affordances described above, and does so in ways linked to concepts of empathy, understanding, and social improvement. It claims, perhaps, to be the most faceless of interfaceless VR, a proposal which I will seek to counter.

VRealities

The envelopment offered by VR dictates elements of its representation and staging. First, as indicated, the mobility of the viewer calls for creators to place visual and auditory cues in ways that direct attention around the 360° space, but in a manner that does not obscure key information. This begets a kind of affective involvement, a sense of being embedded within the unfolding scene, whether this is one of immediate sensation or more sedate environmental observation. Second, and relatedly, the perspective of the camera usually somehow acknowledges this envelopment. Often placed within the centre of the scene, camera perspective will emphasise affective charge – that is, since the user is perceptually transported within this space, the viewpoint of the 360° rig will somehow underscore this presence (rather than taking a more detached or observant positioning). Third, thanks to the potential discomfort that can arise from extended use of the headset, experiences are often short. This leads to a tendency towards relatively simple content with overt goals. As a result, VR is often mapped along the coordinates of the 'cinema of attractions', Tom Gunning's (2006) description of early filmmaking and its emphasis on direct address and brief flashes of spectacle. Viewer comfort in VR also leads a range of other creative decisions – for instance, camera movement and editing patterns are usually tightly controlled in order not to radically unsettle the user's proprioception.

All these traits can be found in a vast range of VR content. For instance, tie-in VR texts such as *Rogue One: Recon – A Star Wars 360 Experience* (2016) and *The Meg: Submersive VR Experience* (2018) place the user within the pilot seat of an X-Wing fighter and a dive suit far beneath the ocean respectively. The participant can look all around within these environments, although their view is directed in both cases by defined apertures (the cockpit window and the front of the diving helmet respectively). Affective spectacles like attacking TIE fighters and circling sharks work in tandem with a powerfully 3D sound design to keep the user enveloped and engaged for the short running time of the experience (a couple of minutes each). Meanwhile, 360° VR experiences not connected to transmedia franchises might provide users the thrill of a spacewalk, rollercoaster, or safari; in these instances, the user is once again placed in the perceptual centre, with the offered thrills of speed, vertigo, or dangerous wildlife directly acknowledged. You are not watching someone else on a rollercoaster – you are yourself on a rollercoaster (or feel as though you are thanks to visual and aural stimuli). Finally, videogames like those included in the compilation *PlayStation VR Worlds* (2016) invite players to complete short passages of at times quite simple gameplay – hitting a virtual ball with their head or manoeuvring a luge down a hill with careful neck movements. These games are clearly 'attractional' in nature, and embed the player within the mise-en-scène much in the manner of 360° experiences. Videogames which offer more complex gameplay and invite longer gameplay sessions nonetheless still centre the player – the aforementioned *Resident Evil 7*, for instance, was the first of the franchise's flagship games to use first- rather than third-person perspective for its gameplay, providing greater affective charge for the zombie-besieged player.

These examples all utilise first-person perspectives to embrace the perceptual transportation of the format. This is not the only possible approach, though. A slightly contrasting example is offered by *Invisible* (2016), an experimental VR show made by VR start-up JAUNT with the brands Condé Nast and Lexus, and with the involvement of director Doug Liman. With episode running times of under ten minutes, this dramatic and at times action-oriented show tells a science-fiction story of invisible villains and threatened world economies (Jaunt 2017). Offering a more cinematic form of address than *Rogue One: Recon* or *Resident Evil 7*, scenes play out with actors moving past (and occasionally through) the camera, requiring the VR user to turn their head to follow the action. When cutting to a new scene (which happens often), the user is also often required to reorient, searching out the relevant point of attention in the new space by twisting and turning their head and upper body. An attack sequence in a hospital in the first episode uses jump cuts, tracking shots, and enveloping staging in ways that force the user to be extremely active in glancing around and reframing their own view; even then, there is the distinct impression that some 'dead air' is being witnessed, that one is looking in the wrong place, if only for a second or two (and this in turn encourages even more frantic head and neck movement). Liman's profile as a cinematic action director, particularly of *The Bourne Identity* (2002) and *Edge of Tomorrow* (2014), suggest that a kind of compromise is being attempted here between the intensified continuity of contemporary blockbuster filmmaking and the sustained perceptual emplacement of VR.

These few brief examples do not cover the wealth of VR material currently available, but they do indicate some consistent aesthetic trends arising from the affordances of the format. If many VR content producers come from, and still work within, the less proximate and less responsive screen-based media of film, television, and advertising, then VR demands the modification of many normalised practices to fit these different affordances. As Holly Willis puts it, 'for filmmakers, VR represents a radical shift in orientation, whether they opt to work in animated space or live-action; in either case, the structuring of time, space, perspective, identification and narrative all require reimagining' (Willis 2016: 151). Creative personnel must consider a wider spatial environment than they would when composing for a particular framed view, and they must also account for the spectatorial position of the 360° camera rig. Likewise, users are required abandon the kind of static viewing position associated with other screen content. They instead actively look around (whether due to prompts or innate curiosity), and in this way implicitly accept their perceptual integration within the scene and the linked affective address.

Milking it

These traits have led to VR's extensive use for documentary and documentary-like projects which raise awareness of a social issue or seek to expose injustice. In a term coined by VR practitioner Nonny de la Peña and her colleagues, this VR content is often called 'immersive journalism', defined as 'the production of news in a form in which people can gain first-person experience of the events or situations described in news stories' (de la Peña et al. 2010). The user of a piece of immersive journalism seems to be present within a contemporary event, usually one presumed to be very far from the social conditions and lived experiences of the intended or expected VR audience.

This use of VR highlights those facets of re-placement touched on above, and marshals this transportation in tandem with the apparent interfaceless nature of the medium to generate emotional understanding in the user. Immersive journalism has therefore given rise to claims that VR is a kind of 'empathy machine'. This label, popularised by VR filmmaker Chris Milk in a 2015 TED talk, seeks to describe VR's ability to rouse viewer engagement, excitement, and compassion (Milk 2015; see also McStay 2018: 95–111; Robertson 2017). A significant body of VR work believes in Milk's suggestion that the spatial re-placement offered by VR allows it to generate these feelings more than perhaps all other media.

In some cases, VR aims to mobilise this empathy by providing its user with the embodied perspective of a different sensory regime or social situation – for instance, conjuring an experience of colour blindness, or putting the user in the shoes of a young child. Some experiences even claim to put the user into a raced body different from the presumed user's (i.e. a non-white body – see Louie et al. 2018). More prominently, though, many VR experiences that foreground empathy offer not bodily alteration but rather bodily re-placement: you are situated among surroundings that are new and somehow ethically weighted. These surroundings are not only verisimilitudinous enough that they can be considered an authentic document of time and space, but are also accessible to the VR user in a physically interactive manner.

Take *Carne y arena* (2017), a multi-sensory VR experience directed by Alejandro G. Iñárritu which situates the viewer within an illegal border crossing from Mexico to the US. Released at the 2017 Cannes Film Festival, the situated experience involves a large, sand-strewn area through which the user can move, and so adds perambulatory geolocation and tactile sensory input to the cranial geolocation of seated (or standing) experiences. After acclimatising to the desert location (and the feeling the sand beneath one's bare feet), helicopters and border patrols appear, while aggressive officers confront the VR user no matter where they have chosen to stand in the open space of the installation.

Given *Carne y arena* was staged at an elite festival, and was sponsored by Prada, the experience it offers is presumed to be quite distant from that of the average user, with its success gauged by the extent to which it can bridge this gap. 'You're *there*', states Owen Gleiberman glowingly in *Variety*, before calling it a 'genuine fiction' which prompts a 'primal empathetic connection' (Gleiberman 2017; emphasis in original). Praising its effectiveness as a sensory encounter, Peter Bradshaw's (2017) review in *The Guardian* calls *Carne y arena* 'a dynamic, kinetic experience in which the audience can roam freely about, looking up and down, and around'. He crucially then connects this freedom with the greater understanding of the plight of undocumented migrants that the experience fosters, as it teaches observers like Bradshaw 'what it feels like to have a gun pointed at you' (Bradshaw 2017).

Installations such as this are expensive, though, and immersive journalism more commonly takes the form of 360° experiences (these can, in a pinch, then be viewed on YouTube or other platforms). For example, in 2015 the United Nations initiated a series of VR projects in line with the organisation's mandate to foster international peace and understanding, with the stated intention of 'bring[ing] the world's most pressing challenges home to decision makers and global citizens around the world, pushing the bounds of empathy' (UN SDG Action Campaign n.d.). Sites of 'challenge' included an Ebola epidemic in West Africa and the Gaza Strip, among others. *Clouds Over Sidra* (2015), in which a young Syrian refugee tells her story from within a Jordanian refugee camp, is perhaps the most widely circulated of these experiences. As already described, this video situates the user within various spaces of the camp, a mostly unacknowledged witness to work and leisure activities that are both mundane and, given the extremity of the situation, remarkable. Designed for VR, the video can nonetheless be watched on the desktop, although this highlights the awkwardness of the clicking and dragging, and the relatively low polish of the visuals.

Co-created by Milk, *Clouds Over Sidra* has received praise for its humanitarian credentials. It is 'a breakthrough in humanity', states Erica Swallow (2015) for *The Tech*, allowing the viewer 'to become part of her setting and empathize more deeply with the characters she encounters'. A humanitarian pledging conference in which it was installed in March 2015 raised $3.8bn in donations for Syrian refugees. Its power to raise this kind of money is linked by its creators to the capacity of the film to make users apparently 'feel like they were really, truly understanding what it's like to walk in someone else's shoes' (Anderson 2015).

Immersive journalism need not map onto a contemporary event, though. In the University of Southern California Shoah Foundation's *The Last Goodbye* (2017), Holocaust survivor Pinchas Gutter provides a tour of the Majdanek concentration camp in Poland, and discusses his lived knowledge of it in the 1940s. Directed by Gabo Arora and Ari Palitz, the twenty-minute experience places emphasis on the forensic accuracy of its location and the authenticity of its central figure. Directly addressing the point of view of the user throughout, Gutter talks about the workings of the camp and his own tragic experiences within it (Figure 7.1). We may choose to look at Gutter or not, but if we look away our gaze alights on the sombre surroundings of the camp. These surroundings are generated from footage of the contemporary location taken by 360° cameras and into which Gutter has been composited; the impression is of an in-person tour of Majdanek today, not a recreation of its existence at the time of the recounted events. But these added layers of distance are designed to be respectful more than alienating. For Joshua A. Fisher and Sarah Schoemann (2018: 583), the experience allows users 'to determine their own engagement' with the subject matter, either peering keenly at the details of the recorded space (craning their necks to look through the window of a gas chamber) or paying respectful attention to Gutter and his eye-line as one might if actually accompanying

Figure 7.1 Pinchas Gutter is composited into the Majdanek concentration camp in *The Last Goodbye* (2017), directly addressing the viewer as he discusses his experience. Frame enlargement from YouTube VR.

him in person. The result is the sense of emplacement commonly expected from VR, with Gutter's direct address, like Sidra's, calling on the user to pay particularly committed attention (whether to him or to the space he is discussing).

In such examples, it seems as though the VR user is moved twice over. As revealed not only by the statements of creative personnel but also the words of reviewers and academics, the *you are there* quality of VR, in tandem with the direct address often featured in the medium, is thought to create a moral encounter of some sort. These videos and their ilk rely on an 'auratic rhetoric' – the sense that the auras of individuals and places have been retained and delivered to the user in some authentic fashion (Fisher and Schoemann 2018: 586). Physical transportation is tied to emotional stimulation, with the re-placement of the user apparently conditional on their capacity to gain new access to the experience of another.

For Milk, VR is an empathy machine because 'through this machine we become more compassionate, we become more empathetic, we become more connected, and ultimately we become more human' (Milk 2015). Through the apparatus we are ethically improved – although it is not clear in Milk's words whether this is because we witness what we otherwise would not, or if the very act of seeing content in VR makes us inherently more compassionate subjects, as the machine's mode of address reshapes our capacity to understand the other. Either assertion is questionable, and they are often problematically conflated; that is, the content of experiences is intrinsically yoked to the mode of their experiencing. Granting temporary access in a disembodied fashion, VR like *Carne y arena*, *Clouds Over Sidra*, and *The Last Goodbye* places excessive emphasis on the fact that this access is possible – from and through such access, ethical understanding is then thought to flow.

In some senses, therefore, immersive journalism can be seen as a kind of corrective to the 'distant suffering' offered by some television news coverage. As various scholars have shown, in this mode of representation images of others in pain are instrumentalised to defuse the political charge of the situation that has led to that pain, including the situation of viewing itself (Downing and Saxton 2010: 67). That is, the act of feeling bad when watching the reporting of real-world tragedy then absolves viewers of further activity in relation to that tragedy. Luc Boltanski (1999: 114) has suggested that the insurmountable gap between television viewer and viewed sufferer in such cases results in a kind of enforced viewer inactivity, and it is this inability to intervene that results in the production of pity. Yet the rhetoric of VR asserts that the viewer – now user or experiencer – *can* in some senses intervene. We are encouraged by the fact of 360° immersion to look and sometimes move around, and in immersive journalism we are often directly addressed by an individual from within the mediated world. Being *in* Sidra's surroundings is a different experience than watching a news reporter interview Sidra with the Zaatari camp as a backdrop.

Summarising the use of VR in these contexts, communication scholar Bimbisar Irom stresses how the technology is thought to overcome usual barriers around humanitarian communication. Under normal circumstances, images of refugees render them vulnerable and distorted, their voices 'either muted or heard only after they pass through ideological frames that perpetuate existing power hierarchies' (Irom 2018: 4273). In VR, that dynamic seems to change:

> VR experiences will allow spectators to be 'present' in the environment of the refugees, thus raising the empathy levels of its users. Further, it will enable spectators to hear and see the refugees directly, without the interference of cultural filters. This discourse plays a central role in humanitarian communication's enthusiastic embrace of the technology. (Iroms 2018: 4273)

Moreover, the very act of being (apparently) present in VR acts as a form of implied agency, an incursion that is – the user feels – not passive. The spatial access and presence granted by the medium operates under the sign of intervention, and industrial and journalistic discourses presume that this apparent immersion and intervention then *automatically* engenders a more ethically engaged viewer. This idea of VR makes it a tool for social improvement as much as, if not more than, mere entertainment.

Does VR make distant suffering less distant? Or is there something else going on? Digital studies academic Lisa Nakamura (2020) describes how immersive journalism helps to rebrand VR as a 'good' technology, and she suggests that this is used by Milk and others to celebrate the moral virtuousness of technology more generally. The widely pronounced claims of the format's empathic possibilities are, for her, ways for Big Tech to deflect from the inequalities and privacy violations structured into their platforms. The world of social media surveillance and gig economy labour disputes apparently vanishes when one dons a self-improving headset. As she states,

> Virtuous VR is a cultural alibi for a digital media culture that has taken a wrong turn, towards distraction, detachment, and misinformation. Hence its industrial strategy to represent it as inherently more ethical, empathetic, and virtuous than any other media has ever been. (Nakamura 2020: 49[1])

Pronouncements of VR's immersion (and the emotional consequences of this immersion) are, then, ways to re-access an earlier idea of digital technology as exciting, connective, and participatory, before it became a site of data violations and clickbait emptiness.

Nakamura and others are deeply sceptical of such claims. Irom (2018: 4287), for instance, notes how the rhetoric of 'framelessness' in relation to VR ignores key aspects of format's mediation, and he rightly argues that VR is permeated by the same power hierarchies and ideologies as other representational tools. For scholar of interactive media Kate Nash (2018: 129), the peculiar intensity of VR can generate 'improper distance' in which the user is prompted not to ethical reflection but rather 'a narcissistic reflection on one's own experience'. Nakamura (2020) calls this 'feeling good about feeling bad': immersive journalism allows those who are distant from events and places to rehearse pity, and so perform their moral duty, without then actually doing anything substantive.

Furthermore, the emplacement provided by VR inculcates a form of spectatorship which is implicitly intrusive. As Nakamura (2020: 57) outlines, VR 'requires the user to constantly pivot in a circle to find the person who is

---

[1] Likewise, for Ken Hillis (1999: xvii), 'VR becomes a narrative of the future that abets forgetting the failed promises of earlier technologies'.

speaking or the point of view described in the audio narration, peeking and snooping within spaces where their physical bodies might not have been welcome'. Relatedly, Nash (2018: 128) describes an ever-present tension between focusing on the subject of an experience on the one hand and looking around to revel in and visually test the completeness of the spatial illusion on the other. Scholars like Joshua Fisher and Sarah Schoemann (2018) may consider this beneficial in relation to *The Last Goodbye*, but it points to the way the immersion of VR users is balanced alongside, or even maintained through, an attention to the media itself and its technological capacities.

Folding together immersion and moral understanding also ignores the *dis*embodiment inherent in VR mediation. Apart from choosing our spatial viewpoint we are not active within the mediated scene. Our presence is implied through the way we are addressed, and in the case of the angry border patrol officers in *Carne y arena* is even authenticated through their capacity to locate us no matter where we physically move. And yet we don't have to pay attention to these other presences as we would in the flesh, and we can choose to appreciate the virtual simulation in which we find ourselves instead. As a result, game designer Robert Yang (2017) suggests that VR is less an empathy machine than an appropriation machine, and that experiences like *Clouds Over Sidra* are 'refugee tourism simulators' furnishing little real compassion, let alone political understanding. In a qualitative sense, the technological excitement of VR is precisely that *we are not there*, even though we feel like we are. If we were actually in a Syrian refugee camp we might certainly be curious about our surroundings, but we would probably not be tempted to squint and examine them even when we are being directly spoken to by a small child.

This is not to claim that the technological dimension of the screening situation straightforwardly compromises any ethical intentions of these experiences. If this was the case, then any mediated content would suffer the same fate. What *is* different is the nature of agency, and the way this is discussed in popular, industrial, and academic discourses. In her book about ethics and cinema, Michele Aaron (2007: 88) describes how 'spectatorial agency' is 'a marker of socio-political responsibility', as the film viewer is prompted to consider her own moral frameworks and her own lived ethical experiences as a result of watching certain content. Through its sensorimotor requirements and perceptual emplacements, VR offers a quite different form of agency than the responsibility Aaron is discussing. But in wider cultural conversations around the medium, these proprioceptive actions supersede or override other forms of engagement, and they are interpreted as having the same effects as the sort of self-reflection Aaron considers. The machine, it seems, automatically performs or encodes the presence of empathy through a facsimile of intervention in the form of head movements and affective address.

If ethical media (of any kind) prompt us to consider 'our personal powers of reasoning and choice' and our relationship to moral conditions (Aaron 2007: 109), then VR is certainly capable of such encouragements. But as Irom, Nakamura, Nash, and Yang all bring to our attention, there is a mismatch between the rhetoric of automated empathy which circulates around VR, and the realities of it as yet another interface. In Jenna Ng's words, this begets a kind of 'moral arrogance', defined as

> the assertion that one may conjoin with another's suffering simply through audiovisual media which represents their reality and the erasure of screen boundaries to carry through that media, or [the assertion] that technology can bridge gaps of understanding where human sympathy has somehow failed. (Ng 2021: 148–9)

If the content of a VR experience operates in a register of empathetic presence, then this still functions to highlight the actual absence the VR technology is overcoming. Revelling in this technological competence implicitly creates further distance. Even though the user is granted some semblance of experiential access and perceptual personalisation, this is always pegged to the distance between the coordinates of the mediated content and the user's own circumstances.

Looking through the Aperture

Unpicking some of the claims around immersive journalism helps us deconstruct some of the myths that circulate around VR and its immersive capacities. Prominent and culturally significant, immersive journalism is associated with what Marie-Laure Ryan above diagnosed as the format's 'hollow channel' model of media, namely a denial of hardware and software in the delivery of content. Far from unique to VR, versions of this misapprehension are often rehearsed in the early days of a media technology's mainstream adoption. Photography and cinema, for instance, were both considered by some at the time of their initial rollout to remove the guiding or interfering hand of the artist. Yet with VR this rhetoric of media transparency, or outright effacement, has been particularly strong. Perhaps, as noted by Nakamura (2020: 49–50), this is because of the opportunity VR offers to rescue a digital technology sector that has moved a long way from its initial utopian promises. Nonetheless, this model of an interfaceless interface is questionable *tout court*, and, as we have seen, can conceal a set of aesthetic affordances and even problematic ethical claims.

The concept of unmediated communication also brings VR into dialogue and explicit contrast with the GUI, which is after all a site of highly overt procedures of mediation. As outlined in Chapter 1, the Apple v. Microsoft court ruling of 1995 legally defined some of these procedures, including multiple simultaneous windows, symbolic icons, and menus. These features – along with links, layering, and user manipulation – all assert the presence of the intervening interface, even if this interface is coded as a representational space, and the world of the screen is implicitly a spatialised site of digital access.

A lot of VR content seems pretty free from this kind of goo. In its efforts to convincingly re-place the user in another environment without apparent mediation, VR strips out obvious interface elements. Outside of some VR videogames or the menu screens that greet a user initially, there are no overlapping windows, no manipulable icons, no menus for possible interaction. In immersive journalism and other enveloping and immediate spatial experiences, we seem very far from what Friedberg called the 'multiple, adjacent, postperspectival' visual vernacular of the GUI (Friedberg 2006: 22). The desktop interface has functional features and platform operations that we can point to; a VR experience like *Clouds Over Sidra* gives us none of this, providing instead just various locations in Zaatari.

But what if these locations are themselves the interface? In Chapter 2, I explored how a Bazinian model of realism shapes discourses on both cinema and the GUI. The amplification of resolution, I argued, was as much about information access as it was about verisimilitude. As a medium in which wide angles, deep focus, and long takes are key affordances, VR of course also appeals to Bazinian concepts of 'integral realism' (Bazin 2005b: 21) and 'objectivity in time' (Bazin 2005a: 14). Can this, too, be viewed as the creation of more functional 'real estate'? Videogame theory is useful in answering this question, and so I want to take a short side-quest into simulations and apertures, before returning finally to VR with some surprising resources in hand.

Whether they are highly detailed AAA titles, schematic 2D platformers, or text-based RPGs, videogames create worlds to display to their players, and they also allow these worlds to be somehow navigated or manipulated. Their interactivity is what makes them distinct as a screen media form, a point Gonzalo Frasca has made using the terms representation and simulation. For Frasca, narrative media like novels, cinema, and television are representational, in that they describe traits and narrate events. Videogames differ in that they offer both representation *and* simulation, with simulation being a dynamic system that models behaviour.[2] As he puts it, using the example of a flight sim game,

> A film about a plane landing is a narrative: an observer could interpret it in different ways (i.e., 'it's a normal landing' or 'it's an emergency landing'), but she cannot manipulate it and influence how the plane will land since film sequences are fixed and unalterable. By contrast, the flight simulator allows the player to perform actions that will modify the behavior of the system in a way that is similar to the behavior of the actual plane. (Frasca 2003: 224)

That is, a film about an event represents that event, showing the viewer what it looked and sounded like. But a videogame about an event simulates that event as a system, and so allows the player to interact with the event, to test inputs and outputs, to learn its dynamics. If we jam the joystick hard to the left, we learn that the plane crashes; if we walk our avatar into a mushroom, we learn that they grow bigger and so can take more damage.

But of course, there are no actual planes or mushrooms involved here. These are representational elements, metaphors that help us interact with the underlying system of the game. Images, sounds, and even narrative content are only the visible coating of the deeper simulation, a series of rules and operations regarding state changes that are stored in code. Players are rarely granted access to the source code of a game, and so they rely on manipulation of these representational elements to impact this system. Jamming the joystick hard to the left prompts the flight sim to visualise a tilted horizon and blaze warning sirens, showing the player repeatable, predictable consequences of this action. The visual and audial content of videogames are therefore ways in which we are granted some inkling of what is happening within the system of a videogame, a process which is by definition reactive.

As a ludological understanding of videogames, this framework foregrounds how gameplay and mechanics shape meaning. Ludology does not necessarily ignore elements of representation (narrative, character, semiotic

---

2 Nash (2018: 123–4) has used Frasca's work along with other discussions of simulation to think about moral distance and VR's first-person address, arguing that the sense of involvement provided by VR's simulation carries with it the aforementioned 'moral risk' of 'improper distance'.

signs, verisimilitude), but it does see these as tightly bound up with the interaction between player and game system. Whatever type of videogame we are playing, it must constantly deliver system information in order to orient and direct our actions. From flight sims to side-scrollers to third-person shooters to city-planning sims, testing the system *is* gameplay, but this testing only occurs thanks to the representational markers provided – otherwise, we'd just be coding.

If visual and aural elements deliver information concerning the status and workings of the videogame's simulation, then in some cases this can be highly schematic. Onscreen text, numbers, and other overt and obvious markers can inform us of changes in system states (our health bar going down, a bobbing arrow or dotted line pointing us to a location, an all-purpose heads-up display). These explicitly provide information about gameplay activities and possibilities in a manner that seems distinct from the actual environment of the videogame. But, as we heard in Chapter 3, videogames deliver information in more general and holistic ways. Both visuals and sounds intermingle diegetic and non-diegetic in ways that leads Kristine Jørgensen (2013) to propose the term 'transdiegetic' in relation to this medium. Jørgensen goes so far as to argue that a game's representational features – no matter how realistic, how diegetic – must be seen as elements of the interface between player and system. Indeed, for her, the boundary between fictional diegesis and system data is highly porous (Jørgensen 2013: 5). We must read the environment of a game, no matter how verisimilitudinous it is as a world, nonetheless as part of its interface.

To demonstrate this, let's compare two first-person videogames with detailed, three-dimensional worlds, but which seem to take different approaches to organising the player's understanding of the game's system. In *Prey* (2017), the player moves through the various levels of the Talos 1 space station, a highly detailed and realistically rendered environment swarming with alien invaders. Our navigation is aided by a wealth of visual overlays: the bottom left edge of the screen contains a series of numbers indicating current amounts of health, armour, and 'psi' points, and if the player comes across an NPC or manipulable item, then simply looking at it will trigger a descriptive statement, a health bar, a colour-coded indication of hostile status, or a pick-up prompt. Further to all this, the player can access sub-screen or full-screen menus that contain multiple tabs, and through which weapons can be selected, inventories managed, powers upgraded, and objectives monitored.

By contrast, *Portal 2* (2011) contains almost nothing of this sort. The player must solve increasingly complex spatial tests set by rogue computer system GLaDOS in Aperture Labs, but do so without recourse to an ammo counter, an objective marker, or an in-game menu of any kind. The player can see only the portal gun bobbing in their hands, the environment in which they find themselves, and a two-coloured disc in the centre of their vision indicating what portals are currently in use.

Is our aperture onto Aperture therefore more translucent and immediate than our outlook onto Talos 1? Far from it. If these two first-person science-fiction videogames organise their information slightly differently, then nonetheless they are both still continually communicating system information to the player, doing so through space itself. In *Portal 2*, the subtle detailing of the various wall panels in the test chambers indicate whether the player's portal gun will have an effect on them: we quickly learn to scan for slightly off-white rectangular panels, avoiding darker or fractured material upon which the portal gun will only splutter unsatisfyingly. Lines on the floor and ceiling give further clues as to the task at hand, guiding the player to see a connection between a button mechanism and a tube which drops weighted plastic cubes. Beyond these features, the lessons learned from previous chambers and even the viewing angles provided by each space all shape the player's understanding of what they can, and indeed should be doing in this environment in order to progress. Equally, the player of *Prey* is not relying solely on the nominalist augmentations and numerical counters contained in their enriched vision; they also look for clues and pointers in the architecture of their surroundings, the sound design, and the behaviour of those they encounter.

Following Frasca and Jørgensen, gameworlds like these are not neutral realities which are then either highly augmented with visible system data (in Talos 1) or not (in Aperture). Rather, the spatial environment we see in these and all videogames are constructs that deliver system information. Pop-ups, menus, and numerical counters might or might not be present, but the world itself is equally an interface that shows us a range of interactive possibilities. Knowing which panels to target with our portal gun in *Portal 2* is as much an example of our interfacing with a game system as is the pop-up notification in *Prey* which informs us of which button to press in order to pick up, store, or throw an item we encounter. The former seems to be less of an interface, but it is just providing us information to access the system in a different way, one which relies more heavily on roughly verisimilitudinous codes.

If, for Jørgensen, there is no game outside the interface, then there is no interface outside the game. The clothes our character wears and the dialogue they speak are as much elements of the interface as are overlain ammo counters or directional pop-ups (Jørgensen 2013: 23–4). It is the combination of all such elements – that is, everything the game provides to help us learn its workings, to act upon its code – that constitutes the game as it is played. This representation is always a lever to access the simulation beneath.[3] There is no transparent interface in any game, no non-obtrusive window through which we peer at and engage with a world, because every game is essentially an interface in its entirety. The menu screens, overlain text boxes, pop-up commands, and peripheral flankings of data that are present in games like *Prey* deflect our attention from the fact that the spatial world that the game displays – no matter how realistically rendered it may be – is equally a data display to facilitate our access to the simulation and its countless variables.[4]

All of which brings us back to VR. As seen, industrial and cultural claims around VR suggest that its envelopment is akin to invisible mediation, that it functions as something like a total cinema of spatial transportation and unique affective power. Immersive journalism is a high-water mark in this regard, marshalling this transportation not for effervescent thrills but for serious, socially engaged education and understanding. If, as noted, critical objections can be raised regarding the ethical dimensions of this transportation, then these can be extended through an interpretation of the enveloping visual and aural spaces of VR as gameworld interfaces. Rather than eradicating the interface, even the most pared down and realistic of VR emplacements is still, at root, an interface, a representational surface providing metaphorical access to a digital system. We then interface with this gameworld through our motility: whether moving our entire bodies or just our head and neck, VR calls on us to confirm our envelopment through changing our position within the represented space. In this way, we explore the dynamics of the system: if I provide the 'input' of moving my head a full 180°, does the VR simulation provide the expected 'output' of visually presenting the opposite side of the represented space?

---

3 As such, Jørgensen follows Galloway (2012: 42–3) in emphasising that the interface is an *effect* rather than a thing. Galloway's own term for the combination of representational and overlain elements is an 'intraface'.

4 As a media object, a film text, by contrast, is not a gameworld interface, because its contents do not adapt or enable active participation in the same way. A science-fiction or social media drama may include a wealth of overlain text or HUD-style augmentations, but these are hard-coded, and for the most part do not change depending on the way the film is watched. However, when embedded within a digital ecology in a user-oriented way – watched on Netflix, for instance, or even on DVD – a film does become an element within a gameworld interface, as the viewer can prompt the appearance of superimposed elements by moving the cursor or using the remote, and the text as a result becomes a navigable gameworld of sorts.

In his writing on digital media, Paul Frosh (2019) uses Holocaust survivor testimony as a key example of the kind of ethical content put under strain by the operative attention of the GUI. How can we pay the required amount of attention when constantly aware of other clickable possibilities? In an example like *The Last Goodbye*, VR would seem to directly resolve this – yes, the testimony of this Holocaust survivor is digitally mediated, but the absence of interface elements allows more concerted, less distracted attention. And yet, if we think about VR as a gameworld interface, we can see how it similarly mobilises operative attention. The comprehensiveness of the interface within the visual and aural field prompts users to test, and so fully experience, this comprehensiveness. The 'sensorimotor restlessness' of GUI use is not here expressed through the hand resting on the mouse, but rather in the eyes, neck, spine, and whole body of the VR user (Frosh 2019: 154). VR spaces may on one level encourage the hermeneutic attention of textual absorption, but the spatialised rendering of this text through screen-based mediation creates the operative dynamic that personifies the GUI.

Whether a spatial experience like *The Last Goodbye*, a 360° video like *Clouds Over Sidra*, or even a digitally-created gameplay environment like *Resident Evil 7* or *SuperHot* (2016), VR's visual interactivity – the capacity it offers us to look and sometimes move around a mediated environment – works in ways that are far from simple realism or immersion. If the multiple windows and menus of the desktop interface create loop of continual alertness that shuttles back and forth between the content of a window (a media clip, say) and the wider interactive possibilities of the GUI, then VR does not quite eradicate this loop (Frosh 2019: 152). Immersive journalism may seem to force attention upon its subject matter, but the technological transportation that occurs becomes just as much a focus of the work. The louder the cries of *you are there!*, the more emphasis is placed on the media wizardry which prompts such cries. Looking around one's VR surroundings then becomes less a confirmation of presence than an active seeking for the contours of the interface.

Conclusion

In VR, the interactivity so central to the operative mode of media attention in the age of the GUI is transformed from a trait of distraction to one of immersion. This is immersion in what is effectively a gameworld, an algorithmically rendered space in which our glances and movements constitute a form of gameplay, an experiment with the workings and limits of the system. These limits are revealed when our interlocutor's eye-line does not follow our craning neck, or when a glowing blue grid materialises to indicate we are seconds away from stepping outside the bounds of the motion sensor array. Traces of the interface like these appear quite frequently, although they do not fit with the rhetoric regarding the medium's faultless perceptual envelopment. Similarly, the idea that VR offers unmediated presence is laughable when we turn our gaze to the VR user observed from without: a spatially limited individual with a large apparatus attached to their head and maybe wires trailing across the floor or into the ceiling, who might need to remove this apparatus after a dozen minutes due to queasiness or perceptual exhaustion.

These and other challenges have prevented the format from becoming as widely adopted as might have been predicted, and more pertinently indicate the vastness of the gap between media lore and media reality. Despite huge investment by key technology companies like as Facebook and Google, VR is yet to become a normalised media experience for the majority of consumers. It is an occasional entertainment novelty for a relative few, and a central technological apparatus for only a slim number of professions and professionals.

This may change in time, but it will require considerable adaptations in media practice on the sides of both production and consumption. This somewhat belies the suggestion that VR denies the role of software and hardware in shaping media content. Considering VR in light of Bazin's myth, meanwhile, reminds us once again that this is indeed a myth, an unattainable North Star in the narrative of media development, one granted a new telling in the Age of Oculus. Just as wide-angle lenses did not render cinema a hollow channel for information circulation, neither does an extremely proximate, gyroscopically enabled, high frame rate stereoscopic screen, nor 3D binaural sound.

This calls our attention to the fact that VR is an interface. And, as an interface, even if it seems to lack a frame, it nonetheless frames what we see in highly particular ways. In this way, although seemingly very different from the GUI, VR nonetheless clearly adopts gooey traits, even if industrial and cultural agents seek to obscure these beneath ideas of empathy and transportation.

Conclusion: Stuck In

A car screeches through busy downtown streets. Controlling a character who sits in the passenger seat, I look behind me and see a host of pursuing vehicles, their occupants climbing onto bonnets to leap in my direction with hostile intent. I take aim with a pistol, and a circular targeting pip flags up exactly when I should pump the trigger on my PS5 remote to blow out tyres and shoot the besuited enemies. The roof of the car I'm in is torn off during this combat, and now I must also contend with a helicopter launching a hail of rockets toward me. Upgrading to a larger weapon, I indiscriminately spray bullets everywhere in sight. The result is an immense explosion which seems to take out all adversaries and draw a line under this action sequence and section of gameplay.

At this point an onscreen logo – Unreal Engine 5 – comes and goes, and after this I float above the same city in which combat just took place (seemingly now clear of the explosions and rubble I so recently generated). Prompts invite me to 'Toggle Mass AI Visualization', 'Toggle Day/Night', or 'Toggle Nanite Visualization', while accompanying text states seemingly related concurrent information about 'automatic open world streaming', 'dynamic global illumination and reflections', 'rule based object placement', 'particle system', 'virtualized geometry', 'procedural audio generation', and more. Pressing x on the controller indeed toggles these values, making traffic appear and disappear, altering the time of the world from midday brightness to night-time halogen glow, or even rendering the entire, extremely verisimilitudinous world into a fractal, primary-coloured cavalcade of tessellated triangles (Figures C1a–b). After this aerial sweep, I am plunged back to street-level, where I control a character who can walk, run, and drive through this Western metropolis. No longer pursued by agents, possible activities to undertake are suggested by map markers (if I reach them I will gain access to more toggling options), but instrumental task completion does not seem to be the primary purpose of this world. Rather, these streets seem to be about wandering and languid aesthetic appreciation – I am

Figures C.1a and b An aerial view of the city created by (and used to announce and advertise) Unreal Engine 5 in *The Matrix Awakens* (2015), offering the user/player/viewer/experiencer the option to toggle visual attributes. Frame enlargement from PS4 gameplay.)

invited to be awed at the size of this map, the realism of the physics, the scale of the AI, the quality of the audio, and so on.

Unreal Engine 5 is a videogame engine developed by Epic Games. Released across 2021–2, UE5 was optimised with the PlayStation 5 in mind (a console released in late 2020, but with a somewhat delayed rollout thanks to the global COVID-19 pandemic and global shortages of crucial chip components; see Byford 2021). It is the fifth iteration of this particular software, but to call it a videogame engine might at this point be somewhat misleading. Yes, past versions of Unreal have been used to create many videogames, including large-scale titles such as *PUBG: Battlegrounds* (2017) and *Gears of War* (2006 – ongoing). But the program is also used to make films and television shows. *The Lion King* (2019), *The Mandalorian* (2019 – ongoing), and *House of the Dragon* (2022 – ongoing), among others, have used so-called 'virtual production', in which Unreal and other engines are used to create digital backdrops which respond in real time to on-set camera movements (Willment 2022). Meanwhile, *John Wick: Chapter 3 – Parabellum* (2019) used Unreal Engine 4 to create virtual sets for pre-production shot planning (Blondin 2019).

The experience described above is that of *The Matrix Awakens*, a download available to those with PS5 and Xbox Series X/S consoles, and seemingly designed to advertise this engine, these consoles, and also the newest cinematic entry in the *Matrix* franchise, *The Matrix Resurrections* (2021). The tagline to the first film in this multimedia saga – the 1999 blockbuster film *The Matrix* – asked 'what is the Matrix?' The answer in that film was: a digital simulation of reality into which malevolent sentient machines have imported the consciousnesses of those humans who survived an apocalyptic war. Our hero Keanu Reeves – playing office drone Thomas Anderson by day, and renegade hacker Neo by night – discovered this early on in the film, then teamed up with other 'awakened' humans to free those still imprisoned by the system.

With this in mind, we might ask, over two decades later, what is *The Matrix Awakens*? There are many possible answers. It is not exactly a game – there are almost no goals, and after the opening chase scene, no enemies or meaningfully interactive components (except crashing cars into one another, or pointlessly hassling AI pedestrians). It might be a kind of virtual reality – the experience is more about existing in this convincing simulation and being awed by the amount of detail and physical transportation offered than it is about actually doing anything specific within it. In some ways, it is a film tie-in, akin to VFX breakdowns in its paratextual promotion of digital spectacle – it features Keanu Reeves and Carrie-Ann Moss (the stars of the franchise), and it extends some of the metacommentary found throughout the film *Resurrections*. It is also a product demo, a proof of concept for an exciting new digital tool that will soon be offered to designers and its products enjoyed more widely by consumers. It could even, possibly, be a form of television, or of television production – it is downloaded to one's domestic viewing screen via a console, and the technologies it foregrounds will no doubt prove central to future virtual productions in the mould of *The Mandalorian*.

Are any of these definitions fit for purpose? Do any of them fully and satisfyingly address the existence of this text, and the various media categories in which it might be placed? I don't think so. This is a polyvalent piece of media which cannot be understood in these kinds of discrete ways.

As such, *The Matrix Awakens* is a very suitable way in which to conclude *Gooey Media*. On the one hand, it is best approached – or can *only* be approached – as a superlative example of the 'goo' described in the preceding pages. More than this, it indicates some future extensions to the previous work through its explicit and urgent embedding within industrial networks of transmedia borrowing and intermingling, and through its commentary upon the corporate (mis)management of all this gooiness. Because of the nature of concluding chapters, my discussion of *Awakens* is relatively broad and brief, principally mapping how the concerns unpacked in the preceding chapters are useful in understanding this media object. Nonetheless, I hope this short discussion helpfully traces the changes to digital screen media entertainment that have happened since we were first asked 'what is the matrix?'

Back to where it all started

The gooiness of *Awakens* makes sense – the franchise of which it forms a part has long had a rebellious relationship with media boundaries of any kinds. A major action film released in 1999, *The Matrix* spawned a raft of ancillary products, and this world became something of a lynchpin or test case for the digitally converged environment of the twenty-first century. Hollywood studio Warner Bros. seized upon the popularity of the original film (which made nearly half a billion dollars on a budget of $63m, and then sold extremely well on VHS and DVD), greenlighting not only sequel films but short films, videogames, comic books, and more. The Matrix became less a film, or even a franchise, and more an enormous digital world that could be accessed through any of a multitude of multimedia doors: never one thing, never one media, it quickly evolved into an overlapping and intermingling profusion of digitally linked elements.

Scholars took note, and the franchise was a central case study in Henry Jenkins's *Convergence Culture* (2006), in which he summarises the scale and intention of this project through the lens of its creators, the Wachowski siblings. These creators, he argued,

> played the transmedia game very well, putting out the original film first to stimulate interest, offering up a few web comics to sustain the hard-core fan's hunger for more information, launching the anime [*The Animatrix* (2003), a series of short animated films] in anticipation of the second films, releasing the computer game [*Enter the Matrix* (2003)] alongside it to surf the publicity, bringing the whole cycle to a conclusion with *The Matrix Revolutions* [2003], and then turning the whole mythology over to the players of the massively multiplayer online

> game [*The Matrix Online* (2005)]. Each step along the way built on what has come before, while offering new points of entry. (Jenkins 2006: 97)

Jenkins's commentary here perhaps unsurprisingly emphasises individual agency, whether of the original creators (who 'put out the first film to stimulate interest') or of fans (to whom the mythology is 'turned over' in 2005). We might turn the tables of this game, though, and accentuate instead industrial factors and financial imperatives: Warner Bros. cultivated a positive relationship with commercial creative voices who had experienced previous success with their first film *Bound* (1996), then mined the resulting intellectual property as extensively as they could, maximising consumer engagement across a range of corporately owned platforms.

Whichever players we focus on, this was not the end of the story. As we have just heard, the game continues beyond *The Matrix Online*, with *The Matrix Resurrections* being released in cinemas in the US on 22 December 2021. In a previously unthinkable move – but one increasingly common as a result of the COVID-19 pandemic – it was also made available in full on the same date on HBO Max, a streaming platform owned by WarnerMedia. Meanwhile, *Awakens* was released concurrently with the film, along with a wider transmedia portfolio of soundtrack CDs, NFTs, a Snapchat AR filter, and even Funko Pops (Thilk 2021; Weprin 2021).

Speaking of earlier entries, Jenkins (2006: 96) states that '[n]o film franchise has ever made such demands on its consumers', and the same remains true of this belated reboot, albeit perhaps in different ways. This tells us much about how, in the twenty-first century, convergence has become gooey. Rather than expecting its viewers to be savvy transmedia surveyors of an exploded textual terrain, for instance, *Resurrections* instead narratively collapses in on itself. Our erstwhile Neo is once again Thomas Anderson, although he is no longer an office drone: apparently seized by some entrepreneurial spirit, he has become one of the most famous videogame designers in this world. His most successful game franchise is called *The Matrix*, allowing Anderson to become a stand-in not only for the Wachowskis (who created this world), but also, in a way, for all those fans to whom the world was, in Jenkins's words, 'turned over'.

More than these plot elements, the in-film videogame itself is explicitly connected to the franchise antecedents of *Resurrections*. Described by characters and glimpsed in passing on occasional screens and through intermittent flashbacks, the game clearly – if quite oddly – consists of the first three films directed by the Wachowskis (or at least their most iconic moments). That is, footage from these films will be projected onto walls, and characters will comment that it is from the diegetic videogame found in this world – even though this footage, to viewers, is explicitly and memorably cinematic. Potentially explainable as nothing more than a bit of convenient semantic slippage, this nonetheless does not account for the instabilities created: why not just make Anderson a film director? Why not just use footage from *Enter the Matrix* or *The Matrix Online*? Why fold together videogame and film as discrete objects and even media forms?

So popular were these games that Neo's business partner Smith (Jonathan Groff) is now pressuring him to make a belated third sequel, some twenty years later. Smith explains the imperative for this mandate:

> Things have changed. The market's tough. I'm sure you can understand why our beloved parent company, Warner Bros., has decided to make a sequel to the trilogy. [...] I have to say I'm kind of excited. After all these years, to be going back to where it all started. Back to the Matrix. I've spoken to marketing ...

This sort of postmodern self-referentiality itself seems like a call-back to a cycle of knowing mainstream genre films released in the years leading up to the original *Matrix* film, with *Last Action Hero* (1993), *Wes Craven's New Nightmare* (1994), and *Scream* (1996) all making continual references to their own conditions of production. But in *Resurrections*, dialogue such as this speech delivered by Smith, as well as wider plot threads, point as much to production disputes and industrial manoeuvring within the franchise as to funky self-awareness. Lana Wachowski, one of the creators and directors of the franchise, stated she would only return if granted creative freedom by Warner Bros. (Weintraub 2021). Seeking a revivification of a highly marketable property by any means necessary at a time when other franchises were losing steam, the studio conceded. The relative autonomy she was given is perhaps reason for the film's unusually direct and slippery metacommentary.

This might be contrasted with *Spider-Man: No Way Home* (2021), which was released theatrically only a few days before *Resurrections*. Since this book began with a bit of web-crawling (the *Spider-Man* videogame of 2018), it is appropriate to return (briefly) to our friendly neighbourhood goo-meister. *No Way Home* is the third entry in the Spider-Man films starring Tom Holland and co-produced by Disney and Sony, but Holland is joined in the film by previous iterations of the character, played then and now by Tobey Maguire and Andrew Garfield. In the film's third act, this trio of converged heroes faces off against a rogue's gallery of villains (and their iconic actors) from over twenty years of Spider-Man films, sticking together a wealth of rebooted and hitherto competing intellectual property. The tone is one of fun and warm nostalgia – a toybox aesthetic in which a parallel universe conceit allows the cherry-picking of elements from different films and eras, and their amalgamation in a light-hearted romp. The imperatives are as much commercial as creative though, with the hype generated through this dazzling mobilisation of Spidey lore and reminiscence resulting in over $2bn at the worldwide box office, a figure double what any previous Spider-Man film had achieved.

In *No Way Home*, then, just as in *Resurrections*, gooiness is pointed to and acknowledged. But the former seems to want to appeal to Jenkins's model of convergence, to be an example of fans getting what they want. Internet speculation about web-shooters is finally laid to rest, and Spider-Man memes are thrillingly brought to life with A-list actors. The 'best' (or most memorable) bits of this franchise iteration and that franchise iteration are brought together and celebrated. Both films are inherently gooey in terms of both their aesthetics and their industrial functioning, but *No Way Home* is gratified with this in a way that *Resurrections* is clearly not.

Despite the valiant efforts of marketing, *Resurrections* met with lukewarm critical reception, even more so than the earlier, widely derided sequels. It also suffered poor cinematic box office ($157m globally, or around 1/13 that of *No Way Home*'s), although this was likely as much to do with its release strategy and marketing as with its thematic approach or quality as a piece of art. As mentioned, the film was used by Warner Bros. to drive subscription to its Netflix rival HBO Max. This approach significantly de-emphasised the cinema as a space of textual reception, bypassing the theatrical window and making it instantly a piece of television as much as a movie. This muddies media boundaries as much as the in-film collapsing of diegetic videogame and earlier cinematic franchise entries.

The intertextual probing undertaken by *Resurrections*, as we might expect at this point, goes far beyond just the film itself. As noted, the film itself functions as a $200m flagship, launching (or possibly caught in the wake of) a range of other products, including a whole new streaming platform. If Smith has spoken to marketing, then one output of that conversation might be *The Matrix Awakens*. However, marketing have either been duped, or they are in on the joke, as throughout *Awakens* the metacommentary relentlessly continues. *Resurrections* is less a film, after all, than one more browser window into the graphic user interface of the Matrix, a resizable tile hyperlinked and overlapping with a wider array of screen products, *Awakens* among them.

Stay away from marketing

After downloading *The Matrix Awakens*, the experience begins on our televisions with a voice-over from Reeves while footage from the first film (or is it a game?) plays:

> Hi, I'm Thomas Anderson. Like many of you, I work with computers. I like the freedom I feel outside the limitations of the real world. But computers are also mirrors, reflecting back who and what we are and the choices we make, the worlds we build. They also confront us with questions about why we want to choose this over that, why we want to make X instead of Y. Where do ideas of who we are and what we want even come from?

Such words point to ideas of the desktop encountered in the preceding chapters – here the screen is another world, but it is also a mirror, a labour device, and a confrontation; it is a map of our personal, interactive choices, choices which may or may not be constrained by a range of factors.

Now standing before us, Anderson keeps up this heady line of questioning, asking us how we know what is real. Then, turning to a mirror, his reflection picks up the theme in a surprising way: 'Hi, I'm Keanu Reeves ...' Only the person talking to us is not Reeves exactly, but a synthespian created within UE5, a digital recreation at times indistinguishable from the real thing. He is joined by a contemporary synthespian of Carrie-Ann Moss, who plays Trinity in the franchise, although they soon become virtual reproductions of the actors circa 2003, with slicker hair and smoother skin ('I sometimes miss this version of us', Reeves/Neo says touchingly to Trinity/Moss) (Figure C.2). These younger versions find themselves suddenly transported into the above-described car chase, prompting the following exchange:

> Neo: Whoa, what just happened?
> Trinity: Yeah, this is what they wanted. They said they were fine with your theoretical mumbo jumbo but they needed some sexy action.
> Neo: Who said?
> Trinity: The marketing people.
> Neo: Marketing? I thought we were supposed to have total creative control?
> Trinity: Welcome to the Matrix.

Marketing is not just a process that happens after something is made, but a powerful force shaping both the content of particular artefacts and also the

242 Gooey Media

Figure C.2 Synthespian versions of Keanu Reeves and Carrie-Ann Moss state that they sometimes miss 'these younger versions of us' in *The Matrix Awakens* (2021). Frame enlargement from PS4 gameplay.

way that multiple transmedia artefacts overlap. While this book has focused on technology and aesthetics, Trinity calls our attention to another kind of glue, namely the commercial imperatives that press down on all media of this scale, whether they be film, videogame, or game engine demo.

If Trinity's fatalistic responses to Neo's complaints merge fictional text and production wrangling, reality and simulation, then this aligns with *Resurrections*, a film which asks fans of its franchise to consider and re-consider their interest and investment in this world. Since 1999, after all, key motifs of the franchise have migrated far beyond its porous borders. The special effect of 'bullet-time' became a pervasive and parodied visual technique in mainstream film and television, and 'red pilling' (the pill Neo chooses in order to wake himself up from the Matrix) became internet slang within hyper-conservative communities for a newfound personal commitment to misogynistic perceptions of the world. Computers, as Anderson/Reeves tells us in *Awakens*, are mirrors as much as they are liberators – but unlike *No Way Home*, the Matrix admits that we might not always like what we see when we look at those screens. In both *Resurrections* and *Awakens*, then, 'Welcome to the Matrix' is not the simple promise of adventure and media immersion, but something much more complicated.

The same is true of the representational world itself. A key selling point of *Awakens* is the scale of world construction that can be undertaken by UE5. After Reeves and Moss depart, the player is left to wander the streets of the New York-style urban space. Exploring the extensive, highly detailed world, the user can run through the streets and fly through the air, looking closely into the windows of every building, inside which there will invariably be rooms, chairs, kitchens, sofas, and televisions. As in VR experiences, the emphasis is on the totality of the simulated space, the capacity to peer at and scrutinise every meticulous and exhaustive detail of this digitised territory. Created using the procedural AI generation offered by Houdini, the detail in *The Matrix Awakens* is impressive, but also inhuman (Epic Games 2021). It may strive for realism but it does not always achieve this goal in unproblematic ways. The furniture does not quite convince as furniture at times, and closer inspection reveals office chairs which lack legs, or sofas which contain bulging protuberances where one would sit down. Meanwhile, room layouts make no sense, as vending machines are positioned in front of the only door.[1]

As much as *Gravity* in 2013, *Awakens* therefore traces the sometimes fraught overlapping of GUI workflow and aesthetics with ideas of realism. Close to creating worlds which are indistinguishable from our own, the GUI and its algorithmic underpinnings nonetheless here show accidental traces of themselves. The result is something like the website 'The Person Does Not Exist', created in 2019 by Philip Wang. This site uses generative adversarial networks (GANs) to fabricate a unique artificial face every time it is accessed or refreshed (Paez 2019). Often extremely realistic, there are nonetheless moments where the GANs have not quite achieved their purpose, and faces are generated with strange metallic tumours or eerily globular hair. Meanwhile, the rest of the image around these faces can be a distorted collection of hodgepodge elements (the GANs seek realism in the faces, not their contexts). Likewise, the image generators DALL-E and DALL-E 2 – named for artist Salvador Dali and the robot from *WALL-E* (2008) and first released in 2021 – create often peculiarly effective artificial images from text prompts. Nonetheless, the illustrations produced by these desktop tools can also be full of uncanny features and unsettling distortions among their more accurate attributes, faces and backgrounds slipping out of precision as we try to focus on them (Figure C.3). It is as if the desktop's goo is seeping through from the substrate here, the pictures deliquescing and dissolving in the humid atmosphere of the GUI.

Neo's final advice to the player of *Awakens* is to 'stay the hell away from marketing', and indeed the distortions of tools like DALL-E highlight how the marketing of digital simulation does not necessarily overlap with the truth. Like the instantaneity of VFX production, the neutrality of Google Maps, the revivification of space through parametric architecture, or the transportation of VR, we need to be sceptical of the hype that comes with

---

[1] I am indebted to Saad Maqbool for bringing this feature of *Awakens* to my attention.

Figure C.3 AI generated image of the prompt 'Neo and Trinity from the Matrix missing the younger versions of themselves,' made using DALL-E 2 (labs.openai.com).

the GUI. The experiences it offers are compelling, overwhelming, and pervasive, but they must also prompt critical reflection.

Time off screen

The *Matrix* franchise has been the subject of much scholarly attention over the past two decades. And yet I hope that the preceding discussion has indicated that this transmedia phenomenon remains a fruitful site of enquiry, especially in relation to the way it exposes ongoing changes to digital screen culture in the twenty-first century. *The Matrix Awakens* is just one more piece of a frothing and churning multimedia ecology, likely destined to be mostly forgotten, even as the tool it deploys and advertises (UE5) becomes ever more crucial to a range of media productions. Nonetheless, it is a pointed example of the kind of media cross-pollination that I have been discussing throughout this book. Videogame, demo, film, TV program, virtual reality, app ... whatever we decide it is, *Awakens* further alerts us to the need to undertake new forms of media analysis. Such analysis must now attend not only to the overlaps between our many screens, but also to the glue sticking these all together – the GUI – and the viscid aesthetic traces it leaves all over them. (And if the preceding discussion of *Awakens* has also emphasised the industrial and commercial contours that are parts of this media web, then this is to assert the importance of these concerns – and their future analysis – in addition to and in close relationship with the aesthetic intermingling that has been my primary concern in earlier chapters.)

Throughout *Gooey Media* I have sought to show that the process of bonding enacted by the GUI changes the content we view on these screens. The graphic user interface is not just there. It is designed in particular ways to particular ends, and these design choices are both drawn from wider media aesthetics and also themselves recursively shape those wider aesthetics. The GUI is somehow both an aesthetic form entirely its own, *and* one assembled from, inspired by, and dynamically interacting with other forms of screen media. As its own form, we must pay attention to its particulars; as a powerful influencing force, we must also be alert to how those particulars bleed and merge with the content found within its borders, and beyond. Indeed, while the GUI certainly offers what Anne Friedberg described in 2006 as a 'new visual vernacular', this vernacular does not stay sealed within the borders of the screen (Friedberg 2006: 22). It bleeds and seeps into the way media artefacts are conceived and produced, into their visual and aural aesthetics, and even into the world around us in the way we conceive of cities, buildings, and matter itself.

The GUI, as I have stated throughout, is not an impartial enabler of content viewing and navigation, despite the computational functionalism that the word interface implies. Ever more central to visual and aural culture, the GUI informs everything from blockbuster cinema aesthetics, television production processes, discourses of digital special effects, cutting-edge architectural design, videogame spatial imaginations, virtual reality experiences, and the sonic practices of entertainment media.

With this in mind, maintaining fixed boundaries is increasingly untenable, or at least unhelpful. This includes distinctions between screen media texts themselves (films, TV shows, videogames, and so on), and between the desktop screen and the other screens that might deliver these entertainments. Yes, there are still discrete media and there are still discrete screens. But walling them off from one another in our perception and analysis is highly limiting, and cuts against the realities of contemporary media culture.

This poses a challenge to scholars, asking them to move outside of disciplinary frameworks: there is simply no way to understand the contemporary screen without blending film studies, television studies, software studies, videogame studies, and more. If our media has come unstuck from specific screens, then our thinking about these media and these screens must become equally runny.

Looking closely at the GUI can be difficult. The graphic user interface seeks to be neutral, invisible, purely functional. But the desktop is central to our lives, and we seem to spend vanishingly little time off screen. Twenty-first-century media analysis has so far overlooked this fact. The GUI shapes the ways our entertainment media are accessed, organised, created, consumed, and manipulated, and its impacts are smeared across the surfaces of so much that we watch and listen to. Rather than wipe these traces away, we need to get stuck in.

Bibliography

100 Gecs (2020a), '100 gecs – ringtone (remix) [feat. Charli XCX, Rico Nasty, Kero Kero Bonito] {LYRIC VIDEO}', [Video], <https://www.youtube.com/watch?v=4NDEZs8UIiYandab_channel=100gecs> (accessed 20 August 2020).

100 Gecs (2020b), '100 gecs – ringtone (remix) [feat. Charli XCX, Rico Nasty, Kero Kero Bonito] {VISUALIZER}', [Video], <https://www.youtube.com/watch?v=OmX4UPiVS-wandab_channel=100gecs> (accessed 20 August 2020).

Aaron, Michele (2007), *Spectatorship: The Power of Looking On*, London: Wallflower.

Acland, Charles R. (2020), *American Blockbusters: Movies, Technology, and Wonder*, Durham, NC: Duke University Press.

Ahern, Mal (2014), 'Body mass index', *The New Inquiry*, 26, <https://thenewinquiry.com/body-mass-index/>.

Åkervall, Lisa (2020), 'Post-cinematic unframing', in Jill Murphy and Laura Rascaroli (eds), *Theorizing Film Through Contemporary Art: Expanding Cinema*, Amsterdam: Amsterdam University Press, pp. 255–75.

Anderson, Mark (2015), 'Can tearjerker virtual reality movies tempt donors to give more aid', *The Guardian*, 31 December, <https://www.theguardian.com/global-development/2015/dec/31/virtual-reality-movies-aid-humanitarian-assistance-united-nations> (accessed 20 August 2020).

Andersson, Johan and Lawrence Webb (2019), 'American cinema and urban change: industry, genre, and politics from Nixon to Trump', in Johan Andersson and Lawrence Webb (eds), *The City in America Cinema: Film and Postindustrial Culture*, London: Bloomsbury, pp. 1–39.

Anon. (2016), 'Barking dogs account for 3,500 Suffolk noise complaints', BBC News, 16 July, <https://www.bbc.co.uk/news/uk-england-suffolk-33534403> (accessed 23 September 2022).

Apple Computer, Inc. v. Microsoft Corp (1995), 35 F.3d 1435 (9th Cir), <https://law.justia.com/cases/federal/appellate-courts/F3/35/1435/605245/>.

Apple Explained (2017), 'Every Mac startup and crash chime', [Video], <https://www.youtube.com/watch?v=n23dp8caq9Aandab_channel=AppleExplained> (accessed 20 August 2020).

Apple Explained (2020), 'Every windows startup and shutdown sound', [Video], <https://www.youtube.com/watch?v=0UUAQiT2-Xcandab_channel=AppleExplained> (accessed 20 August 2020).

Apple Inc. (2017), 'iPad Pro, in 10.5-inch and 12.9-inch models, introduces the world's most advanced display and breakthrough performance', [Press Release], <https://

www.apple.com/newsroom/2017/06/ipad-pro-10-5-and-12-9-inch-models-introduces-worlds-most-advanced-display-breakthrough-performance/> (accessed 9 October 2022).

Apple Inc. (2022), 'Use mission control on your Mac', [Website], <https://support.apple.com/en-us/HT204100> (accessed 9 October 2022).

Arnheim, Rudolf (1957), *Film as Art*, California: University of California Press.

Ash, James (2015), *The Interface Envelope: Gaming, Technology, Power*, London: Bloomsbury.

Atkinson, Michael (2009), 'Parkour, anarcho-environmentalism, and poiesis', *Journal of Sport and Social Issues*, 33(2), 169–94.

AWN Staff Editor (2016), 'Framestore teams with Greg Lynn FORM for Venice Architecture Biennale', *AWN.com*, 3 June, <https://www.awn.com/news/framestore-teams-greg-lynn-form-venice-architecture-biennale> (accessed 18 July 2020).

Ayers, Drew (2019), *Spectacular Posthumanism: The Digital Vernacular of Visual Effects*, New York and London: Bloomsbury.

Barad, Justin (2019), 'Virtual and augmented reality can save lives by improving surgeons' training', *Stat News*, 16 August, <https://www.statnews.com/2019/08/16/virtual-reality-improve-surgeon-training/> (accessed 22 August 2019).

Bazin, Andre (2005a), 'The Ontology of the Photographic Image', in *What is Cinema?*, translated by Hugh Gray, Berkeley, Los Angeles and London: University of California Press, pp. 9–16.

Bazin, Andre (2005b), 'Myth of Total Cinema', in *What is Cinema?*, translated by Hugh Gray, Berkeley, Los Angeles and London: University of California Press, pp. 17–22.

Bazin, Andre (2005c), 'The Evolution of the Language of Cinema', in *What is Cinema?*, translated by Hugh Gray, Berkeley, Los Angeles and London: University of California Press, pp. 23–40.

Belton, John (2014), 'If film is dead, what is cinema?', *Screen*, 55(4), 460–70.

Bennett, Bruce (2015), 'The cinema of Michael Bay: an aesthetic of excess', *Senses of Cinema*, 75, <http://sensesofcinema.com/2015/michael-bay-dossier/cinema-of-michael-bay/> (accessed 11 May 2021).

Benson-Allott, Caetlin (2015), *Remote Control*, New York and London: Bloomsbury.

Berman, Marshall (1983), *All That is Solid Melts into Air: The Experience of Modernity*, London and New York: Verso.

Bible, Thomas (2016), 'Binaural audio for narrative VR', *Oculus Story Studio Blog*, 31 May, <https://www.oculus.com/story-studio/blog/binaural-audio-for-narrative-vr/> (accessed 26 Sept 2022).

Blake, James (2017), 'Second screen interaction in the cinema: experimenting with transmedia narratives and commercialising user participation', *Participations*, 14(2), 526–44.

Blondin, Andy (2019), 'Designing a film set in VR on "John Wick: Chapter 3 – Parabellum"', *Unreal Engine*, 25 October, <https://www.unrealengine.com/en-US/spotlights/designing-a-film-set-in-vr-on-john-wick-chapter-3---parabellum (accessed 23 September 2022).

Bogost, Ian (2010), *Persuasive Games: The Expressive Power of Videogames*, Cambridge, MA: MIT Press.

Boltanski, Luc (1999), *Distant Suffering: Morality, Media and Politics*, Cambridge: Cambridge University Press.

Bolter, Jay David and Richard Grusin (1999), *Remediation: Understanding New Media*, Cambridge, MA: MIT Press.
Bordwell, David (2002), 'Intensified continuity: visual style in contemporary American film', *Film Quarterly*, 55(3), 16–28.
Bould, Mark (2008), 'Transformers', *Science Fiction Film and Television*, 1(1), 163–7.
Bradshaw, Peter (2017), 'Carne y arena review', *The Guardian*, 22 May, <https://www.theguardian.com/film/2017/may/22/carne-y-arena-review-inarritu-virtual-reality-refugee-cannes-2017> (accessed 22 August 2019).
Brown, William (2013), *Supercinema: Film-Philosophy for the Digital Age*, New York: Berghahn.
Burke, Chris (2013), 'Beyond bullet time: media in the knowable space', in Jenna Ng (ed.), *Understanding Machinima: Essays on Filmmaking in Virtual Worlds*, New York: Bloomsbury, pp. 23–39.
Bush, Vannevar (1945), 'As we may think', *The Atlantic*, July, <https://www.theatlantic.com/magazine/archive/1945/07/as-we-may-think/303881/> (accessed 30 January 2021).
Byford, Sam (2021), 'Sony reportedly making even fewer PS5s due to component shortage', *The Verge*, 11 November, <https://www.theverge.com/2021/11/11/22775829/sony-ps5-supply-chip-shortage-forecast-cut> (accessed 18 February 2022).
Carpo, Mario (2013a), 'Introduction: twenty years of digital design', in Mario Carpo (ed.), *The Digital Turn in Architecture 1992–2012*, Chichester: John Wiley, pp. 8–14.
Carpo, Mario (2013b), 'Embryologic houses', in Mario Carpo (ed.), *The Digital Turn in Architecture 1992–2012*, Chichester: John Wiley, pp. 125–31.
CGF (2019), 'Shanghai fortress – VFX breakdown', [Video], <https://www.youtube.com/watch?v=6i90oYtHyY4> (accessed 23 September 2022).
Chamberlain, Daniel (2010), 'Television interfaces', *Journal of Popular Film and Television*, 38(2), 84–8.
Chan, Melanie (2014), *Virtual Reality: Representations in Contemporary Media*, London and New York: Bloomsbury.
Chion, Michel (1994), *Audio-Vision*, translated by Claudia Gorbman, New York: Columbia.
Chun, Wendy (2011), *Programmed Visions: Software and Memory*, Cambridge, MA: MIT Press.
Chung, Hye Jean (2017), *Media Heterotopias: Digital Effects and Material Labor in Global Film Production*, Durham, NC: Duke University Press.
Ciccoricco, David (2012), 'Narrative, cognition, and the flow of *Mirror's Edge*', *Games and Culture*, 7(4), 263–80.
Claypool, Mark and Kajal Claypool (2006), 'Latency and player actions in online games', *Communications of the ACM*, 49(11), 40–5.
Claypool, Mollie (n.d.), 'The digital in architecture: then, now and in the future', *Space10*. <https://space10.com/project/digital-in-architecture/> (accessed 22 June 2020).
Cogle, Jarrad (2014), 'Christopher Nolan's Gotham City and global cinema space', *The Mediated City Conference*, April, <https://architecturemps.com/wp-content/uploads/2013/09/mc_conference_cogle_jarrad.pdf> (accessed 10 June 2022).
Collins, Karen (2013), *Playing with Sound: A Theory of Interacting with Sound and Music in Video Games*, Cambridge, MA: MIT Press.

Control Remedy (2020), 'Control – breaking down real-time visual effects', [Video], <https://youtu.be/6-SRtd9NTvw> (accessed 22 September 2022).

Crecente, Brian (2018), 'Sony: 3 million Playstation VR sold, 21 million PSVR games', *Variety*, 16 August, <https://variety.com/2018/digital/hardware/psvr-sales-2018-1202907159/> (accessed 22 August 2019).

Cresswell, Tim (2006), *On the Move: Mobility in the Modern Western World*, London and New York: Routledge.

Crockett, Tobey (2009), 'The "*Camera* as camera": how CGI changes the world as we know it', in Scott Balcerzak and Jason Sperb (eds), *Cinephilia in the Age of Digital Reproduction: Film, Pleasure and Digital Culture*, London: Wallflower, pp. 117–39.

Cubitt, Sean (2011), 'Current screens', in Oliver Grau and Thomas Veigl (eds), *Imagery in the Twenty-First Century*, Cambridge, MA: MIT Press, pp. 21–36.

Daskalaki, Maria, Alexandra Stara and Miguel Imas (2008), 'The "Parkour organisation": inhabitation of corporate spaces', *Culture and Organization*, 14(1), 49–64.

de Certeau, Michel (1984), *The Practice of Everyday Life*, translated by Steven Rendall, Los Angeles and London: University of California Press.

Dematteis, Giuseppe (2001), 'Shifting cities', in Claudio Minca (ed.), *Postmodern Geography: Theory and Praxis*, Oxford and Malden, MA: Blackwell, 113–28.

Denson, Shane and Jane Leyda (eds) (2016), *Post-Cinema: Theorizing 21st-Century Film*, Falmer: Reframe.

Denson, Shane (2020a), *Discorrelated Images*, Durham, NC, and London: Duke University Press.

Denson, Shane (2020b), 'The horror of discorrelation: mediating unease in post-cinematic screens and networks', *JCMS*, 60(1), 26–48.

Dooghan, Daniel (2019), 'Digital conquerors: *Minecraft* and the apologetics of neoliberalism', *Games and Culture*, 14(1), 67–86.

Douglas, Nick (2014), 'It's supposed to look like shit: the internet ugly aesthetic', *Journal of Visual Culture*, 13(3), 314–39.

Downing, Lisa and Libby Saxton (2010), *Film and Ethics: Foreclosed Encounters*, Abingdon: Routledge.

Dunmer, David and Tim Sluckin (2014), *Soap, Science, and Flat-Screen TVs: A History of Liquid Crystals*, Oxford: Oxford University Press.

Dwyer, Tessa (2017), 'Hecklevision, barrage cinema and bullet screens: an intercultural analysis', *Participations*, 14(2), 571–89.

EA (n.d.), 'SimCity BuildIt', [Website], <https://www.ea.com/games/simcity/simcity-buildit/media-hub/media/simcity-buildit-tips-tricks-part-2-specializations> (accessed 11 October 2022).

El Ranchito Imagen Digital (2015), 'Game of Thrones (HBO) – Hardhome (VFX breakdown)', [Video], <https://vimeo.com/132571771> (accessed 23 September 2022).

Elliott, Kevin (2019), 'The tragic story of the Michigan film industry', *Downtown News Magazine*, 27 March, <https://www.downtownpublications.com/single-post/2019/03/26/the-tragic-story-of-michigan-film-industry> (accessed 18 August 2022).

Elsaesser, Thomas and Malte Hagener (2015), *Film Theory: An Introduction Through the Senses*, London and New York: Routledge.

Elsaesser, Thomas (2013), 'The "return" of 3-D: on some of the logics and genealogies of the image in the twenty-first century', *Critical Inquiry*, 39, 217–46.

Epic Games (2021), 'Introducing *The Matrix Awakens: An Unreal Engine 5 Experience*', *Unreal Engine*, 9 December, <https://www.unrealengine.com/en-US/blog/introducing-the-matrix-awakens-an-unreal-engine-5-experience> (accessed 28 September 2022).

Feuer, Jane (1983), 'The concept of live television: ontology as ideology', in E. Ann Kaplan (ed.), *Regarding Television: Critical Approaches – an Anthology*, Frederick, MD: University Publications of America, pp. 12–22.

FilmIsNow Movie Bloopers and Extras (2017), 'Transformers: Age of Extinction – VFX breakdown by base FX (2014)', [Video], <https://www.youtube.com/watch?v=ligLfcdUfycandab_channel=FilmIsNowMovieBloopers%26Extras> (accessed 27 September 2022).

FilmIsNow Movie Bloopers and Extras (2018), 'Wonder Woman – VFX breakdown by UPP (2017)', [Video], <https://www.youtube.com/watch?v=5PX2GrxSY3o> (accessed 23 September 2022).

FilmIsNow Movie Bloopers and Extras (2021), 'ASSASSIN'S CREED VALHALLA | "Cinematic Commercial" VFX breakdown by Goodbye Kansas (video game)', [Video], <https://youtu.be/OW1zkoiRdpg> (accessed 23 September 2022).

Fisher, Joshua A. and Sarah Schoemann (2018), 'Toward an ethics of interactive storytelling at dark tourism sites in virtual reality', in *Conference Proceedings of the 11th International Conference on Interactive Digital Storytelling*, New York: Springer, pp. 577–90.

Fordham, Joe (2010), 'In dreams', *Cinefex*, 123.

Framestore (2016), 'Venice Architecture Biennale (full length)', [Video], <https://vimeo.com/169009968> (accessed 28 January 2021).

Frasca, Gonzalo (2003), 'Simulation versus narrative: introduction to ludology', in Mark J. P. Wolf and Bernard Perron (eds), *Video/Game/Theory*, London and New York: Routledge, pp. 221–36.

Frearson, Amy (2016), 'Augmented reality "will change the way architects work," says Greg Lynn', *Dezeen*, 3 August, <https://www.dezeen.com/2016/08/03/microsoft-hololens-greg-lynn-augmented-realityarchitecture-us-pavilion-venice-architecture-biennale-2016/> (accessed 18 June 2020).

Friedberg, Anne (2006), *The Virtual Window: From Alberti to Microsoft*, Cambridge, MA: MIT Press.

Friedrich, Kathrin (2016), 'Therapeutic media: treating PTSD with virtual reality exposure therapy', *MediaTropes*, 6(1), 86–113.

Frosh, Paul (2019), *The Poetics of Digital Media*, Cambridge: Polity.

Gaboury, Jacob (2018), 'The random-access image: memory and the history of the computer screen', *Grey Room*, 70, 24–53.

Gaboury, Jacob (2015), 'Hidden surface problems: on the digital image as material object', *Journal of Visual Culture*, 14(1), 40–60.

Galloway, Alexander (2006), *Gaming: Essays on Algorithmic Culture*, Minneapolis: University of Minnesota Press.

Galloway, Alexander (2012), *The Interface Effect*, Cambridge: Polity.

Gane, Nicholas and David Beer (2008), *New Media: The Key Concepts*, London: Bloomsbury.

Geoghegan, Bernard Dionysius (2019), 'An ecology of operations: vigilance, radar, and the birth of the computer screen', *Representations*, 147, 59–95.

Gere, Charlie (2006), 'Genealogy of the computer screen', *Visual Communication*, 5(2), 141–52.

Gibson, James J (1979), *The Ecological Approach to Visual Perception*, Boston: Houghton Mifflin.

Gillies, Craille Maguire (2014), 'Lego: can this most analogue of toys really be a modern urban planning tool?', *The Guardian*, 18 December, <https://www.theguardian.com/cities/2014/dec/18/lego-toys-urban-planning-tool-architects-mit#img-1> (accessed 15 June 2020).

Gitelman, Lisa (2006), *Always Already New: Media, History, and the Data of Culture*, Cambridge, MA: MIT Press.

Glasgow, Dane (2020), 'Google Maps is turning 15! Celebrate with a new look and features', *Google Blog*, 6 February, <https://www.blog.google/products/maps/maps-15th-birthday/> (accessed 27 September 2022).

Gleiberman, Owen (2017), 'Cannes virtual reality review: Alejandro G. Iñárritu's "Carne y Arena"', *Variety*, 20 May, <https://variety.com/2017/film/reviews/carne-y-arena-review-alejandro-g-inarritu-1202438293/> (accessed 22 August 2019).

Gospodini, Aspa (2006), 'Portraying, classifying and understanding the emerging landscapes in the post-industrial city', *Cities*, 23(5), 311–30.

Goss, Jon (1993), 'The "Magic of the Mall": an analysis of form, function, and meaning in the contemporary retail built environment', *Annals of the Association of American Geographers*, 83(1), 18–47.

Graham, Stephen and Simon Guy (2002), 'Digital space meets urban place: sociotechnologies of urban restructuring in downtown San Francisco', *City*, 6(3), 369–82.

Grau, Oliver (2004), *Virtual Art: From Illusion to Immersion*, translated by Gloria Custance, Cambridge, MA: MIT Press.

Greenfield, Adam (2017), *Radical Technologies: The Design of Everyday Life*, London and New York: Verso.

Grubb, Jeff (2016), 'PlayStation 4 Pro is not a real 4K console', *Venture Beat*, 8 September, <https://venturebeat.com/games/ps4-pro-isnt-4k-that-doesnt-matter/> (accessed 23 September 2022).

Gunning, Tom (2006), 'The cinema of attraction: early film, its spectator and the avant-garde', in Wanda Strauven (ed.), *The Cinema of Attractions Reloaded*, Amsterdam: Amsterdam University Press, pp. 381–8.

Gurevitch, Leon (2016), 'Cinema designed: visual effects software and the emergence of engineered spectacle', in Shane Denson and Julia Leyda (eds), *Post-cinema: Theorizing 21st Century Film*, Sussex: Reframe Books, pp. 270–96.

Han, Angie (2015), '"Transformers: Age of Extinction" tops 2015 product placement awards', *SlashFilm*, 4 March, <https://www.slashfilm.com/transformers-age-of-extinction-tops-2015-product-placement-awards/> (accessed 19 August 2021).

Harpold, Terry (2009), *Ex-Foliations: Reading Machines and the Upgrade Path*, Minneapolis: University of Minnesota Press.

Harvey, David (1989), *The Urban Experience*, Baltimore, MD: Johns Hopkins University Press.

Harvey, David (1990), *The Condition of Postmodernity*, Cambridge, MA, and Oxford: Blackwell.

Harvey, David (2006), 'Neo-liberalism as creative destruction', *Geografiska Annaler B*, 88(2), 145–58.

Hesmondhalgh, David and Amanda D. Lotz (2020), 'Video screen interfaces as new sites of media circulation power', *International Journal of Communication*, 14, 386–409.

Hillis, Ken, Michael Petit and Kylie Jarrett (2013), *Google and the Culture of Search*, London and New York: Routledge.

Hillis, Ken (1999), *Digital Sensations: Space, Identity, and Embodiment in Virtual Reality*, Minneapolis: University of Minnesota Press.

Hinds, Julie (n.d.), '"Transformers 5" gets $21 million in Michigan incentives', *Detroit Free Press*, <https://eu.freep.com/story/entertainment/2016/02/26/transformers-5-movie-michigan-film-incentives-mark-wahlberg/80977054/> (accessed 18 August 2022).

Hockenberry, Matthew and Jason LaRiviere (2020), 'On the performance of playback for dead media devices', in Nick Hall and John Ellis (eds), *Hands on Media History: A New Methodology in the Humanities and Social Sciences*, London and New York: Routledge, pp. 110–25.

Hoelzl, Ingrid and Rémi Marie (2014), 'Google Street View: navigating the operative image', *Visual Studies*, 29(3), 261–71.

Hogg, Trevor (2016), 'HALON tackles previs and postvis on "Star Wars: The Force Awakens"', *AWN.com*, 4 February, <https://www.awn.com/vfxworld/halon-tackles-previs-and-postvis-star-wars-force-awakens> (accessed 15 August 2021).

Holmes, Oliver (2019), 'Instagram Holocaust diary Eva.Stories sparks debate in Israel', *The Guardian*, 8 May, <https://www.theguardian.com/world/2019/may/08/instagram-holocaust-diary-evastories-sparks-debate-in-israel> (accessed 12 July 2021).

Holyer, Andy (2019), 'Teletext was slow but it paved the way for the super-fast world of the internet', *The Conversation*, 25 September, <https://theconversation.com/teletext-was-slow-but-it-paved-the-way-for-the-super-fast-world-of-the-internet-124118> (accessed 11 June 2021).

Hornaday, Ann (2013), '"Gravity" works as both thrilling sci-fi spectacle and brilliant high art', *Washington Post*, 3 October, <https://www.washingtonpost.com/goingoutguide/movies/gravity-works-as-both-thrilling-sci-fi-spectacle-and-brilliant-high-art/2013/10/02/cffa11bc-2a03-11e3-97a3-ff2758228523_story.html> (accessed 10 April 2021).

Horwitz, Jeremy (2020), 'How high refresh and frame rates will change phone screens and cameras', *Venture Beat*, 29 June, <https://venturebeat.com/business/how-high-refresh-and-frame-rates-will-change-phone-screens-and-cameras/> (accessed 23 September 2022).

Industrial Light and Magic (2013), 'ILM: behind the magic in Marvel Studios' The Avengers', [Video], <https://www.youtube.com/watch?v=MnQLjZSX7xM> (accessed 23 September 2022).

Insider (2021), 'How Marvel actually makes movies years before filming', [Video], <https://youtu.be/bgvgi3ShcmY> (accessed 4 December 2021).

Irom, Bimbisar (2018), 'Virtual reality and the Syrian refugee camps: humanitarian communication and the politics of Empathy', *International Journal of Communication*, 12, 4269–91.

Isaacson, Walter (2015), *Steve Jobs: The Exclusive Biography*, London: Abacus.

Jaunt (2017), 'Invisible – the director's cut', [Video playlist], <https://www.youtube.com/playlist?list=PL-bklv5cvCu7QSAJsTumVOU20tQxS_nOT> (accessed 20 September 2020).

Jencks, Charles (2005), *The Iconic Building*, New York: Rizolli.

Jenkins, Henry, Sam Ford and Joshua Green (2013), *Spreadable Media*, New York: New York University Press.

Jenkins, Henry (2006), *Convergence Culture: Where Old and New Media Collide*, New York and London: New York University Press.
John McAslan + Partners (n.d.), 'King's Cross Station', [Online], *John McAslan + Partners*, <https://www.mcaslan.co.uk/work/kings-cross-station> (accessed 27 September 2022).
Johnson, Catherine (2019), *Online TV*, London: Routledge.
Johnson, Catherine (2020), 'The appisation of television: TV apps, discoverability and the software, device and platform ecologies of the internet era', *Critical Studies in Television*, 15(2), 165–83.
Johnson, Steven (1997), *Interface Culture: How New Technology Transforms the Way We Create and Communicate*, New York: Basic.
Jones, Nick (2013), 'Quantification and substitution: the abstract space of virtual cinematography', *Animation*, 8(3), 253–66.
Jones, Nick (2015), *Hollywood Action Films and Spatial Theory*, London and New York: Routledge.
Jones, Nick (2018), 'The expansive and proximate scales of immersive media', *International Journal on Stereo and Immersive Media*, 2(2), 36–49.
Jones, Nick (2019a), 'The flexible urban imaginary: postindustrial cities in *Inception*, *The Adjustment Bureau*, and *Doctor Strange*', in Johan Andersson and Lawrence Webb (eds), *The City in American Cinema*, London and New York: I. B. Tauris.
Jones, Nick (2019b), 'Visual productions of urban space: Lefebvre, the city and cinema', in Michael Leary-Ohwin and John P. McCarthy (eds), *The Routledge Handbook of Henri Lefebvre*, New York: Routledge, pp. 230–9.
Jones, Nick (2020), *Spaces Mapped and Monstrous: Digital 3D Cinema and Visual Culture*, New York: Columbia University Press.
Jones, Nick (2023a), 'Far from Houdini: the "magic" of the VFX breakdown', *Animation*, 18(1), 42–58.
Jones, Nick (2023b) 'Empathy machines, indifference engines and extensions of perception', in Lucy Bolton, David Martin-Jones and Robert Sinnerbrink (eds), *Contemporary Screen Ethics: Absences, Identities, Belonging, Looking Anew*, Edinburgh: Edinburgh University Press, pp. 171–87.
Jørgensen, Kristine (2011), 'Time for a new terminology? Diegetic and non-diegetic sounds in computer games revisited', in Mark Grimshaw (ed.), *Game Sound Technology and Player Interaction: Concepts and Developments*, Hershey, PA: IGI Global, pp. 78–97.
Jørgensen, Kristine (2013), *Gameworld Interfaces*, Cambridge, MA: MIT Press.
Jørgensen, Kristine (2017), 'Emphatic and ecological sounds in gameworld interfaces', in Miguel Mera, Ronald Sadoff and Ben Winters (eds), *The Routledge Companion to Screen Music and Sound*, Abingdon: Routledge, pp. 72–84.
Jurgess, Todd (2017), 'Digital cinema and ecstatic technology', *Angelaki*, 22(4), 3–17.
Kalfa, Konstantina (2015), 'Where the spell is chanted (fallacies of contemporary architectural discourses)', *Architecture and Culture*, 3(3), 315–25.
Kenny, Tom (2019), 'The low-end, sensual sound of Apocalypse Now: Final Cut', *Mix*, 3 May, <https://www.mixonline.com/sfp/the-low-end-sensual-sound-of-apocalypse-now-final-cut> (accessed 23 September 2022).
Kerins, Mark (2010), *Beyond Dolby (Stereo): Cinema in the Digital Sound Age*, Bloomington: Indiana University Press.

Kerins, Mark (2013), 'Multichannel gaming and the aesthetics of interactive sound', in John Richardson, Claudia Gorbman and Carol Vernallis (eds), *The Oxford Handbook of New Audiovisual Aesthetics*, Oxford: Oxford University Press, pp. 585–602.

King, Geoff and Tania Krzywinska (eds) (2002), *ScreenPlay: Cinema/Videogames/Interfaces*, London: Wallflower.

Kirkpatrick, Graeme (2011), *Aesthetic Theory and the Video Game*, Manchester: Manchester University Press.

Klerk, Rui de, André Mendes Duarte, Daniel Pires Medeiros, José Pinto Duarte, Joaquim Jorge and Daniel Simões Lopes (2019), 'Usability studies on building early stage architectural models in virtual reality', *Automation in Construction*, 103, pp. 104–16.

Klinger, Barbara (2006), *Beyond the Multiplex: Cinema, New Technologies, and the Home*, Berkeley and Los Angeles: University of California Press.

Kłosiński, Michał (2016), 'SimCity: where the city ends', in Ksenia Olkusz, Michał Kłosiński and Krzysztof M. Maj (eds), *More After More: Essays Commemorating the Five-Hundredth Anniversary of Thomas More's Utopia*, Krakow: Ośrodek Badawczy Facta Ficta, pp. 134–46.

Koepnick, Lutz (2018), *Michael Bay*, Urbana: University of Illinois Press.

Kolarevic, Branko (2001), 'Designing and manufacturing architecture in the digital age', *Architectural Information Management, Proceedings of the 19th eCAADe Conference*, Helsinki University of Technology: Helsinki, pp. 117–23.

Kolarevic, Branko (2003), 'Introduction', in Branko Kolarevic (ed.), *Architecture in the Digital Age: Design and Manufacturing*, New York and London: Spon, pp. 1–11.

Kolson, Kenneth (1996), 'The politics of SimCity', *PS: Political Science and Politics*, 29(1), 43–6.

Korsgaard, Mathias Bonde (2013), 'Music video transformed', in John Richardson, Claudia Gorbman and Carol Vernallis (eds), *The Oxford Handbook of New Audiovisual Aesthetics*, Oxford: Oxford University Press, pp. 501–21.

Korsgaard, Mathias Bonde (2017), *Music Video After MTV: Audiovisual Studies, New Media, and Popular Music*, New York: Routledge.

Kuhn, Virginia (2021), 'Hamilton anyone? Lyrical kinetic typography', *InMediaRes*, 26 April, <http://mediacommons.org/imr/content/hamilton-anyone-lyrical-kinetic-typography-0> (accessed 18 August 2021).

Kuleshov, Lev (1974), 'Art of the cinema', in Ronald Levaco (ed. and trans.), *Kuleshov on Film: Writings by Lev Kuleshov*, Berkeley, Los Angeles and London: University of California Press.

Kulezic-Wilson, Danijela (2019), *Sound Design is the New Score: Theory, Aesthetics, and Erotics of the Integrated Soundtrack*, Oxford: Oxford University Press.

Kushigemachi, Todd (2020), 'Fake 3D, Real work: rethinking the creative labor and cultural perception of 3D conversion', unpublished PhD thesis, University of California.

Lageat, Thierry, Sandor Czellar and Gilles Laurent (2003), 'Engineering hedonic attributes to generate perceptions of luxury: consumer perception of an everyday sound', *Marketing Letters*, 14(2), 97–109.

Leach, Neil (2009), 'Introduction', *Architectural Design*, 79(4), 6–13.

Lee, Kevin B. (2016), 'De-coding or re-encoding?', in Malte Hagener, Vinzenz Hediger and Alena Strohmaier (eds), *The State of Post-Cinema: Tracing the Moving Image in the Age of Digital Dissemination*, London: Palgrave, pp. 211–24.

Lefebvre, Henri (1991), *The Production of Space*, translated by Donald Nicholson-Smith, Oxford: Blackwell.

Levine, Yasha (2018), 'Google's Earth: how the tech giant is helping the state spy on us', *The Guardian*, 20 December, <https://www.theguardian.com/news/2018/dec/20/googles-earth-how-the-tech-giant-is-helping-the-state-spy-on-us> (accessed 10 August 2021).

Lewis, Michael (2014), *Flash Boys: A Wall Street Revolt*, New York and London: Norton.

Linde, Charlotte and William Labov (1975), 'Spatial networks as a site for the study of language and thought', *Language*, 51, 925–39.

London, Barbara (2010), 'Looking at music', in Henry Keazor and Thorsten Wübbena (eds), *Rewind, Play, Fast Forward: The Past, Present and Future of the Music Video*, Bielefeld: Transcript Verlag, pp. 59–66.

Louie, Alan K., John H. Coverdale, Richard Balon, Eugene V. Beresin, Adam M. Brenner, Anthony P.S. Guerrero and Laura Weiss Roberts (2018), 'Enhancing empathy: a role for virtual reality?', *Academic Psychiatry*, 42(6), 747–52.

Lynn, Greg (1999), *Animate Form*, New York: Princeton Architectural Press.

Lynn, Greg (2013), 'Architectural curvilinearity', in Mario Carpo (ed.), *The Digital Turn in Architecture 1992–2012*, Chichester: John Wiley, pp. 29–44.

McCormack, Tom (2013), 'Did "Vertigo" introduce computer graphics to cinema?', *Rhizome*, 9 May, <https://rhizome.org/editorial/2013/may/9/did-vertigo-introduce-computer-graphics-cinema/> (accessed 23 September 2022).

McHenry, Jackson (2016), 'Does a normal frame rate make *Billy Lynn* a better movie?', 14 November, <http://www.vulture.com/2016/11/billy-lynn-high-frame-rate-120-fps-vs-24-fps.html> (accessed 22 September 2022).

McLaren, Laura (2019), 'Katy Perry's "Wide Awake": the lyric video as genre', in Lori A. Burns and Stan Hawkins (eds), *The Bloomsbury Handbook of Popular Music Video Analysis*, London and New York: Bloomsbury, pp. 163–80.

McStay, Andrew (2018), *Emotional AI: The Rise of Empathic Media*, Thousand Oaks, CA: Sage.

Manovich, Lev and Jeremy Douglass (2011), 'Visualizing change: computer graphics as a research method', in Oliver Grau (ed.), *Imagery in the 21st Century*, Cambridge, MA: MIT Press, pp. 315–38.

Manovich, Lev (2012), 'The back of our devices looks better than the front of anyone else's: on Apple and interface design', in Pelle Snickars and Patrick Vonderau (eds), *Moving Data: The iPhone and the Future of Media*, New York: Columbia University Press, pp. 278–86.

Manovich, Lev (2001), *The Language of New Media*, Cambridge, MA: MIT Press.

Mapes, Jillian (2020), '"Ringtone (remix)" [ft. Charli XCX, Rico Nasty, and Kero Kero Bonito]', *Pitchfork*, 25 February, <https://pitchfork.com/reviews/tracks/100-gecs-ringtone-remix-ft-charli-xcx-rico-nasty-and-kero-kero-bonito/> (accessed 18 August 2021).

Marshall, Paul (2019), 'Making old television technology make sense', *VIEW Journal of European Television History and Culture*, 8, <https://doi.org/10.18146/2213-0969.2019.jethc163>.

Marzola, Luci (2021), *Engineering Hollywood: Technology, Technicians, and the Science of Building the Studio System*, Oxford: Oxford University Press.

Maxwell, Richard and Toby Miller (2012), *Greening the Media*, Oxford: Oxford University Press.
Mazzarella, Sharon R. and Rebecca C. Hains (2019), '"Let there be LEGO!": an introduction to *Cultural Studies of LEGO*', in Sharon R. Mazzarella and Rebecca C. Hains (eds), *Cultural Studies of LEGO: More Than Just Bricks*, London: Palgrave, pp. 1–20.
Menkman, Rosa (2010), 'A vernacular of file formats', [Website], <http://rosa-menkman.blogspot.com/2010/08/vernacular-of-file-formats-2-workshop.html> (accessed 15 July 2021).
Menkman, Rosa (2011), *The Glitch Moment(um)*, Amsterdam: Colophon.
Michelle, Carolyn, Charles H. Davis, Craig Hight and Ann L. Hardy (2017), 'The Hobbit hyperreality paradox: polarization among audiences for a 3D high frame rate film', *Convergence*, 23(1), 229–50.
Microsoft (n.d.), 'Guided help: troubleshoot Aero problems in Windows 7', [Website], <https://support.microsoft.com/en-us/topic/guided-help-troubleshoot-aero-problems-in-windows-7-deeb0541-7fd1-aec9-e7a4-877dc8fde8cd> (accessed 9 October 2022).
Milk, Chris (2015), 'How Virtual reality can create the ultimate empathy machine', *TED*, March, <https://www.ted.com/talks/chris_milk_how_virtual_reality_can_create_the_ultimate_empathy_machine?language=en> (accessed 22 August 2019).
Mitchell, William (1982), *The Reconfigured Eye*, Cambridge, MA: MIT Press.
Moore, Rowan (2016), 'Zaha Hadid's successor: my blueprint for the future', *The Observer*, 11 September, <https://www.theguardian.com/artanddesign/2016/sep/11/zaha-hadid-architects-patrik-schumacher-blueprint-future-parametricism> (accessed 17 June 2020).
Morris, Tatiana (2017), 'Game of Thrones' Kings Landing in Minecraft 3 years later is bigger and better', *GameZone*, 17 July, <https://www.gamezone.com/news/game-of-thrones-kings-landing-in-minecraft-3-years-later-is-bigger-and-better-3455577/> (accessed 10 June 2022).
Myers, Joseph (1995), 'Casenote: *Apple v. Microsoft*: Virtual identity in the GUI wars', *Richmond Journal of Law and Technology*, 1(1), <http://scholarship.richmond.edu/jolt/vol1/iss1/8> (accessed 30 January 2021).
Nakamura, Lisa (2020), 'Feeling good about feeling bad: virtuous virtual reality and the automation of racial empathy', *Journal of Visual Culture*, 19(1), 47–64.
Nash, Kate (2018), 'Virtual reality witness: exploring the ethics of mediated presence', *Studies in Documentary Film*, 12(2), 119–31.
Ndalianis, Angela (2004), *Neo-Baroque Aesthetics and Contemporary Entertainment*, Cambridge, MA: MIT Press.
Nead, Lynda (2005), 'STRIP', *Early Popular Visual Culture*, 3(2), 135–50.
Ng, Jenna (2013), 'Introduction', in Jenna Ng (ed.), *Understanding Machinima: Essays on Filmmaking in Virtual Worlds*, New York: Bloomsbury, pp. xiii–xxvii.
Ng, Jenna (2021), *The Post-Screen Through Virtual Reality, Holograms and Light Projections: Where Screen Boundaries Lie*, Amsterdam: Amsterdam University Press.
Nicoll, Benjamin and Brendan Keogh (2019), *The Unity Game Engine and the Circuits of Cultural Software*, Basingstoke and New York: Palgrave, pp. 95–6.
Nitsche, Michael (2009), *Video Game Spaces: Image, Play, and Structure*, Cambridge, MA: MIT Press.

Nochimson, Martha P. (2002), 'Mulholland Drive', *Film Quarterly*, 56(1), 37–45.

Nvidia (n.d.,), 'Frames Win Games', [Website], <https://www.nvidia.com/en-gb/geforce/campaigns/frames-win-games/?nvid=nv-int-billgfe-31145#cid=gf56_nv-int-billgfe_en-gb> (accessed 23 September 2022).

Paez, Danny (2019), 'This person does not exist is the best one-off website of 2019', *Inverse*, 14 February, <https://www.inverse.com/article/53280-this-person-does-not-exist-gans-website> (accessed 18 February 2022).

Page Six (2018), 'Tom Cruise warns against "soap opera effect" of "motion smoothing" in PSA', 5 December, <https://www.youtube.com/watch?v=SDjQySUMqCoandab_channel=PageSix> (accessed 23 September 2022).

Paramount Movies (2017), 'TRANSFORMERS: THE LAST KNIGHT | The Packard Plant | Official Behind the Scenes', [Video], <https://www.youtube.com/watch?v=BFcmE3tvI9g> (accessed 27 September 2022).

Parisi, Luciana (2013), *Contagious Architecture: Computation, Aesthetics, and Space*, Cambridge, MA, and London: MIT Press.

Pasek, Anne (2017), 'The pencil of error: glitch aesthetics and post liquid intelligence', *Photography and Culture*, 10(1), 37–52.

Patches, Matt (2019), 'No movie theater in America will play Gemini Man as it was meant to be seen', *Polygon*, 8 October, <https://www.polygon.com/2019/10/8/20896194/gemini-man-hfr-3d-120-fps-showtimes-movie-theaters> (accessed 23 September 2022).

Peña, Nonny de la, Peggy Weil, Joan Llobera, Elias Giannopolous, Ausiàs Pomés, Bernhard Spanlang, Doron Friedman, Maria V. Sanchez-Vives and Mel Slater (2010), 'Immersive journalism: immersive virtual reality for the first-person experience of news', *Presence*, 16(4), 291–301.

Pierson, Michele (2002), *Special Effects: Still in Search of Wonder*, New York: Columbia.

Plaza, Beatriz, and Silke N. Haarich (2015), 'The Guggenheim Museum Bilbao: between regional embeddedness and global networking', *European Planning Studies*, 23(8), 1456–75.

Polygon (2020), 'How looting sounds are made', [Video], <https://www.youtube.com/watch?v=sqoylzFvxXsandab_channel=Polygon> (accessed 20 August 2020).

Poon, Linda (2015), 'Using Legos as a legitimate urban planning tool', *Bloomberg UK*, 16 October, <https://www.citylab.com/life/2015/10/legos-as-a-legitimate-urban-planning-tool/410608/> (accessed 23 September 2022).

Prince, Stephen (1996), 'True lies: perceptual realism, digital images, and film theory', *Film Quarterly*, 49(3), 27–37.

Purse, Lisa (2013), *Digital Imaging in Popular Cinema*, Edinburgh: Edinburgh University Press.

Purse, Lisa (2015), 'Rotational aesthetics: Michael Bay and contemporary cinema's machine movement', *Senses of Cinema*, 75, <https://www.sensesofcinema.com/2015/michael-bay-dossier/michael-bay-machine-movement/> (accessed 11 May 2021).

Purse, Lisa (2018), 'Layered encounters: mainstream cinema and the disaggregate digital composite', *Film-Philosophy*, 22(2), 148–67.

Raban, Jonathan (1974), *Soft City*, New York: E. P. Dutton.

Rehak, Bob (2018), *More Than Meets the Eye: Special Effects and the Fantastic Transmedia Franchise*, New York: New York University Press.

Reynolds, Daniel (2016), 'The Vitruvian thumb: embodied branding and lateral thinking with the Nintendo Game Boy', *Game Studies*, 16(1), <http://gamestudies.org/1601/articles/reynolds>.
Rizov, Vladimir (2021), 'PlayStation photography: towards an understanding of video game photography', in Marc Bonner (ed.), *Game/World/Architectonics: Transdisciplinary Approaches on Structures and Mechanics, Levels and Spaces, Aesthetics and Perception*, Heidelberg: Heidelberg University, pp. 49–62.
Robertson, Adi (2017), 'VR was sold as an "empathy machine" – but some artists are getting sick of it', *The Verge*, 3 May, <https://www.theverge.com/2017/5/3/15524404/tribeca-film-festival-2017-vr-empathy-machine-backlash> (accessed 22 August 2019).
Robertson, Barbara (2012), 'How ILM built a blasted-out NYC', *StudioDaily*, May 10, <https://www.studiodaily.com/2012/05/how-ilm-built-a-blasted-out-nyc/> (accessed 12 December 2020).
Rosa, Miriam de and Catherine Fowler (2019), 'Creating entangled histories of museum collections: Isaac Julien's *Vagabondia* (2002), and Camille Henrot's *Grosse Fatigue* (2013)', in Diego Cavallotti, Simone Dotto and Andrea Mariani (eds), *Exposing the Moving Image: The Cinematic Medium across World Fairs, Art Museums, and Cultural Exhibitions*, Milan: Mimesis International, pp. 293–99.
Rose, Gillian, Monica Degen and Clare Melhuish (2016), 'Looking at digital visualizations of urban redevelopment projects: dimming the scintillating glow of unwork', in Shirley Jordan and Christoph Lindner (eds), *Cities Interrupted: Visual Culture and Urban Space*, London: Bloomsbury, pp. 105–20.
Rotten Tomatoes Coming Soon (2016), 'Billy Lynn's long halftime walk featurette – immersive (2016), – Joe Alwyn Movie', [Video], <https://www.youtube.com/watch?v=ftsCUruuj-0> (accessed 9 October 2022).
Ryan, Marie-Laure (2015), *Narrative as Virtual Reality 2: Revisiting Immersion and Interactivity in Literature and Electronic Media*, Baltimore: Johns Hopkins University Press.
Sanjiv Creation (2016), 'How to use Aero Flip 3D in Windows 7', [Video], <https://www.youtube.com/watch?v=oGG6VGGh9Mwandab_channel=SanjivCreation> (accessed 2 October 2022).
Schiller, Melanie (2018), 'Transmedia storytelling: new practices and audiences', in Ian Christie and Annie van den Oever (eds), *Stories: Screen Narrative in the Digital Era*, Amsterdam: Amsterdam University Press, pp. 97–107.
Schroeer, Dietrich (2000), 'GPS: military technology to consumer good', in Dietrich Schroeer and Mirco Elena (eds), *Technology Transfer*, New York: Routledge, pp. 67–89.
Secor, Anna (2013), 'Topological city (2012 Urban Geography Plenary Lecture)', *Urban Geography*, 34(4), 430–44.
Sergi, Gianluca (2013), 'Knocking at the door of cinematic artifice: Dolby *Atmos*, challenges and opportunities', *The New Soundtrack*, 3(2), 107–21.
Setoodeh, Ramin and Brent Lang (2016), 'Inside "Billy Lynn's" troubled walk to the big screen', *Variety*, 4 November, <http://variety.com/2016/film/news/billy-lynns-long-halftime-walk-ang-lee-tom-rothman-1201908845/> (accessed 20 September 2021).
Seymour, Mike (2012), 'VFX roll call for The Avengers (updated)', *FXguide*, 6 May, <https://www.fxguide.com/fxfeatured/vfx-roll-call-for-the-avengers/> (accessed 4 December 2021).

Seymour, Mike (2016), 'Doctor Strange's magical mystery tour in time', *FXguide*, 14 November, <https://www.fxguide.com/featured/dr-stranges-magical-mystery-tour-in-time/> (accessed 20 July 2020).
Seymour, Mike (2019), 'Replicas that i Clone', *FXguide*, 29 January, <https://www.fxguide.com/quicktakes/replicas-that-i-clone> (accessed 15 August 2021).
Shaviro, Steven (2010), *Post-Cinematic Affect*, Winchester and Washington: Zero Books.
Shirr, Bertram (2017), 'Godly noises – resounding divine materiality in contemporary trailer culture', *Journal of Religion and Popular Culture*, 29(1), 69–85.
Shubert, Howard (2009), 'Embryological house', *Canadian Center for Architecture*, April, <https://www.cca.qc.ca/en/articles/issues/4/origins-of-the-digital/5/embryological-house> (accessed 27 January 2021).
Skelly, Tim (2009), 'Foreword', in Bernard Perron and Mark J. P. Wolf (eds), *The Video Game Theory Reader 2*, New York: Routledge, pp. vii–xx.
Smith, Jeff (2013), 'The sound of intensified continuity', in John Richardson, Claudia Gorbman and Carol Vernallis (eds), *The Oxford Handbook of New Audiovisual Aesthetics*, Oxford: Oxford University Press, pp. 331–56.
Smith, Jo T. (2008), 'DVD technologies and the art of control', in James Bennett and Tom Brown (eds), *Film and Television after DVD*, London and New York: Routledge, pp. 129–48.
Smith, Neil (1984), *Uneven Development: Nature, Capital, and the Production of Space*, Athens, GA: University of Georgia Press.
Soja, Edward (2001), 'Exploring the postmetropolis', in Claudio Minca (ed.), *Postmodern Geography: Theory and Praxis*, Oxford and Malden, MA: Blackwell.
Sontag, Susan (1996), 'The decay of cinema', *New York Times*, 25 February, <https://www.nytimes.com/1996/02/25/magazine/the-decay-of-cinema.html> (accessed 6 November 2021).
Sterne, Jonathan (2012), *MP3: The Meaning of a Format*, Durham, NC: Duke University Press.
Stewart, Susan (1993), *On Longing: Narratives of the Miniature, the Gigantic, the Souvenir, the Collection*, Durham, NC: Duke University Press.
Steyerl, Hito (2009), 'In defense of the poor image', *e-flux*, 10, <https://www.e-flux.com/journal/10/61362/in-defense-of-the-poor-image/>.
Stork, Matthias (2013), 'Space-wars: mapping the aesthetics of post-cinematic city space in action films and video games', *Mediascape*, Fall, <http://www.tft.ucla.edu/mediascape/Fall2013_SpaceWars.html>.
Summers, Tim (2017), 'Dimensions of game music history', in Miguel Mera, Ronald Sadoff and Ben Winters (eds), *The Routledge Companion to Screen Music and Sound*, Abingdon: Routledge, pp. 139–52.
Sutherland, Ivan E. (1965), 'The ultimate display', in Wayne E. Kalenich (ed.), *Proceedings of International Federation of Information Processing (IFIP)*, vol. 2. Washington DC: Spartan/London: Macmillan, pp. 506–8.
Swallow, Erica (2015), 'United Nations' first VR film pushes the bounds of empathy', *The Tech*, 7 May, <https://thetech.com/2015/05/07/sidra-v135-n15> (accessed 20 August 2020).
Swift, Brendan (2014), 'Mixed reviews for cinema tech tools', *Financial Review*, 30 September, <https://www.afr.com/technology/mixed-reviews-for-cinema-tech-tools-20140929-jkwli> (accessed 23 September 2022).

Szczepaniak-Gillece, Jocelyn (2020), 'Introduction', in Richard Grusin and Jocelyn Szczepaniak-Gillece (eds), *Ends of Cinema*, Minneapolis and London: University of Minnesota Press, pp. vii–xiv.

Territory Studio (2019), 'Shanghai Fortress | VFX and motion graphic reel | Territory Studio', [Video], <https://vimeo.com/366448271> (accessed 23 September 2022).

Thilk, Chris (2021), 'The matrix resurrections – marketing recap', *Cinematic Slant*, 22 December, <https://cinematicslant.com/2021/12/22/the-matrix-resurrections-marketing-recap/> (accessed 26 August 2022).

Third Floor (n.d.), 'About Us', [Website], <https://thethirdfloorinc.com/about-us> (accessed 21 Dec 2021).

Tryon, Chuck (2009), *Reinventing Cinema: Movies in the Age of Media Convergence*, New Brunswick: Rutgers University Press.

Tudor, Deborah (2008), 'The eye of the frog: questions of space in films using digital processes', *Cinema Journal*, 48(1), 90–110.

Turnock, Julie (2013), 'Removing the pane of glass: *The Hobbit*, 3D high frame rate filmmaking, and the rhetoric of digital convergence', *Film Criticism*, 37–8 (3/1), 30–59.

UN SDG Action Campaign (n.d.), 'UN Virtual Reality', [Website], <http://unvr.sdgactioncampaign.org/home/about/> (accessed 22 August 2019).

UPP (Universal Production Partners) (n.d.), 'Wonder Woman', [Video], <https://www.upp.cz/film/wonder woman> (accessed 23 September 2022).

Väliaho, Pasi (2014), *Biopolitical Screens: Image, Power, and the Neoliberal Brain*, Cambridge, MA: MIT Press.

Verhoeff, Nanna (2012), *Mobile Screens: The Visual Regime of Navigation*, Amsterdam: Amsterdam University Press.

Vernallis, Carol and Amy Herzog (2013), 'Introduction', in Carol Vernallis, Amy Herzog and John Richardson (eds), *The Oxford Handbook of Sound and Image in Digital Media*, Oxford: Oxford University Press, pp. 1–10.

Vernallis, Carol (2013), *Unruly Media: YouTube, Music Video, and the New Digital Cinema*, Oxford: Oxford University Press.

Vernallis, Carol (2014), 'Toward the limit: Michael Bay's *Transformers: Age of Extinction*', *Film International*, 25 October, <http://filmint.nu/toward-the-limit-michael-bays-transformers-age-of-extinction/>.

Vernallis, Carol (2017), 'Beyonce's overwhelming opus; or, the past and future of music video', *Film Criticism*, 41(1), <https://quod.lib.umich.edu/f/fc/13761232.0041.105/--beyonce-s-overwhelming-opus-or-the-past-and-future-of-music?rgn=main;view=fulltext>.

Vox Creative (2018), 'How the human eye processes pixels', *The Verge*, 26 November, <https://www.theverge.com/ad/18113053/pixels-human-vision-8k-television> (accessed 23 September 2022).

Walden, Jennifer (2019), 'How the incredible sound of "Avengers: Endgame" was made [interview with Shannon Mills]', *A Sound Effect*, 7 May, <https://www.asoundeffect.com/avengers-endgame-sound/> (accessed 5 July 2021).

Walker, Bruce N. and Michael A. Ness (2011), 'Theory of sonification', in Thomas Herman, Andy Hunt and John G. Neuhoff (eds), *The Sonification Handbook*, Berlin: Ambient, pp. 9–39.

Wasson, Haidee (2007), 'The networked screen: moving images, materiality, and the aesthetics of size', in Janine Marchessault and Susan Lord (eds), *Fluid Screens, Expanded Cinema*, Toronto: University of Toronto Press, pp. 74–95.

Watts, Catrin (2021), 'Music and the formal structures of contemporary action film trailers', in James Deaville, Siu-Lan Tan and Ron Rodman (eds), *The Oxford Handbook of Music and Advertising*, Oxford: Oxford University Press, pp. 286–302.

Webb, Lawrence (2016), 'When Harry met Siri: digital romcom and the global city in Spike Jonze's *Her*', in Johan Andersson and Lawrence Webb (eds), *Global Cinematic Cities: New Landscapes of Film and Media*, New York: Columbia University Press, pp. 95–118.

Weintraub, Steve (2021), '"The Matrix Resurrections": James McTeigue on the Meta dialogue, how Lana Wachowski has changed as a director, and future movies', *Collider*, 26 December, <https://collider.com/matrix-resurrections-sequels-meta-dialogue-james-mcteigue-interview-lana-wachowski/> (accessed 26 February 2022).

Weprin, Alex (2021), 'Warner Bros. plans "The Matrix Resurrections" NFT project (exclusive)', *Hollywood Reporter*, 2 November, <https://www.hollywoodreporter.com/business/digital/warner-bros-the-matrix-resurrections-nfts-1235040166/> (accessed 26 August 2022).

Whissel, Kristen (2016), 'Parallax effects: epistemology, affect and digital 3D cinema', *Journal of Visual Culture*, 15(2), 233–49.

Wilkinson, Alissa (2019), 'Gemini Man, starring Will Smith, spells catastrophe for the future of movies', *Vox*, 9 October, <https://www.vox.com/culture/2019/10/9/20905020/gemini-man-review-will-smith> (accessed 2 July 2020).

Williams, Christopher (2011), 'The $300m cable that will save traders milliseconds', *The Telegraph*, 11 September, <https://www.telegraph.co.uk/technology/news/8753784/The-300m-cable-that-will-save-traders-milliseconds.html> (accessed 23 September 2022).

Williams, Evan Calder (2017), *Shard Cinema*, New York: Repeater.

Williams, Raymond (2003), *Television: Technology and Cultural Form*, New York: Routledge.

Willis, Holly (2016), *Fast Forward: The Future(s) of the Cinematic Arts*, London: Wallflower.

Willment, Nina (2022), 'House of the Dragon: how virtual production is helping actors say goodbye to green screens', *The Conversation*, 13 September, <https://theconversation.com/house-of-the-dragon-how-virtual-production-is-helping-actors-say-goodbye-to-green-screens-190469> (accessed 23 September 2022).

Wirz, Fulvio (2014), 'Foreword', in Ming Tang, *Parametric Building Design Using Autodesk Maya*, Abingdon and New York: Routledge, pp. 7–9.

Wolf, Mark J. P (2011), 'Theorizing navigable space in video games', in Stephan Günzel, Michael Liebe and Dieter Mersch (eds), *DIGAREC Keynote-Lectures 2009/10*, Potsdam: University Press, pp. 18–49, <http://pub.ub.uni-potsdam.de/volltexte/2011/4980/> [urn:nbn:de:kobv:517-opus-49809].

Wood, Aylish (2007), *Digital Encounters*, London and New York: Routledge.

Wood, Aylish (2012), 'Recursive space: play and creating space', *Games and Culture*, 7(1), 87–105.

Wood, Aylish (2015), *Software, Animation and the Moving Image: What's in the Box?*, Basingstoke and New York: Palgrave.

Xenon (n.d.), 'Nvidia DGX A100 <<New>>', [Website], <https://xenon.com.au/product/nvidia-dgx-a100/> (accessed 23 September 2022).

Yang, Robert (2017), '"If you walk in someone else's shoes, then you've taken their shoes": empathy machines as appropriation machines', *Radiator*, 5 April, <https://www.blog.radiator.debacle.us/2017/04/if-you-walk-in-someone-elses-shoes-then.html> (accessed 22 August 2021).

YouTube (n.d.), 'YouTube VR', [Website], <https://vr.youtube.com/> (accessed 27 September 2020).

Zero (n.d.), 'Little Women before and after reel', [Video], <https://www.zerovfx.com/video/little-women> (accessed 23 September 2022).

Zonaga, Anthony and Marcus Carter (2019), 'The role of architecture in constructing gameworlds: intertextual allusions, metaphorical representations and societal ethics in Dishonored', *Loading ...* , 12(20), 71–89.

Zuboff, Shoshana (2019), *The Age of Surveillance Capitalism*, London: Profile.

Zylinska, Joanna (2020), *Perception at the End of the World, or, How Not to Play Video Games*, Pittsburgh and New York: Flugschriften.

Index

Note: 'n' indicates note.

100 gecs, 85, 111–13
300: Rise of an Empire (2014 film), 64
6 Underground (2019 film), 108, 113

Aaron, Michele, 225–6
Acland, Charles, 34
Adobe After Effects, 85, 115, 119n
Adobe Premiere, 87
Aeon Flux (2005 film), 107–8
Ahern, Mal, 66
Åkervall, Lisa, 41, 42
Al Jazeera, 32
algorithms, 32, 46, 48, 80, 133–4, 167–8, 171, 176, 178–80, 182–7, 191, 193, 205, 243
Amazing Spider-Man, The (2014 film), 9
Amazon, 30, 172
Android (platform), 1, 19, 49, 60
Andromeda Galaxy, 67–8
Angry Birds (2009 videogame), 163
Animals on the Loose: A You vs. Wild Movie (2021 television program), 30
animatics *see* previsualisation
Animatrix, The (2003 short film series), 237
Apocalypse Now: The Final Cut (2019 re-edit of 1979 film), 58n
App (2013 film), 35
Apple (company), 23–5, 41, 59, 74, 82, 227
Apple Computers (2013 video essay), 41, 46
Arcade Fire, 47

architecture
  in action cinema, 190–3
  and CAD (computer-aided design), 16, 176, 177–86, 193–8, 201, 205–7
  and flexibility, 16, 177, 182–5, 187, 205–7
  parametric, 179–86, 190, 191, 192, 194–6, 198, 203, 204–7, 243
  and topology, 180–1, 198
  speculative, 193, 198
Arnheim, Rudolf, 56n
Arora, Gabo, 221
Ash, James, 4
Atari 2600, 57
Atkinson, Bill, 59
attention, modes of, 47
augmented reality, 156, 158, 169n, 173, 193, 194, 238
Autodesk 3ds Max (program), 115
Avatar (2009 film), 70–1
Avengers, The (2012 film), 117, 121, 122, 123–4, 127, 128, 129–30, 137–8, 142–4
Avid, 87, 103

Babbage, Charles, 21
Bad Boys for Life (2020 film), 77n
Baltimore, 151
Bandersnatch *see Black Mirror: Bandersnatch*
Barron, Bebe, 118
Barron, Louis, 118
Base FX, 196

Bass, Saul, 118
Batman (2005, 2008, 2012 film franchise), 153
Bay, Michael, 42, 189, 190
Bazin, Andre, 14, 65, 72, 136, 167
   and myth of total cinema, 14, 53–4, 55–6, 58, 62, 65, 86, 209, 216, 227, 231, 233
Beer, David, 4
Beijing, 153, 179
Belton, John, 7
Bennett, Bruce, 189
Benson-Allott, Caetlin, 30
Best Years of Our Lives, The (1946 film), 55
Big Hero 6 (2014 film), 154
Bilbao, 151, 178–9
Billy Lynn's Long Halftime Walk (2012 film), 77
Birds Nest Olympic Stadium, 179, 189
Black Mirror: Bandersnatch (2018 television program), 30
Black or White (song by Michael Jackson), 183
Black Panther (2018 film), 137
Blade Runner (1982 film), 201
Blair Witch Project, The (1999 film), 37
Bloomberg (channel), 32
Blu-ray, 57, 79, 127, 137–8
   interface organisation of, 137–8
Bogost, Ian, 163
Bolter, Jay David, 3, 36
Bordwell, David, 103
Bound (1996 film), 238
Bourne Identity, The (2002 film), 218
Bradshaw, Peter, 220
Brasilia, 150
Briz, Nick *see Apple Computers* (2013 video essay)
Brown, William, 139–40
bullet-screens, 35
Burke, Chris, 142
Bush, Vannevar, 22–3

Call of Duty (b.2003 videogame franchise), 67n, 75, 82, 98
Cannes Film Festival, 220

Cam (2018 film), 40n
Captain America: Civil War (2016 film), 91, 106
Carne y arena (2017 VR experience), 220, 223, 225
CCTV Building, 153, 179, 185, 187–90
Certeau, Michel de, 168, 171
CGF Studio, 121, 124, 128, 131
Chamberlain, Daniel, 30
Charli XCX, 85, 111–13
Chicago, 42, 153, 175, 187–9, 192
Children of Men (2006 film), 139n
China, 42
Chion, Michel, 106
Chun, Wendy Hui Kwong, 23, 134, 149, 159–60, 164, 169
Chung, Hye Jean, 146
Chrome (internet browser), 1, 46
cinema
   and array aesthetics, 64–5, 71–2, 117
   cinema of attractions, 217
   and the 'cinematic', 2, 35, 46
   and the city, 152–4
   definition of, 213
   frame rate of, 73, 77–83
   and the GUI, 26
   history of, 21
   as index, 55, 226
   and intensified continuity, 103–9
   as place, 20, 33–5, 240
   and post-cinema, 7, 41, 104, 109, 140
   and shard cinema, 64–5, 68–9, 71–2
   soundtrack of, 101–9
   splitscreen, 63–4
   threat from other platforms, 36
   and workflow cinema, 67–72
   see also film studies
Citizen Kane (1941 film), 55
City of Culture of Galicia, 179
Clouds Over Sidra (2015 VR experience), 17, 208–9, 212, 221, 223, 225, 227, 232
codecs, 88
Cogle, Jared, 153n2
Collins, Karen, 96, 100–1
collision boxes, 96

ComiXology (platform), 12
computer-generated imagery (CGI) *see* VFX
computers
  as black boxes, 22
  and code, 22, 133, 159–60
  and command-line interface, 21–2, 26, 27, 31, 62, 133–4, 160
  as dynamic, 149
  and graphics processing, 74–5
  history of, 21–2, 117–18
  sounds of, 89
  see also interface; GUI
Condé Nast, 218
Constantine (2005 film), 64
Content (2019 web series), 46
Control (2018 videogame), 155
convergence
  convergence culture, 5, 237–8, 240
  and fluidity of media, 2–3, 104
  and media distinctions, 2, 13, 54, 72, 78–84, 245–6
  of media environment, 1–2, 5–7, 11, 28–35, 36, 51, 105, 140
  and screen technology, 12
crafting (videogame mechanic), 98–9
Criterion (app), 47
Cruise, Tom, 79–80

Dali, Salvadore, 243
DALL-E, 243–4
Daredevil (2015–18 television program), 139n
Dark City (1998 film), 157n
Deleuze, Gilles, 182
Dematteis, Giuseppe, 151
Denson, Shane, 46, 49n, 88, 189–90
Detroit, Michigan, 153, 191
Digital Domain, 196
Disclosure (1994 film), 210
Dishonored (2012 videogame), 155
Disney, 12, 30, 47, 154, 239
Doctor Strange (2016 film), 16, 64, 159–61, 164, 166, 170, 179, 187
Doctor Strange and the Multiverse of Madness (2022 film), 12

documentary (genre), 36, 40–3
Dooghan, Daniel, 164
Doom VFR (2017 videogame), 167n
Douglas, Nick, 111–12
Douglass, Jeremy, 182
Dredd (2012 film), 64
DVD, 32n, 33, 56n, 57

Echochrome (2008 videogame), 155
Edge of Tomorrow (2018 film), 218
Eiffel Tower, 178, 188–9
Eisenman, Peter, 179
El Ranchito, 121
Elektroplankton (2006 videogame), 96
Embryologic House, 185–6, 197
  see also Greg Lynn
Empire State Building, 189
Engelbart, Douglas, 22, 210
  see also mother of all demos, the
ENIAC (Electronic Numerical Integrator and Computer), 22
Enter the Matrix (2003 videogame), 237, 239
E.T. the Extraterrestrial (1982 film), 118
Eva.Stories, 46
Excel (program), 32

Face Changer, 145
Facebook (platform), 37, 39, 46, 66, 233
Fast and the Furious, The (2001 film), 139
Feuer, Jane, 32
Fight Club (1999 film), 139
film studies
  and the end of cinema, 6–7
  videographic, 42
Final Cut (program), 87
Fisher, Joshua A., 221, 225
FMOD, 87
Forbidden Planet (1956 film), 118
Ford, Sam, 42
Forza Horizon 4 (2018 videogame), 141
Foster, Norman, 179
found footage, 37, 42, 49
Fowler, Catherine, 41
Framestore, 193–4, 196, 198–9

Frasca, Gonzalo, 227–8, 230
Friedberg, Anne, 2, 3, 26, 27, 160, 245
Frosh, Paul, 47, 114, 169, 209, 232
Fruit Ninja (2010 videogame), 163
Funko Pop, 238

Gaboury, Jacob, 4, 21, 130
Galloway, Alexander, 4–5, 75, 231n
Game of Thrones (2011–2019 television
    program), 121–2, 124–5, 126, 139n
GameBoy, 74
Gamer (2009 film), 66
Gane, Nicholas, 4
Gears of War (b.2006 videogame
    franchise), 75, 235
Gehry, Frank, 178, 183, 196
Gemini Man (2019 film), 77, 81–2
Generative Adversarial Network (GAN),
    243
Geoghegan, Bernard, 26
Gere, Charlie, 21n, 26
Gibson, James J., 24
Gilbreth, Frank, 135
Gilbreth, Lilian, 135
Gitelman, Lisa, 213–15
Gleiberman, Owen, 220
glitch, 40, 49
Global Positioning System (GPS), 156,
    165–6, 169n, 171
Google, 37, 39, 44, 111, 165–72, 233
  DeepMind, 171
  Google Cardboard, 211
  Google Earth, 1, 10, 42, 149, 165,
    166–7, 169, 171
  Google Maps, 10, 16, 42, 145, 148, 156,
    165, 166–7, 168, 171, 243
  Google Street View, 10, 16, 148, 149,
    165, 166–7, 168–9, 171
  And surveillance, 170–2
Graphic User Interface (GUI)
  aesthetic of, 13, 20, 24–5, 29, 59–61, 67,
    71, 144–6, 245
  and building design, 184–5, 187, 199,
    204, 205–7
  central to lived experience, 1, 6, 39, 41,
    169

  central to visual and aural culture, 1,
    3–4, 11, 17, 42, 51, 118–19, 245–6
  in cinema, 36–40, 50, 64, 70
  depth of, 53, 60
  frame rate of, 73–4, 82–3
  history of, 21–6
  interactivity of, 10, 27–8, 41, 46, 47, 82,
    134, 168, 216, 232
  legal definition of, 24–5, 50, 227
  as new visual vernacular, 3, 27–8, 227,
    245
  and personalisation, 47, 52, 53, 60, 62,
    119, 149, 156, 160
  and physical matter, 176–7, 200, 205–7
  soundscape of, 86, 88, 89–90, 96, 102,
    106, 109, 113–14
  and task management, 54, 61–2, 66–7,
    71, 76, 83, 144–5
  untidiness of, 68
  and urban space, 147–9, 152, 158–9,
    164, 165 72
  in video essays, 40–6, 50
  in videogames, 48–51
  and visual overlapping, 20, 27–8, 38–40,
    50–1, 52, 60
  and VR, 209, 211, 227
  and VFX breakdowns, 117–19, 144–6
  see also computers; interface;
    interactivity; screens
Gravity (2013 film), 14, 54, 65–72, 80–1,
    83, 193, 243
  production process of, 65–6
  3D in, 72
Green, Joshua, 42
Greenfield, Adam, 214
Grosse Fatigue (2013 video essay), 41
Grusin, Richard, 3, 36
Guangzhou Opera House, 183, 198
Guggenheim Museum Bilbao, 178–9, 183,
    185, 187, 190
Gunning, Tom, 217
Gurevitch, Leon, 190
Gutter, Pinchas, 221–2

Hadid, Zaha, 178, 183, 198
Hanke, John, 166

Hardcore Henry (2015 film), 66
Harpold, Terry, 27
Harvey, David, 150, 164
Hausmann, Baron, 150
HBOMax, 238, 240
hecklevision, 35
Henrot, Camille *see Grosse Fatigue* (2013 video essay)
Her (2013 film), 154
Her Story (2015 videogame), 47, 50
Herzog, Amy, 103
Herzog and de Meuron, 179
Hibernia Networks, 76
High-frame rate (HFR), 15, 54, 72–84
   aesthetic tendencies of, 80–1
   definition of, 73
   realism of, 72–3
   and soap opera effect, 79–80
high-frequency trading, 76
Hobbit, The (2012–2014 film trilogy), 77, 80, 81
Hong Kong, 153, 191
HoloLens, 194, 196
Host (2020 film), 36
Houdini (program), 176–7, 190, 243
House of the Dragon (2022 television program), 235
HTC Vive, 211
Hulk (2003 film), 63–4

iClone, 119n
IMDb, 44
immersive journalism *see* VR, immersive journalism
Iñárritu, Alejandro G., 220
Inception (2010 film), 16, 157–60, 164–5, 166, 170, 179, 187, 196–7
Industrial Light and Magic (ILM), 117, 121, 122, 123–4, 127–8, 143, 144, 145, 196
Instagram, 46
interface
   as concept, 4
   as effect, 4–5
   of mobile phone, 19
   as tactile, 22, 23–4, 60–2, 133, 160–1, 164, 176
   videogames as, 230–1
   VFX as, 116
   see also computers
interactivity, 9–10, 28–30, 32, 33, 35, 38–9, 50, 71–2, 82–3, 87, 96, 102, 141, 156, 168–9, 229, 232
internet ugly, 111–12
Invisible (2016 VR series), 218
iPad, 74, 82
iPhone X, 57
Irom, Bimbisar, 223, 224, 226

JAUNT, 218
Jenkins, Henry, 5, 11, 42, 237–8, 240
Jobs, Steve, 59
John Wick: Chapter 3 – Parabellum (2019 film), 236
Johnson, Catherine, 31
Johnson, Steven, 5, 22, 23, 24
Jørgenson, Kristin, 28, 92, 96, 99, 229–31
Jurgess, Todd, 78

Kalfa, Konstantina, 206
Kerins, Mark, 87n, 88–9, 106–7
Kero Kero Bonito, 85, 111
Keyhole, 166
Khan, Albert, 191
King Arthur: Legend of the Sword (2017 film), 101
King's Cross Train Station, London, 198–9
Kingdom Hearts III (2019 videogame), 154
Kirkpatrick, Graeme, 96
Klinger, Barbara, 34
Koepnick, Lutz, 189–90
Kolarevic, Branko, 178–9, 180, 181
Koolhaas, Rem, 178, 179, 183, 185, 187–9
Korsgaard, Mathias Bonde, 110
Kowloon Bay, 153
Kuleshov, Lev, 152
Kulezic-Wilson, Danijela, 101

labour, 132–4, 145–6, 206–7
Lake Michigan, 153

Last Action Hero (1993 film), 239
Last Goodbye, The (2017 VR experience), 221–2, 223, 225, 232
Last of Us, The (2014 videogame), 141
Last of Us Part II, The (2020 videogame), 15, 93–5, 97–9, 102
Late Shift (2016 film), 35
latency, 74
Launchpad *see* Mac (operating system)
Lawnmower Man, The (1992 film), 210
Le Corbusier, 150, 180
Leach, Neil, 198, 203
Lee, Kevin B. *see Transformers: The Premake* (2014 video essay)
Lefebvre, Henri, 150
Lego, 172–4
Lego Movie, The (2014 film), 173–4
Lexus, 218
LIDAR scanning, 122–3, 199–200
Life of Pi (2012 film), 70
Little Women (2019 film), 121, 122–3, 126, 128
Liman, Doug, 218
Lion King, The (2019 film), 235
London, 131, 151, 153, 159, 198–9
London, Barbara, 105
Los Angeles, 154, 201
Lovelace, Ada, 21
Lynn, Greg, 16, 180–7, 191, 193–7, 198–9, 203
lyric videos, 46, 85–6, 109–13; *see also* music video

Mac (operating system), 1, 10, 19, 52–3, 60, 67–71, 161
 Aqua, 24n5
 Launchpad, 10, 52, 69–70
 Mission Control, 60, 61, 144
 Start-up noise, 89
McAslan, John, 198–9
McGoff, Jessica *see My Mullholland* (2020 video essay)
McHenry, Jackson, 78
machinima, 141–2, 146
McLaren, Laura, 86, 109–10
McQuarrie, Christopher, 79–80

Mandalorian, The (b.2019 television program), 235, 236
Manifold Garden (2019 videogame), 155
Manovich, Lev, 5, 6, 24n, 26, 28, 133, 135–6, 182, 183n
Maquette (2020 videogame), 155
Marey, Etienne-Jules, 135
Markel, Nick, 142–3
Marvel, 7, 8, 12, 15, 47, 91, 154
Marvel's The Avengers (2020 videogame), 143n
Marxism, 150
Marzola, Luci, 21n
Matrix, The (1999 film), 64, 139, 236, 237, 239
Matrix Awakens, The (2021), 17, 234–45
Matrix Online, The (2005 videogame), 238, 239
Matrix Resurrections, The (2021 film), 236, 238–40, 242
Matrix Revolutions, The (2003 film), 237
Maya (program), 1, 10, 65, 115, 117, 119, 132–4, 137, 140, 144, 161, 176–7, 179, 184, 185, 187
 interface organisation of, 132–3
Max Payne (2001 videogame), 64–5
media agnosticism (as method), 13–14, 17
Meg: Submersive VR Experience, The (2018 VR experience), 217
Memex, 22–3
Menkman, Rosa, 88
Metal: Hellslinger (2022 videogame), 96
Metro: Exodus (2019 videogame), 97n
Michelle, Carolyn, 78
Microsoft, 24–5, 227
MicroStation, 185
Milk, Chris, 219, 221, 222, 224
Mills, Shannon, 91
Minecraft (2009 videogame), 161, 164
Mirror's Edge (2008 videogame), 201–3
Mirror's Edge Catalyst (2016 videogame), 179, 201–3, 203n
Mission: Impossible – Fallout (2018 film), 79–80
Mitchell, William, 57n
Moore, Rowan, 206

Mosaic (2018 television program), 30
Moscow, 152
Moses, Robert, 150, 180
Moss, Carrie-Ann, 236, 241–4
Mother of all Demos, the, 22, 23–4, 210
MP3, 88, 109
Mulholland Drive (2004 film), 44
multi-user dungeon (MUD), 28
music video, 85–6, 104–5, 110
mutoscopes, 135
Muybridge, Eadweard, 135–6, 186
My Mullholland (2020 video essay), 44–5, 50
Myers, Joseph, 25

Nakamura, Lisa, 224–5, 226, 227
Napster, 88
NASA, 67, 198n
Nash, Kate, 224–5, 226, 228n
Nead, Lynda, 134
neoliberalism, 150–1, 163–4
Netflix, 1, 29, 30, 32n, 89, 114, 240
    interface organisation of, 31–2
Neuromancer (1986 novel), 210
New York City, 8–11, 122, 124, 143, 150, 152, 153, 159, 189
Ng, Jenna, 141–2, 226
Niantic, 166
NieR: Automata (2017 videogame), 203–4
Nintendo, 74
No Man's Sky (2016 videogame), 161
Noah (2013 short film), 37
Nolan, Christopher, 153, 157
Non-fungible tokens (NFTs), 238
NowTV, 32
Nuke (program), 115, 117
NURBS, 181–2, 187
Nvidia, 74–6

Oculus Rift, 211
Open Windows (2014 film), 36, 39–40
Oz: The Great and Powerful (2013 film), 64

Pacific Rim (2013 film), 137
Packard Plant, 16, 191–7
Palitz, Ari, 221

Panic Room (2002 film), 139
panoramas, 213–14, 215
Paranormal Activity (2007 film), 37
Paris, France, 150, 157
Paris, Texas, 192
parkour, 202–3
participatory culture, 42–3
Pasek, Anne, 88
peepshows, 134–5, 136
Peña, Nonny de la, 219
perceptual realism, 120, 127, 138–9, 189, 196, 197, 203–4
    see also realism
Perry, Katy, 46, 110–11
phenakistoscopes, 135
photo mode, 141, 143
Pierson, Michele, 203–4
planned obsolescence, 12
Playstation (console), 57, 208, 211, 234–6
PS 4 Pro (gaming console), 58
PlayStation VR Worlds (2016 videogame), 218
Pokémon GO (2016 videogame), 156, 166, 169n
polymers, 16, 176–7, 186, 193–6, 197–205
Pong (1972 videogame), 74, 100
poor images, 34–5, 42
Portal 2 (2011 videogame), 229–31
Post-cinema *see* cinema
PowerAnimator, 133
Prada, 220
Prey (2017 videogame), 229–31
pre-visualisation (previz), 119–20, 139–40, 142–4
    and techviz, 140, 144
    see also machinima
Prince, Stephen, 120
procedural rhetoric, 163
Profile (2021 film), 36
Pro Tools, 87, 103
ProMotion, 74, 82
PUBG:Battlegrounds (2017 videogame), 235
Purse, Lisa, 64, 117, 137, 145, 189
Pyramids, the, 153, 191
Python (programming language), 119

Quicktime, 94

Raban, Jonathan, 151
realism, 14–15, 25–6, 27, 48, 53–84, 127, 169, 229, 243
   and high frame rates, 77–8
   as moving target, 56
   and sound design, 86, 88, 97–102
   see also perceptual realism
Rear Window (1954 film), 39
Reeves, Keanu, 236, 241–4
Rehak, Bob, 116, 119
remediation, 3, 36
Replicas (2018 film), 119n
Resident Evil 2 (2019 videogame), 141
Resident Evil: Afterlife (2010 film), 64
Resident Evil: Biohazard (2017 videogame), 212, 218, 232
resolution, 53–4, 56–62, 68, 72, 78–9, 83, 227
   and human vision, 58
Rez (2001 videogame), 96
ringtone (remix) (song by 100 gecs), 85, 111–13
Roar (song by Katy Perry), 110
Rogue One: Recon – A Star Wars 360 Experience (2016 VR experience), 217, 218
Rohe, Mies van der, 158
Rosa, Miriam de, 41
Ryan, Marie-Laure, 216, 226

SAGE (Strategic Air Ground Command), 21n
Sage Music Centre Gateshead, 179
San Francisco, 154
Sara is Missing (2016 videogame), 14, 19–20, 47–9, 83
Saving Private Ryan (1998 film), 107
ScanLAB, 199
Schoemann, Sarah, 221, 225
Scream (1996 film), 239
screamer videos, 44
screens
   absence of in early computers, 21
   as active forces, 6
   and CRT (cathode ray tube) displays, 21, 26
   materiality of, 12, 148
   as multipurpose, 20
   portability of, 12, 170
   as real estate, 54, 61–2, 83, 227
   as synecdoche of computer, 23
   and transparency, 3, 27
   and urban space, 147–8, 156, 194
   and VR, 209, 214–15, 233
Searching (2018 film), 36, 37, 39, 44n
Secor, Anna, 181
Shadow in the Cloud (2020 film), 101
Shadow of the Tomb Raider (2018 videogame), 141
Shanghai, 124, 128, 154
Shanghai Fortress (2019 film), 121, 124–5, 126, 127, 128, 131, 137, 138
Shaviro, Steven, 64n8, 104, 108
Sherlock Holmes: A Game of Shadows (2011 film), 64
Showscan, 77
Sign O the Times (song by Prince), 110
SimCity (videogame series), 10, 16, 161–5, 166, 170, 172n, 187–9
   interface design of, 162
SimCity: BuildIt (2014), 147–9, 162–5, 196–7, 200–2, 205
   interface design of, 162–3, 200
   procedural rhetoric of, 163–4
Sims, The (videogame series), 161
Simulacra (2017 videogame), 47
skeuomorphism, 3, 25, 59
Skype, 12, 37–9, 89, 90, 114
Smith, Jeff, 103, 108
Smith, Jo, 33
Snapchat, 238
Soja, Edward, 151
sonification, 10, 90, 102, 106
Sontag, Susan, 6–7
Sony, 239
Soundcloud, 89
soundtracks, 15, 86–7, 90–114
   dynamic range, 92, 106
   musicality of, 101–2
   transdiegetic, 99–101, 114

soundtracks (*cont.*)
    and synchronisation, 103–14
    and the ultrafield, 106–7, 114
Spider-Man (2002 film), 9
Spider-Man (2018 videogame), 8–11, 13, 141
Spider-Man: No Way Home (2021 film), 239–40
Spotify, 37, 52, 156
Star Trek (multimedia franchise), 116, 210
Star Wars (multimedia franchise), 90n, 119n, 116, 118, 217
Steam (platform), 1, 89
stereoscopes, 213–14, 215
stereoscopic 3D, 15, 66, 67, 71, 72, 80n, 135, 196, 215
Sterne, Jonathan, 58, 88
Steyerl, Hito, 34–5, 42
Stork, Matthias, 140
Sucker Punch (2011 film), 139, 140
Summers, Tim, 100
Super Mario Bros. (1985 videogame), 92–3, 228
SuperHot (2016 videogame), 232
surveillance capitalism, 170–2
Suspense (1913 film), 63
Sutherland, Ivan, 27, 176, 210
Swallow, Erica, 221
Swordfish (2001 film), 64
Syria, 208, 221, 225

Taking of Pelham 123, The (1974 film), 103–4
Taking of Pelham 123, The (2009 film), 103–4
Tarr, Bela, 47
tax incentives, 192
techviz *see* previsualisation
television (TV)
    as appliance, 12, 21, 26, 28, 29–33, 53, 57, 72, 209
    in cinema, 35
    and flow, 29
    frame rate of, 73, 79–80
    and liveness, 32
    and news broadcasting, 32, 223
    programs of, 34, 236
    remote control, 30
    smart TVs, 30
    teletext and, 26, 27
Telling Lies (2019 videogame), 47
Terminator 2: Judgement Day (1991 film), 183–4, 185, 190, 196, 204
Tetris (1984 videogame), 154
Third Floor, 142–3
Thumper (2016 videogame), 96
TikTok, 105
Timecode (2000 film), 63
TimeShift (2007 videogame), 65
tourism, 149
trailers, 109
Transformers (fictional characters), 176, 187–92, 195–7
    in film theory, 189–90
Transformers: Age of Extinction (2014 film), 42, 105n, 153, 175–7, 190–1, 192, 195, 205
Transformers: Dark of the Moon (2011 film), 153, 187–8, 190, 192
Transformers: The Last Knight (2016 film), 192, 196
Transformers: The Premake (2014 video essay), 41–3, 44, 175
Trumbull, Douglas, 77–8
Trump Tower, 153
Tryon, Chuck, 132
Tudor, Deborah, 63–4, 117
tunnel books, 134–5
Turnock, Julie, 77, 78–9

Unfriended (2014 film), 14, 36, 37–9, 40, 46, 49n, 50, 83
Unfriended: Dark Web (2018 film), 36, 40
United Nations, 220–1
Unity (program), 96
Universal Production Partners (UPP), 115–16, 121, 122, 145
Unreal (program), 96, 234–6, 241–4
ultrafield, 87
urban form, 15–16, 149–52, 157–60, 163–5
    and creative destruction, 150, 164, 175

and flexibility, 16, 150–1, 156, 173–4
and gentrification, 151, 163
imagination of, 151–2, 170, 174
and the postmetropolis, 151
and videogames, 147–9, 161–5, 170

Väliaho, Pasi, 75, 216
Vancouver, 152
Venice Architecture Biennale, 193, 194, 196
Verhoeff, Nanna, 6, 156
Vertigo (1958 film), 118
Vernallis, Carol, 103, 105n, 104–5, 111
VFX (visual effects), 15, 64–6, 69, 103, 114, 115–46, 175, 179, 189–91, 193–4, 196, 205
  association with post-production, 118–20
  bullet-time, 242
  history of, 117–20, 203–4
  keyframing, 184
  as magic, 159, 206
  morph effect, 183–4
  and seamlessness, 120
  as 'special', 118
  synthespians, 241–2
VFX breakdowns, 15, 65, 115–46, 160, 161, 164–5, 196, 197, 199, 200, 204, 236
  absences within, 132–4, 183, 206
  and assembly, 127, 131–2, 135–6, 143
  and blending, 121–4, 130, 131–2
  and credit sequences, 136–8
  and fly-throughs, 128–30, 141, 143, 184
  historical precursors of, 134–6
  influence of GUI on, 116–17
  and iterations, 124–7, 131, 132
  soundscapes of, 120–1, 128
  speed of, 131, 243
  and visual mapping, 122–3, 130, 143
VHS, 32n, 33, 56n
Vib-Ribbon (2004 videogame), 96
video essays, 40–6
videogames
  as 'cinematic', 34, 93
  and First Person Shooters, 74–6, 82

frame rates of, 74–6, 82
as gameworld interface, 29, 92, 99–100, 227–31
and graphic resolution, 53, 57
overlap with GUI, 28–9, 50, 97–8
as persuasive, 163
as recursive spaces, 154–5, 161, 210
as simulations, 228–9
soundscapes of, 93–102, 114
and VR, 211–12, 218
Vimeo, 41, 121
virtual production, 235–6
Virtuosity (1995 film), 210
VR (virtual reality), 16–17, 28, 29, 208–33, 236, 243
  aesthetic of, 217–19, 227, 233
  definitions of, 212–17
  as empathy machine, 219, 222–6
  and ethics, 210
  as faceless interface, 216, 227, 233
  frame rate of, 215
  as gameworld interface, 232
  history of, 210–11
  immersion of, 214, 232
  immersive journalism in, 17, 207–9, 217, 219–26, 231–3
  soundscapes of, 215, 217
  and transportation, 209, 218, 219–26, 243
  uses of, 211
Virtuosity (1995 film), 204

Wachowski siblings, 237–9
WALL-E (2008 film), 243
Walt Disney Concert Hall, 185
Wang, Philip, 243
Warner Bros., 237–8, 240
Washington, DC, 152
Wasson, Haidee, 2, 5–6
Watch Dogs 2 (2016 videogame), 179
Wayback Machine, 44
Webb, Lawrence, 154
Weber, Lois *see Suspense* (1913 film)
Wes Craven's New Nightmare (1994 film), 239
West, Ben, 193–4

WhatsApp, 110–11
Whissel, Kristen, 66, 67
Whitney, John, 118
widescreen, 57
Wikipedia, 44
Wild Palms (1993 television program), 210
Wilkinson, Alissa, 82
Williams, Evan Calder, 64–5
Williams, Raymond, 29
Willis, Holly, 119–20, 140n, 199–200, 219
Willis Tower, 153
Willow (1988 film), 183
Windows (operating system), 1, 19, 25–6, 59–60
  Flip 3D, 60, 144–5
  Start-up noise of, 89
Wired (magazine), 210
Wonder Woman (2017 film), 115–16, 119, 121, 122, 124, 128–9, 131

Wood, Aylish, 5, 29, 63–4, 116, 133, 154–5
Word (program), 52
Wright, Frank Lloyd, 158
Wwise, 87

Xbox (console), 57, 236
Xerox, 24

Yang, Robert, 225, 226
Yoh, Shoei, 183–4
YouTube, 12, 15, 29, 30, 40, 42, 44, 85, 89, 105, 109, 112, 113, 114, 115, 117, 121, 127
  YouTube VR, 214, 220

Zero FX, 121, 122–3, 126, 128
zoetropes, 135, 136
Zuboff, Shoshana, 170–2

EU representative:
Easy Access System Europe
Mustamäe tee 50, 10621 Tallinn, Estonia
Gpsr.requests@easproject.com

www.ingramcontent.com/pod-product-compliance
Lightning Source LLC
Chambersburg PA
CBHW050211240426

43671CB00013B/2292